SYSTEM CRIMINALITY IN INTERNATIONAL LAW

International crimes, such as crimes against humanity, genocide and war crimes, are committed by individuals. However, individuals rarely commit such crimes for their own profit. Instead, such crimes are often caused by collective entities. Notable examples include the 'dirty war' in Argentina in the 1970s and 1980s, the atrocities committed during the Balkan Wars in the early 1990s and the crimes committed during the ongoing armed conflicts in the Darfur area in Sudan. Referring to Darfur, the Prosecutor of the ICC noted in 2008 that although he had indicted a few individuals, 'the information gathered points to an ongoing pattern of crimes committed with the mobilization of the whole state apparatus'.

This book reviews the main legal avenues that are available within the international legal order to address the increasingly important problem of system criminality and identifies possible improvements.

ANDRÉ NOLLKAEMPER is Professor of Public International Law and Director of the Amsterdam Center for International Law at the Faculty of Law, University of Amsterdam.

HARMEN VAN DER WILT is Professor of International Criminal Law at the Faculty of Law, University of Amsterdam.

SYSTEM CRIMINALITY IN INTERNATIONAL LAW

Editors

HARMEN VAN DER WILT

and

ANDRÉ NOLLKAEMPER

Assistant editors

MENNO DOLMAN

and

JANN KLEFFNER

CAMBRIDGE UNIVERSITY PRESS
Cambridge, New York, Melbourne, Madrid, Cape Town, Singapore, São Paulo, Delhi

Cambridge University Press
The Edinburgh Building, Cambridge CB2 8RU, UK

Published in the United States of America by Cambridge University Press, New York

www.cambridge.org
Information on this title: www.cambridge.org/9780521763561

First published 2009

Printed in the United Kingdom at the University Press, Cambridge

A catalogue record for this publication is available from the British Library

Library of Congress Cataloguing in Publication Data
System criminality in international law / Harmen van der Wilt (editor),
André Nollkaemper
p. cm.
Includes index.
ISBN 978-0-521-76356-1 (hardback)
1. Criminal jurisdiction. 2. International offenses.
I. Wilt, Harmen van der, 1955– II. Kleffner, Jann K. III. Title.
K5036.S97 2009
345'.0235–dc22 2009010961

ISBN 978-0-521-76356-1 hardback

CONTENTS

PREFACE

This book explores the state of international law in respect of situations of system criminality, that is: situations where collective entities such as states or organised armed groups order or encourage international crimes to be committed, or permit or tolerate the committing of international crimes. The book emanated from a widely felt discomfort with the mismatch between the dominant role of collective entities in situations where international crimes are committed, on the one hand, and the current fashionable focus on individual (criminal) responsibility, exemplified by the mushroom of international criminal tribunals, on the other.

Against the background of a discussion of the mechanisms through which collective entities induce or cause international crimes to be committed, the book focuses in particular on the power and limitations of forms of international responsibilities in regard to system criminality, covering individual responsibility, responsibility of organizations and organized armed groups, and state responsibility.

While separate aspects of the role of collective entities in regard to international crimes have been subject to scholarly analysis, we felt that there was a lack of comprehensive assessments of the state of the law, the lacunas in the law of international responsibility and the prospects for strengthening the law. This book aims to fill part of the gap and contribute to an understanding of this increasingly important area of law.

The chapters in this book were originally presented at a conference held at the Amsterdam Center for International Law, University of Amsterdam, on 20 and 21 October 2006. They were reworked on the basis of the discussions at the conference and in light of later developments. The conference was made possible by contributions from the Universiteit van Amsterdam, the Amsterdam Center for International Law, the Department of Criminal Law of the Universiteit van Amsterdam and the Royal Netherlands Academy of Arts and Sciences (KNAW).

We would like to thank Stefanie Küfner and Caitilin McGivern for their excellent editorial assistance in the preparation of the book.

André Nollkaemper and Harmen van der Wilt (editors)
Menno Dolman and Jann Kleffner (assistant editors)
1 July 2009

TABLE OF CASES

International Courts

European Court of First Instance

European Court of Human Rights

Inter-American Court of Human Rights

ICC

ICTR

ICTY

International Court of Justice

Permanent Court of Arbitration

Permanent Court of International Justice

SCSL

National Courts

Argentina

Chile

Columbia, Supreme Court

Germany, Constitutional Court

Germany, Supreme Court

Greece, Supreme Court

Israel, District Court

Italy, Court of Cassation

Netherlands, District Court

Peru

Poland, Supreme National Tribunal

United Kingdom, British Military Court (sitting at Luneburg)

United Kingdom, British Military Court (sitting at Essen)

United Kingdom, Divisional Court

United Kingdom, House of Lords

United States of America, District Court

United States of America, Federal Court

United States, Military Court

United States of America, Supreme Court

TABLE OF TREATIES AND INTERNATIONAL INSTRUMENTS

Treaties

Hague Regulations (1907)

Treaty of Versailles (1919)

German-Polish Convention (1922)

IMT Charter (1945)

UN Charter (1945)

Chapter VII 253, 318–20, 322, 324, 325, 328, 331, 332, 335
Article 1(1) 318, 319
Article 2(4) 335, 336
Article 2(7) 318
Article 17(1), (2) 335
Article 27(3) 330
Article 39 320, 322, 328
Article 40 322
Article 41 322, 332
Article 42 323, 332
Article 43 332
Article 48 332
Article 51 301
Artice 53 335
Article 103 318, 335

Geneva Convention I (1949)

Geneva Convention for the Amelioration of the Condition of the Wounded and Sick in Armed Forces in the Field (12 August 1949) 75 UNTS 35, entered into force 21 October 1950 14, 30, 36, 90, 303, 305
Article 1 267
Article 3 239, 247, 257, 258, 267
Article 49 303

Geneva Convention II (1949)

Geneva Convention for the Amelioration of the Condition of Wounded, Sick and Shipwrecked Members of Armed Forces at Sea (12 August 1949) 75 UNTS 81, entered into force 21 October 1950 14, 30, 36, 90, 303, 305
Article 1 267
Article 3 239, 247, 257, 258, 267
Article 50 303

Geneva Convention III (1949)

Geneva Convention relative to the Treatment of Prisoners of War (12 August 1949) 75 UNTS 135, entered into force 21 October 1950 14, 30, 36, 90, 303, 305
Article 1 267
Article 3 239, 247, 257, 258, 267
Article 4(a)2 132
Article 129 303

Geneva Convention IV (1949)

Additional Protocol I (1977)

Additional Protocol II (1977)

Genocide Convention (1948)

San Francisco Peace Treaty (1951)

ICERD (1965)

ICCPR (1966)

Torture Convention, CAT (1984)

ICTR Statute (1994)

ICTY Statute (1994)

International Convention for the Suppression of Terrorist Bombings (1998)

Rome Statute (1998)

African Union Treaty (2000)

UN Convention against Transnational Organized Crime (2000)

EU Council Framework Decision on Combating Traffic in Human Beings (2002)

UN Convention on State Immunity (2004)

Instruments

Control Council Law No 10 (1945)

Potsdam Protocol (1945)

Nuremberg Principles (1947)

International Law Commission Draft Articles on the Responsibility of States for Internationally Wrongful Acts (1996)

International Law Commission, Draft Code of Crimes Against the Peace and Security of Mankind (1996)

International Law Commission Draft Articles on the Responsibility of States for Internationally Wrongful Acts (2001)

International Law Commission, Draft Articles on Diplomatic Protection (2006)

Resolutions

United Nations Security Council

United Nations General Assembly

ABBREVIATIONS

AFRC	Armed Forces Revolutionary Council
AJIL	American Journal of International Law
ARIEL	Austrian Review of International and European Law
AU	African Union
AUC	United Self-Defense Forces/Group of Colombia
BLA	Baluchistan Liberation Army
BGHSt	Bundesgerichtshofs in Strafsachen
Cal L Rev	California Law Review
CUP	Cambridge University Press
CrimLR	Criminal Law Review
DINA	Direccion de Intelegencia Nacional (Chilean Secret Police)
ECOWAS	Economic Community Of West African States
ECtHR	Europea Court of Human Rights
EJIL	European Journal of International Law
EU	European Union
EWHC	High Court of England and Wales
FARC	Revolutionary Armed Forces of Colombia
FIS	Islamic Salvation Front
GA	General Assembly
GA	Goltdammer's Arhiv fur Strafrecht
IACHR	Inter-American Court of Human Rights
IAEA	International Atomic Energy Agency
ICCPR	International Covenant for Civil and Political Rights
ICC	International Criminal Court
ICLQ	International Comparative Law Quarterly
ICJ	International Court of Justice
ICL	International Criminal Law
ICLR	International Criminal Law Review
ICTR	International Criminal Tribunal for Rwanda
ICTY	International Criminal Tribunal for the former Yugoslavia
ILC	International Law Commission
ILR	International Law Reports

IMT	International Military Tribunal
IRA	Irish Republican Army
JCE	Joint Criminal Enterprise
JEM	Justice and Equality Movement
JICJ	Journal of International Criminal Justice
JZ	Juristenzeitung
LTTE	Liberation Tigers of Tamil Eelam
NATO	North Atlantic Treaty Organization
NGO	Non-Governmental Organisation
NILR	Netherlands International Law Review
NJ	Nederlandse Jurisprudentie
NJ	Neue Justiz
NJIL	Netherlands Journal of International Law
NJW	Nieuw Juridisch Weekblad
NJW	Neue Juristische Wochenzeitschrift
NMRD	National Movement for Reform and Development
NStZ	Neue Zeitschrift fur Strafrecht
NYIL	Netherlands Yearbook of International Law
NYPD	New York Police Department
OAS	Organization of American States
OED	Oxford English Dictionary
ONLF	Ogaden National Liberation Front
ÖJZ	Österreichische Juristenzeitung
OKW	Oberkommando der Wehrmacht
OTP	Office of the Prosecutor
OUP	Oxford University Press
OWIG	Gesetz über Ordnungswidrigkeiten
P5	(the countries that compose the UN Security Council)
PCIJ	Permanent Court of International Justice
PKK	Partiya Karkerên Kurdistan (Kurdistan Workers Party)
POW	Prisoner Of War
RGDIP	Revue Générale de Droit International Public
RUF	Revolutionary United Front
SCSL	Special Court for Sierra Leone
SD	Sicherheitsdienst
SLM/A	Sudan Liberation Movement/Army
SS	Schutzstaffel
SSRN	Social Science Research Network
UKHL	United Kingdom House of Lords
UN	United Nations
UNCC	United Nations Compensation Commission
UNGA	United Nations General Assembly

UNOG	United Nations Office at Geneva (UNOG)
UNSC	United Nations Security Council
UNSCR	United Nations Security Council Resolutions
USA	United States of America
VbVG	Verbandverantwörtlichkeitsgesetz
WISTRA	Zeitschrift für Wirtschafts-und Steuerstrafrecht
WTO	World Trade Organisation
Yale LJ	Yale Law Journal
YBILC	Yearbook of the International Law Commission
ZEuS	Zeitschrift fur Europarechtliche Studien
ZRP	Zeitschrift fur Rechtspolitik
ZStW	Zeitschrift für die gesamte Strafrechtswissenschaft

LIST OF CONTRIBUTORS

KAI AMBOS is Chair of Criminal Law, Criminal Procedure, Comparative Law and International Criminal Law at the Georg-August-Universität Göttingen (since May 2003); Head of Department of Foreign and International Criminal Law, Institute of Criminal Law & Justice, University of Göttingen. Judge at the State Tribunal Göttingen (24 March 2006); and Student Dean of the Law Faculty (since 30 April 2007). Legal education at the Universities of Freiburg i.Br., Oxford (UK) and Munich. First State Exam, 1990. Legal Preparatory Service, 1992–94. Second State Exam, 1994. Dr. iur 1992 (Munich), Habilitation (Post-Doc) 2001 (Munich), venia legendi in Criminal Law, Criminal Procedure, Criminology, Comparative Law & Public International Law. Former (senior) research fellow at the Max-Planck-Institute for Foreign and International Criminal Law, Freiburg im Breisgau, Germany, in charge of the sections 'International Criminal Law' and 'Spanish-speaking Latin America' (1991–2003).

MENNO DOLMAN (1967), LLM MA PhD is a graduate of the Law (1990) and Social Sciences (1991) faculties of the University of Amsterdam. Since graduation he has been a law clerk at the Netherlands' Supreme Court (1991–98) and a post-doctoral researcher at Tilburg University (1998–99); since 1999 he has been Lecturer in Criminal Law at the University of Amsterdam. His research interests include substantive criminal law, culminating in his 2006 Ph.D. thesis on the functions of duress and necessity in Dutch criminal law, military criminal law and the law of evidence. Dr Dolman has also been a regular contributor to the series Annotated Leading Cases of the International Criminal Tribunals.

ALBIN ESER is Professor Emeritus at the University of Freiburg/Germany. From 1982 until 2003 he served as Director at the Max-Planck-Institute for Foreign and International Criminal Law and from 2004 to 2006 as Ad-Litem judge at the International Criminal Tribunal for the Former Yugoslavia in The Hague/Netherlands. In the summer term of 2008 he taught as Visiting Professor at the Ritsumeikan University in Kyoto/Japan. He has widely published in criminal law and procedure and in medical law, with particular attention to homicide, abortion, suicide and euthanasia, human genetics and, more recently, in international criminal law, environmental protection and corruption. Many of his publications are published in various languages beyond English particularly in Spanish and in Japanese. He is co-editior of a European colloquium on 'Individual, Participatory and Collective Responsibility in Criminal Law' (1998) and of 'Criminal Responsibility of Legal and Collective Entities' (1998).

ANDREA GATTINI, born in 1959, has been since 2005 Full Professor of International law at the Law Faculty of the University of Padua. His previous academic positions were at the Universities of Sassari and Urbino, where he taught international law, EEC law and international trade law. He holds degrees in law and in political sciences from the universities of Padua and Bologna, and a doctorate in international law at the University of Munich. He has written extensively on international responsibility of states in international leading journals and is the author of a monograph in Italian on war reparations. He is often invited to give lectures in German universities.

NINA H. B. JØRGENSEN is currently the Senior Judicial Coordinator of the Pre-Trial Chamber at the Extraordinary Chambers in the Courts of Cambodia. Previously, she worked for three years at the Special Court for Sierra Leone and prior to that at the International Criminal Tribunal for the Former Yugoslavia. She has a DPhil, from the University of Oxford and did post-doctoral research at the University of Leiden. She is a member of the Bar of England and Wales.

HERBERT C. KELMAN is Richard Clarke Cabot Professor of Social Ethics, Emeritus, and co-chair of the Middle East Seminar at Harvard University. A pioneer in the development of interactive problem solving – an unofficial third-party approach to the resolution of international and intercommunal conflict – he has been engaged for more than thirty-five years in efforts toward the resolution of the Israeli-Palestinian conflict. His writings on interactive problem solving received the Grawemeyer Award for Ideas Improving World Order in 1997. His major publications include *International Behavior: A Social-Psychological Analysis* (editor and co-author, 1965); *A Time to Speak: On Human Values and Social Research* (1968); and *Crimes of Obedience: Toward a Social Psychology of Authority and Responsibility* (with V. Lee Hamilton, 1989).

JANN K. KLEFFNER is Assistant Professor of International Law at the Faculty of Law of the University of Amsterdam. He is Managing Editor and Member of the Editorial Board of the *Yearbook of International Humanitarian Law*, member of the Committee on 'Compensation for Victims of War' of the

International Law Association, Committee Member of the Interest Group on Peace and Security of the European Society of International Law, co-convenor of the Netherlands Research Forum on the Law of Armed Conflict and Peace Operations (LACPO), and executive member of the The Hague Initiative for Law and Armed Conflict. He has also served as expert for a number of international governmental and non-governmental organizations.

ANDRÉ NOLLKAEMPER is Professor of Public International Law at the Faculty of Law of the University of Amsterdam, the Netherlands. He is general editor *of the Netherlands Yearbook of International Law* and Editor-in-Chief of *International Law in Domestic Courts*. He is also Member of the Advisory Committee for Public International Law of the Netherlands. As counsel to the Amsterdam based law firm Böhler, Franken Koppen Wijngaarden, he has frequently been involved in litigation in international and Dutch courts, including international criminal law cases. He has published widely on legal questions pertaining to international responsibility, including 'Internationally Wrongful Acts in Domestic Courts', *American Journal of International Law* (2007) and 'Multi-level Accountability: A Case-Study of Acountability in the Aftermath of the Srebrenica Massacre' (in *The Shifting Allocation of Authority in International Law* (Broude and Shany, eds., 2008).

MAURICE PUNCH studied and worked in the UK before moving to the Netherlands in 1975. He has researched police corruption (*Conduct Unbecoming*, 1985) and corporate crime (*Dirty Business: Exploring Corporate Misconduct*, 1996; and *Rethinking Corporate Crime*, 2003, with Jim Gobert). He is currently writing books on police corruption and on police and Army deviance in Northern Ireland during the 'Troubles'. After twenty years in Dutch universities he became a Visiting Professor at the Mannheim Centre for Criminology, London School of Economics, and now also in the School of Law at King's College London.

FELIX RETTENMAIER, Attorney-at-Law, was born in 1976 at Waiblingen, Germany. He is a graduate of the Johannes-Gutenberg-University, Mainz and also studied at the University of Glasgow, School of Law. His practical experiences include internships in Frankfurt, London and New York. During his legal clerkship he attended the German University of Administrative Sciences, Speyer and was a Research Fellow at the Max-Planck-Institute for Foreign and International Criminal Law, Freiburg. He joined the firm of Knierim & Kollegen, Mainz in 2006. His practice focuses on white collar criminal defence, corporate criminal law as well as advising companies affected by criminal acts. He is a regular contributor to the bi-weekly C. H. Beck-Criminal Law Report (Fachdienst Strafrecht).

IAIN SCOBBIE is the Sir Joseph Hotung Research Professor in Law, Human Rights and Peace Building in the Middle East at the School of Oriental and African Studies, University of London. He studied at the Universities of Edinburgh and Cambridge, and at the Australian National University. Professor Scobbie maintains a special interest in international humanitarian law; international adjudication, particularly the role of the International Court of Justice; and in the theory of international law. He is a member of the Executive Board of the European Society of International Law; the Scientific Advisory Board of the *European Journal of International Law*; the Governing Board of the Scottish Centre for War Studies; the Executive Council of the Lieber Society on the Law of Armed Conflict; and the International Advisory Council of Diakonia's International Humanitarian Law Programme.

GERRY SIMPSON divides his time between London, where he is a Professor of Public International Law at the London School of Economics, and Australia, where he holds a Chair in Law at the University of Melbourne. He is also a Senior Associate at the Centre for Human Rights in London. Gerry is the author of *Great Powers and Outlaw States* (Cambridge, 2004) (awarded the American Society of International Law's annual prize for Pre-eminent Contribution to Creative Legal Scholarship) and is co-editor (with Tim McCormack) of *The Law of War Crimes: National and International Approaches* (1997). His latest book is *Law, War and Crime; War Crimes Trials and the Reinvention of International Law* (2007).

ELIES VAN SLIEDREGT is Professor of Criminal Law at Vrije Universiteit Amsterdam. She is a member of the editorial boards of the *Leiden Journal of International Law* and of the *European Constitutional Law Review* and sits as a part-time judge in the extradition chamber of the District Court in Amsterdam. Her research interests lie in the field of international and European criminal law, comparative criminal law, and human rights law.

MICHAEL TEICHMANN is Legal Clerk (Rechtsreferendar) at the Higher Regional Court of Hamburg and a PhD candidate in international law at the University of Kiel (under the supervision of Professor Dr Andreas Zimmermann). He graduated in law from Humboldt University of Berlin and research positions held include, *inter alia*, at Helmut Schmidt University – University of the Federal Armed Forces Hamburg.

NIGEL D. WHITE is Professor of International Law at the University of Sheffield and Director of the Centre for Law in its International Context. In addition to publishing numerous articles and essays, he is author of several books including *Keeping the Peace: The United Nations and the Maintenance of International Peace and Security* (1997), *The Law of International Organisations* (2005) and *The UN System: Toward International Justice* (2002). He is also editor of a number of leading collections, primarily *Collective Security Law* (2004), and co-editor of *The UN, Human Rights and Post Conflict Situations* (2005), *International Conflict and Security Law* (2005), *European Security Law* (2007). He is co-editor-in-chief of the *Journal of Conflict and Security Law.*

HARMEN VAN DER WILT: PhD in 1993 (Maastricht University) on trade union freedom in Latin America. Former part-time judge. District Court of Roermond (1999–2000). Edmond Hustinx price for research, 1999. Since 2001, Associate Professor, and since 2004, Full Professor in International Criminal Law, University of Amsterdam. Van der Wilt has been involved in professional training programmes for judiciary and public prosecutors in Addis Abeba (Ethiopia) and training programmes for young staff-members of Lobatchevski University of Nijni Novgorod (within the framework of TEMPUS-TACIS and VOLGADOC Programme). He has been a member of the Research Council of an EU-project on the European Arrest Warrant and is a member of the Steering Committee of the EU-project DOMAC (Impact of International Procedures on Domestic Criminal Procedures in Mass Atrocity Cases). Van der Wilt has published extensively on extradition, international criminal tribunals and concepts of substantive international criminal law. Currently, he is chairman of the Department of Criminal Law, University of Amsterdam.

ANDREAS ZIMMERMANN: Walther-Schücking-Institute of International Law, University of Kiel; Dr. jur. (Heidelberg), LLM (Harvard); former Member of the German delegation to the Preparatory Committee and the United Nations Diplomatic Conference on the Establishment of an International Criminal Court; member of the Permanent Court of Arbitration; counsel in various cases before the ICJ; judge ad hoc in various cases before the European Court of Human Rights; arbitrator under the annex to the Vienna Convention on the Law of Treaties; member of the advisory board on UN issues of the German Ministry of Foreign Affairs; *inter alia,* co-editor of *The Statute of the International Court of Justice – A Commentary* (2006).

1

Introduction

ANDRÉ NOLLKAEMPER*

This book reviews the main legal avenues that are available within the international legal order to address the increasingly important problem of system criminality, and to identify the need and possibilities for improving such avenues.

The term system criminality refers to the phenomenon that international crimes – notably crimes against humanity, genocide and war crimes – are often caused by collective entities in which the individual authors of these acts are embedded.[1] Notable examples of situations of system criminality after the Second World War include the 'dirty war' in Argentina in the 1970s and 1980s,[2] the atrocities committed during the Balkan Wars of the early 1990s of the previous century, in which states and organized armed groups played a dominant role,[3] and the crimes committed during the ongoing armed conflicts in the Darfur area in Sudan.[4]

While in many situations of system criminality the legal response of the international community has focused on individual perpetrators, who for instance have been the subject of criminal proceedings at the ICTY, ICTR, ICC or domestic courts, such individuals were often small cogs in larger systems that may be beyond the reach of individual responsibility. With regard to the international crimes committed in Darfur, for example, the Prosecutor of the ICC has indicted

* Professor of Public International Law and Director of the Amsterdam Center for International Law, University of Amsterdam. I thank Erik Kok, Mark Osiel and Harmen van der Wilt for comments on an earlier draft of this introduction.

1 See for further discussion of this definition section II below.

2 M. Osiel, *Mass Atrocity, Extraordinary Evil and Hannah Arendt: Criminal Consciousness in Argentina's Dirty War* (Yale University Press, New Haven & London 2001).

3 A. J. Vetlesen, *Evil and Human Agency: Understanding Collective Evildoing* (Cambridge University Press, Cambridge 2005).

4 Report of the International Commission of Inquiry on Darfur to the United Nations Secretary-General, Pursuant to Security Council Resolution 1564 of 18 September 2005 [25 January 2005].

two individuals whom he thought were responsible for international crimes.[5] But it is hard to believe that Ahmad Muhammed Harum, former Minister of State for the Interior of the Government of Sudan,[6] was, on his own, responsible for the crimes that have been committed in Sudan, or even for the crimes in respect of which he was charged. It is equally hard to believe that Ali Muhammed Ali Adb-Al-Rahman, a leader of the Janjaweed and also indicted by the ICC,[7] caused, on his own, the various crimes that have been attributed to the Janjaweed. Indeed, in his 2008 report to the Security Council, the Prosecutor of the ICC had to conclude that these two individuals were part of a much larger organizational context:

> [T]he information gathered points to an ongoing pattern of crimes committed with the mobilization of the whole state apparatus. The coordination of different bureaucracies, ranging from the military to the public information domains, suggest the existence of a plan approved and managed by GoS authorities at the highest level.[8]

In examining the systemic context of international crimes, this book focuses in particular on the relevance, potential and limits of the law of international responsibility. We use the term 'international responsibility' as an umbrella term to refer to the various forms of responsibility under international law, including responsibility of individuals, states, international organizations and, much less well-established, organized armed groups like the Lord Resistance Army in Uganda or the Revolutionary United Front in Sierra Leone.[9]

This introductory chapter will explain the context in which this book is situated and identify the key aspects of the phenomenon of system

[5] See 'The Prosecutor of the ICC opens investigation in Darfur', ICC Press Release (The Hague, 6 June 2005) at www.icc-cpi.int/pressrelease_details&id=107&l=en.html, accessed 14 January 2008.

[6] *Prosecutor v Ahmad Muhammad Harun* and *Ali Muhammad Ali Abd-Al-Rahman*, ICC-02/05-01/07.

[7] See (n. 5).

[8] Seventh Report of the Office of the Prosecutor of the International Criminal Court to the UN Security Council Pursuant to UNSCR 1593 (2005) para 98, available at www.icc-cpi.int/library/organs/otp/UNSC_2008_En.pdf, accessed 3 July 2008.

[9] See further section III below. Note that the term 'international responsibility', as used here, is broader than its common use as equivalent for responsibility of states, where the term 'international' is used to indicate that responsibility is not civil, criminal, or any other form known in domestic systems, but *sui generis* and in fact, simply 'international'; see A. Pellet, 'The New Draft Articles of the International Law Commission on the Responsibility of States for Internationally Wrongful Acts: a requiem for states' crime?' (2001) 32 NYIL 59.

criminality and its manifestations in international law. It will explain, first of all, the working hypothesis of this book: that, in cases of international crimes, responsibility should not (only) be located at individual level, but should also address the system within which individual behaviour is embedded (section 1). It then will review the concept of system criminality (section 2) and the role, objectives and main forms of international responsibility in relation to system criminality (section III). The chapter closes with a roadmap of the book (section IV).

I. Working hypothesis

1. *The role of systems in international crimes*

This book is based on the hypothesis that, in certain cases, responsibility in relation to system criminality should be allocated to the level of 'the system', in its various manifestations, rather than only to the individual level.

This hypothesis in certain respects challenges the dominant approach to international crimes. The Nuremberg Tribunal held that: 'Crimes against international law are committed by men, not by abstract entities, and *only* by punishing individuals who commit such crimes can the provisions of international law be enforced.'[10] Since this judgment, the dominant response of international law to international crimes has been individualistic. This also was expressed in the prosecutor's opening statement in the trial of Slobodan Milosevic in the ICTY:

> The accused in this case, as in all cases before the Tribunal, is charged as an individual. He is prosecuted on the basis of his individual criminal responsibility. No state or organisation is on trial here today. The indictments do not accuse an entire people of being collectively guilty of the crimes, even the crime of genocide.[11]

The individualist nature, and antipathy against collective responsibility, pervades other fields of international law. An illustration is the Security Council's response to North Korea's nuclear policies, targeting

[10] *The Trial of Major War Criminals: Proceedings of the International Military Tribunal Sitting at Nuremberg Germany, Part 22*, p. 447 (emphasis added).

[11] *Prosecutor v Slobodan Milosevic*, Prosecution Opening Statement, 8 IT-02-54-T [12 February 2002]. This statement is also cited by G. Simpson, 'Men and abstract entities: individual responsibility and collective guilt in international criminal law', this volume, Chapter 4.

the sanctions at luxury goods with the aim of affecting the rich individual leaders, rather than the population of North Korea.[12]

This book assumes that, for all its virtues, targeting responses to system criminality at individual authors of crimes is only a partial solution, and one which does not always take away the need to address the larger entities of which individuals are a part. If the goal is termination of the crimes and prevention of their recurrence, individual responsibility is unlikely to do the job.[13] Holding Saddam Hussein individually responsible in, say 1991, probably would not have made much of a difference to the system that continued to foster crimes.

Individuals who transgress fundamental norms of international law often are not acting on their own initiative or for their own cause. In some cases, individuals will carry out the plans of other, higher placed individuals. This may, under the doctrines of superior or command responsibility, result in prosecutions of higher ranked officials that supplement the prosecution of the lower ranked official or may lead to a decision not to prosecute such lower ranked officials.[14] Such prosecutions still may fall within the paradigm of individual responsibility.

In other cases, individuals do what they do because they act on behalf, or as part, of a state or other larger collective entity. In situations where state authorities consider that the security of the state is under severe threat, or fear they may lose power,[15] when they have a powerful apparatus at their disposal charged with protecting the security of the state, and when they have identified groups that are defined as enemies of the state, collective entities themselves can turn into actors that commit, or further the commission of, international crimes.[16] This was what happened, for example, in relation to the criminal acts orchestrated or supported by Belgrade during the Balkan Wars.[17]

[12] UNSC Resolution S/RES/1718 (2006). See generally on smart sanctions: D. Cortright and G. A. Lopez (eds.), *Smart Sanctions: Targeting Economic Statecraft* (Rowman & Littlefield, Lanham 2002); M. E. O'Connell, 'Debating the law of sanctions' (2002) 13 EJIL 70.

[13] See, on the objectives of international law with regard to situations of system criminality, A. Nollkaemper and H. van der Wilt, 'Conclusions and outlook', this volume, Chapter 15.

[14] E.g. *Prosecutor v Krstic*, IT-98-33-T [2 August 2001] para. 724.

[15] Hannah Arendt noted that 'loss of power becomes a temptation to substitute violence for power', H. Arendt, *On Violence* (Harvest Book, New York, London 1970) 54. She also wrote that: 'every decrease in power is an open invitation to violence – if only because those who hold power and feel it slipping away from their hands, be they the government or the governed, have always found it difficult to resist the temptation to substitute violence for it'; *ibid.*, p. 87.

[16] H. C. Kelman, 'The policy context of international crimes', this volume, Chapter 2.

[17] Vetlesen (n. 3) 178.

Individual authors of international crimes, then, are often part of a context in which a variety of actors participate, and which are properly dealt with at the level of the state, or other entity, as such.[18] Hannah Arendt wrote on the acts of Eichmann: 'crimes of this kind were, and could only be, committed under a criminal law and by a criminal state.'[19] Tallgren writes that: 'instead of being exceptional acts of cruelty by exceptionally bad people, international crimes are typically perpetrated by unexceptional people often acting under the authority of a state or, more loosely, in accordance with the political objectives of a state or other entity.'[20] Fletcher exposes what he calls a 'romantic view of history and personality', in which the individual's behaviour is motivated by, and can only be understood by reference to, larger communities of nation, state or tribe.[21] The emphasis on individual responsibility 'obscures a basic truth' about war crimes, that these are 'deeds that by their very nature are committed by groups and typically against individuals and members of groups'.[22]

Our starting point, then, is that collective entities can, as causal mechanisms, cause or contribute to individual international crimes. This is not much different from the familiar problems of structure and agency and of structural analysis that arise in case of ordinary criminality.

[18] See I. Brownlie, *System of the Law of Nations: State Responsibility. Part I* (Clarendon Press, Oxford 1983), p. 130; G. Arangio-Ruiz, 'State fault and the forms and degrees of international responsibility: questions of attribution and relevance, contribution to M–langes Michel Virally', in *Le Droit International au Service de la Paix, de la Justice et du Développement* (A. Pedone, Paris 1991), p. 35.

[19] H. Arendt, *Eichmann in Jerusalem: A Report on the Banality of Evil* (Viking Press, New York 1963), p. 240; K. Jaspers, 'Who should have tried Eichmann' (2006) 4 JICJ 854; C. Wells, *Corporations and Criminal Responsibility* (Oxford University Press, Oxford 1993), p. 135 (noting that many proceed from the belief that 'in general, corporate criminal acts are not the result of the isolated activity of a single employee, but arise "from the complex interactions of many agents in a bureaucratic setting"' (internal reference omitted)).

[20] I. Tallgren, 'The sense and sensibility of international criminal law' (2002) 13 EJIL 575.

[21] G. P. Fletcher, *Romantics at War: Glory and Guilt in the Age of Terrorism* (Princeton University Press, Princeton, MA 2002).

[22] G. P. Fletcher, 'The Storrs Lectures: liberals and romantics at war: the problem of collective guilt' (2002) 111 Yale LJ 1499; L. E. Fletcher and H. M. Weinstein, 'Violence and social repair: rethinking the contribution of justice to reconciliation' (2002) 24 *Human Rights Quarterly* 618; M. A. Drumbl, 'Collective Violence and Individual Punishment: The Criminality of Mass Atrocity' (2005) 99 *Northwestern University Law Review* 570–1. See also: *Bosnia and Herzegovina v Serbia and Montenegro*, Application of the Convention on the Prevention and Punishment of the Crime of Genocide ('Genocide Case') General List No. 91, ICJ Judgment (26 February 2007).

2. *Causal mechanisms*

Several factors may connect the system with international crimes. A dominant factor appears to be the emergence of a normative climate within a collectivity. Röling noted that the characteristic feature of system criminality is that it corresponds with the 'prevailing climate in the system'.[23] Punch, in this volume, points to processes of neutralization and rationalization that may influence individual behaviour.[24] A crucial aspect of system criminality, then, is that individual crimes are not, as is commonly the case for domestic crimes, contrary to a norm, but rather in conformity with norms that result from collective processes.[25]

The transformation of the normative climate, and the resulting erosion of individual moral inhibitions against international crimes, may, as argued by Kelman and Bauman, in particular arise when there is an authorization of acts of violence, a routinization of violence by rule-governed practice, and a dehumanization of victims of violence by indoctrination.[26] It may be much aided by the existence of large bureaucracies.[27] However, it can be assumed that this may also hold for particular organized forms of non-state actors, such as organized armed groups, though much will depend on the organized nature of such groups.[28]

A related factor that may help explain how collectivities may contribute to international crimes in particular cases is that, in the kind of (often military) acts that may generate individual crimes, individual autonomy may give way to group coherence. Hannah Arendt wrote that: 'in military as well as revolutionary action "individualism is the first [value]

[23] B. V. A. Röling, 'The significance of the laws of war', in A. Cassese (ed.), *Current Problems of International Law: Essays on UN Law and on the Law of Armed Conflict* (Dott A. Giuffrè Editore, Milan 1975), p. 138. Also: Fletcher (n. 21) 1541, referring to the 'climate of moral degeneracy' produced by the 'collective' contributes to the crime.

[24] M. Punch, 'Why corporations kill and get away with it: the failure of law to cope with crime in organizations', this volume, Chapter 3.

[25] Tallgren (n. 20) 575. Similarly, H. C. Kelman, 'The policy context of international crimes', this volume, Chapter 2. It is to be added, though, with Wells, that this in general will involve a two-way process, with acts of criminality not only using a climate for justification, but at the same time contributing to that climate: Wells (n. 19) 126. This is also implied in Fletcher (n. 21) 1541, referring to the 'climate of moral degeneracy' *produced* by the "collective" contributes to the crime'.

[26] H. C. Kelman, 'The policy context of international crimes', this volume, Chapter 2; Z. Bauman, *Modernity and the Holocaust* (Cornell University Press, Ithaca, NY 1989) 21; Vetlesen (n. 3) 16. See also Osiel (n. 2) 64.

[27] Vetlesen (n. 3) 16.

[28] J. Kleffner, 'The collective accountability of organized armed groups for system crimes', this volume, Chapter 11.

to disappear"'[29] and that once a man is admitted to group action, 'he will fall under the intoxicating spell of "the practice of violence [which] binds men together as a whole, since each individual forms a violent link in the great chain, a part of the great organism of violence which has surged upward"'.[30]

Beyond the influence of normative climate and group cohesion, the ways in which the system level may contribute to international crimes will differ significantly between various cases. Collective entities such as states or rebel movements may provide aid and assistance to individual authors of crimes, for example by providing weapons or funding.[31] A system may also contribute to crimes by doing little else than sitting still and acquiescing to the crimes.[32] Alvarez notes that there was nothing secret about what was done in Rwanda in 1994 and that: '[t]he attempt to involve as many perpetrators within Rwanda and to make the international community indirectly complicit was intended to preclude the possibility of prosecution on the premise that "[if] all are guilty, no one is guilty".'[33]

In view of the various ways in which systems can contribute to the commission of international crimes, the basis of the dogma of individual responsibility, that 'crimes against international law are committed by men, not by abstract entities, and *only* by punishing individuals who commit such crimes can the provisions of international law be enforced'[34] is doubtful. Jennings rightly noted that the words of the Nuremberg Tribunal are 'net and high sounding but dangerous, not to say dishonest, half-truth' that has 'a considerable currency with the great and the

[29] Arendt (n. 15) 67, citing F. Fanon, *The Wretched of the Earth* (Macgibban 1961), p. 47.

[30] Arendt (n. 15) 67, citing Fanon (n. 29) 93. See also J. Kleffner, 'The collective accountability of organized armed groups for system crimes', this volume, Chapter 11.

[31] That may make it appropriate to label the involvement of the system in terms of complicity; see Wells (n. 19) 139. The international law of responsibility would not in technical terms recognize such involvement as aid or assistance in the sense of Art. 16 of the Articles on State Responsibility, as that only applies between states; see Genocide Case (n. 22) para. 420. In the specific case of genocide, where the court found that a state can act in breach of the principle of complicity as that applies to individual responsibility, this may be different however: see (n. 22) para. 420.

[32] J. Alvarez, 'Crimes of states/crimes of hate: lessons from Rwanda' (1999) 24 *Yale Journal of International Law* 367 (noting that international lawyers characterize offences in Rwanda regions as crimes of states, because such offences, either by definition or because of their scale or scope, tend to require the connivance or at least acquiescence of governmental authority).

[33] Alvarez (n. 32) 399–400.

[34] *The Trial of Major War Criminals* (n. 10) 447 (emphasis added).

good, who have been willing to deceive themselves into believing that this aphorism represented the essence of wisdom'.[35]

3. *Some possible objections*

A few objections may be ventured to the line of argument developed here that international law should address the level of systems rather than that of individuals. One objection is that this argument leads to collective accountability and that 'if all are accountable, no one is accountable'.[36] If individual responsibility is valued for its contribution to retribution and possibly reconciliation, collective accountability may be inadequate.[37] Moreover, collective responsibility has been said to undermine the efficacy of international law. Hersch Lauterpacht wrote that 'there is cogency in the view that unless responsibility is imputed and attached to persons of flesh and blood, it rests with no one'.[38] Philip Allott said: 'the moral effect of the law is vastly reduced if the human agents involved are able to separate themselves personally both from the duties the law imposes and from the responsibility which it entails.'[39]

However, responses at the collective level do not exclude responses at the individual level.[40] Moreover, in particular cases reconciliation may require precisely responses at the collective level.[41] Punishment of a relatively limited number of political and military authorities of the Third Reich would have been unlikely to allow for reconciliation between victimized groups and the German state.

[35] R. Jennings, 'The Pinochet extradition case in the English courts', in L. Boisson de Chazournes and V. Gowlland-Debbas (eds.), *The International Legal System in Quest of Equity and Universality: Liber Amicorum George Abi-Saab* (Martinus Nijhoff Publishers, The Hague 2001), p. 693.

[36] C. Kutz, *Complicity: Ethics and Law for a Collective Age* (Cambridge University Press, Cambridge 2000), p. 113.

[37] M. P. Scharf and P. R. Williams, 'The functions of justice and anti-justice in the peace-building process' (2003) 35 *Case Western Reserve Journal of International Law* 170; M. Ignatieff, *The Warrior's Honour* (Penguin, Canada 1999), p. 178.

[38] H. Lauterpacht, *International Law and Human Rights* (Archon Books, Hamden, reprint 1968) (1950), p. 40.

[39] P. Allott, 'State responsibility and the unmaking of international law' (1988) 29 *Harvard Journal of International Law* 14.

[40] Article 58 of the Articles on State Responsibility. The Articles on the Responsibility of States for Internationally Wrongful Acts (hereafter Articles on State Responsibility) are contained in the Annex of UN Doc A/Res/56/83 of 28 January 2002. Genocide Case (n. 22) para. 173. See further A. Nollkaemper and H. van der Wilt, 'Conclusions and outlook', this volume, Chapter 15.

[41] Fletcher and Weinstein (n. 22) 601.

A second objection to responsibility of a group, state or other collectivity is that it may confront innocent individual members of that collectivity with the consequences of the criminal acts of a few. Non-responsible persons are made to bear the responsibility for (or rather the consequences of) the acts of others.[42] It is a standard critique on traditional (say, pre-Second World War) international law that it located responsibility at the level of collectivities rather than individuals.[43] It often has been maintained that the idea of collective responsibility was primitive and immoral, in view of its effects on innocent members of a collectivity.[44] Modern international criminal law is premised on the idea that no individual may be held accountable, or be punished, for offences that he himself did not commit. In principle, members of a group are not criminally liable for acts performed by other members (notably leaders) of such a groups in which these members themselves did not participate.[45] Scharf and Williams note that 'the first function of justice is to expose the individuals responsible for atrocities and to avoid assigning guilt to an entire people'.[46] Cassese writes: 'Collective responsibility is no longer acceptable.'[47] Resorting to

42 S. Darcy, *Collective Responsibility and Accountability Under International Law* (Transnational Publishers, Leiden 2007), p. xvi; Vetlesen (n. 3) 158. Cf. the remarks by John Dugard, Special Rapporteur on Situation of Human Rights in the Occupied Palestinian Territories on the effects of the sanctions against Hamas on the Palestinian people (noting that that it was not the Hamas government that was being punished, but the Palestinian people). See presentation by John Dugard, held at the Human Rights Council Special Session on Human Rights Situation on Occupied Arab Territories, 5 July 2006, UNOG Press Release, available at www.unog.ch/unog/website/news_media.nsf/(httpNewsByYear_en)/C9422B675B9EC069C12571A2004F2783?OpenDocument, accessed 3 July 2008.

43 See e.g. F. Parisi and G. Dari-Mattiacci, 'The rise and fall of communal liability in ancient law' (2004) 24 *International Review of Law and Economics* 489–505, available at SSRN: http://ssrn.com/abstract=451581, accessed 3 July 2008; D. J. Levinson, 'Collective sanctions' (2003) 56 *Stanford Law Review* 351–60. More generally: G. F. Mellema, *Collective Responsibility* (Rodopi Press, Atlanta 1997), ch. 4.

44 H. Kelsen, *Law and Peace in International Relations. The Oliver Wendell Holmes Lectures, 1940–41* (Harvard University Press, Cambridge, MA 1942), pp. 97–8. See also S. Levinson, 'Responsibility for crimes of war' (1973) 2 *Philosophy and Public* 246 (stating that: 'No sanction can be directed at an organization – whether the method chosen is a fine or dissolution – without also affecting at least some of the individuals with ties to the entity').

45 But note that development of the joint criminal enterprise doctrine had expanded the possibility that individuals could be held responsible for acts they did not themselves commit; see H. van der Wilt, 'Joint criminal enterprise and functional perpetration', this volume, Chapter 7 and E. van Sliedregt, 'System criminality at the ICTY', this volume, Chapter 8.

46 Scharf and Williams (n. 37) 170.

47 A. Cassese, *International Criminal Law* (Oxford University Press, Oxford 2003), p. 136.

collective responsibility would thus be a step back to the primitive collective responsibility from which the international legal order has just liberated itself.

A partial response to this objection is that, in particular situations, responses targeted at the level of the collectivity are justified because a large part of the population or 'members' of a group were in fact co-responsible for failing to prevent, for instance, the rise of a political party or a leader who led the collectivity into the criminal acts.[48] In some cases, a substantial part of the group was indeed involved in the crimes, as was the case in Rwanda during the genocide in the early 1990s.[49] Also, Jaspers recognized, in the form of political guilt, the responsibility of members of a collectivity for the acts that resulted from their active or passive behaviour.[50]

Another part of the answer is that collective sanctions do not necessarily have effects for all members of the collectivity.[51] While, in theory, it may be true that sanctions imposed on a collectivity affect members of that collectivity, in the practice of international reparations that certainly does not seem to be the case in any substantial way. Darcy notes that, 'for citizens who are the constituent members of a State, the impact upon them of any consequences of state responsibility is usually negligible'.[52]

A third objection is that collective responsibility would (re-)introduce the notion of collective guilt in international law. However, responses targeted at the level of the system, particularly if these do not entail criminal responses, need not carry the connotation of collective guilt. They can be

[48] G. Arrangio-Ruiz, *Fifth Report on State Responsibility, Extract from the Yearbook of the International Law Commission* (vol. III(1) 1993) para. 266, available at http://untreaty.un.org/ilc/documentation/english/a_cn4_453.pdf, accessed 3 July 2008.

[49] Alvarez (n. 32) 467–8 (noting that: 'When one percent of a country's population is under arrest for such offences, amid credible charges that millions were involved in atrocities, an attempt to dissemble on the scope of likely complicity is likely to fail'); M. A. Drumbl, 'Pluralizing international criminal justice' (2005) 103 *Michigan Law Review* 1311. Compare H. Mannheim, *Group Problems in Crime and Punishment* (Routledge & Kegan Paul, London 1955), p. 44 (distinguishing various connections between individual and collective responsibility and singling out 'collective responsibility for mass crime', in which the larger group is held responsible 'for crime committed by some considerable section of its members').

[50] K. Jaspers, *The Question of German Guilt* (trans., Fordham University Press, New York, NY 2000); Mannheim (n. 49) 62.

[51] C. Tomuschat, *International Law: Ensuring the Survival of Mankind on the Eve of a New Century* (vol. 281, Recuil des Cours, The Hague 1999), p. 293.

[52] Darcy (n. 42) xvii. See e.g. International Crisis Group, 'After Mecca: engaging Hamas', Middle East Report No. 62 (28 February 2007) available at www.crisisgroup.org/home/index.cfm?id=4677, accessed 3 July 2008 (discussing effects of the sanctions on Hamas).

of a fundamentally different nature than individual criminal responsibility, to which the idea of guilt is inherent.[53] As noted by Michael Walzer, the distribution of costs over a population that may result from state responsibility for international crimes 'is not the distribution of guilt'.[54]

A fourth objection is that focusing on the level of collectivities rather than on individuals may have destabilizing effects.[55] It might undermine the efforts of newly formed democracies or governments to stabilize a society after a period of reconstruction. The punishment of the German state (and society) in Versailles may be blamed for the breakdown of the European order in the 1930s and 1940s.[56] The effects of the isolation of Hamas in Palestine may be a modern case in point,[57] as is the adverse effects of 'de-Bathification' on the stabilization and development of Iraq.[58] Larry Cata Backer argues that, for this reason, individual responsibility often indeed prevails: the individual is sacrificed so that the group can continue.[59] This may explain the one-dimensional (because mainly focused on individuals) international responses to the crimes committed by Serbian agents or by groups and individuals that acted with the support of Serbia – the international community had a prime interest in letting the state of Serbia continue and re-establish itself quickly as a stable political entity.

53 T. Franck, 'Individual criminal liability and collective civil responsibility: do they reinforce or contradict one another' (2007) 6 *Washington University Global Studies Law Review* 570.

54 M. Walzer, *Just and Unjust Wars* (Basic Books, New York, NY 1977), p. 297.

55 M. Osiel, 'Why prosecute? Critics of criminal punishment for mass atrocity' (2000) 22 *Human Rights Quarterly* 120. See e.g. 'The Struggle for Iraq: Reconstruction; U.S. Generals Fault Ban on Hussein's Party' in *New York Times* (15 January 2008), available at http://query.nytimes.com/gst/fullpage.html?res=9F05E7DC163AF932A15757C0A9629C8B63, accessed 3 July 2008 (citing a US general, who stated that the 'de-Baathification' policy had caused many Sunnis to feel 'disenfranchised' from the emerging Iraqi government, which had created a destabilizing effect).

56 G. Simpson, 'Men and abstract entities: individual responsibility and collective guilt in international criminal law', this volume, Chapter 4.

57 N. J. Brown, 'The Peace Process has no clothes – the decay of the Palestinian and the international response' (2007) *Carnegie Endowment Web Commentary, Middle East Program*, available at www.carnegieendowment.org/files/BrownCommentaryjune072.pdf, accessed 3 July 2008; Division for Palestinian Rights (DPR), 'United Nations Seminar on Assistance to the Palestinian People' (Doha 5 and 6 February 2007), available at http://unispal.un.org/UNISPAL.NSF/fd807e46661e3689852570d00069e918/9b020962bbde8ee2852572f8005f11f3!OpenDocument, accessed 3 July 2008.

58 See e.g. W. Phares and R. G. Rabil, *De-Bathification Went too Far*, at http://hnn.us/articles/4624.html, accessed 3 July 2008.

59 L. Catá Backer, 'The Fuhrer principle of international law: individual responsibility and collective punishment' (2003) 21 *Penn State International Law Review* 509–67, available at SSRN: http://ssrn.com/abstract=410460, accessed 3 July 2008.

This objection needs to be taken seriously. However, it will have to be balanced against the objectives of responsibility in relation to system criminality: is stability more valuable than incapacitating a regime that is responsible for mass atrocities? More fundamentally, it will have to be taken into account that, while responses to system criminality may delegitimize regimes, they do not necessarily incapacitate them.[60]

Each of these objections in particular cases may carry weight and may influence the fashioning of legal policy in regard to situations of system criminality. However, none of them fundamentally undermines the hypothesis that underlies this book: that in situations were international crimes are committed, the relevant actors' law should not only pursue individual responsibility but also target the system in which the individuals concerned were embedded.

4. *The individualistic nature of international law with regard to system criminality*

Proceeding from the working hypothesis that responsibility in relation to system criminality should recognize the role of 'the system', this book is based on our preliminary assessment that international law in its present form does not adequately deal with the role of systems in international crimes.

The systemic nature of international crimes is recognized in the definitions of international crimes.[61] That is certainly true for crimes of genocide[62] and crimes against humanity.[63] Although a Trial Chamber

[60] See A. Nollkaemper and H. van der Wilt, 'Conclusions and outlook', this volume, Chapter 15.

[61] O. Triffterer, 'Prosecution of States for Crimes of State' (1996) 67 *Revue Internationale de Droit Penal* 346; *Democratic Republic of the Congo v Belgium*, Case Concerning the Arrest Warrant of 11 April 2000, ICJ Judgment (14 February 2002) dissenting opinion of Judge Al-Khasawneh (noting that such acts 'are definitionally State acts') (para. 6). This last remark should be qualified to encompass other organized groups that may oppose the state.

[62] Article 6, ICC Statute. During the negotiations of the Genocide Convention, the United Kingdom took the position that the Convention should be directed at states and not individuals, as it was impossible to blame any particular individual for actions for which whole governments or states are responsible. W. Schabas, *Genocide in International Law* (Cambridge University Press, Cambridge 2000), p. 419. Also, Denmark considered that in cases of genocide or aggression, the responsibility cannot be limited to the individual acting on behalf of the state, *ibid.*, 442.

[63] Article 7, ICC Statute (defining crimes against humanity as acts 'when committed as part of a widespread or systematic attack directed against any civilian population').

of the ICTY deemed the case of the 'lone génocidaire' theoretically possible,[64] genocide as such does not seem possible without the involvement of a larger collectivity.[65] The situation for war crimes is slightly different in that, compared with genocide and crimes against humanity, these are more likely to be committed as individual acts. However, war distinguishes itself from individual ordinary crimes by its organized nature, and more often than not war crimes will have the systemic element as required by the definition of system criminality.[66] Note also that the ICC Statute provides that the Court has jurisdiction over such crimes 'in particular when committed as part of a plan or policy or as part of a large-scale commission of such crimes'.[67] The systematic nature of crimes is particularly clear for aggression. Though not (yet) within the jurisdiction of the ICC, most definitions of aggression assume that perpetrators can commit aggression only if they order or participate actively in the planning, preparation, initiation or waging of aggression by a state.[68] Finally, torture is also characterized as an official act. Though acts of torture of course can be committed by state officials against official policy (and, as such, would not be part of system criminality as defined in this book), there would seem to be many cases where torture indeed has a systematic character and is condoned and perhaps supported by the policy of an organization, exemplified by the events in *Abu Ghraib*.[69]

[64] *Prosecutor v Jelisic*, IT-95–10-T, Judgment, Trial Chamber I (14 December 1999) paras. 100, 101.

[65] Van der Wilt notes: 'It would be simply preposterous for an individual to boast that by his actions alone he could achieve the goal of destroying a whole group. In the normal situation, the perpetrator of genocide may at the most feel confident that his conduct might contribute to the concerted action of annihilating the group'; see H. van der Wilt, 'Genocide, complicity in genocide and international v. domestic jurisdiction. Reflections on the *van Anraat* Case' (2006) 4 JICJ 242.

[66] See section II below.

[67] Article 8(1), ICC Statute.

[68] Preparatory Commission for the International Criminal Court (11 October 2001) UN Doc. PCNICC/2002/WGCA/RT.1/Rev.1, 10 July 2002 Discussion Paper proposed by the Coordinator, www.un.org/law/icc/documents/aggression/aggressiondocs.htm, accessed 3 July 2008; see also D. N. Nsereko, 'Agression under the Rome Statute of the International Criminal Court' (2002) 71 NJIL 518.

[69] S. Strasser (ed.), 'The Abu Grahib investigations, the official Independent Panel and Pentagon Reports on the shocking prisoner abuse in Iraq' (Public Affairs, New York 2004). See further, H. C. Kelman, 'The policy context of international crimes', this volume, Chapter 2.

However, while the law of individual responsibility thus recognizes the systematic nature of international crimes, the responsibility that it envisages (whether under the ICC Statute or under the various conventions such as the Geneva Conventions or the Torture Convention) is focused on the individual, rather than on the level of the system. The systemic level may be relevant for the jurisdiction of the ICC, but the principles and procedures of individual responsibility do not affect that level as such.[70]

The law of international criminal responsibility increasingly has attempted to address the collective nature of international crimes, through such concepts as joint criminal enterprise. The international criminal law paragdigm of individual responsibility has thus widened its scope.[71] These attempts will be explored in various chapters in this book. But the question is whether these criminal law approaches will be enough to address the causal mechanisms referred to in section I.2 of this introduction and reach the level of the system.

Of course, the international community does not entirely neglect these organizational contexts. In regard to the conflict in Darfur, the UN, the AU, the EU and individual states have addressed the government of Sudan and to a lesser extent rebel groups as relevant actors who may have the power to change the course of events. However, compared to the relatively organized way in which the international community deals with individual suspects, responses that target these collective entities are unorganized and definitively legally less developed.[72] The *Genocide case* before the ICJ was a rare exception to the predominantly political responses to the role of organized entities in situations of system criminality.[73] The fact

70 Note, however, that it has been held that punishment of individuals may in effect constitute punishment of state. P. M. Dupuy, 'International Criminal Responsibility of the Individual and International Responsibility of the State', in A. Cassese, P. Gaeta and J. R. W. D. Jones (eds.), *The Rome Statute of the International Criminal Court: A Commentary* (Oxford University Press, Oxford 2002), p. 1085 (noting that: 'the promoters of the various international criminal courts undoubtedly intended, by punishing individuals, also to punish the actions of the State to which the acts may be attributed'.) Also, A. A. Cancado Trindade, 'Complementarity between state responsibility and individual responsibility for grave violations of human rights: the crime of state revisited', in M. Ragazzi, *International Responsibility Today: Essays in Memory of Oscar Schachter* (Martinus Nijhoff, Leiden and Boston 2005), p. 265.

71 A. Clapham, 'Issues of complexity, complicity and complementarity: from the Nuremberg trials to the dawn of the new International Criminal Court', in P. Sands (ed.), *From Nuremberg to the Hague* (Cambridge University Press, Cambridge 2003), p. 62; Drumbl (n. 49) 1305.

72 N. White, 'Responses of political organs to crimes by states', this volume, Chapter 14.

73 Genocide Case (n. 22).

that, largely due to the jurisdictional limitations, neither the ICJ nor any other court was able to identify a collectivity that was responsible for the genocide illustrates the shortcoming of the law of international responsibility in dealing with collectivities in situations of system crimes and the need for rethinking the connection between international law and system criminality.[74] Addressing the level of the system is essential if the power of the causal mechanisms identified above is to be mitigated. There is also a more pragmatic reason to supplement individual with collective forms of responsibility. The group as a whole may be better positioned to cause a change in behaviour: it is in a better position to monitor and control individuals whose actions matter.[75]

It is for these reasons that the present book addresses the main legal avenues that are available within the international legal order to address the increasingly important problem of system criminality, and to identify the need and possibilities for improving such avenues.

II. The concept of system criminality

Until now, we have used the term system criminality in a rather loose way to refer to the organizational context of individual crimes or to collectivities of which individuals form part. It is now necessary to consider the concept in more detail, so as to provide a conceptual basis for the chapters that follow.

1. General definition

According to the *Oxford English Dictionary*, the term 'system' refers to 'an organized or connected group of objects', and '[a] group, set, or aggregate of things, natural or artificial, forming a connected or complex whole'.[76] The definition is pertinent for our purposes, as it underlines the concept that systems which are involved in mass atrocities are more than collections of isolated individuals – key factors are connection and organization.

[74] E.g., P. Gaeta, 'On what conditions can a state be held responsible for genocide?' (2007) 18 (4) EJIL 631; C. Kreß, 'The International Court of Justice and the elements of the crime of genocide' (2007) 18 EJIL 619; C. Tomuschat, 'Reparation in cases of genocide' (2007) 5 (4) JICJ 905; A. Gattini, 'Evidentiary issues in the ICJ's Genocide judgment' (2007) 5 JICJ 889.

[75] Levinson (n. 43) 348.

[76] OED Online Database, available at http://dictionary.oed.com/entrance.dtl, accessed 3 July 2008.

The term 'system criminality' has not often been used in literature on international crimes. The most notable exception is B. V. A. Röling, who used the concept to refer to situations where 'governments order crimes to be committed, or encourage the commitment, or favour and permit or tolerate the committing of crimes'.[77] He argued that the commission of war crimes 'serves the system, and is caused by the system'.[78] In this book we build on this definition of Röling, and define system criminality as a situation where collective entities order or encourage international crimes to be committed, or permit or tolerate the committing of international crimes.[79]

Three aspects of this definition need further clarification: the forms of involvement of collectivities with international crimes (II.2), the nature and forms of collectivities that may be involved in system criminality (II.3), and the focus on international crimes (II.4).

2. *Modes of involvement*

Collective entities can be involved in the commission of international crimes in an active or passive manner. Active involvement may take the form of ordering or encouraging international crimes to be committed, for instance by orders from military or civilian commanders, whose acts in term may be attributable to states or other collectivities. Encouragement may also take more subtle forms, as incitement and propaganda, dehumanisation of victims of violence by indoctrination, and policies directed

[77] Röling (n. 23) 138. [78] Röling (n. 23).

[79] The definition is closely related to Kelman's concept of crimes of obedience; see H. C. Kelman, 'The policy context of international crimes', this volume, Chapter 2. Note that the concept of 'system' can also be used in a wider meaning. It does not then relate to the structure of separate collective entities (such as rebel movements, states, international organizations), but rather to the structural relationship *between* such entities. In this sense, the term 'system' has been applied to the anarchical structure of international relations that may explain behaviour of states and perhaps also of individual state agents. See K. N. Waltz, *Man, the State and War: A Theoretical Analysis* (Columbia University Press, New York, NY 1959) chs. 4 and 5 and K. N. Waltz, *Theory of International Politics* (Addison-Wesley, Reading, MA 1979). It also may be extended to structural relationships between rebel movements, or between such groups and the government – in that respect any proper analysis of events in Darfur should extend to this level of analysis. However, this level is not easily addressed by the principles of international responsibility. It is for this reason that the discussions of the phenomenon of system criminality in this book focus primarily on the former meaning of system: the collectivity and its structure, institutions and processes as such, that in principle can meaningfully be subjected to the law of international responsibility, rather than on the relations between them.

as changing the normative climate.[80] Passive involvement may take the form of permitting or tolerating the committing of international crimes, by systematically not acting when individuals commit international crimes which further the objectives of the state.[81]

In general, the involvement of states or other collective entities will be 'systematic' in terms of our definition of system criminality if it is supported by a plan or policy. In line with the definition of Röling, we are interested in situations where the commission of international crimes 'serves the system, and is caused by the system'.[82] Though formally an *ultra vires* act of a commander to commit an international crime will be attributed to the state, and in that respect can then be said to be on the order of a state, this is not the type of state involvement that falls within the concept of system criminality. What we are concerned with is involvement of a collectivity that is based on a plan or policy and that remains in place, even when an individual author of a criminal act is removed.[83]

3. *Types of collectivities*

Collective entities that are involved in system criminality can take many different forms. Röling confined himself to states.[84] We believe this to be unduly narrow in view of the wide variety of organizational contexts and collective entities in which international crimes are committed. Collective entities that order or encourage international crimes to be committed may also include organized armed groups,[85] ruling political parties, as in the case of Nazi-Germany,[86] and perhaps also international organizations. As to the latter: while we tend to relate international organizations to noble objectives, experience has shown that, like any

[80] Text to notes 23–8, above.

[81] Christenson notes: '[...] benign neglect of State may serve many subjective political purposes. Indeed, through loose reins government inaction can function as easily as a conscious part of the prudent exercise of power': G. A. Christenson, 'Attributing acts of omission to the state' (1991) 12 *Michigan Journal of International Law* 316–17. See also Alvarez (n. 32).

[82] Röling (n. 23).

[83] Compare Art. 8(1) of the ICC Statute, which uses this qualification to limit the jurisdiction of the ICC in regard to international crimes.

[84] Röling (n. 23).

[85] J. Kleffner, 'The collective accountability of organized armed groups for system crimes', this volume, Chapter 11.

[86] Vetlesen (n. 3) 44–5 (discussing the impact of the Nazi party on the German state and highlighting that the explanatory variable for the holocaust was to be found at the level of the party rather than of the state).

other bureaucracies and institutions, they may slide into policies that condone systematic crimes – perhaps exemplified by the UN's failure to protect the populations in Srebrenica and Rwanda.[87] While this in itself may not be sufficient to engage international responsibility of the organization in relation to system crimes, the situation may be different where an organization provides aid to acts that violate peremptory norms of international law. The NATO bombardments of the FRY in 1999 may be a case in point. It is noteworthy that the ILC did envisage the possibility of a 'serious breach by an international organization of an obligation arising under a peremptory norm of general international law'.[88]

The collective entities that may be involved in system criminality can be differentiated on a number of dimensions. First, they may vary in size. In some cases, crimes may be committed or caused by a small group of individuals that constitute the leadership of collectivity. Tomuschat notes that, mostly, the commission of crimes by a state 'means that a people has fallen pray to a criminal leadership'.[89] An example may be the case of Liberia in the 1990s under the leadership of Charles Taylor. On the other extreme, a collectivity may take the form of a regime that extends through various layers of government, such as that of Saddam Hussein in the 1990s.

Collective entities involved in system criminality may also vary in organizational nature, ranging from the highly organized bureaucracy of Nazi-Germany to the seemingly loosely organized collective action by clans in Somalia.[90] Though the presence of some form of institutions and rules normally is a defining feature of system criminality, the degree of organization may vary, with obvious consequences for the proper legal responses.

Finally, collective entities involved in system criminality may differ in legal nature, as they may or may not possess legal personality. This is a matter of some relevance, as it is only when the collectivity has legal

[87] For the former, see Report of the Secretary-General pursuant to General Assembly Resolution 53/35, 'The Fall of Srebrenica' (1999) UN Doc A/54/549. For Rwanda, see the remark by Kofi Annan that he could and should have done more to stop the genocide in Rwanda ten years ago and that: 'The international community is guilty of sins of omission'; see *UN chief's Rwanda genocide regret*, http://news.bbc.co.uk/1/hi/world/africa/3573229.stm, accessed 3 July 2008.

[88] Article 44 of the draft Articles on Responsibility of International Organizations, ILC, Report of the fifty-ninth Session (2007), UN Doc. A/62/10, 199.

[89] Tomuschat (n. 51) 290.

[90] J. Kleffner, 'The collective accountability of organized armed groups for system crimes', this volume, Chapter 11. See, on the influence of a state apparatus in producing the conditions for individual criminality, Vetlesen (n. 3) 16.

personality that responsibility (under domestic or international law, depending on the question whether the personality is recognized by domestic or by international law) may be attached to that legal person as such.[91] This explains major differences between the way in which the international legal order deals with states, on the one hand, and rebel movements, on the other.[92]

4. *System criminality and international crimes*

There is one other aspect in which our definition differs from that by Röling. Our definition, and this book, is confined to the narrow category of crimes that international law recognizes as international crimes under customary law. This category also has been referred to as 'core crimes'.[93] Though the category of crimes in which systems are involved may well be broader (it may, for instance, include corruption), there are good reasons for confining the book to this narrow category of 'core crimes'.

First, it is precisely these crimes that are defined in terms of their systemic nature and that more often than not will involve system criminality.[94] Second, as this category of crimes threatens the fundamental values of the international community,[95] the legal responses to such crimes are largely influenced by the involvement of the international community. This is illustrated by the fact that a large number of states has brought such crimes within the jurisdiction of the International Criminal Court[96] and that, when involving the responsibility of a state, the ILC thought it proper to subject them to a separate chapter on serious breaches of peremptory norms of international law.[97] The effectuation of responsibility is, in the final analysis, thus not in the hands of individual states but can be 'pulled' by the international community.[98] In regard to state

[91] Wells (n. 19).

[92] See, respectively, Chapters 12, 13 and 11 in this volume. Legal personality also may mean that individuals may hide behind the legal person and that their acts can only be attributed to the legal person, though this generally will not hold for international crimes, see Art. 27 of the ICC Statute. Individuals may still be shielded if a case would be brought before a domestic court of a foreign state.

[93] E.g. W. N. Ferdinandusse, *Direct Application of International Criminal Law in National Courts* (TMC Asser Press, The Hague 2006), p. 10.

[94] Text to notes 61–69 above.

[95] Pellet (n. 9) 65–6; Jaspers (n. 19) 853.

[96] Text to notes 62–7 above.

[97] Articles 40–41 of the Articles on State Responsibility.

[98] However, responsibility of individuals or collectivities against the international community of course can coexist with responsibilities in or towards particular states. In criminal law, it coexists with responsibility of individuals in states that have jurisdiction over the crimes. In the law of state responsibility, it coexists with responsibility towards

responsibility, this follows from the fact that in the ILC Articles on State Responsibility injured states are not, as is the case in regard to 'normal breaches', allowed to waive a claim that they may have against a responsible state[99] as well as from the rights of non-injured states.[100] In regard to individual responsibility, this follows from the principles of complementarity in the ICC Statute[101] and primacy in the ICTY and the ICTR Statutes.[102] Our focus is largely on the ways in which the international community can develop, organize and enforce the proper legal responses to situations of system criminality.

III. The role of international responsibility in respect of system criminality

The focus of this book is on one relatively narrow set of legal responses to system criminality, those provided by the law of international responsibility. We recognize that the law of international responsibility has only a relatively minor role in regard of system criminality. The international legal order has at its disposal a variety of 'tools' to address causes and effects of system criminality. International legal responsibility is one use of those tools, alongside such instruments as military intervention, economic sanctions, political pressure by states or international organizations, development aid, etc.

Many states, including the United States, have taken the position that the proper responses of the international community towards cases of system criminality are to be left to political organs, rather than to the domain of international responsibility.[103] This explains the demise of the concept of 'state crimes',[104] but also more generally the virtual non-use of

the injured state(s). The result may often be a coexistence of latent claims to effectuate international responsibility at the international level and competing and more effective claims at domestic level.

[99] Articles 20 and 45 of the Articles on State Responsibility. See also Pellet (n. 9) 70.

[100] Article 48 of the Articles on State Responsibility.

[101] E.g. Art. 17 of the ICC Statute. Although the principle protects sovereignty and jurisdiction of states parties, it also allows for the ICC to pull the case if national prosecution does not satisfy the criteria set forth in the ICC Statute.

[102] Article 9(2) of the Statute of the ICTY; Art. 8(2) of the Statute of the ICTR.

[103] Comments United States in UN Doc. A/CN.4/515 (2001) 53. See also J. Crawford, *The International Law Commission's Articles on State Responsibility* (Cambridge University Press, Cambridge 2002), commentary to Art. 40, para. 9.

[104] See e.g. E. Wyler, 'From "State Crime" to Responsibility for "Serious Breaches of Obligations under Peremptory Norms of General International Law"' (2002) 13 EJIL 1147–60.

state responsibility in situations of system criminality. The law of responsibility was not a major factor in, for instance, dismantling the regimes of Pol Pot, Slobodan Milosevic or Saddam Hussein. Several scholars, including Jennings and Koskeniemmi, have pointed out that, in this area, international law may be better served by political processes than by formal responsibility.[105]

At this point there is a noticeable difference between the domestic level and the international level. While domestically, responsibility (notably individual criminal responsibility) is seen as the harshest intervention, this certainly is not true at the international level (though it may be true for an individual targeted). Other means target the state much more directly; e.g. sanctions and military intervention.[106] Tallgren observes: 'Criminal law is not the *ultima ratio* for the international community. It is, instead, a subsequent means in addition to the mere exercise of military and economic power.'[107]

Despite the relatively modest role of international responsibility in relation to system crimes, this book is based on the assumption that international responsibility, in both its manifestations – criminal responsibility and as state responsibility – may play a distinct and potentially significant role in the responses of the international community to situations of system criminality. The law of international responsibility may, at least in theory, serve each of the aims to which international law in general may aspire in regard to situations of system criminality: termination, prevention of recurrence, prevention in other cases, reconciliation and reparation in regard of international crimes.[108] Moreover, we proceed from the assumption that against the overwhelming dominance of political responses to situations of system criminality (only to a relatively limited extent subjected to and embedded in legal procedures and safeguards),[109] the law of international responsibility can bring

[105] See R. Jennings, 'International Law Reform and Progressive Development', in G. Hafner *et al.* (eds.), *Liber Amicorum Professor Seidl-Hohenveldern – in Honour of his 80th Birthday* (Kluwer Law International, The Hague 1998), p. 328; M. Koskenniemi, 'Solidarity Measures: State Responsibility as a New International Order?' (2002) 72 *British Yearbook of International Law* 337.

[106] Tallgren (n. 20) 589.

[107] Tallgren (n. 20) 590.

[108] W. M. Reisman, 'Legal responses to genocide and other massive violations of human rights' (1996) 59 *Law and Contemporary Problems* 75. See further discussion in A. Nollkaemper and H. van der Wilt, 'Conclusions and outlook', this volume, Chapter 15.

[109] N. White, 'Responses of political organs to crimes by states', this volume, Chapter 14.

an important rule of law quality to the legal responses to situations of system criminality.[110]

Within the law of international responsibility there exists a variety of options that will be considered in this book. Some of these remain within the paradigm of individual responsibility, based on the notion that collective action is, after all, the product of individual action,[111] but seek to widen the net so as to cover more persons involved and to make it easier to make individuals responsible.[112] These forms include command responsibility, responsibility based on the principle of joint criminal enterprise and responsibility based on membership of criminal organizations.[113] Moving beyond the paradigm of individual responsibility, various forms of collective responsibility are available that concern acts of the group or system as a whole, rather than responsibility of the collectivity for acts of individuals.[114] These forms include criminal responsibility of organizations,[115] responsibility of rebel groups,[116] and responsibility of states.[117] The responsibility of international organizations for situations of system criminality is not discussed in this book.

The various forms of international responsibility differ not only in their subjects, but also in regard to the nature of responsibility. Responsibility towards a community (a defining feature of international responsibility in regard to system criminality) may lead one quickly into associating responsibility with criminal law. However, in international law that only holds for the responsibility of individuals. The conceptual structures of existing law of international responsibility pose limits to what we can

110 I. Brownlie, *The Rule of Law in International Affairs: International Law at the Fiftieth Anniversary of the United Nations* (Martinus Nijhoff Publishers, The Hague, Boston and Cambridge, MA 1988), pp. 79–80.

111 Kutz (n. 36) 67.

112 Clapham (n. 71).

113 See K. Ambos, 'Command responsibility and *Organisationsherrschaft:* ways of attributing international crimes to the "most responsible"', this volume, Chapter 6; H. van der Wilt, 'Joint criminal enterprise and functional perpetration', this volume, Chapter 7; E. Sliedregt, 'System criminality at the ICTY', this volume Chapter 8 and N. Jørgenson, 'Criminality of organizations under international law', this volume, Chapter 9.

114 See, on the distinction, M. Bovens, *The Quest for Responsibility* (Cambridge University Press, Cambridge 1998), p. 96.

115 A. Eser, 'Criminality of organizations: lessons from domestic law – a comparative perspective', this volume, Chapter 10.

116 J. Kleffner, 'The collective accountability of organized armed groups for system crimes', this volume, Chapter 11.

117 I. Scobbie, 'Assumptions and presuppositions: state responsibility for system crimes', this volume, Chapter 12 and A. Zimmermann and M. Teichmann, 'State responsibility for international crimes', this volume, Chapter 13.

reasonably conceive as the aims of the law of international responsibility. The ill-fated history of the concept of state crimes illustrates the point.

However, it by no means is necessary to identify international responsibility for system crimes with criminal responsibility. It is to be recalled that the term system criminality refers to the involvement of systems, as described above, in criminal acts, not to the criminality of that system. It is not the system that is criminal – is it in the nature of criminality that is systematic. This implies that it is not necessary that the system (e.g. a state or organised armed group) is subject to criminal sanctions. Legal responses to cases of system criminality may also be modelled on a tort analogy, perhaps apart from the fact that criminal responses have the added value of moral condemnation.[118]

In view of the rather distinct nature of legal responses to the involvement of organized armed groups in situations of system criminality, this book extends the rather narrow legal concept of responsibility to the broader concept of accountability. While accountability, like responsibility, involves an assessment of conduct of actors against prior established norms and are generally followed by some sort of sanction, it does not, as responsibility, involve a determination of an internationally wrongful act.[119]

The book as a whole takes as its starting point that the various forms of international responsibility are not mutually exclusive and may supplement each other. Trindade rightly observed that the current 'compartmentalized conception of international responsibility – of States and individuals – leads … to the eradication of impunity in only a partial way'.[120] His observation can be extended to include other actors who may engage in, or be involved in, system criminality – international organizations and perhaps even rebel movements such as the Revolutionary United Front in Sierra Leone and terrorist networks such as Al Quaida (which, after all, is addressed as one entity by states and international organizations) – even though these latter entities are not generally subjected to the law of international responsibility but rather to the looser concept of accountability. In the majority of cases in which international law takes an interest in situations of system criminality, international law could thus address both the collectivity and individuals. The result is, in a

[118] Levinson (n. 44) 247–8.

[119] D. Curtin and A. Nollkaemper, 'Conceptualizing accountability in international and European Law' (2007) 36 NYIL 3; J. Brunée, 'International legal accountability through the lens of the law of state responsibility' (2007) 36 NYIL 21.

[120] Trindade (n. 70) 259.

situation that is confined to responsibility of states and individuals, what the ICJ in the *Genocide case* called a 'duality of responsibility'[121] – a situation that can be more complex if more actors are involved.[122]

IV. Roadmap

After this introduction, Chapters 2 and 3 (Kelman and Punch) discuss the policy context of international crimes. A major focus of the discussion in these chapters will be on the different ways in which individual responsibility is influenced by demands from system authorities and by other factors that may explain situations of system criminality. These chapters provide the essential background for a proper assessment of the legal options in regard to system criminality and indeed are key to assessing the validity of the working hypothesis of this book that, in certain cases, responsibility in relation to system criminality should be allocated to the level of 'the system', in its various manifestations, rather than only at the individual level. Though outside the purview of the legal discipline in the strict sense, and requiring excursions into political science, sociology and social-psychology, they are highly relevant for our understanding of proper legal policies in response to situations of system criminality.

Based on the working hypothesis that international crimes can often be explained with reference to the system in which the individual operates, the contributions in this book explore the main legal avenues that are available within the international legal order to address the various forms and manifestations of system criminality.

Chapters 4 and 5 by Simpson and Gattini provide a bridge between the extra-legal chapters and those dealing with more specific legal issues. Simpson and Gattini examine the historical development from the notion of collective responsibility to, post-Nuremberg, the emergence of individual responsibility and in recent years, a renewed recognition of the structural elements of international crimes.

Chapters 6–8 (Ambos, Van der Wilt and Van Sliedrecht) examine the power of key principles of the law on individual responsibility with regard to system criminality. They deal with the concepts of command

[121] Genocide Case (n. 22) para. 173. See also Franck (n. 53) 573 (noting that 'genocide is a hydra-headed monster. It warrants a multifaceted response. The heralded advent of individual liability should not cloud our understanding of the continued importance of state responsibility').

[122] See further, A. Nollkaemper and H. van der Wilt, 'Conclusions and outlook', this volume, Chapter 15, section III.

responsibility, 'functional commission' and joint criminal enterprise. Though each of these concepts is intended to provide a basis for individual responsibility, they also recognize that individuals operate in larger contexts that may explain their acts.

Chapters 9 and 10 by Jørgensen and Eser address criminality of organizations. Specifically, they address the questions whether international criminal law should provide for criminal liability of organizations, either as a basis for holding individual members responsible (Jorgensen) or in regard to the organization as such (Eser). These questions are reviewed both from an international law and a comparative law perspective.

Chapters 11–14 by Kleffner, Scobbie, Zimmerman and White address problems and possibilities of collective entities. Kleffner focuses on the accountability of non-state entities, in particular rebel movements. Zimmerman and Scobbie discuss state responsibility with regard to system criminality and more in particular how, given the absence of a concept of state crimes, the law of state responsibility can be useful or should be developed to address problems of state criminality. Nigel White discusses the appropriateness of the procedures within political organs, notably the United Nations, for dealing with system criminality.

In Chapter 15, the editors synthesize the main outcomes, examine the relationship between the various options and suggest some ways for further developing international law in respect of system criminality.

2

The policy context of international crimes

HERBERT C. KELMAN*

Genocide, mass killing, torture, ethnic cleansing, and other gross violations of human rights are defined as war crimes or crimes against humanity under international law. To develop an adequate explanation of such actions, which is the task of social psychology, and an adequate legal response to them, which is the task of international law, requires going beyond the characteristics of individual perpetrators or even of the situations in which these practices take place. It requires close examination of the political system and of the policy process in which these actions are embedded and that provide the larger context for them.

I. Crimes of obedience

As a first step in this examination, we must define the special nature of the crimes under consideration. Some instances of such crimes may well constitute 'ordinary' crimes – that is, crimes committed in violation of the expectations and instructions of authority. Participation in massacre, torture, or ethnic cleansing would be an ordinary crime in this sense if it were carried out by individual perpetrators on their own initiative and in disregard of the policies and orders of the authorities under which they function. Even a crime committed in the context of an authorized activity – such as a military operation or interrogation of prisoners – could be treated as an ordinary crime if the perpetrator went beyond legally permissible limits: if, for example, a soldier on a reconnaissance mission indiscriminately shot civilians, or if an interrogator used means of pressure in excess of what the rules permitted.

* Richard Clarke Cabot Professor of Social Ethics, Emeritus, Harvard University, USA. The paper draws extensively on two earlier publications: H. C. Kelman, 'The social context of torture: policy process and authority structure' in R. D. Crelinsten and A. P. Schmid (eds.), *The Politics of Pain: Torturers and their Masters* (COMT, University of Leiden, Leiden 1993); H. C. Kelman, 'The policy context of torture: a social-psychological analysis' (2005) 857 *International Review of the Red Cross* 123.

The essence of international crimes, such as war crimes and crimes against humanity, however, is that they are generally not ordinary crimes, but *crimes of obedience*: crimes that take place, not in opposition to the authorities, but under explicit instructions from the authorities to engage in these acts, or in an environment in which such acts are implicitly sponsored, expected, or at least tolerated by the authorities. Lee Hamilton and I have defined a crime of obedience as 'an act performed in response to orders from authority that is considered illegal or immoral by the larger community'.[1] Torture provides a clear example of a crime of obedience: it is considered illegal and immoral by the international community; it is a crime under the UN Convention against Torture of 1984[2] and other relevant international frameworks; and it is similarly defined in the national legal codes of many of the UN's member states. Yet it is the authorities of these very states that often order, encourage, or tolerate systematic policies or sporadic acts of torture.

When does an ordinary crime become a crime of *obedience?* It is often the case – in acts of torture as much as in massacre and other gross violations of human rights – that the perpetrators engage in the action willingly, enthusiastically, and with varying degrees of innovation. But 'the fact that a criminal action serves various personal motives or is carried out with a high degree of initiative and personal involvement does not necessarily remove it from the category of crimes of obedience',[3] as long as the action is supported by the authority structure: as long as the perpetrators believe and have good reason to believe that the action is authorized, expected, at least tolerated, and probably approved by the authorities – that it conforms with official policy and reflects what their superiors would want them to do. To be sure, those who commit these crimes with enthusiasm and initiative are more culpable, from a legal and moral point of view, than those who commit them reluctantly in response to explicit orders. However, whether the action is *caused* or merely *justified* by explicit or implicit orders from superiors, it can be described as a crime of obedience, on the presumption that it would not have taken place without authorization.

1 H. C. Kelman and V. L. Hamilton, *Crimes of Obedience: Toward a Social Psychology of Authority and Responsibility* (Yale University Press, New Haven and London 1989), p. 46; compare the definition of system criminality in A. Nollkaemper, 'Introduction', this volume, Chapter 1, p. 1.

2 J. H. Burgers and H. Danelius, *The United Nations Convention against Torture: A Handbook on the Convention against Torture and Other Cruel, Inhuman or Degrading Treatment or Punishment* (Martinus Nijhoff, Dordrecht/Boston/London 1988), pp. 177–8.

3 Kelman and Hamilton (n. 1) 50.

Recognizing these actions as crimes of obedience immediately directs our attention to the other side of the coin: to the crimes of authority that invariably accompany crimes of obedience. For every subordinate who performs criminal acts under official orders or with the encouragement or toleration of the authorities, there is a superior – or typically an entire hierarchy of superiors – who issue the orders and who formulate the policies that require or permit these acts. Higher-level superiors may in fact not have issued specific orders to engage in these criminal acts, but they are the ones who formulate the policies, create the atmosphere, and establish the framework within which officials at intermediate levels of the hierarchy translate general policy directives into specific orders and actions on the ground.

The fact that crimes of obedience take place within a hierarchical structure makes it especially difficult to pinpoint responsibility for them. Subordinates deny responsibility by reference to superior orders. Superiors are often able to deny responsibility because they are various steps removed from the actions themselves and can claim that the initiative was taken at a lower level or that their instructions were misunderstood. The top leadership is protected by the difficulty in establishing causal links between the general atmosphere and policy directives they convey and the practices designed and carried out at lower levels of the hierarchy. The issue of assignment of responsibility in such situations is a central theme of the work reported in *Crimes of Obedience*,[4] which began with a national survey of the US population on public reactions to the conviction of Lt. William Calley for the My Lai massacre in Vietnam[5] – a prime example of what I have called *sanctioned massacres*.[6]

The important question in determining responsibility is not 'who is responsible?' – the actor or the authority – but 'who is responsible for *what?*' When the question is framed that way, it becomes clear that both ought to be held responsible. The actors themselves are properly held responsible for the actions they perform and the harm they cause, even if they are acting under superior orders. Since the adoption of the

[4] Kelman and Hamilton (n. 1).

[5] H.C. Kelman and L. Hamilton Lawrence, 'Assignment of responsibility in the case of Lt Calley: preliminary report on a national survey'(1972) 28(1) *Journal of Social Issues* 177; H. C. Kelman and V. L. Hamilton, 'Availability for violence: a study of US public reactions to the trial of Lt Calley', in J. D. Ben-Dak (ed.), *The Future of Collective Violence: Societal and Intersocietal Perspectives* (Studentlitteratur, Lund 1974).

[6] H. C. Kelman, 'Violence without moral restraint: reflections on the dehumanization of victims and victimizers'(1973) 29(4) *Journal of Social Issues* 25.

Nuremberg Principles after World War II, which have been incorporated into the military codes of all western states, superior orders cannot be used as an absolute defense for criminal actions on the part of subordinates. The UN Convention against Torture specifically applies this principle to torturers when it states that 'an order from a superior officer or a public authority may not be invoked as a justification of torture'.[7] Subordinates have the obligation to evaluate the legality of orders and to disobey those orders that they know, or should have known, to be illegal.

Superiors, for their part, have the obligation to consider the consequences of the policies they set and to oversee the ways in which those policies are translated into specific orders and actions as they move down the ladder. The authorities' obligation of oversight makes the defense of ignorance of, or lack of control over, the actions of subordinates generally unacceptable, since they are expected to know and to control what their subordinates are doing. Of course, more often than not, massacre and torture do not result from negligence at the top, but from deliberate policy – or perhaps deliberate inattention at the top to the way in which policy is carried out below.

II. The policy context

Conceptualizing international crimes as crimes of obedience implies that they must be understood in the context of the policy process that gives rise to them and of the authority structure within which this policy is carried out. To concretize my analysis of the policy context of international crimes, I focus specifically on torture as a case in point. The same logic applies, however, to sanctioned massacres, to systematic expulsions, and to other war crimes and crimes against humanity.

The issue of torture – particularly in situations of armed conflict or in the fight against terrorism – received widespread international attention when the abuses of Iraqi prisoners by US soldiers at Abu Ghraib came to light in the spring of 2004. Torture, of course, is not a peculiarly American phenomenon. Unfortunately, it is widely practiced in many parts of the world; moreover, it is endemic to autocratic states and is far less prevalent in democratic ones. Abu Ghraib serves as a reminder, however, that even democratic states may resort to torture when a particular set of social conditions is in place, and it illustrates the policy context in which the practice of torture is embedded.

[7] Burgers and Danelius (n. 2) 178.

In the case of Abu Ghraib, the findings of the investigative reporter, Seymour Hersh[8] – the same man, incidentally, who broke the story of the My Lai massacre and its cover-up[9] – make it evident that the abuses were part of a systematic process. They took place in the context of interrogation and were apparently designed to 'soften up' prisoners for questioning by intelligence officers. No doubt, some of the perpetrators engaged in these actions with a greater degree of initiative and sadistic enjoyment than others, but they were operating in an atmosphere of pressure to produce intelligence information from prisoners presumed to be guilty. Whether or not some of the specific abuses and acts of torture were directly ordered, indications are that they were expected, condoned, and encouraged by higher officers. Commanding officers along the different tiers of the hierarchy have been accused, at the least, of exercising insufficient oversight of the conditions of detention and procedures of interrogation that prevailed in Abu Ghraib and other military prisons for suspected terrorists.

In the months following the exposure of the Abu Ghraib abuses, it became increasingly evident that the treatment of the Abu Ghraib prisoners was not an isolated occurrence, nor was it simply the product of decisions and actions (or inaction) at the local level. Similar patterns of abuse, linked to aggressive interrogation techniques, occurred in prisons elsewhere in Iraq, and – going back to 2002 – in Afghanistan and Guantánamo Bay. Numerous documents show that the techniques and practices revealed in Abu Ghraib had 'migrated' from Guantánamo and Afghanistan and that they were authorized or justified at various points by high-ranking officials in the Pentagon and the White House.[10] For example, memos circulating in upper echelons of the administration authorized harsh interrogation techniques; defined torture so narrowly that many forms of painful, debilitating, and degrading treatment became permissible; and suggested that the Geneva Conventions did not apply to 'unlawful combatants.'[11] The mistreatment of prisoners revealed by the various reports, particularly given the context in which it occurred, has

[8] S. Hersh, 'Torture at Abu Ghraib'(2004) 80(11) *The New Yorker*; S. Hersh, 'Chain of command'(2004) 80(12) *The New Yorker.*

[9] S. Hersh, *My Lai 4: A Report on the Massacre and its Aftermath* (Vintage Books, New York, NY 1970); S. Hersh, *Cover-Up* (Random House, New York, NY 1972).

[10] M. Danner, *Torture and Truth: America, Abu Ghraib, and the War on Terror* (New York Review of Books, New York 2004); S. Strasser, *The Abu Ghraib Investigation: The Official Independent Panel and Pentagon Reports on the Shocking Prisoner Abuse in Iraq* (Public Affairs, New York 2004).

[11] Cf. K. Zernike, 'Newly released reports show early concern on prison abuse', *New York Times*, 6 January 2005.

all the earmarks of physical and mental torture. And, indeed, the accounts presented in these reports are highly reminiscent of what is known about the conditions that have given rise to torture so often in the past anywhere in the world.

While I look to the policy process and the authority structure to identify the major determinants of acts of torture as well as the major correctives against these practices, I do not minimize the role of individual and cultural differences. With respect to individual differences, I am sure there is a certain degree of self-selection of individuals who gravitate to the role of torturer. Moreover, those operating within the role vary in their amount of enthusiasm, diligence, and innovativeness that they bring to the task. No doubt differences in personality and background play an important part in determining who becomes a torturer and who acts out that role eagerly and with evident enjoyment. But a focus on structural factors helps us understand why many, perhaps most, torturers are not sadists but ordinary people, doing what they understand to be their jobs. I might add that individual differences in readiness to engage in torture may be related as much to people's orientation toward authority as they are to their propensity toward aggression or their sense of compassion.[12]

Cultural differences – particularly differences in political culture – no doubt also play an important role. Thus, Berto Jongman[13] showed that human rights violations, including torture, were much more likely to occur in non-democratic than in democratic societies (84 per cent v. 25 per cent); and in countries at low levels than in those at high levels of development (84 per cent v. 31 per cent). Democratic countries are less likely to practice torture precisely because of the nature of their policy process and authority structure. But torture does occur even in highly developed democratic societies, usually in the context of counter-terrorist activities or armed conflict, as the experiences of Guantánamo Bay and Abu Ghraib well illustrate. There are social conditions under which democratic cultures that ordinarily respect human rights may sanction torture, just as there are social conditions under which ordinary, decent individuals may be induced to take part in it. Thus, while individual and cultural factors are important determinants of torture, they operate in interaction with the policy process and the authority structure that ultimately give rise to the practice.

12 Kelman and Hamilton (n. 1) chs. 11 and 12.

13 B. Jongman, 'Why some states kill and torture while others do not'(1991) 3(1) *PLOOM Newsletter*.

How can we account for torture and its characteristic manifestations within this framework – both at the macro-level and at the micro-level? At the macro-level, what are the structural and situational conditions that encourage and enable the relevant authorities to use torture as an instrument of policy? At the micro-level, what are the conditions that encourage and enable individuals and organizations to participate when asked to implement this policy?

III. The use of torture as an instrument of policy

Torture has been practiced by collective actors other than states, such as guerrilla groups or liberation movements, but it has been analyzed primarily as a phenomenon linked to the state. The emergence or reemergence of torture as an instrument of policy in the twentieth century is directly related to the nature of the modern state. In particular, as Edward Peters[14] argues in his historical study, torture arises from the combination of two features of the modern state: its vast power and its enormous vulnerability to state enemies, internal and external. The power of the modern state rests in the extent to which it affects all aspects of the life of its citizens and the resources that it can mobilize to control its population. The vulnerability of the modern state stems from the high degree of interdependence of the political, economic, and social institutions required to run a modern society and the resulting ease with which social order can disintegrate and the political authorities can lose control when their legitimacy declines in the eyes of their population or when they confront terrorism and insurgency.

The conditions conducive to the rise of torture as an instrument of state policy are the authorities' perception of an active threat to the security of the state from internal and external sources; the availability of a security apparatus, which enables the authorities to use the vast power at their disposal to counter that threat by repressive means; and the presence within the society of groups defined as enemies of or potential threats to the state (see table 2.1).

The recourse to repression is particularly likely in situations in which opposition represents a challenge to the *legitimacy* of those in power and thus a fundamental threat to their continued ability to maintain power, such as states in which the rulers' legitimacy rests on a unitary, unchangeable ideology (political or religious), or states run by a ruling clique with

[14] E. Peters, *Torture* (Basil Blackwell, New York and London 1985).

an extremely narrow population base (in socioeconomic and/or ethnic terms) but with the support of military forces. However, torture may also be used, sporadically or sometimes systematically, by democratic regimes that find themselves in charge of ethnically distinct populations or subpopulations that do not accept their rule – such as Israel in the occupied territories or Britain in Northern Ireland.

When state authorities resort to torture, they can often point to a history of violence directed against the state: in the form of insurgency, guerrilla operations, or terrorist acts. To be sure, torture may at times be applied to individuals whose only crime is political or religious dissent, or even mere membership in a religious or ethnic community that does not fit into the ruling group's scheme of things. Even where there is a history of violence, the apparatus of torture is not particularly discriminating in the selection of its victims. Individuals who have not participated in violent action at all may be singled out for torture for any number of reasons: because they are members of, or supporters of, political opposition groups; because they belong to an ethnic, religious, or even professional category – as happened in Argentina during its 'dirty war'[15] – that is generally suspect; because they are deemed guilty by association (perhaps because they are related to suspects); or simply because they are picked up at random or on the basis of mistaken identity. Still, the occurrence or perceived threat of violence against the state is central to the rationale for a policy of torture.[16]

Given the centrality of the threat of violence in the rationale for a policy of torture in modern times, it is not surprising that torture is particularly likely to occur in the context of war or armed conflict. Although my analysis so far has focused on torture within the state, aimed at repressing domestic groups or populations whom the authorities perceive as internal threats to the security of the state or as agents and allies of external enemies of the state, it is equally applicable to situations of war and occupation, in which torture may be used against members or suspected supporters of the enemy camp. The use of torture in war situations – often directed at civilians, as well as at military personnel – has become more probable as war has moved from the classical clash between organized armed forces to a clash between whole populations, in which civilian

[15] See A. Elon, 'A letter from Argentina', *The New Yorker*, 21 July 1986.

[16] W. S. Heinz, 'The military, torture and human rights: experiences from Argentina, Brazil, Chile and Uruguay' in R. D. Crelinsten and A. P. Schmid (eds.), *The Politics of Pain: Torturers and their Masters* (COMT, University of Leiden, Leiden 1993).

groups are often specifically targeted.[17] Torture in this context may be used as part of a state's policy of control and repression of the population and as an instrument of interrogation or psychological warfare. The conditions conducive to the use of torture in situations of armed conflict are identical to those outlined in table 2.1. Once again, democratic regimes are not immune to the use of torture under these conditions, as the US actions in Afghanistan and Iraq so clearly illustrate.

IV. Social processes facilitating a policy of torture

At the level of policy formation, there are three important points at which the perceived threat to the security of the state provides the rationale for a policy of torture, and the power of the state enables it to implement that policy: in establishing the purpose and justification of the torture, in recruiting the agents or perpetrators of the torture, and in defining the targets of the torture (see table 2.1).

First, the essential justification of torture, as has already been proposed, is the protection of the state against internal and external threats to its security – which often means the maintenance in power of those more or less narrow elements of the population that have gained control of the

Table 2.1 The policy context of torture[18]

Conditions Conducive to the Use of Torture as an Instrument of Policy	Social Processes Facilitating Torture	
	At level of policy formation	*At level of implementation*
Perception of a security threat	Justification of a policy of torture	Authorization of acts of torture
Existence of a security apparatus	Development of professional torture cadres	Routinization of torture practices
Presence of groups defined as enemies of the state	Exclusion of target groups from protection of the state	Dehumanization of targets of torture

[17] M. Shaw, *War and Genocide: Organized Killing in Modern Society* (Polity Press, Cambridge UK 2003).

[18] H. C. Kelman, 'The policy context of torture: a social-psychological analysis' (2005) 87(857) *International Review of the Red Cross* 128. Reprinted by permission of the publisher, the International Committee of the Red Cross.

state apparatus. The practice of torture is justified by reference to the particular doctrine of the state's legitimization: maintaining law and order or stability, or the rule of 'the people' whom the state claims to embody, or the rule of God, or the survival of western civilization, or the integrity of national institutions. In war situations, of course, the justification for taking up arms, generally couched in terms of defense against threats to national security and to the vital interests of the state, also covers whatever steps are deemed necessary – including torture – to achieve the military objectives.

Second, the agents of torture are defined as a professional force with a significant role in protecting the state against internal threats to its security. The power of the state allows it to mobilize the necessary resources to establish a torture apparatus. A central component of that mobilization process is the recruitment of a cadre of torture practitioners through the development of what is in effect an organized profession – a profession that is wholly owned by the state, that operates within the state's internal security framework, and that is dedicated to the service and protection of the state. Like other professionals, torturers undergo a rigorous process of professional training, socialization, and indoctrination to prepare them for their roles.[19] Typically, this process includes torture resistance training, which acclimatizes them to cruelty.[20] (In war situations, it might be noted here, acclimatization to violence and cruelty is a daily occurrence, requiring no specialized training.) Another element of the professionalization of torture is that it has become an international enterprise. Torturers from different parts of the world come together in international meetings in which they share information about training procedures and torture techniques. The similarity in the techniques of torture used across the world is startling. Some of this is probably due to independent discovery and innovation, but much of it can be credited to professional exchange.

Third, the targets of torture are defined as enemies of the state who constitute serious threats to the state's security and survival. For that, as well as for other reasons, such as their ethnicity or ideology, they are

[19] H. Radtke, 'Torture as an illegal means of control', in F. Bockle and J. Pohier (eds.), *The Death Penalty and Torture* (Seabury Press, New York, NY 1979); J. T. Gibson, 'Factors contributing to the creation of torture', in P. Suefeld (ed.), *Psychology and Torture* (Hemisphere, New York, NY 1990).

[20] Radtke (n. 19); R. D. Crelinsten, 'In their own words: the world of the torturer', in R. D. Crelinsten and A. P. Schmid (eds.), *The Politics of Pain: Torturers and their Masters* (COMT, University of Leiden, Leiden 1993).

placed outside the protection of the state. In the modern state, individual rights in effect derive from the state. Thus, to be excluded from the state – to be denied the rights of citizenship – is tantamount to becoming a non-person vulnerable to arbitrary treatment, to torture, and ultimately to extermination. Targets of torture in the context of armed conflict are, by definition, placed in the category of enemies, who are not entitled to the protection of the state. In principle, enemy combatants and civilian populations are protected against torture and other violations of their human rights by the Geneva Conventions.[21] In practice, people categorized as enemies in a war situation are vulnerable to being targeted for torture.

V. Social processes facilitating participation in torture

The three points at which the security concerns and power of the state contribute to a policy of torture at the *macro-level* – i.e., the justification for torture, the agents of torture, and the targets of torture – can be linked to three social processes that facilitate participation in torture at the *micro-level*: the processes of authorization, routinization, and dehumanization, which I distinguished in my earlier analysis of sanctioned massacres and other crimes of obedience.[22] The justification of torture as a means of protecting the state against threats to its security helps to *authorize* the practice; the development of a profession of torturers as part of the state's security apparatus helps to *routinize* the administration of torture; and the designation of the targets of torture as enemies of the state who are excluded from the state's protection helps to *dehumanize* the victims (see table 2.1, right-hand column).

In the analysis of sanctioned massacres I argued that, to understand participation in massacre or genocide, it is less important to explore the forces that push people into performing such violent acts than to explore those forces that contribute to the weakening of moral restraints against performing these acts – acts that people would normally find unacceptable. Within this framework, *authorization* helps to define the situation in a way that makes standard moral principles inapplicable: the individual is not acting as an independent moral agent and therefore feels absolved of the responsibility to make personal moral choices. Through

[21] Geneva Convention Relative to the Treatment of Prisoners of War (Geneva Convention III) 75 UNTS 135, (Geneva 12 August 1949). Geneva Convention Relative to the Protection of Civilian Persons in Time of War (Geneva Convention IV) 75 UNTS 287 (Geneva 12 August 1949).

[22] Kelman (n. 6); Kelman and Hamilton (n. 1).

routinization, the action becomes organized in a way that eliminates the opportunity to raise moral questions and make moral decisions: the action is divided among many individuals and sub-units of the organization; each individual carries out routine tasks without having to think of the overall product to which these tasks contribute; euphemisms further enable individuals to ignore the overall meaning of the tasks they are performing; altogether, the actions come to be seen as part of a normal job rather than participation in massacre or genocide. Finally, *dehumanization* of the victims makes it unnecessary for perpetrators to relate to them in moral terms, since it excludes the victims from the perpetrators' moral community.

These three social processes apply to torturers as much as to participants in massacre or other crimes of obedience. In the case of torture, it is particularly clear that these processes are mediated to a significant degree by the torturers' relationship to the state.

The role of *authorization* is strengthened by the fact that torturers, typically, are not just acting within a hierarchy in which they are expected to obey – and have indeed been trained to obey without question[23] – but they are participating in an action that represents a *transcendent mission*. They have come to share the view of the authorities that the task they are engaged in serves a higher purpose that transcends any moral scruples they might bring to the situation. They have come to see themselves as playing an important part in an effort to protect the state: to ensure its security and continued integrity, to maintain law and order, or to keep alive the fundamental values of the state that are being subjected to a merciless onslaught by ruthless enemies who are intent on destroying it. This view of the purpose of the torture project as part of a noble effort, in which the perpetrators are prepared to play their role despite any moral reservations and feelings of repugnance they might have, greatly enhances the legitimacy of the enterprise.

An additional element of the torture situation that contributes to its perceived legitimacy is the participation of medical professionals, who often play an active role by evaluating victims' physical capacity to go through the process, by making sure that the torture does not go beyond the point of causing the victim to die, and by performing other functions.[24]

[23] Gibson (n. 19).

[24] S. V. Faraone, 'Psychology's role in the campaign to abolish torture: can individuals and organizations make a difference?', in P. Suedfeld (ed.), *Psychology and Torture* (Hemisphere, New York, NY 1990); see also J. M. Arrigo, 'A utilitarian argument against torture interrogation of terrorists'(2004) 10(3) *Science and Engineering Ethics* 543.

Incidentally, the role of physicians in interrogations that are tantamount to torture has also been noted in the Abu Ghraib situation.[25] Physicians have also played a role in developing torture techniques, including brainwashing and related psychological methods of torture. An extreme example of the role of physicians in legitimizing torture and the systematic killing of 'undesirables' and enemies of the state is the case of the Nazi doctors, who helped to formulate the biomedical vision underlying the Nazi genocidal programs.[26]

The justification of torture as a necessary means of ferreting out 'the truth' also helps to surround it with an aura of legitimacy, as does the legal context in which it often takes place. One of the common uses of torture is as an adjunct to judicial proceedings, where it is designed to obtain evidence to be introduced into trials. This practice goes back to the early uses of torture – in the Roman period and in the Middle Ages – as a central part of the process of producing a confession, which was deemed necessary to establish the guilt of the accused.[27]

Routinization of torture is enhanced by the establishment of torturers as a professional group (as described in the previous section), which contributes to normalizing and ennobling their work. Torturers come to see themselves as performing a job, as doing their duty. It is a job that often involves hard work, that can lead to promotion and other rewards, that may offer opportunities to demonstrate innovativeness, that one can excel in and become expert in. Above all, it is a job that one can be proud of because it is perceived as a special profession that provides a significant service to the state and often carries with it membership in an elite corps. Although some torturers may seek out this occupation because of their sadistic inclinations, many are ordinary people who come to this work through a number of different routes.

The torture process itself also shows signs of considerable routinization. It usually involves a series of steps, clearly identified, and following each other in regular sequence. The different torture techniques, as well as the different torture chambers, are typically designated by special names, often with a euphemistic or ironic quality. These names are not so much designed to hide the reality of what is actually taking place as to give

[25] E.g. M. G. Bloche and J. H. Marks, 'When doctors go to war' (2005) 29(11) *New England Journal of Medicine* 3.

[26] R. J. Lifton, *The Nazi Doctors: Medical Killing and the Psychology of Genocide* (Basic Books, New York, NY 1986).

[27] Peters (n. 14).

expression to a professional culture with its own rituals and language.[28] The procedures used by torture organizations – including a variety of psychological techniques – are often quite sophisticated. All of this helps to give the work an aura of professionalism, which allows the torturer to perceive it, not as an act of cruelty against another human being, but as the routine application of specialized knowledge and skills.

In *dehumanization,* too, the state is an important part of the equation. The exclusion of torture victims from the torturer's moral community goes back, in fact, to the early history of torture. In the Roman legal system, torture – as a means of obtaining confessions – was originally applied only to slaves and foreigners, but not to citizens.[29] In contemporary practice, as well, torture victims are or are treated as non-citizens. The main source of their dehumanization is their designation as enemies of the state who have placed themselves outside the moral community shared by the rest of the population. They are described as terrorists, insurgents, or dissidents who endanger the state and are bent on undermining law and order and destroying the community. The view of torture victims as non-citizens, who are not entitled to the protection of the state, was evident in interviews that Heinz[30] conducted with 'masters of torture' in Latin America: once they identified guerrillas as Communists, they saw them as foreign agents and thus, in effect, 'denaturalized.' Furthermore, torture increased when guerrillas began killing military officers and their families, because they came to be seen as not only outsiders, who are not entitled to the community's protection, but as dangerous elements, against whom the community had a right to protect itself.

A central assumption in the contemporary practice of torture – just as in the early days, when it was used as a systematic part of criminal legal procedures – is that the victims are guilty. The torture apparatus operates on the assumption that those who are brought in for torture are guerrillas, insurgents, or terrorists, who have committed and/or are about to commit dangerous crimes against the state. Thus, torture is designed only to punish the guilty, to warn their accomplices, and – most important – to elicit the truth from them. Indeed, torture is often justified on the grounds that it is the only way to elicit information necessary for the protection of the state and its citizens – such as information about the identity and whereabouts of terrorist leaders or about planned terrorist operations – that the torture victims are presumed to have in their possession.

[28] Radtke (n. 19). [29] Peters (n. 14). [30] Heinz (n. 16).

A contributing factor to the dehumanization of torture victims is the fact that – even when they are citizens of the state that tortures them – they are often outside the ethnic or religious community of the torturers and of the dominant sector of the society. This has been the case, among many others, for Kurds in Iraq, for Bahais in Iran, for Palestinians in Kuwait and in the Israeli-occupied territories, for Irish Catholics in Northern Ireland, or for Bosnian Muslims in the former Yugoslavia. In many cases, the victims' ethnic or religious identity is itself the primary reason for their vulnerability to torture. In other cases, ethnic or religious identity is a factor in dissent or insurgency. In all cases, it facilitates exclusion and dehumanization, thus removing one of the constraints against torture and other serious violations of human rights.

VI. Conclusion

Using torture as the primary illustration, the present analysis suggests some of the conditions under which practices constituting international crimes can become instruments of state policy and the authority structure of the state is fully mobilized to implement that policy: the perception by state authorities that the security of the state is under severe threat – which, at the macro-level, serves to justify these practices and, at the micro-level, contributes to their authorization; the existence of an elaborate and powerful apparatus charged with protecting the security of the state – which, at the macro-level, provides the infrastructure for implementing such practices and, at the micro-level, contributes to their routinization; and the existence of groups within the state or under its control that are defined as enemies of the state – which, at the macro-level, excludes them from protection of the state and, at the micro-level, contributes to their dehumanization.

These conditions are endemic to the autocratic security state. Thus, torture and other gross violations of human rights are much less likely to take place in states governed with the consent of the governed, whose leaders and officials are accountable for their policies and actions. However, even western democratic societies are not invulnerable to the conditions that tempt state authorities to adopt such practices as policy instruments and that enable them to implement policies that rely on these practices: the perception of fundamental threats to the security and integrity of the state; the existence of bureaucratic organizations charged with ensuring state security, staffed by professionally trained security specialists, and allowed to operate with greater secrecy and less accountability than is customary in democratic societies; and the presence of foreign, poorly integrated, or non-citizen elements within the population or under the state's control that can easily be seen as outside of the contract that obligates citizens and state to one another in a democratic polity. These conditions are particularly likely to arise in the context of armed conflict – whether civil or international – in which the threat to the state is readily personified in an internal or external enemy, bent on violence and destruction. The combination of these conditions can override the constraints and bypass the scrutiny, imposed by democratic values and institutions that usually stand in the way of gross violations of human rights in democratic societies. These, then, are the conditions that must be addressed – wherever they manifest themselves – as we seek to develop approaches to enhancing accountability for system-generated international crimes, not only on the part of individuals at all levels of the system's hierarchy, but on the part of the system itself.

3

Why corporations kill and get away with it: the failure of law to cope with crime in organizations

MAURICE PUNCH*

I. Introduction

It is a sad truism that there is nothing that people will not do to other people. This may be at the individual level, as with the psychopathic serial murderer, but it is particularly the case with regard to collective behaviour. This can occur in groups, institutions and organizations driven by ideology, patriotism, extreme belief in a leader, kinship or clanship, by racial hatred or by religious fanaticism. People become absorbed in the group and, within its solidarity, restraints are removed and they commit acts they would almost certainly never contemplate doing as individuals. To a degree then, the organization or collective is complicit. Indeed, I argue that there is ample evidence to support the contention that 'organizations kill'.[1] In essence, I will maintain that there are no 'individuals' in organizations and that organizations commit 'crimes'. This draws attention to the social-psychology of 'deviant'[2] behaviour in organizations and I will illustrate this with regard to policing and the business corporation. And in relation to the latter, I will argue that the law seems unable, or unwilling, to tackle the issue of corporate blame. It remains fixated on

* Visiting Professor, Mannheim Centre for the Study of Criminology and Criminal Justice, London School of Economics and Political Science, and School of Law, King's College London, UK.

[1] M. Punch, 'Suite violence: why managers murder and corporations kill' (2000) 33 *Crime, Law and Social Change* 243–80.

[2] 'Deviant' behaviour is a widely used concept in Sociology to refer to violations of norms and rules which are perceived to de deviant by a particular audience: if a group of police officers collude to accept bribes or favours then, in that social circle, the 'deviant' is the officer who declines to take bribes or gifts: but, if exposed, the group will be held to have violated police regulations, and possibly the criminal law, and will be labeled deviant (P. Rock, *Deviant Behaviour* (Hutchinson University Library, London 1973).

the individual and the organization too often manoeuvres successfully to evade the criminal label.

In addressing collective behaviour, Kelman argues that people within institutional settings are pressurised or persuaded into obedience.[3] Those settings are rather like large-scale replications of Milgram's famous, or infamous, laboratory experiments.[4] In them he induced ordinary people to cause pain to others – the 'pain' was in fact simulated – by putting them under pressure to follow instructions despite their evident qualms. Most people followed the instructions even though they could see that the subject of the experiment was apparently 'suffering'. In the harsh reality of war-time combat and other armed conflict situations, Kelman maintains, the institutionalization of obedience makes subordinates susceptible to following commands from above to commit what others might label cruel and illegal acts. Certain individuals may even be attracted to the 'dirty work' of torture and execution in combat or other conflict situations (coming to justify it, seeing it as a part of a 'noble effort', while perhaps even relishing it). But there is also considerable evidence that, when ordinary individuals are put into certain pressing contexts, they are capable of being actively involved in genocide, mass murder, torture, extreme cruelty and the systematic abuse of women.[5] Their victims may well be the innocent and vulnerable in society: they pose no threat to anyone – women, children, the sick and the elderly – or may even be neighbours, colleagues and close friends. Yet this vulnerability or closeness does not seem to quell their ardour or their viciousness.[6]

This was true, for instance, of Stalin's Soviet Union with its rapacious appetite for mass deportations, campaigns of terror with mock trials, torture and executions and for large-scale, arbitrary banishment to the Gulag.[7] And there was no shortage of 'helpers' or 'willing executioners' who were only too eager to exceed the quotas for deaths and torture and who were often sadistic, ruthless and without pity. This industry of terror produced its own enthusiastic cadre of technicians of evil: they slotted into their allotted roles and mouthed the prescribed scripts with no sign of

[3] H. C. Kelman, 'The Policy Context of International Crimes', this volume, Chapter 2.

[4] S. Milgram, *Obedience to Authority* (Harper and Row, New York 1974).

[5] H. C. Kelman and V. L. Hamilton, *Crimes of Obedience* (Yale University Press, New Haven, CT 1991).

[6] P. Green and T. Ward, *State Crime: Governments, Violence and Corruption* (Pluto, London 2004).

[7] S. S. Montefiore, *Stalin: The Court of the Tsar* (Weidenfeld & Nicolson, London 2003); A. Appelbaum, *Gulag: A History* (Penguin, London 2004).

individual conscience. They doubtless saw themselves, like Eichmann, as merely impersonal 'cogs' in a mighty machine.[8] One assumes that people can only be appalled by this conduct and ask: 'how could they possibly commit such terrible deeds'?

This painful issue is explored in this volume by academic lawyers as well as legal practitioners from international tribunals. What unites them is the conviction that the collective crimes against humanity – in the Balkans, in Rwanda, Sierra Leone and elsewhere – were systemic. For these mass killing fields were plainly not the work of individuals but constituted 'system crimes'.[9] In Rwanda, for example, some 500,000 people, if not more, were slaughtered in about 100 days.[10] The system crimes under consideration were deliberate and planned: they extended over time; they were on a large scale and were systematically executed; they attracted the moral revulsion and unequivocal condemnation of the international community; and they indisputably broke domestic and international law.[11]

In practice, however, the accused are generally prosecuted as individuals. Indeed, it seems as if the criminal law in western society is geared primarily towards the individual and has considerable difficulty in attributing criminal fault and liability to a collective entity, institution or organization.[12] The legal mind has difficulty in determining *mens rea* and the *actus reus* when a crime is not committed by an individual but by an organization or other collective. Indeed, the criminal law was not developed with an organization like the company in mind, and in English law *mens rea* is imputed to a company via an individual through the 'identification principle'.[13] Not only is intent perceived to be essentially a human characteristic rather than an organizational one, but many legal concepts – like malice and recklessness – are fundamentally based on the notion of the autonomous individual taking a conscious decision.

In the context of this volume, for instance, the concern is with 'system crimes', mainly committed by states and particularly genocide and war

[8] H. Arendt, *Eichmann in Jerusalem* (Penguin Books, London 2006).

[9] See definition in A. Nollkaemper, 'Introduction', this volume, Chapter 1, p. 1.

[10] Green and Ward (n. 6).

[11] A. Nollkaemper, 'Concurrence between individual responsibility and state responsibility' (2003) 52 *International Criminal Law Quarterly* 615–40; see also the definition of system criminality in A. Nollkaemper, 'Introduction', this volume, Chapter 1, p. 1.

[12] C. Wells, *Corporations and Criminal Responsibility* (2nd edn, Oxford University Press, Oxford 2001); D. D. Caron, 'State crimes: looking at municipal experience with organized crime', in M. Ragazzi (ed.), *International Responsibility Today: Essays in Memory of Oscar Schachter* (Martinus Nijhoff, Leiden, Boston 2005), pp. 23–30.

[13] J. Gobert and M. Punch, *Rethinking Corporate Crime* (Butterworths, London 2003).

crimes. For example, in the Nuremburg International Military Tribunal of some sixty years ago, the crimes of the Nazis may seem to have been collective ones, whereas the defendants were prosecuted as individuals for conspiracy.[14] This was despite the fact that the SS and the Nazi Party were defined as criminal organizations. Van der Wilt, furthermore, draws attention to this reluctance to prosecute collectives (from the view *societas delinquere non potest*) and that it is 'second nature' in criminal law and prosecutions to look for the individual component.[15] Arendt illustrates this in her renowned analysis of the Eichmann trial: 'The prosecution, unable to understand a mass murderer who had never killed ... was constantly trying to prove individual murder.'[16]

Some people may find it almost perverse that individuals are prosecuted for being a member of a criminal organization, or criminal state, but the organization itself is not prosecuted, convicted, sanctioned and branded as criminal.[17]

In this chapter, I will show that precisely the same dilemma occurs in corporate crime. If one replaces 'state' with 'corporation' then there are near identical arguments, for the offences are committed in an organizational context and in concert with others. But the law in some jurisdictions remains stubbornly locked largely at the individual level. For instance, when the industrial enterprises of nineteenth-century Britain were first held to account for deaths and injuries in the workplace, the legislators avoided the issue of intent for a collective, *mens rea,* by simply sidestepping it with legislation defining these as strict liability offences. Yet in English jurisprudence, there are a number of cases going back for almost a century and a half which hold that the company as a legal entity can be held responsible for a crime (but clearly not all crimes).[18] This is also true in a number of countries, including the Netherlands.[19] But those countries with a civil law tradition have somewhat more difficulty attributing a crime to an enterprise. 'Crimes' can only be committed by humans, in

[14] P. Calvocoressi, *Nuremberg: The Facts, the Law and the Consequences* (Chatto and Windus, London 1947), p. 81: 'The prosecution did not indict an organisation as such or ask that any organisation should be punished ... In the last resort the objects of the prosecution's attacks remained against individuals and not collectives.'

[15] H. van der Wilt, *Het kwaad in functie* (2005) Inaugural lecture, Faculty of Law, University of Amsterdam.

[16] Arendt (n. 8) 215. [17] The UN Security Council can impose sanctions on states.

[18] G. Slapper and S. Tombs, *Corporate Crime* (Longman, London 1999).

[19] S. Field and N. Jörg, 'Corporate liability and manslaughter: should we go Dutch?' (1991) 11 CrimLR 156–71.

this view, although companies can be accused, prosecuted and sanctioned for 'administrative' or economic offences but not for manslaughter.[20]

I will examine this issue in relation to 'corporate violence', when corporations are held to account for the deaths of people.[21] Of course, people are all considered to be unique individuals and are answerable to others socially, morally and legally as individuals (assuming they are capable of taking responsible decisions): but through the lenses of the sociological paradigm it is possible to perceive that, once people enter into interaction with others, they tend to alter their behaviour and surrender some of their individuality.[22] This is particularly the case when people become members of a collective, an institution or organization which in some powerful way demands conformity to group norms and in which people have to 'suppress' some aspects of their individuality (such as a school, corporation, army, church, religious sect, criminal gang or political party). In some situations people can even feel that they have adopted a new identity in an institution or have become totally subordinate to it, as in the mass suicide of over 700 sect members at Jonesville in 1978 on orders from their spiritual leader.

In this chapter I will illustrate this process with two examples which illustrate how individuals in some way give up some of their individual responsibility and end up breaking the law 'for' the group and/or the organization. The first example relates to police corruption and the second to crime in corporations.

II. Organizational deviance: police corruption and corporate crime

1. *Police corruption*

Around thirty years ago, I was involved in research on policing in the inner-city of Amsterdam at a time when it came to light that there was some corruption taking place within the force.[23] If one delves into the literature on this subject, then one can only come to the conclusion that some forms of 'corruption', in its wider sense of abuse of power rather than in the narrower sense of bribery, crop up at some time in almost

[20] KPMG, *Compliance Programma* (KPMG, Amstelveen 2001).
[21] Punch (n. 1) 243–80.
[22] A. Giddens, *Sociology: A Brief but Critical Introduction* (Macmillan, London 1986).
[23] Particularly in relation to bribery by Chinese criminals involved in the drug trade; M. Punch, *Conduct Unbecoming* (Tavistock, London 1985).

every police force.[24] Indeed, policing has often been associated with other grave forms of deviance such as excessive violence and systemic racial discrimination. There does, then, appear to be something in the nature of police work and the institutional context of policing which fosters deviance from internal rules, and even the law, in the people who join the police across time and in many cultures and many societies.[25]

This cannot just be a few 'bad apples' – a few corrupted individuals, as is so often maintained by officialdom – because often large numbers of officers and even entire units are involved on a long-term, systemic basis. In New York, for example, there has been a corruption scandal roughly every twenty years since the founding of the city's police force (New York Police Department or NYPD) in 1845. This implies that the deviance is cyclical and cannot be individual because the personnel have changed substantially since the previous cycle. Then, when a young officer called Serpico entered plain-clothes work in the NYPD, he found that everyone was 'on the take': because he would not accept bribes, he became the deviant and, when he blew the whistle, was subject to serious sanctions.[26] This cannot, then, be dismissed as a case of bad apples: more likely the metaphor should be of a bad barrel – or even a bad orchard.[27] Indeed, some areas of police work are associated with a predictably high risk of corruption – as in drugs enforcement, 'vice' (gambling and prostitution), undercover work, licensing of premises and businesses and running informants. Individuals entering these areas run an enhanced risk of becoming part of a system of corruption. Then some units employ excessive force across time, meaning that it is not incidental and individual but repetitive and institutionalised. The Mollen Report on the NYPD, for instance, detailed that some officers routinely beat up suspects and sometimes assaulted people at random just to display their control of the streets: they even used violence consciously as a *rite de passage* into deeper corruption for newcomers.[28] Their younger colleagues were carefully manipulated and coached on to the 'slippery slope' of deviance where, often after initial reserves, it became

[24] T. Newburn, *Understanding and Preventing Police Corruption: Lessons from the Literature* (Home Office, London 1999).

[25] L. W. Sherman, *Scandal and Reform: Controlling Police Corruption* (University of California Press, Berkeley, CA 1978).

[26] P. Maas, *Serpico* (Fontana, London 1974).

[27] M. Punch, 'Rotten orchards: pestilence, police misconduct and system failure' (2003) 13(2) *Policing and Society* 171–96.

[28] Mollen Commission, *The City of New York Commission to Investigate Allegations of Corruption and the Anti-Corruption Procedures of the Police Department* (City of New York, New York 1994).

progressively easier to commit offences. Then in the Louima scandal in New York, the victim was exposed to gross violence: he incurred serious internal injuries as a result of being sodomised with a broom handle. Yet this happened within a police station in sight of other officers who did not intervene. In the well-known Selmouni affair in France, the severe and degrading abuse of a suspect also took place visibly inside a police station over several days and with a number of officers observing it: in fact one of them publicly urinated on him when he was tied to a staircase. But, again, no-one intervened while this 'cruel and degrading' treatment took place over a considerable period of time. Several officers were prosecuted for a number of offences against Selmouni and the French government was subsequently held responsible by the European Court of Human Rights for the ill-treatment.[29]

The sociological conclusion drawing on a wealth of research on police deviance is that people were prepared to enter a collective entity where they ceased behaving as autonomous individuals and were prepared to accept the systematic breaking of rules and even of the law in latent or overt concert with others.[30] The result is that officers in the police organization, who are meant to enforce the law, end up not only breaking the law but even becoming criminals. They display contempt for the law and find creative ways to get around it. They lie in court, manipulate or destroy evidence, take or extort bribes, steal drugs and sell them, beat up the defenceless, ensure that the guilty go unpunished and the innocent go to prison, cooperate with criminals and even commit murder. And somehow they can justify this to themselves (through 'vocabularies of motive'[31]).

The sociological and criminological conclusion is that the organizational context and occupational culture of policing can be so powerful that they in some way sponsor and even encourage deviance, which can be no less than a perversion of the expressed aims of the organization, and induce individuals to take deviant and even criminal paths. These recurring patterns, which are extensively documented, simply cannot be

[29] *Selmouni v France*, Judgment (28 July 1999) Reports 1999-V.

[30] Punch (n. 27) 171–96.

[31] C. Wright Mills, 'Situated actions and vocabularies of motive' (1940) 5(6) *American Sociological Review* 904–13: vocabularies of motive are the scripts or accounts used by people to justify their deviant or criminal behaviour such as 'everyone was doing it' or 'it didn't hurt anyone': S. Cohen, *States of Denial* (Polity, Cambridge 2001) gives a masterful analysis of the accounts that states use when accused of violations of human rights, including torture, from outright denial ('it never happened'), to qualified denial ('it was never as extensive as you claim'), to justification ('they had it coming to them').

viewed as an individual phenomenon: I and others would rather refer to 'organizational deviance'.[32]

By this concept sociologists and criminologists draw attention to the manner in which organizations can be 'criminogenic' and can provide the context for crime for those who are its members, workers, operational managers or senior executives. The organization, in fact, provides the holy trinity of standard criminal investigation – Motive, Opportunity and Means.[33] Without the corporation, the individuals could not have taken part in the crimes; and their defence is often 'but I did it for the corporation'.[34] And yet, in practice, the law seems unable to cope with this and, hence, it is mainly the individual who is prosecuted rather than the organization.

2. *Corporate crime*

The second area to be examined is that of corporate crime. Later I will also scrutinise the explanations as to how managers take decisions which lead to avoidable death and injury and which could be attributed to organizational fault. First, I wish to clarify what I mean by 'corporate crime'.

Any venture into this area must start with the lapidary work of Sutherland[35] in 1949. Although he used the confusing term 'white-collar crime', in order to make a contrast with the emphasis in criminology on lower class, 'blue-collar' crime, Sutherland was effectively describing corporations that broke the law. In short, his findings were that many leading American corporations broke the law (criminal, civil and administrative laws); they did so deliberately; some were 'recidivists' or repeat offenders; and they frequently evaded conviction. His material maintained that, often, senior managers were involved, that they displayed contempt for the law and their 'consciences did not normally bother them'. His pioneering work has been criticized for two main reasons. Many of the offences he considered in his survey of court decisions were not technically crimes but more often regulatory offences; and some of the cases that did go to a criminal trial did not lead to a conviction. Some have argued that it is

[32] D. Ermann and R. Lundman (eds.), *Corporate and Governmental Deviance* (3rd edn, Oxford University Press, New York 1996).

[33] J. Bologna, *Corporate Fraud* (Butterworths, Boston 1984).

[34] G. Geis, 'White collar crime: the heavy electrical equipment antitrust cases of 1961', in M. Ermann and R. J. Lundman (eds.), *Corporate and Governmental Deviance* (Oxford University Press, New York 1978).

[35] E. H. Sutherland, *White Collar Crime* (Dryden Press, New York, NY 1949).

incorrect to speak of crimes without a conviction. The counter-argument is that many corporations are wealthy and powerful and use their legal muscle to stay out of the criminal courts and, by plea bargaining, reach a settlement (this is common in financial crime and regulatory offences). Generally, then, corporate 'crime' refers to accusations, investigations, prosecutions and convictions for criminal offences against legitimate corporations or for serious regulatory offences. The latter refers to the fact that much economic and industrial activity is regulated by an alternative body of regulatory law which is heard in the criminal courts but which is hardly perceived as 'criminal' in terms of stigma and sanctions.

Since Sutherland's research and publication in the 1940s, a range of studies has supported his pioneering insights.[36] But there is one feature of his work that has attracted revision in recent years: namely, that much of his evidence alluded to 'clean hands' crime of a financial nature where the victims suffered financial loss rather than physical harm. He does not bestow much attention on the extent to which companies can cause avoidable death and suffering through, say, accidents as a result of negligence or a product defect.[37]

But, of importance here, is that he did show that much corporate crime was not incidental and episodic (as is much common crime), but was fully conscious, deliberate, extending over time and highly damaging. It is, for instance, in the nature of price-fixing, industrial espionage, cartel-forming, insider trading, some environmental offences and market manipulation, that they are carefully constructed conspiracies, involving senior management, and requiring covert campaigns with sophisticated camouflage. In brief, there is a swathe of evidence from Sutherland onwards that executives in business organizations consciously and deliberately intend to break the law.[38]

Intent, *mens rea*, is important if not crucial in criminal law and these crimes were clearly intended and premeditated. But, for a number of reasons, including the legal resources of large companies and the willingness of regulators and prosecutors to bargain a settlement, many offences by corporations and their executives evade the criminal arena. In fact, some corporations are ingenious at evading the law: they hire corporate lawyers to explore the 'holes' in legislation and the opportunities those

[36] M. B. Clinard and P. C. Yeager, *Corporate Crime* (Free Press, New York 1980).

[37] R. Mokhiber, *Corporate Crime and Violence* (Sierra Club Books, San Francisco 1988).

[38] F. Pearce and L. Snider (eds.), *Corporate Crime: Contemporary Debates* (Toronto University Press, Toronto 1995); N. Shover and J. P. Wright (eds.), *Crimes of Privilege* (Oxford University Press, New York and Oxford 2001).

holes supply for illicit activities or for the 'grey area' between legality and illegality (e.g. via off-shore tax-havens or countries with banking secrecy). And international law, in particular, provides a playground for astute and cynical lawyers because of complex issues of jurisdiction, rules of evidence, standards of proof, problems of extradition, diversity in court procedures (as in the difference between jury or non-jury trials), difficulties of obtaining witnesses, language difficulties with regard to documentation and cross-examination of witnesses and issues of 'double criminality' (that an offence is not similar in different countries).[39]

The ship *Salem*, for instance, illegally delivered oil to South Africa in 1979 and broke the international embargo against the apartheid regime. The ship was registered in Liberia; its officers were Greek; the oil was loaded by an Italian company in Kuwait; this was sold to the Anglo-Dutch Shell firm but delivered to South Africa after which the ship was scuttled in international waters off the African coast leading to a fraudulent insurance claim. The main suspects were American, German and Dutch and prosecutions followed in the USA, Greece and the Netherlands. Eight years after the incident, the case was heard in court in Rotterdam but the defendant was found not guilty, largely because the South African authorities refused to cooperate and denied access to witnesses.[40] No wonder that some firms prefer restitution rather than seeing a lengthy and uncertain prosecution being mounted. Also offenders may be 'transnational' but the law and law enforcement are primarily national enterprises and international cases outside of national jurisdictions may founder on institutional weaknesses or political and judicial corruption in national enforcement. As a result, many internationally operating companies do not take the law seriously: and they can get away with doing so all too easily. Green and Ward,[41] for instance, provide examples from South America and Africa where major multinationals, including the Dutch-British Shell oil-company, engage in what some perceive to be serious human rights offences for which they are not brought to court.

Once more, this is related to their political and economic power but also because the law tends to focus on individuals. But in large, complex companies it is difficult to isolate which individual is responsible for what decision: the decision-making may be genuinely intricate and opaque but it may also be that ingenious devices are created to make sure that blame cannot be attributed to those at the top (perhaps even including

[39] Gobert and Punch (n. 13). [40] M. Punch, *Dirty Business* (Sage, London 1996).
[41] Green and Ward (n. 6).

straw-men or the 'Vice-President for going to jail').[42] Senior executives are powerful, shrewd and manipulative people, who have had a long schooling in organizational politics as they have moved up the hierarchy, making them amoral chameleons who fully understand the game of 'deniability' (like politicians making sure that there is no trace of personal blame with no footsteps in the sand leading to their door).[43] Even if an individual is prosecuted and found guilty, he can doubtless fall back on a large measure of 'social capital' – a university education at a prestigious establishment (perhaps the same institute as the judge!), exemplary career, no criminal record, voluntary involvement in good works and a respectable and a deeply contrite persona carefully constructed by the defence team to impress the jury. This is likely to mean that he (or she) will receive a mild sentence such as a fine, a suspended custodial sentence or, at worst, a short stay at a minimum security jail (sometimes referred to as 'country-club' prisons).[44]

In effect, managers have a good chance of getting away with it, or getting off lightly; but corporations have an even better chance of evading a conviction and sanctioning. In effect, the individual can hide behind the company and the company can hide behind the individual.

For in corporate crime the law is often weak, if not impotent. The law is in a sense merely paper, a statement of moral disapproval or intent, or what is referred to as the 'law in the books'. In contrast, the 'law in action' revolves around sound legislation, strong enforcement, determined investigation, skilful prosecution, successful conviction and deterrence through convincing sanctions.[45] But here is an area of crime in which many of these elements are weak and inadequate and this is especially so in the international legal arena.

This is assuming the law is designed to work. Reisman talks of *lex imperfecta* for those laws which are a swift response to some scandal or moral panic – as a legally expedient fig-leaf – and are not meant to be fully enforced or turn out to be largely unenforceable.[46] This makes the study of corporate crime something of a gloomy if not depressing occupation. For if the criminal justice system is founded on notions of justice, and of punishing the guilty, then in this area the law and the courts do not

[42] J. Braithwaite, 'White collar crime' (1985) 11 *Annual Review of Sociology* 1–25.

[43] R. Jackall, *Moral Mazes: The World of Corporate Managers* (Oxford University Press, New York and Oxford 1989).

[44] Punch (n. 40). [45] G. Gurvitch, *Sociology of Law* (Transaction, Somerset NJ 2001).

[46] M. W. Reisman, *Folded Lies* (Free Press, New York 1979).

always deliver justice: indeed, it is often criminal how often the system fails to deliver justice.

To a large extent this is related to the difficulty of associating companies with 'crime'. There are some who argue that the criminal law is inappropriate to economic activity and that corporate offences should be dealt with solely by civil or regulatory law.[47] Indeed, organizations cannot, by definition, be accused of a number of crimes committed by humans, while many offences attributed to corporations are *male prohibita* rather than *male in se*. There is even a separate system of two-tier criminal law, in that many offences involving companies are dealt with by regulatory agencies with a 'compliance' strategy and a general reluctance to prosecute and these offences are typically not seen as 'real' crime.[48] Even if a company is taken to a criminal court, it will be physically represented by a company executive exuding respectability. To the extent that the criminal court is an exercise in moral theatre, particularly in the Anglo-Saxon adversarial system with juries, the executive and the company he or she represents simply do not fit the criminal stereotype.[49] The Department of Justice in the USA may have pursued Microsoft on anti-trust grounds, but it must have been difficult for anyone to see Bill Gates (then CEO of Microsoft) as a 'criminal' when he was one of the most successful entrepreneurs of recent times. But in a court or hearing he would have visualized the company, as the company has no concrete identity other than the executives who represent it, and he would have brought a great deal of 'social capital' to the encounter. In practice, then, we see that many potential crimes are 'plea-bargained' out of the criminal arena,[50] enforcement is patchy and under-resourced, regulators focus on compliance and avoid prosecution, investigations and prosecutions are complex and prolonged and can easily end in failure, given the high standards of proof and sanctions are pitiful. Sutherland's message sixty years ago was effectively that companies were getting away with it; and they are still getting away with it.

[47] Gobert and Punch (n. 13).

[48] K. Hawkins, *Law as Last Resort* (Oxford University Press, Oxford 2002).

[49] Wells (n. 12).

[50] For instance, with a plea of *nolo contendere*. A regulatory agency such as the Security and Exchange Commission in the USA cannot itself prosecute, so it confronts a company under suspicion with the evidence and with the threat of recommending prosecution in order to come to a deal with a fine: this could be defined as 'bargain and bluff' as the Justice Department does not have the capacity to pursue too many cases: *nolo contendere* is not an admission of guilt and prevents other civil or criminal procedures on the base of it. In effect, the law, the regulators and the prosecutors 'go easy' on corporate crime; F. Partnoy, *Infectious Greed* (Holt, New York 2003).

Surely, one might think, this might be true of cases involving false advertising, price fixing and fraud where no-one is physically harmed, but can that be the picture when a company is held liable for causing death or serious injury?

3. *Corporate violence*

Indeed, how can we explain that managers take decisions that end in serious physical harm and even fatalities? Of importance is that in corporate crimes of violence there is, one assumes, no fully conscious intent to cause suffering and death. In a sense, then, they cannot be directly compared with violent conventional crime or the killing machines of massacre, genocide and illegal warfare where the perpetrators deliberately set out to kill. Nevertheless, I would briefly like to touch on such institutionalized barbarity to illustrate that also in such cases there can scarcely be talk of 'individual' involvement, even though western societies remain tied to the notion of individual guilt. And perhaps there are parallels between the social psychology of organizational deviance in the international and corporate crime areas.

For, to a certain extent, the social dynamics of deviating from rules – whether or not from the criminal law as a young delinquent, the Geneva Conventions on the laws of war, or the moral code of a social group – are similar.[51] These mechanisms can be summed up around the key concepts of neutralization and rationalization. The assumption is that people know what is wrong and, in order to engage in deviant behaviour, have to neutralize and rationalize their conduct. These mental processes are amplified when individuals are placed in an organizational context that reduces their individuality and that puts them into opportunities where alternative 'rules of engagement' apply (e.g. in a guerrilla war, where soldiers respond by treating all civilians as potential combatants who can be fired on at will). Also, when the small groups to which these individuals belong, the larger units or indeed the institution itself, provides them with rationalizations. These 'vocabularies of motive' not only justify the misconduct but also provide scripts for participants to assuage their consciences.[52] This will also be the case with irregular soldiers engaged in 'ethnic cleansing' operations, civilians slaughtering neighbours from

[51] D. Downes and P. Rock (eds.), *Understanding Deviance* (4th edn, Oxford University Press, Oxford 2003).

[52] Cohen (n. 31).

a different ethnic group or radical Muslim terrorists involved in mass casualty attacks on targets where innocent civilians will be the victims. In brief, the harm done to others is neutralized and then rationalized.[53]

Then, when it comes to excesses, it is often specific units, like the SS in World War II or certain paramilitary units in the recent Balkan conflicts, that indulge in extreme violence, mutilation, torture, group rape, mass killing or in the industrialised murder of the Nazi concentration camps.[54] This brings two further concepts to explain how soldiers and irregulars could indulge in such gross barbarity: namely, dehumanization and routinization. Victim groups are dehumanized and demonized by negative stereotyping: and then murder and mutilation on a large scale simply becomes a daily and taken-for-granted routine.[55] One German *Einsatzgruppe*, for instance, had killed some 250,000 people within a year on the Eastern Front in World War II, meaning they probably shot about a thousand innocent civilians a day.[56] This illustrates how mass killing can become taken for granted, as standard operating practice: and this was 'blood on the hands' killing, manhandling the victims and watching them die, so that the individual officer cannot claim distance from the scene of crime or lack of knowledge of the carnage. And yet they learned to accept this callous butchery as part of their routine duties, even on occasion laughing and joking as they went about their grisly task.

Of importance is that it is group pressure in an institutional context that is paramount here to explaining behaviour, and not the individual who is effectively subsumed in the collective. As Kelman suggests, it may well be that certain types of people are attracted to specific units – like the SS, irregular paramilitary units or Special Forces – but there is ample evidence that ordinary people are capable of being rapidly transformed into doing extreme things in extreme conditions.[57] Indeed, Browning's book *Ordinary Men*, details how an ordinary battalion of the German Police was stationed in Poland in World War II and, within a very short

[53] Cf. G. Sykes and D. Matza, 'Techniques of neutralization: a theory of delinquency' (1957) 22 *American Sociological Review* 664–70 on 'techniques of neutralization': they argued that delinquents were aware that their misdeeds were 'wrong' but were able to neutralize and rationalize their deviant behaviour.

[54] Green and Ward (n. 6).

[55] The use of the term 'cockcroaches' in Rwanda legitimized exterminating the Tutsis as if they were vermin: van der Wilt (n. 15).

[56] Arendt (n. 8) 73.

[57] H. C. Kelman, 'The policy context of international crimes', this volume, Chapter 2.

time after leaving home, was engaged in routine, mass murder.[58] In short, warfare and other serious conflict situations reveal that 'ordinary' people will do extraordinarily cruel things in what are perceived to be extraordinary situations.

In a way, then, the military institution in combat provides the training, equipment, opportunities, rationalizations, motives and group dynamics that can turn ordinary citizens into routine killers. Armies in combat form a vast and highly successful social laboratory in mass obedience; they provide replications of Milgram's experiment. People, who would probably loathe killing a chicken bare-handed as an individual in normal society, can become enthusiastic group murderers and highly motivated, sophisticated torturers. But then one might conclude: 'it's not really them as individuals but the organization that has done it – and should carry the blame.'

III. Corporate killing

With that in mind, I would like to switch attention back to the business organization and specifically in relation to violence and corporate killing. This is obviously not to suggest that there is a direct comparison between the excesses of an army in a war zone and a legitimate corporation under normal circumstances. Business managers clearly cannot be placed in the same category as dictatorial leaders who sponsor mass violence (such as Pol Pot, Idi Amin, Stalin or Charles Taylor); and executives do not share the 'bloody hands' experiences of front-line soldiers or paramilitaries.

But this material does provide a contrasting and illustrative backcloth to companies that kill. Although some managers use martial metaphors – and speak forcefully and abrasively of fighting wars, going into battle, achieving victory and defeating the enemy[59] – we generally view corporate decision-making as taking place far from the action, in comfortable boardroom suites and cloaked in economic rationality. The executives are mature people, educated at elite universities, who may appear to be exemplary, responsible, restrained individuals. They do not have a record of personal violence, have never been convicted of a crime and perhaps even their chauffeurs have never had a parking ticket. And yet they may engage in decision-making which leads to the injury and death of their

[58] C. Browning, *Ordinary Men: Reserve Battalion 101 and the Final Solution in Poland* (Harper Perennial, New York 1998).

[59] Punch (n. 40).

own employees and members of the public. To a certain extent, business organizations demand obedience from employees and managers learn to rationalize misconduct with it becoming routine, as when price-fixing is seen as the 'normal way' to conduct business.[60]

In the field of white-collar and corporate crime, moreover, there is palpable and convincing evidence that companies 'kill'. This awareness is partly related to increasing scholarly interest in avoidable deaths and injuries in the workplace,[61] but is also fostered by attention to serious accidents and disasters.[62] With regard to the latter we can mention some of the leading cases:

- In 1973 a McDonnell Douglas DC 10 plane crashed outside Paris with some 300 fatalities: a product defect, which the company was said to have been aware of, was held to be the cause.
- In the 1970s some 8,000 children were born deformed in a number of countries because the drug Thalidomide had been marketed as a tranquilliser that was harmless, even for pregnant women: the warning signals had been ignored.
- Also in the 1970s, the Ford Motor Company produced a car, the Pinto, which was susceptible to fire following a rear-end collision because of the design which made the petrol tank vulnerable to rupture: there was a series of accidents in which people were severely burned, or burnt to death, in such rear-end collisions.
- In 1987 the ferry *Herald of Free Enterprise* capsized outside Zeebrugge Harbour causing some 200 deaths: the ship sailed with the bow doors open which allowed water to enter the car deck.
- In the Netherlands, the company Vos BV delivered glycerine to Haiti for use in cough medicine for children but, due to contamination in a batch of the glycerine, some sixty children died.
- In 1997 a train crash at Southall killed seven passengers: the driver had gone through a red light; the warning system (AWS: see below) against this happening was defective in the train's cab; but the driver had been pressurised into driving the train by operational managers who wanted no delay to schedules as delay might lead to fines for lack of punctuality; he had never driven a train before without the warning system in operation.
- And in the worst chemical accident in history, an explosion at the Union Carbide plant at Bhopal in India killed several thousand people

[60] Geis (n. 34). [61] Slapper and Tombs (n. 18). [62] Punch (n. 40).

(estimates vary between 3,000 and 5,000) with around 200,000 injured, while people are still dying and suffering as a result of the accident twenty years later. Union Carbide was held not to have kept to maintenance standards as the company was looking to sell off the plant.

There is no doubt that the legitimate and highly rated companies concerned in these accidents and disasters were linked in some way to the deaths and injuries with varying levels of responsibility and culpability. And it is an established fact that economic enterprises carry various forms of potential harm: there are certain high-risk elements associated with transport, pharmaceuticals, waste disposal, asbestos, tobacco, food, medical care, weapons and munitions, radiation, chemicals and explosives. Also consumers accept part of that risk when they use certain products or forms of transport, while cigarette packets even carry dire warnings of the health risks of tobacco.

But can these companies be held criminally accountable and liable? It is assumed that no management board would consciously set out to kill people; indeed, the deaths, injuries and deformities that occur are precisely what the executives would never willingly want to encounter. In that sense, then, full and deliberate intent and premeditation, *mens rea*, is absent. Thus companies cannot technically commit 'murder'. This leaves manslaughter in relation to gross negligence or recklessness. But, once more, the issue arises: is it the executives as individuals who are to be held liable or can the company as an entity also be prosecuted?

For instance, all of the cases above are highly complicated incidents, with much attention being paid in the extensive literature to causal relations linking blame to corporate decision-making, while they also raise complex legal issues. I shall not enter that terrain in detail here, but it is noticeable that none of the major cases above led to a criminal conviction of an individual or a company, and a number not even to a criminal trial. Several of the cases were dealt with in civil actions for compensation. Ford, for instance, made a deal with the regulators to withdraw the Pinto for modifications; and none of the criminal cases related to the incidents above achieved a conviction. The degree of culpability of Union Carbide for the negligence at the plant in Bhopal, and for the huge number of casualties, has never been properly contested in a court of law. This was largely because the legal power of Union Carbide outgunned and outwitted the Indian government that was representing the victims: an American judge ruled that the case could be held in India and rather than face a prolonged battle the Indian government effectively capitulated with a settlement agreed between the two parties which absolved Union Carbide from any future criminal prosecution or civil actions.[63] It is difficult to decipher this action but an unwillingness to alienate multinationals and future investors in the Indian economy may have played a role.[64] In such international legal disputes the playing field is not level and the teams are unevenly matched: in the Bhopal 'match' it was simply no contest between the lawyers representing Union Carbide and the lawyers of the Indian government.

In effect, large corporations facing likely prosecution domestically or internationally marshal their legal 'dream team' from the leading law companies and plea-bargain themselves out of the criminal arena. They endeavour, usually successfully, to come to a deal with the authorities or pursue their interests in civil courts, where they can settle at any moment with the other parties and where there is no statement of blame. And if there is high compensation or swinging punitive damages, then they will strenuously oppose them on appeal.

The legal difficulties in securing a criminal conviction generally remain twofold, although this will depend to a certain extent on the jurisdiction in question. First, if the *actus reus* is located at the scene of crime, is there a clear causal link from the 'smoking gun' (as in the capsized ferry-boat at Zeebrugge) through individuals to decision-making at the board level, with explicit evidence of gross negligence or awareness of undue risk? And, second, can then the *mens rea* of the crime be traced to the collective decision-making of the board?

For example, the current law in England and Wales demands that an individual is fully aware of the specific risk at the moment the incident takes place and that he or she has taken negligent or reckless decisions that implicate the board in culpability in relation to that specific incident. In practice, it proves almost legally impossible to identify a direct casual link between a single major accident and the decision-making of a management board. Large corporations are complex structures with intricate decision-making processes by committees. They will carefully couch all corporate statements on a new product in terms of justifiable risk; will seek regulatory permission before going to market; and will, as a matter of routine when faced by an inquiry, have their lawyers scrutinize all documents closely for anything even remotely incriminating before they are released. But, in essence, the main legal paths to attaching blame to

63 Punch (n. 40).

64 P. Shrivastava, *Bhopal: Anatomy of a Crisis* (Ballinger, Cambridge, MA 1987), pp. 35–47.

corporations are derivative: that is they are cast through forms of individual liability, with a stubborn reluctance to tackle organizational fault.[65]

But in a number of cases there does appear to be some connection between corporate decision-making and substantial harm. Indeed, there have been a handful of prosecutions for 'gross negligence manslaughter', as it is currently referred to in England and Wales, while the Ford Motor Company was prosecuted for homicide in the USA. What explanations can be offered for a company taking decisions that may later bring them to court for killing and injuring people?

Within large companies the board members may feel far distant from the end product or service provided: they encapsulate themselves in 'strategic' mode, basing their choice on the long-term viability of the company in relation to competitors and the market. Safety, for example, did not play an important role in the American automobile industry in the 1960s and this was exposed by Ralph Nader in his book 'Unsafe at Any Speed': presumably the managers responsible dissociated themselves from the consequences of their actions and also looked down on consumers. Indeed, Ford executives took a calculated risk with the Pinto and argued that they were doing none other than what their competitors were doing while the Pinto had also passed the required safety tests.[66]

In Britain the deregulated rail industry decided not to install 'ATP' (Automatic Train Protection), which is standard on trains in many Continental European countries and which enables a train to stop automatically on going through a red light, primarily on grounds of cost. They opted for the retention of 'AWS', which requires the driver's intervention after a warning claxon has alerted him or her to having driven through a warning or red light. There is no doubt on the evidence of several accidents that ATP would have saved lives, as in the Southall train crash and other incidents, but the industry was entitled to make this decision on strategic grounds. And the government, having deregulated the industry, could not intervene.[67] Profit, it could be argued, prevailed over lives.

Similarly, Townsend Thoreson, the owners of *The Herald of Free Enterprise*, which capsized at Zeebrugge, was a new-style, deregulated, cost-cutting, anti-union, entrepreneurial company of the 1980s, in which

[65] And, as Gobert points out, the company may be held accountable, say through vicarious liability, despite having behaved in a highly compliant fashion; J. Gobert, 'The evolving test of corporate criminal liabilty', in J. Minkes and L. Minkes (eds.), *Corporate and White-Collar Crime* (Sage, Los Angeles, London, New Delhi and Singapore 2008), p. 63.

[66] R. Nader, *Unsafe at Any Speed* (Grossman, New York 1965).

[67] I. Jack, *The Crash that Stopped Britain* (Granta Books, Cambridge 2001).

Margaret Thatcher's Conservative governments pursued neo-liberal, monetarist and 'no-nonsense' policies. It may well have gone for profit first, and may have pared back safety, but it would have had to have done so within industry regulations in order to receive a licence to sail and to gain insurance cover. It could be said that the firm was awful but lawful.

In all these cases there are a battery of external environmental and contextual factors related to the nature of the market, the strength of the competition, the level of technical or medical expertise at the time, the style of regulation, and so on. But these were also true for other companies that did not break the law (or did not get caught). So there must be other factors at work. For when things go wrong in companies it is possible in the post-mortem to discern a number of socio-psychological processes in management boards and their decision-making.[68] These can contain an element of 'group think', of tunnel vision, of executives distancing themselves from the end user, of depersonalizing the customer and of cloaking risk within the stratosphere of a 'strategic' mind-set which puts the interests of the company first.

As Jackall puts it, executives 'leave their consciences behind' them when they leave home as moral individuals and enter through the portals of the company where they do what the corporation requires of them (and if they do not, they are squeezed aside and ignored).[69] In the light of subsequent accidents, and loss of life and limb, the dispassionate observer – 'the man [*sic*] on the Clapham omnibus' is the British expression used in courts for the opinion of the average person – may view this style of operating as morally reprehensible and that it demands a criminal conviction. And although it may be that later there are successful prosecutions for regulatory offences, these are not the same as having sufficient evidence for a criminal prosecution and a conviction in court.[70] In fact, it is precisely that social and organizational distance from the 'smoking gun' which proves valuable in allowing executives to evade criminal liability.

A different mechanism is at work in another set of cases where, typically, the management of small companies is directly involved in the

[68] Punch (n. 40).

[69] R. Jackall, *Moral Mazes: The World of Corporate Managers* (Oxford University Press, New York and Oxford 1989).

[70] The GWR rail company, having escaped conviction for manslaughter, subsequently admitted to a number of offences and was fined £1.5 million for Health and Safety offences (I. Jack, *The Crash that Stopped Britain* (Granta Books, Cambridge 2001); U. Report, *The Southall Rail Accident Report* (Department of Transport, London 2001).

primary processes and are in close face-to-face contact with customers and/or employees. One would, then, naturally assume that they must be fully aware of the consequences of something going wrong: and yet they take undue and even reckless risks. For example, OLL was an adventure holiday enterprise that was effectively a one-person company with low standards for the few young and inexperienced people that it did employ, a poor record with personnel (who received little training and who complained in writing about the lack of a safety culture), and with small attention to risk. Then, in stormy weather, four young people drowned while canoeing in coastal waters: the owner had ignored the storm warnings and was lax in responding to the alarm about the missing children. This did lead to a conviction and a custodial sentence against the owner, and his company; largely because the chain of control was miniscule, his negligence palpable and the link between him and the company transparent.

The conditions for 'reckless manslaughter', as it then was, were readily established beyond reasonable doubt in court. But what might be an explanation for this irresponsible behaviour? Why would the owner take such risks with the lives of young people in a manner which might lead to prison and the collapse of his company?

The answer in such cases appears to be 'wilful blindness'. Some managers in some companies appear to almost literally blind themselves to the consequences of their actions. There have been several cases, for example, where managers of blood banks have continued to use blood which they must have known was contaminated with the HIV virus: this had catastrophic consequences for those who received transfusions of infected blood.[71] And, in transport, there have been occasions when managers have insisted that planes fly to schedule despite insistent warnings from mechanics about serious deficiencies in safety requiring immediate repair.[72] In both situations, in order to keep to performance targets, to keep up production or to stick to timetables, managers risk the lives

[71] Police brought criminal charges against the Canadian Red Cross Society and a US pharmaceutical company after an investigation into tainted blood: in one of the worst public health scandals in Canada, thousands of blood transfusion recipients contracted the AIDS and hepatitis C viruses from contaminated blood during the 1980s. Many of them died. The police claimed that the accused failed to inform the public about the risk of HIV and hepatitis infections from unscreened blood and failed to test donated blood for the hepatitis C virus. The charges included criminal negligence causing bodily harm. Cf. 'Doctor at center of Canadian tainted blood scandal must stand trial despite poor health, judge says' (*Ottawa Sun*, 7 August 2005).

[72] Parlementaire Enquête Bijlmerramp, *Eindrapport* (Staatsuitgeverij, Den Haag 1999).

of hundreds of people and, in the blood bank scandals, effectively issued their death warrants.

Then, in the Roy Bowles Transport Company, managers were encouraging and rewarding drivers to drive considerably above the legal limit of hours of work at the wheel. On the surface, this was a respectable firm that complied with safety standards, yet on another level there was systemic deviance involving stimulating drivers to go well beyond the legal and safe limit for driving. To camouflage this, there was the routine doctoring of the 'tachometers' in the trucks' cabs which record a driver's hours behind the wheel; these devices are ostensibly strictly regulated. In practice, people were able to operate within a sort of 'split-personality' environment: one had a respectable and compliant face to the outside world while the other one was breaking all the rules.

But what this meant was the company was sending out 'time-bombs' on to the roads every day. Everyone involved must have 'known' this, as the risk of accident due to driver exhaustion is common knowledge in the industry. Moreover, the drivers themselves were likely victims in a serious road accident yet willingly colluded with management in return for financial rewards. As well as wilful blindness, there was a form of routinization leading to risk-taking: each time a manager and a driver got away with it, that would reinforce their belief that drivers could drive adequately with little rest.

One metaphor to describe this pathway into rule-breaking is the 'slippery slope': the first few violations may cause some qualms but each further infringement becomes less and less a matter of conscience until the culprit is sliding further down the slope, and soon he or she reaches a point of no return and accommodates to the deviance as 'normal' and 'routine'.

But this 'normal' situation came abruptly into the open when, on the M25 London ring-road, a Bowles truck rammed another vehicle, causing two deaths. Eyewitnesses said that the Bowles' driver had been driving erratically prior to the crash as if he was periodically nodding off. The police and Crown Prosecution Service decided, after an investigation had revealed systemic deviance, to prosecute for individual manslaughter. Two managers and the driver were convicted of manslaughter: both managers received suspended sentences for their complicity in killing two people (and the driver a custodial sentence).[73] But prosecuting for corporate manslaughter was consciously avoided, although the chances might have

[73] Gobert and Punch (n. 13).

seemed promising with a small company and strong evidence of systemic deviance, because of the negative example of recent failed prosecutions.[74] So the company got away with it. And this in an industry about which there is a common feeling that such risky practices are widespread.

Finally, there is a range of psychological explanations – group thinking, depersonalization, routinization and wilful blindness – to explain why managers in organizations can take decisions that lead to harm. But there is one further mechanism to be added: in the Thalidomide and Dalkon Shield scandals, companies brought products on the market which caused injury and other serious side-effects. The drug Thalidomide led to thousands of seriously deformed children being born with consequential considerable difficulties of immediate care for their parents and the prospect of long-term support for the disabled children. And the Dalkon Shield, an inter-uterine contraceptive device for women, caused bleeding, infections, unwanted pregnancies and even a number of deaths. Both companies received warnings about these defects and side-effects, yet both not only ignored the alarm signals but even pushed on with increased marketing and advertising. It was as if the management simply could not abandon a highly successful product and so filtered out the bad news. This approximates to 'cognitive dissonance', whereby disconfirming evidence is not only dismissed but also leads to a strengthening of the belief in one's cause (or, in this case, product).[75]

In effect, the argument is that, while decision-making in corporations may ostensibly be cloaked within a rational, economic, 'strategic' paradigm, it can also be distorted by a number of psychological mechanisms which, in turn, foster undue risk and promote a culture of negligence. In some instances, where the operational managers are close to the primary processes, it is almost unfathomable that they risk the lives of members of the public, their customers but also of their own personnel. In OLL the owner must have 'known' the risk he was placing the young canoeists in: and the Roy Bowles managers must have 'known' the risk they were taking of a bad crash with possible fatalities involving their own personnel. And that is doubtless why this 'must have known' element, which is typical of such small companies with a close relation at the board level

[74] The reasoning for this decision was conveyed by the police officers responsible for the investigation at a University of Essex/Essex Police seminar on 'corporate manslaughter' 1999.

[75] Mokhiber (n. 37); L. Festinger, *The Theory of Cognitive Dissonance* (Stanford University Press, Stanford, CA 1957).

to the likely consequences of faulty risk assessments, that the handful of convictions for what is effectively 'corporate killing' are reached.

But even if there is the occasional conviction of a small company, there still remains the sense of injustice that large companies which kill manage to evade conviction. In England and Wales this is related to an interpretation of the law which almost grants immunity to large companies against conviction. This is, however, a more universal problem and a similar picture emerges of the difficulty of securing a conviction from offences of violence against large companies in a number of countries including the USA, the Netherlands and Italy.

IV. Getting away with murder

In this section I wish to sum up the conspiracy of variables which permit companies that kill to get off the legal hook and effectively to 'decriminalise' this area of corporate crime.[76] For instance, there have been almost no successful prosecutions for corporate manslaughter of large firms in England and Wales. Earlier, I set out some reasons for this – including a complex organizational structure cloaking responsibility coupled with the companies' awesome and intimidating legal 'muscle' – but a major component in this record of failure is the law itself.

In a nutshell, it is possible to take a company to court for the common-law offence of 'manslaughter' in England and Wales. But to secure a conviction against the company, there has to be a conviction against a manager who is considered to be 'the directing mind' of the company: this is known as the 'identification principle'. That person has to be of sufficient status and managerial level to be identified with the decision-making elite of the firm. He or she also has to be aware at the time of the accident of the risk being taken, or the negligence being perpetrated, and has to have taken some decisions on behalf of the board which directly led to that particular accident. In legal practice it often proves extremely difficult to define who is the 'controlling mind and will' of the company and almost impossible to determine if there were decisions taken by specific individuals directly related to that particular accident which are indisputably traceable to the board.

In the *Herald of Free Enterprise* case, for instance, the ship had left port with the bow doors open. On a 'roll-on roll-off' ferry this leaves the entire vehicle deck exposed if water should enter. The employee responsible for

[76] D. Bergman, *The Case for Corporate Manslaughter* (CCA, London 2000).

closing the doors was not at his station, but asleep in his bunk, and the first officer who was meant to supervise him had already gone to the bridge on the assumption that the employee was doing his job properly and had shut the doors. The master of the vessel could not see if the bow doors were closed because there was no warning light for this installed on the bridge: in fact, several requests from the Master of the fleet for a simple warning device had been rejected by the managing board on grounds of cost. Then a court of inquiry on the accident brought out a damning report on the neglect of safety within the company.[77]

In short, there really can be no dispute about the actual negligence: the gaping bow doors on the capsized vessel lying on its side outside of Zeebrugge Harbour were palpable evidence for all to see of failure to follow safety guidelines. And yet there was no conviction in court and, when the case was dismissed against the company, the Crown Prosecution Service withdrew the cases against the individuals, presumably to avoid their becoming scapegoats. In the end, then, no-one was ever convicted for the deaths of some 200 people: this leaves a strong after-taste that justice was not done and that this would not be tolerated if the deaths had been related to common crime. Indeed, the judge in another trial against a railway company for 'corporate manslaughter' following a serious accident lamented that it was almost impossible to convict a large company under the then existing law. As the judge in the *Herald* case put it:

> Whether the defendant is a corporation or a personal defendant, the ingredients of manslaughter must be established by proving the necessary *mens rea* and *actus reus* of manslaughter against it or him by evidence properly to be relied upon against it or him. A case against a personal defendant cannot be fortified by evidence against another defendant. The case against a corporation can only be made by evidence properly addressed to showing guilt on the part of the corporation as such.[78]

Present law can be viewed as virtually a form of *lex imperfecta*, which seems almost designed not to work. But there is new legislation which is meant to make it easier to take a company to court for a new statutory offence of 'corporate killing' based on 'management failure'; the Corporate Manslaughter and Corporate Homicide Act 2007.[79]

[77] Sheen Report, *M v Herald of Free Enterprise: Report of Court No. 8074* (Department of Transport, London 1987).

[78] Quoted in J. Gobert, 'The Evolving Legal Test of Corporate Criminal Liability' forthcoming in J. Minkes and L. Minkes (eds.), *White Collar Crime* (Sage, London 2008).

[79] The Labour Government, which came into office over ten years ago with the intention to introduce new legislation on this, has been dragging its feet and it only recently came into

This followed from the example of Australia and the proposals of the Law Commission in 2000.[80] This is clearly, in the eyes of many, a legislative step in the right direction: but the real difficulty has been with the legal mind which struggled with locating *mens rea* in an aggregate because, as mentioned before, the criminal law is fundamentally posited on the individual. Or, as Wolf puts it in her defence of individualism, 'how can a flow chart be guilty'?[81] Gobert, in contrast, argues strongly for an 'aggregation theory of corporate liability' where aggregation represents 'a first step towards an approach to corporate criminal liability where a company's liability is not derivative, where the company is liable in it own right for its own fault'.[82] Here, crucially, corporate fault would be unrelated to individual criminality.

V. Conclusion

What this chapter has tried to convey is the fact that 'system crimes', understood as crimes not only by states but also by corporations, suffer from the fact that the criminal law has considerable difficulty in recognising collective guilt and in applying liability to an institution or organization.[83] In both areas this leaves one with the feeling that the criminal law and the criminal justice arena (enforcement, investigation, prosecution, trial and sanctions) simply does not deliver justice. The law courts are not a benign arena but are the playground of the powerful, the crafty, the wealthy and the unscrupulous. Too often the 'real crooks' get away with it.

Crimes against humanity and war crimes are horrendous and often on a massive and almost unimaginable scale of misery. The scale of corporate crime leading to avoidable death and injury is clearly not on the same level and plainly does not have the same measure of intent. Yet the offences are of deep concern because the victims are often ordinary citizens, in their own countries and in peacetime: they are going about their normal, daily business using the same modes of transport that everyone does: and they hold the expectation that the legitimate company involved

force in early 2008: J. Gobert, 'The Corporate Manslaughter and Corporate Homicide Act 2007' (2008) 71(3) *Modern Law Review* 413–63.

80 Wells (n. 12).

81 S. Wolf, 'The legal and moral responsibility of organizations', in J. Pennock and J. Chapman (eds.), *Criminal Justice* (New York University Press, New York 1985), p. 273.

82 Gobert (n. 65).

83 D. D. Caron, 'State crimes: looking at municipal experience with organized crime', in M. Ragazzi (ed.), *International Responsibility Today: Essays in Memory of Oscar Schachter* (Martinus Nijhoff, Leiden and Boston 2005), pp. 23–30.

is concerned about their welfare and safety, is concerned with its obligation to provide a 'duty of care', is competently run and adheres fully to regulatory standards.

But, as we have seen, there are firms where the management is able to disassociate itself from the consequences of its actions, in underestimating risk and in fostering a culture and practice of negligence, in ways which echo the unscrupulousness of organized criminals and callousness of the 'snake-heads' who traffic their human cargoes in horrendous conditions.[84] Although I have drawn largely on England and Wales for my examples of the weaknesses in the law of 'corporate manslaughter', I believe that the thrust of my argument is broad if not universal. It simply seems intrinsically unjust that corporate, and state, crimes are interpreted primarily as offences committed by individuals because the criminal law is so conservative and is rooted in antiquated, nineteenth-century notions of a corporation.

The implication of this chapter is, then, that there should an exploration of a much tougher notion of organizational fault. It may well be argued that we are then left with the problem of sanctions; for a corporation has 'no body to kick and no soul to be damned'.[85] But apart from stimulating more creative ways of sanctioning collectives, there should be a much stronger emphasis on applying the criminal label to collectives and on applying the moral stigma of a criminal conviction to organizations.[86]

[84] J. Katz, *The Seductions of Crime* (Basic Books, New York 1988).

[85] J. C. Coffee, '"No soul to damn, no body to kick": an unscandalized inquiry into the problems of corporate punishment' (1981) 79 *Michigan Law Review* 397–400.

[86] Braithwaite (n. 42) 1–25.

4

Men and abstract entities: individual responsibility and collective guilt in international criminal law

GERRY SIMPSON*

> Trials that reach the hearts and minds of Iraqis reinforce other important social and political messages. By establishing individual rather than collective responsibility for these crimes, they will place blame where it belongs: on the shoulders of Hussein and his cabal, and not on the Sunnis collectively or any particular village or clan.[1]
>
> ... the latest and most formidable form of...dominion: bureaucracy or the rule of an intricate system of bureaus in which no men, neither one nor the best, neither the few nor the many, can be held responsible ...[2]
>
> The true culprits are those who misled public opinion and take advantage of the people's ignorance to raise disquieting rumours and sound the alarm bell, inciting the country and, consequently, other countries into enmity. The real culprits are those who by interest or inclination, declaring constantly that war is inevitable, end by making it so, asserting that they are powerless to prevent it. The real culprits are those who sacrifice the general interest to their own personal interest.[3]

I. Bosnia v Serbia

On 26 February 2007, the International Court of Justice handed down its decision in the *Bosnia v Serbia (Genocide)* case.[4] The Court declared

* Professor of International Law, London School of Economics. Part of this essay was published previously as a chapter entitled 'Law's Subjects' in G. Simpson, *Law, War and Crime: War Crimes Trials and the Reinvention of International Law* (Polity, Cambridge 2007).

1 E. Ward and M. Hieman, 'Iraqi run tribunal is major progress towards rule of law system' *Christian Science Monitor*, 19 July 2005: www.csmonitor.com/2005/0719/p09s02-coop.html, accessed 12 June 2008.

2 H. Arendt, *On Violence* (Harcourt, Brace and World, New York 1970), p. 38.

3 Baron d' Estournelles de Constant, Chairman, *International Commission to Inquire into the Causes and Conduct of the Balkan Wars*, 'Opening Statement' (1914).

4 *Bosnia and Herzegovina v Serbia and Montenegro*, Application of the Convention on the Prevention and Punishment of Genocide ('*Genocide Judgment*') Merits, Judgment (26 February 2007). From now on, I will use 'Bosnia' and 'Serbia' as shorthand for the two states involved (now three, since Montenegro's declaration of independence).

that there had been a genocide in Bosnia but evidence for that genocide existed only in relation to one place: Srebrenica.[5] Other attacks on civilian populations (in Sarajevo, in Goradze) were 'ethnic cleansing' (to use the political term) and, in all probability, crimes against humanity (to use the legal term) but they did not rise (or sink) to the level of genocide (in the technical, legal sense). In the case of Srebrenica, there had been a genocide but the Serbian state was not directly responsible for this genocide.[6] Instead, Serbia had violated the Genocide Convention by failing to prevent this genocide (it had failed to exercise its influence over the likes of Karadzic and Mladic) and by failing to facilitate the punishment of those responsible for it (Serbia has not, despite repeated requests, surrendered General Mladic to the ICTY).[7]

The substantive part of the judgment begins on what must seem, from the perspective of interested laymen, an unusual note. The Court asks whether the Genocide Convention prohibits genocide carried out by states.[8] While the majority in the Court agrees that it does, a significant minority takes the view that the Genocide Convention is not, to any significant extent, directed at the activities of states at all. For this latter group of judges, the Convention outlaws genocide when carried out by *individuals*; it is personal intent that is decisive for the purposes of assessing the nature of a particular offence (i.e. was there intent, on the part of an individual perpetrator, 'to destroy in whole or in part a particular group'?). In the end, a majority of judges accepted that the Genocide Convention had imposed obligations on states but they held that these were of a delictual nature. No judge envisaged state criminal responsibility for genocide.

What I want to explore in this chapter is the relationship between individual responsibility and state responsibility (and, in particular, state criminal responsibility) under international law. It is clear that this relationship is one of the keys to understanding the *Bosnia v Serbia* case but it is also central to the way in which international criminal law itself plays out. For example, the Court, while assessing the responsibility of Serbia as a state, relies, to a great extent, on the findings of the International Criminal Tribunal for the former Yugoslavia in cases implicating individual responsibility (in particular, the *Krstic* case).[9]

[5] *Genocide Judgment* (n. 4) para. 297. [6] *Genocide Judgment* (n. 4) para. 415.

[7] *Genocide Judgment* (n. 4) para. 438. [8] *Genocide Judgment* (n. 4) para. 166.

[9] One topic I do not touch on to any great extent in this chapter concerns the distinction between collective groups with legal personality and those lacking it. The international system is founded on a demarcation between states and collective groups lacking

This cross-pollination is somewhat typical of an international legal order in which state responsibility and individual culpability are symbiotic. Indeed, a number of those judges who were reluctant to read the Convention as imposing direct responsibility nonetheless accepted that states would incur responsibility where acts of individuals could be attributable to the state.

The Court, perpetually juggling the demands of statism with the imperatives of individual culpability, was concerned also to show that any finding of complicity to commit genocide depended on a prior finding that Serbia (or one of its organs) had acted 'knowingly' in aiding the Bosnian Serbs at Srebrenica.[10] Again, this application of concepts of individual responsibility to state behaviour will appear odd to lay observers but entirely unremarkable to those familiar with international law's recurring patterns.

Ultimately, the relationship between individual and collective accountability rests on a dilemma facing those who seek to perform international criminal justice. This dilemma, in turn, reflects our intuition that mass criminality in war or peace is *both* collective and individual in nature. And this combination is present whether we consider the position of the perpetrator or victim. The perpetrator is both individually culpable (perhaps 'evil') and yet also embedded in a social structure or organizational matrix that, to some extent, 'determined' his crimes. The *Jelisic* court imagined a lone genocidal maniac[11] but there is no record, in law or history, of such a person existing. Equally, the victims are individual human beings. Each death or injury is a personal disaster for the victim and the victim's family. But, in the case of genocide, the victim's status as a victim of genocide depends on her membership of a social group. No longer merely an individual victim, she acquires her special status because of the fact that she is part of a 'national, ethnic, religious or racial group'.

This chapter emphasizes one particular aspect of collective responsibility; namely state responsibility. However, international criminal law's collective 'face' encompasses more than simply states. And, as I discuss

statehood. This issue arose in Serbia's *Application for Revision of the 1996 Judgment*, wherein Serbia claimed that, in 1993, when proceedings were instituted by Bosnia, it lacked the legal personality that would permit it to be brought before the court. The Court rejected this argument in 2003 on *res judicata* grounds (there were five dissenting arguments).

[10] *Genocide Judgment* (n. 4) para. 421.

[11] *Prosecutor v Jelisic*, IT-95–10-A, Judgment, Appeals Chamber (5 July 2001).

later, collective identities at a sub-state level (criminal enterprises, state organs) provide a linking point between the abstractions of state responsibility and the particularities of individual liability. It is important to understand, too, that system criminality (in the version articulated in this book) applies to both states and state (and non-state) organs. Culpability extends beyond the individual, and implicates (and is influenced by) the cultural, political and bureaucratic groupings of which the individual is, necessarily, a part. Before exploring more fully this relationship between group and personal victimhood and, more especially, collective and individual responsibility, let me begin this chapter by presenting an orthodox account of international criminal law's roots in a conception of individual responsibility.

II. Men not abstract entities

War crimes trials are understood and imbibed as dramas of individual human reckoning. The indelible imagery of the trial is that of the defendant facing up to his responsibility; accountable for his crimes before the court and the eyes of the world. In Jerusalem, there was Adolf Eichmann behind his glass booth looking out at his '6 million accusers'.[12] At Nuremberg, two rows of variously dazed, defiant, emotionally crippled, high-ranking Nazis slowly absorbed a picture of the gross misdeeds contained in the accusations. In The Hague, there was Slobodan Milosevic bullishly facing down his accusers, and in Baghdad, the personality of an apparently remorseless Saddam Hussein has come to dominate the process of legalized retribution. But if popular understandings of the war crimes field are dominated by notorious individuals, this simply reflects an inclination in the academic and professional world of international law to think of international criminal law as an expression of the growing role of the individual in international law generally. International criminal law, indeed, is often understood as the application of individual responsibility to international law. While most international legal norms subject states to certain behavioural constraints and hold states accountable for breaches of these constraints, international criminal law has been regarded as controversial and innovative precisely because it makes individuals liable for infractions of international law's most fundamental norms. At Nuremberg, the International Military Tribunal declared, in its final judgment, that the hideous crimes under investigation were committed

[12] G. Hausner, *Justice in Jerusalem* (Harper & Row, New York 1966), p. 392.

not by abstract entities but by men.[13] This apparently commonsensical idea has by now become central to international criminal lawyers' self-understandings.[14]

Putting the individual at the centre of the international law project has been a distinguishing motif in much commentary in the field, but it is linked, too, to some other effects of the law of war crimes on the wider discipline. To take the most obviously significant, punishing individuals through criminal sanction is important because it promises the renewal, perhaps completion, of international law; because it links international law explicitly to international human rights law and anticipates the future enforceability of these norms; and because it contributes further to the recession of sovereignty (in the latter case, international criminal law is recruited to wider processes of globalization). Let me take each of these in turn.

First, international criminal law represents at least one possible future for international law.[15] International lawyers have long been assailed by anxieties arising out of the apparent unenforceability of international law. This is, of course, partly a problem built into the very structure of international society. In particular, in a world in which many are sovereign, there is no single site of ultimate sovereignty. Many international lawyers have accepted that the international system is an anarchical society[16] in which states must work to achieve certain global ends while at the same time preserving their freedom. To the extent that compliance is secured, it is done so through reciprocal sanctions,[17] through the establishment of coalitions of like-minded states,[18] through the self-identifications of states[19] or through the work of global networks of state and non-state actors.[20] Often, though, what appears to be missing from even the rosiest

[13] Nuremberg IMT, 'Judgment and sentence' (1947) 41 AJIL 221.

[14] G. Robertson, *Crimes Against Humanity: The Struggle for Global Justice* (The New Press, New York 1999), p. 655.

[15] F. Mégret, 'Justice in times of violence' (2003) 14 EJIL 327; Robertson (n. 14).

[16] J.S. Watson, *Theory and Reality in the International Protection of Human Rights* (Transnational Publishers, Inc., Ardsley, NY 1999).

[17] A. D'Amato, 'Is international law really 'law'?' (1984/85) *Northwestern University Law Review* 75; F. Kratochwil, 'Thrasymmachos revisited: on the relevance of norms and the study of international law for international relations' (1984) 37 *Journal of International Affairs* 343.

[18] F. Teson, 'A Kantian theory of international law' (1992) 92(1) *Columbia Law Review* 53.

[19] C. Reus-Smit, *The Politics of International Law* (Cambridge University Press, Cambridge 2004).

[20] A.M. Slaughter, *The New World Order* 2004 (Princeton University Press, Princeton, NJ 2004), pp. 14–44.

portrayals of international law's muscularity or relevance is the possibility of simple criminal repression or top-down enforcement. In the case of the Iraq war, the tragedy of international law for most international lawyers lay in the breach of the law by two of the Great Powers.[21] The system of habitual compliance and institutional fidelity had been violated. The solution for one group of international lawyers was the re-invigoration of international society through confidence-building among estranged allies and institutional renewal.[22] This, indeed, was the official response of the United Nations in its *High-Level Panel Report*,[23] and in the Secretary-General's *In Larger Freedom* document, where the accent is firmly on avoiding future transgressions by strengthening the UN system and by elaborating principles that would make decisions concerning the use of force more transparent.[24]

Among other lawyers, though, there was a sense that law could only function if there was some sort of *ex post facto* punishment meted out to those who violated the rules.[25] The solution to the problem of the unlawfulness of the 2003 Iraq war lay not just in finding the states concerned responsible but in the punishment of individual violators. In other words, this comprehensive system of rules elaborated over centuries was capable of completion only when it could offer the possibility of some form of retribution towards those individuals who disregarded its most fundamental precepts. But who is to be punished?

The structure of international society makes it difficult to punish states. International law is largely auto-interpretive and states are beholden to no super-sovereign. As the ICTY said in *Blaskic*: 'under international law States could not be subject to sanctions akin to those provided for in national criminal justice systems'.[26] States make and enforce international law and they have shown a marked reluctance to devolve powers of punishment to international organizations. In any case, states may not be a suitable object of punishment. The project of completing international

[21] P. Sands, *Lawless World* (Penguin, Harmandsworth 2005).

[22] J. Brunnée and S. J. Toope, 'The use of force: international law after Iraq' (2004) 53 *International and Comparative Law Quarterly* 785–806.

[23] See Report of the Secretary-General's High Level Panel, *A More Secure World: Our Shared Responsibility*, available at www.un.org/secureworld, accessed 8 July 2008.

[24] See Report of the Secretary-General of the United Nations for Decision by Heads of State and Government in September 2005, available at www.un.org/largerfreedom, accessed 8 July 2008.

[25] D. Bacher and B. Weston, *Bush's Illegal War* (30 May 2003) at www.counterpunch.org/bacher05302003.html, accessed 12 July 2008.

[26] *Prosecutor v Tihomir Blaskic*, IT-95–14-T (3 March 2000).

law, or making it more like domestic law, seemed to require, then, the punishment of individual violators. Bad men were to be incarcerated. This was the thrust of much commentary around the Iraq War. If the US and the UK really were guilty of breaching international law then, surely, the natural consequence of this was the indictment of the war leaders. This approach was reflected in the questions asked by journalists, in the anti-war banners carried by protesters ('The war is illegal, Bush and Blair are war criminals') and by the various efforts to have US and UK officials indicted before the international criminal court. Only individualized justice could ensure the relevance and meaningfulness of international law. Abstract entities were out, flesh and blood human beings were in.

The personalization of international law through international criminal law is linked to a second, broader trend: the emergence of human rights as a field. The move from thinking of international law in terms of 'abstract entities' to conceiving of it as a legal order about individual human beings begins at Nuremberg, and transforms the soul of international law. No longer exclusively about states (or, to a much lesser extent, organizations), it now becomes fixated on the rights and duties of individuals. This is so much so that there is an equation in the public mind of 'human rights' with 'international law'. At least since Nuremberg, states have been seen as potentially self-destructive, rapacious and violent. Initially, at least, the human rights system, while it attempted to place the security and integrity of individual human beings centre stage, still made respect for human rights a matter of state responsibility. The perceived early failure of human rights instruments can be traced to an erroneous assumption that states would hold each other responsible for any breaches of personal rights. This has happened only very rarely. Greece was taken to the European Court of Human Rights by Denmark, Sweden, Norway and the Netherlands,[27] and the UK was sued by Ireland over the treatment of IRA detainees,[28] but overall the record has been patchy. Even where mechanisms of individual petition were established, such as under the International Covenant for Civil and Political Rights, states found to be in breach of human rights obligations remained under only a weak obligation to remedy any abuses. And, of course, it was states themselves, despite the Nuremberg judgment, that continued to be the relevant 'entities' for the purposes of attributing responsibility,

[27] *Denmark, Norway, Sweden and the Netherlands v Greece*, The Greek Case, Application No. 3321/67, 3322/67, 3323/67 and 3344/67, Council of Europe, European Commission of Human Rights (5 November 1969).

[28] *Ireland v The United Kingdom*, ECtHR, Application No. 5310/71 (18 January 1978).

even if it was individuals who were doing the torturing or killing. The International Law Commission had exercised itself with the question of state responsibility for almost half a century before its Articles on that topic were adopted by the General Assembly in 2001.[29] The move to individual responsibility, then, in international criminal law, modifies this tendency and has been hailed as a way of giving human rights law the bite it was thought to lack.

Third, international criminal law promises to further advance the demise of sovereignty. In this sense, the recent explosion of institutional innovation in criminal law is hitched to wider trends in the direction of globalization. As the state recedes in importance in the economic, cultural and political spheres, it seems appropriate that its centrality in international law should also disappear.[30] Thus, the trials of Milosevic and Kambanda, and the decision in Pinochet, seem explicitly to deny states some of the privileges they once held in the international order. This is why in encomiums to globalization, the ICC is frequently invoked alongside the WTO, the loosening of state ownership and the deregulation of trade and capital. Sometimes, too, international criminal law is associated with the triumph of global individualism or some form of cosmopolitanism. The Statute of the International Criminal Court reveals the lineaments of a new global justice order.[31] Daniele Archibugi makes this link explicit: 'For all their flaws, existing bodies [of international criminal law] are the embryos of more robust ones that will be needed to guarantee global legality … a fully-fledged international criminal court needs to be set up'.[32]

But it turns out that, despite the claims and promises made by its keenest proponents, international criminal law or the law of war crimes is not, and has not been at its origins, exclusively dedicated to this methodological individualism that lies at the heart of much international justice rhetoric, human rights law and cosmopolitan enthusiasm for international criminal law. Instead, what we find, and what I want to discuss in the remainder of this essay, is a perpetual movement between

[29] *ILC Articles on State Responsibility* (2001): http://lcil.law.cam.ac.uk/ILCSR/articles(e).doc, accessed 12 June 2008.

[30] M. Koskenniemi, 'The future of statehood', in G. Simpson, *The Nature of International Law* (Ashgate, Aldershot 2001); H. Koh, 'Transnational law', in G. Simpson, *The Nature of International Law* (Ashgate, Aldershot 2001).

[31] D. Hirsh, *Cosmopolitan Trials* (Glasshouse Press, London 2003).

[32] D. Archibugi and M. Koenig-Archibugi, *Debating Cosmopolitics* (Verso, London 2003), p. 268.

the collective and the individual.[33] This manifests itself in a number of different relationships. In section III, below, I discuss a series of institutional choices made throughout modern history between the criminalization of states (what I call, the Versailles Model) and the punishment of individuals (the Nuremberg Model). I conclude that these two models now coexist rather uncomfortably in the contemporary practice of international law with the paradigm instances in each case being the treatment of Iraq after 1991 (and, in particular, Security Council Resolution 687) and the establishment of the *ad hoc* and permanent Tribunals in The Hague and Arusha.

Next, in section IV, I turn to the way in which collective responsibility tends to be built into the doctrinal architecture of much of international criminal law even in its putatively individualistic mode. International criminal law, understood as the trial of individual violators by international courts, cannot escape into individualism entirely. It finds itself perpetually drawn back to group responsibility and communal guilt. In an analysis of the work of tribunals at Nuremberg and The Hague (and here I advert to the Rome Statute, too), I show how doctrines such as Joint Criminal Enterprise, organizational criminality and conspiracy betray international criminal law's roots in what George Fletcher has called a romantic view of history and personality, i.e. one in which the individual's behaviour is motivated by, and can only be understood in reference to, larger communities of nation, state or tribe.[34] Finally, in section V, I turn to broader questions around the structure of war crimes trials and the way in which that structure itself reflects our moral intuitions about responsibility for mass atrocity as well as our apparent allergy to collective punishment and our willing recourse to it. And I show, too, how the relationship between individual evil, structural deformity and the tragedy of being human is implicated in all this.

Ultimately, this chapter presents the field of international criminal law, or war, law and crime, as a perpetual bargain (played out in institutional history, in doctrinal innovation and in the structuring principles of

[33] This resolves itself as (at least) four models of criminality. The first is the responsibility of individuals *qua* individuals. Here I refer to the trial of soldiers who commit extraordinary crimes of war without any authority from their superiors. Second, is the liability of officials who commit crimes on behalf of the state. Here the collective and the individual become mixed. The third model is organizational criminality of the sort seen at Nuremberg, and the fourth model is state crime (a fifth model might attribute some responsibility to the very structure of international society itself).

[34] G. Fletcher, 'The Storrs Lectures: liberals and romantics at war: the problem of collective guilt' (2000) 111 *Yale Law Journal* 1501–73.

both international society and our moral intuitions) between individual blameworthiness and collective guilt.

III. State crime and individual responsibility

The modern institutional trajectory of international criminal law can be understood as a series of movements between collective guilt and individual responsibility. This history begins at Versailles with the peace imposed on Germany following the First World War, a model of peace repeated to some extent in criminalization efforts at the end of the twentieth century in Iraq, in Libya and in Serbia.[35] The Versailles settlement represents, then, the first such *de facto* criminalization of pariah states in international legal history. Previous post-war rearrangements had contemplated forms of demilitarization or sanctions imposed on defeated states (e.g. the Congress of Vienna in 1815, the peace imposed on France at the end of the Franco-Prussian war of 1872) but none before had placed a state under such intense levels of scrutiny nor applied a regime as punitive as that found at Versailles. Versailles represents the moment when the modern international law of institutions begins, and with it the possibility of applying the machinery of institutional oversight to whole nations. Narrow definitions of criminal law (requiring criminal courts[36] or incarceration (*Blaskic*)) need to be modified when we contemplate the way in which certain states are stigmatised and punished by international society.[37] Prior to Versailles, and it is a view that persists to this day, violations of international law were understood as largely bilateral: one state's acts caused injury to a second or third state. Such breaches were dealt with at an inter-state level through a negotiated settlement of claims, or, occasionally, a form of arbitration or through the employment of counter-measures by the injured state.[38] Civil or private law is the appropriate model for understanding international law in

[35] D. Bederman, 'Collective security, demilitarization and "pariah states"' (2002) 13(1) EJIL 121.

[36] R. Higgins, *Problems and Processes* (Clarendon Press, Oxford 1995).

[37] G. Simpson, *Great Powers and Outlaw States: Unequal Sovereigns in the International Legal Order* (Cambridge University Press, Cambridge 2004).

[38] This was the case even in the laws of war. Violations of these laws was a matter of inter-state responsibility. E.g. Art. 3 of Hague IV (1907) states: 'A belligerent party which violates the provisions... shall, if the case demands, be liable to pay compensation.' This includes compensation for individuals. See also C. Greenwood, 'International humanitarian law', in F. Karlshoven (ed.), *The Centennial of the First Peace Conference* (Kluwer Law, The Hague 2000).

this traditional mode. This legal order is composed of a matrix of bilateral relations with the civil suit being paradigmatic (represented by the inter-state dispute settlement mechanism at the International Court of Justice).

By the time of Versailles, though, the Great Powers had begun to see themselves as an incipient international community. Serious violations of that community's dominant mores were no longer thought to be a matter of merely dyadic concern but were understood or reconfigured into a breach of the rights of all states acting as an international society. At least one of the conditions for the existence of the criminal law was now satisfied – the self-consciousness (and self-righteousness) of a moral community (albeit one largely directed by the Great Powers). This self-righteousness translated into a new belief that victory and defeat in war was not simply matter of luck or strategy but also implicated questions of collective virtue and criminality.[39] This combination of institutional self-confidence, community self-awareness, and legalism produced the Versailles settlement and the criminalization of Germany. Germany was punished by the society of states, and the extent and intensity of its punishment was akin to that of the criminal sanctions found in many domestic legal orders. The Versailles model of state criminality was marked by a number of highly distinctive qualities.

First, the criminal state was adjudged to have breached one of the fundamental norms of the international legal order. It was never made absolutely clear what norm had been breached but there was general confidence among the statesmen of the time that the German state and its leadership were responsible for a war that the Canadian Prime Minister, Robert Borden, rather misleadingly, called a 'crime against humanity'.[40] Second, the contractual relationship usually found in armistice and peace agreements with accompanying amnesties[41] (between two private parties, *justi hostes*) was transformed into a relationship between representatives of the legitimate political order and the outlaw state.[42] International law underwent a shift from sovereign equality to centralized enforcement and from society to community. Third, the state in question (Germany in this case) was deprived of some of its basic

[39] C. Schmitt, *The Nomos of the Earth, in the International law of the Jus Publicum Europeaeum* (Telos Press, New York, NY 2003); R. Pal, *Crimes in International Relations* (University of Calcutta Press, Calcutta 1955).

[40] G. J. Bass, *Stay the Hand of Vengeance: The Politics of War Crimes Tribunals* (Princeton University Press, Princeton, NJ and Oxford 2000), p. 65.

[41] Pal (n. 39) 399. [42] Schmitt (n. 39) 262.

sovereign prerogatives. In Germany's case, the state lost some of its territory, was forced to pay highly punitive damages (in the Entente Note of 10 January 1917, the Allies declared that Germany's liabilities were without limit because it had engaged in an aggressive war) and was obliged to undergo a process of demilitarization underwritten by the international community and overseen by, often *ad hoc*, international bureaucracies (e.g. the Inter-Allied Commissions of Control charged with ensuring that Germany disarmed). In addition, the criminal state in this case was placed under notice that any breach of the enhanced regime of oversight could result in a resumption of hostilities or an enforcement of treaties of guarantee.[43]

This Versailles model, of course, fell into serious disrepute shortly after it was imposed. Many contemporary critics blamed it for the breakdown in the European order less than two decades later. John Maynard Keynes famously predicted the dire consequences of criminalising Germany, the United States displayed a marked reluctance to support the more punitive aspects of the settlement, and, of course, the effects of the peace on the German population at large were felt by many people to have been fundamentally unjust. Some of the fault for the rise of the Nazis and the onset of war was laid at the door of the Versailles settlement. It is little wonder, then, that when the Second World War ended, the Allies appeared to renounce the idea of state criminality and resorted to a rejuvenated model of individual responsibility. Nuremberg was a riposte not only to conventional international law with its relentless focus on states' 'civil' liability but also to the state crime model pursued without much success at Versailles.

The orthodox account, then, of the war crimes trials at Nuremberg and Tokyo argues that they were fashioned with a view to cleansing Japan and Germany of collective guilt. The absence of the Emperor from the list of defendants at Tokyo, for example, can be viewed as a symptom of this effort, since he was viewed as a symbol of the nation rather than an individual capable of having committed a crime. At Potsdam on 26 July 1945, the Allies offered the following reassurance: 'We do not intend that the Japanese shall be enslaved as a race or destroyed as a nation'. At Nuremberg, too, there was a rhetorical tendency to shift responsibility from the German state to individual Germans and specifically Nazi institutions. The apparent exoneration of the *Wehrmacht* at Nuremburg and at the post-war Control Council Trials can be understood as part of this

[43] Bederman (n. 35) 128.

process of ridding Germany of the guilt of nations.[44] The development of international criminal law after the Second World War was heavily influenced by the Cold War requirement that Japan and Germany be acquitted of any state crime. Alongside this, the failure to define and criminalize aggression during debates at the United Nations in the 1950s meant that the focus of war crimes prosecutions would return to crimes capable of being carried out by individuals (war crimes, crimes against humanity and genocide).

The above account does not quite accord with the historical record, though. In 1944, the 'Nuremberg solution' was still in some important quarters a minority position. Churchill and Stalin had favoured summary executions of large numbers of Germans who were to be deprived of the right of a trial, and plans were underway to occupy and emasculate Germany. The most developed of these proposals adopted an even more punitive version of the Versailles model. This was US Treasury Secretary, Henry Morgenthau's Memorandum of September 1944. Here was a classic Carthaginian Peace.[45] Under the Morgenthau proposal, Germany was to be de-industrialized and returned to a largely agrarian state denuded of military capability. This pastoralization of a great European state was to be accompanied by a series of 'political' actions against high-ranking Nazis (they were to be shot under summary procedure). The Morgenthau Plan was defeated by an unlikely coalition of American legalists (notably, Secretary of State Stimson) who wanted war crimes trials and Soviet officials who were happy to see the Nazis disposed of after some sort of show trial.[46] The British reluctantly joined with the group seeking trials, and Morgenthau was left isolated and disappointed. The defeat of the Morgenthau Plan is sometimes taken to represent the triumph of liberal legalism and individual responsibility over vengeful politics and collective guilt.

However, elements of Morgenthau's Plan survived alongside Nuremberg. Most notably, of course, the state of Germany was divided into four zones and then two political entities. It was, in effect, temporarily extinguished as a state (this was accompanied by the brutal treatment accorded to German POWs).[47] But, alongside this, there was the designation of Germany (and Japan) in the United Nations Charter

[44] D. Boxham, *Genocide on Trial: War Crimes Trials and the Formation of Holocaust History and Memory* (Oxford University Press, Oxford 2001).

[45] M. Beschloss, *The Conquerors* (Simon & Schuster, New York 2002); Bass (n. 40).

[46] Beschloss (n. 45).

[47] J. Bacque, *Other Losses* (Stoddart Publishing Co. Ltd, Toronto 1999).

as ‘enemy states’, against whom military action could be undertaken without reference to the UN’s standard provisions restricting the use of force.[48] In any case, at least as far as the US Zone was concerned, the Morgenthau Plan was supplanted by JCS Directive 1067[49] and the Potsdam Protocol (1945).[50] The Directive, which was recommended as practice for the other four controlling authorities, contemplated a highly intrusive programme of economic control, decentralisation of indigenous political power and complete military and ‘industrial’ disarmament (indeed, the directive cautions controlling authorities from taking any action that would enhance German economic power). The Potsdam Protocol (1945), meanwhile, set out the conditions for Four-Power Occupation. These included action to permanently prevent ‘the revival or reorganisation of German militarism’ (Principle 3(a)) and the encouragement of primarily agricultural production (Principle 13). The Potsdam agreement, then, to a certain extent, undercut the apparent purpose of the Nuremberg Tribunal by setting out as its core principle the need to:

> Convince the German people that they have suffered a total military defeat and that they cannot escape responsibility for what they have brought upon themselves, since their own ruthless warfare and the fanatical Nazi resistance have destroyed German economy and made chaos and suffering inevitable.
>
> (Principle 3ii)

This was far removed from the IMT’s move from abstract entities or collective responsibility to individual guilt. Here, the romantic idea of attributing agency to the nation had supplanted (or, at least, supplemented) the liberal project of punishing individualized and autonomous moral behaviour.

It is clear, then, that the origins of contemporary international criminal law in post-war Germany are found in both the ‘stern [individualized] justice’ (Moscow 1943) meted out at the IMT and the broader notions of collective responsibility applied at Potsdam. It is no surprise that the present period is one in which these two conceptions of

[48] This provision has been recommended for removal in the *World Summit Report* (2005); see also F. Kirgis, *International Law Aspects of the 2005 World Summit Outcome*, available at www.asil.org/insights/2005/10/insights051004.html, accessed 8 July 2008.

[49] Directive of the Commander-in-Chief of United States Forces of Occupation Regarding the Military Government of Germany (April 1945).

[50] Potsdam Protocol (2 August 1945).

accountability – individual responsibility and state crime – have both come to occupy prominent positions in the international legal armoury. By the time of the revival of international criminal law in the 1990s at The Hague, individual responsibility was an important means by which the Great Powers could respond to mass atrocity and rogue states could be rehabilitated. In emphasizing the subjective roots of criminality and deviance, the turn to individual responsibility had the potential to cleanse the state of responsibility (and, at the same time, exonerate the state system). We need only think of the way the states drafting the statute for an international criminal court sometimes imagined their task. In order to proceed effectively, states parties negotiators had to envisage themselves as acting on behalf of states and the state system against rogue individuals apparently disconnected from these same states. So, the call was for 'international cooperation' and for states to exercise their duty to punish perpetrators (Preamble). The field of struggle was to be between states applying the techniques of criminal repression (jurisdiction, coordination, detection) and rogue individuals determined to disrupt that system by committing gross violations of the public order (often on behalf of rogue groups or outlaw states). In Security Council Resolution 1593, referring the Darfur human rights abuses to the International Criminal Court, the Council, in Operative Paragraph 2, called on Sudan to cooperate with and provide assistance to the Court in its investigations. International criminal law relies on the fiction of detachability. The state, whether it is Serbia or Sudan, is imagined as an entity distinct from its bad apples and rogue statesmen. For Carla Del Ponte, this was the message of the Milosevic Trial. The Serbian people were the innocent dupes of a powerful criminal mind. Indeed, the Serbs, too, had been wronged by Milosevic. At the beginning of her opening statement, the Prosecutor provides a perfect summation of the individualised version of international criminal law:

> The accused in this case, as in all cases before the Tribunal, is charged as an individual. He is prosecuted on the basis of his individual criminal responsibility. No state or organisation is on trial here today. The indictments do not accuse an entire people of being collectively guilty of the crimes, even the crime of genocide. It may be tempting to generalise when dealing with the conduct of leaders at the highest level, but that is an error that must be avoided. Collective guilt forms no part of the Prosecution case.[51]

[51] See Del Ponte's Words: 'An almost medieval savagery', *The New York Times*, 13 February 2002, available at http://query.nytimes.com/gst/fullpage.html?res=9407E0D91F3CF930A25751C0A9649C8B63, accessed 8 July 2008.

She goes on to say however: 'I do, of course, intend to explore the degree to which the power and influence of the accused extended over others.' It is this 'exploration' that is the subject of the next section, in which I consider those doctrines of international criminal justice that seek to situate the individual accused within a criminal enterprise or community of responsible persons. Historically, as I have noted, the attention given to collective guilt has resolved itself as a focus on the societal liability found, for example, at Versailles and at Potsdam. This inclination has not disappeared, and indeed, seemed newly invigorated at precisely the point when the idea of individual justice through international criminal tribunals was itself undergoing a revival.

This re-invigoration happened largely in three domains. First, at the United Nations, the premier law reform body in the international system, the International Law Commission, elaborated a set of principles to which sought to distinguish ordinary wrongs committed by states with a group of breaches that appeared to be more fundamental than mere delicts. In other words, the ILC considered whether to import the distinction between tort and crime from domestic law into public international law. As one commentator asked: 'Can a state commit a crime?'[52] In its 1996 Draft, the Commission defined a series of acts that would give rise to criminal liability on the part of states.[53] These included genocide, aggression and serious environmental offences (Article 19). More importantly, the Commission developed rules outlining the consequences to be attached to such criminal acts. The most significant of these, found in Articles 43, 45 and 52 of the Draft Articles, contemplate placing criminal states within a special juridical category whereby any reparations or sanctions imposed on them would have seriously deleterious effects on the sovereignty, immunity and dignity of such states.[54]

These principles resembled, in some respects, the Versailles Model discussed earlier. States were to be subject to uniquely punitive quasi-penal sanctions and, in a rather unfortunate nod to the Versailles Treaty, Article 52 declared that sanctions directed against criminal states (or restitution claimed from the criminal state) would not be subject to the normal limitations set out in Article 42 (typically, and for cases involving mere delictual liability, restitution was only permissible to the extent

[52] A. Pellet, 'Can a state commit a crime? Definitely, yes!' (1999) 10 EJIL 425.

[53] Draft Articles on State Responsibility, Official Records of the General Assembly, Fifty-First Session, Suppl. No. 10, A/51/10 and Corr, 1 International Law Commission (1996) Art 19.

[54] Simpson (n.37).

that it '... would not seriously jeopardize the political independence or economic stability of the State which has committed the internationally wrongful act, whereas the injured State would not be similarly affected if it did not obtain restitution in kind'). Criminal states under the system envisaged by the ILC would be in a similar situation to post-Versailles Germany. As was the case with Germany, then, sanctions would be applied to contemporary criminal states regardless of the consequences on the internal politico-economic order. A critical attribute of state sovereignty, the dignity of states, would be denied the outlaw state in the name of enforcing higher order international law.

Five years prior to the drafting of the 1996 Articles, the Security Council passed Resolution 687.[55] From at least that point onwards, Iraq became a criminal state and its people subject to collective punishment. The second domain in which the idea of collective responsibility re-emerged was that of the Security Council. The Council deprived Iraq of part of its territory and prohibited it from acquiring certain types of weaponry. The people of Iraq, meanwhile, suffered seriously as a result of sanctions. The UN Population Fund released a report in 2003, stating that the number of women dying in childbirth had tripled between 1989 and 2002 and the respected British medical journal, *The Lancet*, published research in 1995 suggesting that 567,000 Iraqi children had died as a result of sanctions.[56] In the succeeding decade, the outlawry of whole states became a favoured technique of international administration in Serbia, in Afghanistan and in relation to Iraq. These states were confined within a system of surveillance and oversight, deprived of the traditional privileges of sovereignty and reduced to a state of impoverishment. This was the state system's equivalent of 'incarceration' (Blaskic), and, despite the protestations of the Great Powers and the international community, the result was a form of old-fashioned collective punishment directed at a population at large.

Alongside all this, and this representing the third sphere in which the idea of state crime has emerged, the Great Powers themselves began to deploy the image of the criminal state in their rhetoric (Prime Minister Blair's 'irresponsible states' and President Bush's 'enemies of civilization', each recalling Roosevelt's description of the Nazi State as an

[55] Resolution 687, adopted by the Security Council on its 2981st meeting (3 April 1991).

[56] A. F. Presse, 'Death rate of Iraq mothers triples, UN survey finds' (4 November 2003): according to the study the number rose from 117 cases of maternal death per 100,000 live births in 1989 to 310 in 2002; S. Zaidi and M. C. Smith Fawzi, 'Health of Baghdadi children', *The Lancet*, 2 December 1995, p. 356.

'international outlaw'[57] and 'not a military enemy but an enemy of all law',[58] in the work of government bureaucracies (the State Department's 'states of concern'), in legislation (the US Anti-Terrorism and Effective Death-Penalty Act 1996), a statute suspending the operation of sovereign immunity in cases where a designated terrorist state is sued in the United States by (American) victims of acts of terrorism, placed a group of states on a terrorist list),[59] and in legal memoranda seeking to justify the illegal detention of enemy combatants on Guantánamo Bay (Gonzales Memorandum). These developments were reflected in turn by scholarship that sought to draw distinctions between civilized, democratic or decent states, and indecent outlaws,[60] and in the turn to reparations in the UN's Human Rights system.[61]

The 1990s, then, was a decade in which the idea of individual responsibility certainly underwent an astonishing revival (the ICTY, ICTR and ICC).[62] But, at the same time, and less visibly and self-consciously, the system was also embracing, again, the Versailles Model of state criminalization. The institutional history of international criminal law is captured in the Commentary on the 1996 Draft Code on Crimes Against the Peace and Security of Mankind where the ILC notes: 'The state may thus remain responsible and be unable to exonerate itself from responsibility by invoking the prosecution or punishment of the individuals who committed the crime',[63] and in Article 25(4) of the ICC Statute: 'No provision in this Statute relating to individual criminal responsibility shall affect the responsibility of States under international law.'[64] The apparent historical inevitability and moral appeal of individual criminal responsibility is undermined by the temptations of collective responsibility. It may be that

[57] R. Woetzel, *The Nuremberg Trials in International Law* (Stevens & Son, London 1960).

[58] G. Schwarzenberger, *Totalitarian Lawlessness and International Law* (Jonathan Cape, London 1943), p. 85.

[59] US Anti-Terrorism and Effective Death-Penalty Act, section 221.

[60] Teson (n. 18); J. Rawls, *The Law of* Peoples (Harvard University Press, Cambridge, MA 1999).

[61] E.g. the UN Commission on Human Rights adopted *Basic Principles and Guidelines on the Right to a Remedy and Reparations for Victims of Gross Violations* (UN Doc E/CN.4/RES/2005/35).

[62] Even Security Council Resolutions began to name individual violators of international law. This began with Osama bin Laden but there are now many individuals named in similar resolutions: E.g. SC Resolution 1521 (2003).

[63] Commentary to Art. 4 of the Draft Code of Crimes against the Peace and Security of Mankind (1996).

[64] Though it is not clear whether this provision refers only to state civil liability or whether 'responsibility' here can encompass forms of criminal responsibility.

the tension between state crime and individual responsibility (exemplified by the fact that on 27 February 2006, in The Hague, two cases were being heard simultaneously: one, *Prosecutor v Milosevic*, concerned the individual responsibility of the former Serb leader; the other, the aforementioned *Bosnia v Serbia*, also about genocide but this time state responsibility for the crime of genocide) cannot be resolved because the structure of international society and the suppositions of our own belief systems rest upon that tension.

IV. The liability of men and things

The coexistence of collective guilt and individual responsibility, identified in the discussion of institutional preferences in the field, is reflected at the level of doctrine even if, at first blush, international criminal law seems wedded to modes of liability that are highly individualistic. In some respects, it is a declaration of intent concerning personal liability – a turn from structure to agency – that marks off the international criminal law enterprise from the rest of the field of public international law. International criminal law's core instruments are concerned to advertise the centrality of individualized justice, just as the key commentaries are keen to enumerate its virtues. The statutes of the ICTY, ICTR and ICC follow the Nuremberg Principles by placing individual accountability centre-stage. The Charter of the IMT gives the Tribunal (in Article 6) jurisdiction over 'persons' who, acting as 'individuals', commit any of the listed crimes. The ICTY Statute states at Article 7(1): 'A person who planned, instigated, ordered, committed … [a crime] … shall be individually responsible for the crime.' Article 6 makes clear that this jurisdiction is to be found over 'natural persons' not abstract entities. The Rome Statute, too, refers consistently to natural persons and individual responsibility (Article 25). The law of war crimes, then, seems to mark a switch from the abstractions of the general field of public international law to the flesh and blood corporeality of human culpability. As Antonio Cassese puts it, the central idea behind individualized liability is that a defendant ought not to be punished for acts perpetrated by other individuals. Collective responsibility, as he puts it, is 'no longer acceptable'.[65] These doctrinal efforts promise simplicity (it is no longer necessary to explain the reasons why crimes are committed – 'motive', as the Court in *Jelisic* noted, is not

[65] A. Cassese, *International Criminal Law* (Oxford University Press, Oxford 2003), p. 137.

relevant to questions of intent), parsimony (the question of guilt is pared down to an investigation of one person's mental state and capacity) and depoliticization (the central questions become narrowly psychological rather than expansively political).[66]

These doctrinal projects, like the institutional ones discussed above, are frequently undone by the fact that the very acts criminalized under international law are those least susceptible to individualized justice. International criminal law's core offences are crimes against humanity, serious violations of the laws of war (war crimes), genocide and aggression. This is reflected in the IMT Charter at Nuremberg, and in the crimes included under Article 5 of the ICC Statute. In each of these cases, the typical crimes are, what Jose Alvarez called 'crimes of state', i.e. crimes arising from organizational tendencies or collective choices.[67]

Indeed, the rhetorical attention international criminal lawyers devote to individual responsibility is ill-matched to the mood of the general public when it comes to questions of responsibility. An example of precisely this tension occurred in 2005, when the UK government announced that it would begin prosecuting British soldiers for alleged war crimes committed during the occupation of Iraq in 2003. There was almost universal condemnation of this decision in the UK media. Many commentators and letter-writers, while conceding that the soldiers were accused of very grave crimes, could not imagine an international criminal law that applied to one-off acts of murder or assault committed by the personnel of states engaged in largely lawful combat. The commanding officer of the regiment most closely involved stated that: 'From the moment that Mr Baha Mousa lost his life while in our custody, the regiment has made clear that this was an isolated, tragic incident that should never have happened and which I and every member bitterly regret.'[68] In the House of Lords, similar sentiments were expressed:

> What is now hanging over him and other soldiers is that the case may be referred to the International Criminal Court. That court was not set up for that purpose. It was set up to deal with cases of genocide and with war criminals. That that gallant officer [Colonel Mendoca, the Commanding Office of the soldiers accused of killing Baha Mousa in custody] could be

[66] *Prosecutor v Jelisic* (n. 11) para. 49.

[67] J. Alvarez, 'Crimes of states/crimes of hate: lessons from Rwanda' (1999) 24 *Yale Journal of International Law* 365.

[68] N. Tweedie, 'Uproar over war crimes trials' *Daily Telegraph* 21 July 2005, available at www.telegraph.co.uk/news/main.jhtml?xml=/news/2005/07/21/narmy21.xml, accessed 12 June 2008.

> in the same dock as that in which Milosevic has appeared must be wrong in itself.[69]

These commentators equate the idea of war crimes with the practice of mass atrocity. The Nazi genocide, and its contemporary variants, loom over the field as ideal types. The critics of the Willams and Mendoca investigations are responding to a legitimate sense that war crimes law, in its broadest sense, is about with mass criminality. This is a well-founded intuition. International criminal law, it turns out, even in its individualistic mode, is very often deeply concerned with structure. At a very obvious level, the Rome Statute restates this in its Preamble, and elsewhere. The negotiators were at pains to emphasise that the Court would have jurisdiction over only 'the most serious crimes of concern to the international community'. How are such crimes to be understood? In the case of aggression and genocide there is an in-built presumption against the idea that an individual can commit either of these crimes acting independently of a state apparatus. Aggression is an inter-state crime, defined as such in countless international instruments, and capable of being committed only if a group of individuals captures the machinery of the state. The discomfort expressed by the Commission on the Authorship of War in 1919[70] is reflected in the continuing lack of agreement found in the negotiations for an international criminal court.

Likewise, the classic genocides of the twentieth century have been carried out either by states or state-like entities. One of the distinguishing elements of genocide is its sheer scale (in *Jelisic*, the ICTY discusses the possibility of the 'lone genocidal maniac'[71] but this figure is really more hypothetical than real and even the Court sounds unconvinced about the monster it has created). The mass killing of national, ethnical, racial or religious groups requires a degree of planning and organization typically beyond the capacity of all but state or state-like instrumentalities.[72]

[69] Lord Hoyle, Column 1223 (14 July, 2005) *Hansard*, available at www.publications.parliament.uk/pa/ld199900/ldhansrd/pdvn/lds05/text/50714-05.htm, accessed 12 June 2008.

[70] The Commission on the Responsibility of the Authors of the War and on Enforcement of Penalties.

[71] *Prosecutor v Jelisic* (n. 11).

[72] There is nothing in the Genocide Convention itself to exclude the possibility of individual action. The Convention, after all, in the case of murder, refers only to the requirement that the accused has killed members of the group with an intent to destroy it in whole or in part. There is no requirement in the Statute that the killings be in any way substantial. Courts, though, have tended to understand genocide in precisely this way, e.g. the court

Crimes against humanity and, in particular, war crimes appear at first glance to be quite different. The acts associated with these crimes – murder, torture, hostage-taking, improper use of a flag of truce – are capable of being committed by individuals acting in an individual capacity. These crimes appear, then, to represent international criminal law's true face: the face of individualized justice. However, even here, at the definitional level, there are qualifications and conditions that disclose again this coexistence of the collective and the individual.

The International Criminal Court Statute defines crimes against humanity as acts (including murder, extermination and rape) committed 'as part of a widespread or systematic attack directed against any civilian population'.[73] An earlier draft had made 'widespread and systematic' conjunctive but even in their eventual formulation it is clear that a requirement of collective action is retained. A systematic or widespread attack, after all, is not something that can be readily undertaken by a single individual. The definition of war crimes comes attached with a similar qualifier. While war crimes are defined as grave breaches of the Geneva Conventions and other analogous offences, the ICC is to possess jurisdiction only over such crimes in particular when committed 'as part of a plan or policy or as part of a large-scale commission of such crimes'.[74] This suggests that the ICC would lack jurisdiction over the likes of Mendoca and Williams (regardless of the substance of the accusations). Critics of the UK government, then, are simply drawing on a tradition in international criminal law, reflected in the Rome Statute, which understands 'war crimes' and 'crimes against humanity' as references to organized mass atrocity perpetrated in the Balkans and in the Second World War rather than the aberrant behaviour of British soldiers in Iraq.

This tension between individual agency and collective responsibility has been a powerful influence on the development of international criminal law since its putative inception at Nuremberg. The Nuremberg Trial represents a particular paradox in this regard because at the very moment when individual responsibility (the accountability of, what Churchill called the 'gang' of Nazis) was introduced onto the international scene in the form of individual trials, the American delegation was working behind the scenes to formulate charges that would imply a form of

in *Krstic* noted that 'the destruction in part must be of a substantial nature so as to affect the entirety' (para. 10).

[73] Art. 7 ICC Statute. [74] Art. 8 ICC Statute.

collective guilt. These ideas formed the backbone to the IMT Charter. In Article 6, the crime of aggression included the offence of participating 'in a common plan or conspiracy' for the accomplishment of planning or prosecuting aggressive war, and the final provision of that Article charged that those who participated in the formulation or execution of the common plan or conspiracy to commit Charter crimes would be 'responsible for all acts performed by any persons in execution of such a plan'. The purposes of the trial thereby began to work against each other. On the one hand, in order to precipitate the rehabilitation of Germany as a state, the Allies were keen to extract the poisonous elements from German society by identifying the ways in which the Nazi state had been captured and utilized for evil ends. On the other hand, the American conspiracy plan was meant to strike at the heart of that same society, and the broader the conspiracy claim became, the less plausible was its core proposition: that the conspirators were guilty of a massive organised conspiracy but the German people was innocent of participation in it. The idea that the leading German war criminals could be prosecuted with 'joint participation in a broad criminal enterprise' also contradicted one of the central pillars of the idea of individual responsibility because high-ranking Nazis would be prosecuted for acts committed by other individuals: 'Under such a charge there are admissible in evidence the acts of any of the conspirators done in furtherance of the conspiracy, whether or not these acts were in themselves criminal.'[75] The central core of individual responsibility, the mental culpability of the accused, was slowly stripped away by the drafters of the Statute.

The turn to the collective gathered pace around the idea of criminal organizations, too. When Stettinius met Eden and Molotov in San Francisco in the middle of 1945, the Americans had already formulated their plan to criminalize whole strata of German society:

> We proposed to put on trial the Nazi organizations themselves rather than the individuals and convict them all of criminal conspiracy to control the world... Once having provided the organisation to be guilty, each person who had joined the organisation voluntarily would *ipso facto* be guilty of a war crime.[76]

The mass criminality outlined and envisaged in these plans, and in the core ideas of conspiracy and criminal organization, departed from western standards of individual guilt and personal responsibility at

[75] Stimson *et al.*, 'Memorandum for the President' (22 January 1945).

[76] M. Marrus, *The Nuremberg War Crimes Trials* (St Martin's Press, Bedford 1997), p. 35.

the very moment of international law's apparent and much-trumpeted transformation from a body of law exclusively concerned with state responsibility to one in which individual humans and not abstract entities would be judged by the ideals of the international legal order.

International criminal law is revealed at its origins as a composition of collective and individual notions of responsibility, and this carries over to the trials in The Hague, where there are engineered a number of successor doctrines to those elaborated in the 1940s. At the ICTY, for example, the Court has developed a doctrine of 'joint criminal enterprise' (a phrase not even found in the ICTY's Statute).[77] The Court deployed this in convicting Dusko Tadić, where it conceded that many crimes committed in war, rather than being individual acts of wrong-doing: 'constitute a manifestation of the collective criminality.'[78] Joint Criminal Enterprise is attractive to war crimes courts because it is sensitive to the reality of organized crime during periods of armed struggle.[79] More controversially, however, the doctrine is used by courts to avoid the responsibility of determining who actually killed or tortured in specific cases. It is sufficient that the court is able to show that the accused was involved in the system of criminality and had some knowledge of its ultimate criminal purpose. It has not always been necessary for the accused to have shared in that criminal purpose. As Verena Haan argues, Joint Criminal Enterprise is useful in difficult cases 'where the accused had acted in the sphere of politics'.[80] But this means criminalising political behaviour and, as well as the corollary of this, the politicization of criminal law.[81]

The scale of crime contemplated by international criminal law means that there is often likely to be present some element of organizational or mass criminality. Prosecutors and judges, particularly those concerned to steer a course between an absurd and a historical individualism (the idea that one person commits genocide or carries out ethnic cleansing) and a reductive structural determinism (the idea that the state or culture or people are guilty of these crimes at some collective level), are left with two awkward tasks. They must be satisfied that there is proof of personal guilt

77 See also the contributions by H. van der Wilt, 'Joint criminal enterprise and functional perpetration', this volume, Chapter 7 and E. van Sliedregt, 'System criminality at the ICTY', this volume, Chapter 8.

78 *Prosecutor v Tadić*, Appeal Judgment, IT-94-1 (27 February 2001) para. 191.

79 M. Osiel, 'The banality of good' (2005) 105 *Columbia Law Review* 1751.

80 V. Haan, 'The development of the concept of joint criminal enterprise at the ICTY' (2005) 5 *International Criminal Law Review* 167–201.

81 See *Prosecutor v Milosevic*, Rule 98 *bis* Decision, IT-02-54-T, Trial Chamber (16 June 2004) para. 288 *et seq.*

without ignoring the broader context in which crimes take place and they must limit the contextual investigations in order to secure the innocence of the society from which the perpetrators emerged.

V. Three Eichmanns

Amis: 'What is it with Americans and the death penalty?'
He goes on 'Instead of talking about Karla Faye Tucker, they're all talking about Monica Lewinsky'
[Saul remained silent]
Amis: 'Don't tell me *you're* not against it either'
Bellow: 'Well. Look at... Eichmann. What are you supposed to *do* with a son of a bitch like that?'
Amis: 'Christ, you're really Old Testament, aren't you?'
And he [Bellow] shrugged, and gave a sideways nod.[82]

The discussion up to this point has been concerned with the institutional and doctrinal responses to a complex relationship between individual guilt and collective responsibility. But this conflict, perhaps, reflects deeper tensions in the structure of international society and in our ethical predispositions. This is a chapter about international law and society not a philosophical treatise so I only have a limited amount to say about the latter question but it clearly animates and underpins the narrower questions of institutional (section IV) and doctrinal (section V) choice. Who, or what, commits war crimes, crimes against humanity or crimes against peace? This is a question with ethical, legal and political answers. As I have argued, the Nuremberg and Tokyo war crimes trials represented an attempt to individualize responsibility for war. Of course, prior to Nuremberg, lawyers had developed rules on the proper conduct of warfare but only very few criminal prosecutions associated with this body of norms had, by then, taken place (e.g. in Leipzig after the Second World War (*Llandovery Castle*, *Dover Castle*)) and these were highly unsatisfactory.[83] Indeed, it was doubtful whether the existing legal rules anticipated or permitted criminal prosecution at all. Arguably, then, as we have seen, Nuremberg introduced into international law, the conceit of individual responsibility for gross crimes. But it also, and even more contentiously, developed principles of organizational criminality. So, while the Tribunal convicted von Ribbentrop, Goring, Streicher, Keitel *et al.* of having committed individual offences against the law of nations, it also

[82] M. Amis, *Experience* (Jonathan Cape, London 2000), p. 260.
[83] Woetzel (n. 57); Bass (n. 40).

declared whole organizations, such as the SS and the SD, criminal. This declaration, in turn, created the possibility of 'fixing the criminality of its members'.[84] However, this hardly solved, what David Luban called, 'the central moral challenge of our time the problem of moral responsibility in a bureaucratic setting'.[85]

In thinking about criminality at the level found in the Nazi era or, to a lesser extent, during the Vietnam War and in Serbia, one is faced with a problem of structure and agency. The structural analysis of criminality inevitably focuses on processes, social behaviour, institutions, hierarchies and so on (i.e. deviance through the eyes of Kafka and Edelman). There are variations on this theme of structural explanation in Arendt's 'rule by nobody'[86] in Marx's bureaucratic mind[87] and in Raul Hilberg's contention that: 'The killing…was no atrocity in the conventional sense. It was infinitely more, and that "more" was the work of a far-flung, sophisticated bureaucracy.'[88] In the light of this, war crimes trials at best can appear as partial justice, at worst a form of 'scapegoating'.

Structural analysis can yield important insights but it is not without its failings, particularly when translated into legal norms attributing structural responsibility. On one hand, collective responsibility might result in a situation where everyone is guilty and, therefore, no-one is. Daniel Ellsberg, quoted by Sanford Levinson, speaks of the tendency to see Vietnam as 'a tragedy without villains, war crimes without criminals, lies without liars, a process of immaculate deception'.[89] On the other hand, the result of collective responsibility might be the criminalization of conduct that lacks the components of crime as traditionally understood by the liberal mind (*mens rea* and *actus reus*).

In approaching this dilemma, George Fletcher identifies a liberal bias in international criminal law's emphasis on agency or individual responsibility. This bias, he argues, 'obscures a basic truth' about war crimes. These are 'deeds that by their very nature are committed by groups and typically against individuals and members of groups'.[90] For Fletcher, the tension between collective and individual notions of guilt or responsibility can

[84] Judgment of the International Military Tribunal at Nuremberg, Vol. 22 (1948), p. 500.

[85] D. Luban, 'The Legacies of Nuremberg' (1987) 54(4) *Social Research* 779–829.

[86] Arendt (n. 2) 38. [87] Marx, *Critique* (quoted in Luban (n. 85) 68 *et seq.*)

[88] R. Hilberg, *The Politics of Memory* (Ivan Dee, Chicago 2002), p. 59.

[89] S. Levinson, 'Responsibility for crimes of war' (1973) 2 *Philosophy and Public Affairs* 244–73.

[90] G. Fletcher, 'The Storrs Lectures: liberals and romantics at war: the problem of collective guilt' 111 *Yale Law Journal* 1501–73.

be understood through a contrast between what he calls 'romantic' and 'liberal' views of war and guilt. The liberal conception of responsibility is, of course, familiar enough. Liberals focus on individuals as free agents capable of making political choices, consuming freely, and, crucially, of doing wrong as individuals abstracted from the social group to which they belong. Criminal concepts like 'intent' go to the heart of this liberal view of individual human agency. Yet, a less familiar, romantic ontology also pervades international criminal law. This emphasises the role of the collective will and the idea of the people as the 'folk' or as an independent actor capable of greatness and, of course, great evil.

International criminal lawyers might be less surprised than Fletcher to discover this romantic sensibility permeates their work. After all, international law is replete with assumptions about 'the collective will'. The creation of legal norms through customary practice, for example, involves an acceptance that there can be such a thing as 'state consent'. Group guilt, however, is an idea that has made international lawyers uneasy since Versailles and criminal lawyers anxious since the onset of modernity. Fletcher wants to rehabilitate this idea but he does so with understandable caution. The individual and his or her responsibility 'remain central'. The danger of collective guilt (its vivid historical and biblical connotations and its ill-suitedness to criminal procedure and the rule of law) is obvious. However, Fletcher believes collective guilt has a role to play in mitigating the punishment of those individuals whose acts are both individual and also collective. To put it bluntly, an Eichmann or Milosevic who commit mass atrocities in the context of a diverse and decent society in which there is a clear possibility of self-correction is more culpable than the real historical Eichmanns and Milosevics. The 'climate of moral degeneracy'[91] produced by the 'collective' contributes to the crime.

International criminal law, however, seems to work in the opposite direction. The prosecution of Milosevic was a way of punishing Milosevic for his crimes *and* the crimes of the Serbian state. Instead of mitigation we have exacerbation.[92] Because there is a desire to see Serbia rehabilitated (in international society, individuals are disposable but states much less so) and to ward off the dangers of Serbian revanchism, the emphasis is on producing some sort of closure through trial. Thus the oscillations of subjective and collective guilt were likely, prior to the former President's death, to resolve themselves, at least formally, through the conviction of Milosevic. But the credibility of this conviction from the perspective

[91] Fletcher (n. 90) 1541. [92] Fletcher (n. 90) 1542.

of international criminal justice would have depended largely on how well the prosecution and Court were able to uncover the criminality of the Serbian state. After all, mass murderers are known for their notorious reluctance to kill people. Eichmann was famously squeamish at the sight of blood, and Albert Speer found his visits to concentration camps impossibly confronting. Likewise, it is possible that Milosevic had no history of direct killing. The emphasis, then, was on Milosevic's indirect responsibility, with the prosecution case resting largely on Milosevic's command responsibility for illegal acts committed by subordinates and for his leadership role in a joint criminal enterprise dedicated to the commissions of genocide, crimes against humanity and war crimes against Kosovar Albanians, Bosnian Muslims and Croats. Paradoxically, then, the more effective the Court was in building a record of mass atrocity and securing a conviction, the more likely it was to, indirectly at least, indict the Serbian people.

Coming to this dilemma from the opposite direction, Sanford Levinson, in an article written during the Vietnam War, argued that the problem lies not with a lack of mitigation but rather the absence of any responsibility at all.[93] The dilemmas identified by Levinson are largely those of Fletcher, though the problem is presented differently. How is individual culpability and responsibility to be secured in the context of bureaucratic enterprises? Levinson believes this can be accomplished through a teasing out of individual command responsibility in times of war. He begins by rejecting three other possibilities. The first is to engage in collective criminal punishment. This is deemed unsatisfactory because of over-inclusiveness. Innocent citizens would become criminally liable. A second possibility is to impose civil liability on the state. This fails because tort-based remedies cannot capture the moral opprobrium associated with war crimes. The third possibility is to do nothing. Levinson worries about this option on the grounds that there would be no opportunity to 'restore a moral harmony which is dislocated when justice is done'.[94]

According to Levinson, then, the preferred model is to be derived from the existing jurisprudence at Nuremberg and in particular at the trials following Nuremberg. War criminality depends on finding and prosecuting discrete criminals.[95] The guilt of military and civilian leaders will be determined by their level of involvement in policy-making and implementation, the power they possess over that policy and the opposition they express

[93] Levinson (n. 89). [94] Levinson (n. 89) 273. [95] Levinson (n. 89) 251.

towards criminal policies. (e.g. *High Command Case*). Armed with principles derived from the substantive jurisprudence of the tribunals and the law of command responsibility, a reasonable effort can be made to secure individual responsibility. Of course, as Levinson knows, this will work best in judging a regime dedicated to the meticulous documentation of state policy and its enactment (e.g. Nazi Germany) and will work less well in relation to a system in which power is diffuse, commands are informal and constitutional authority is enigmatic (the US in Vietnam). In the latter case, Levinson seems to argue for some informal procedures along the lines of the Russell Tribunal and the recently convened 'comfort women' trial. These trials have demonstrated that the failure of official criminal law to punish may not be fatal to efforts at stigmatising those guilty of international crimes.

Perhaps this debate, and international criminal law itself, simply reflects a wider need in the culture to see war criminals as at the same time uniquely evil ('no-one but Milosevic could have led the Serbs to such moral depths'), culturally representative ('Milosevic simply anthropomorphises a system gone horribly wrong') and typically human ('what would I have done in Milosevic's shoes?'). In the trial of Adolf Eichmann, these debates came to a head. If the law, war and crime dilemma at Nuremberg involved applying law to the problem of exceptional, unprecedented criminality, then the Eichmann trial revealed another perhaps more disturbing symptom of modern industrial society: the figure of the unexceptional political mass murderer. At Nuremberg and Tokyo, there are traces of the idea of 'ordinary' criminality but, the trials were largely dedicated to proving the existence of a criminal enterprise dictated by a small, but powerful, elite within Germany's heavily militarized and ideologically deformed society. Eichmann, though, presented a problem. Was he exceptional? Banal? Human?

In the most famous picture of Adolf Eichmann, he sits, inside the courtroom, in a glass booth, staring impassively ahead. The evil of the Holocaust is heaped upon this Eichmann. This Eichmann was portrayed in his trial as a 'hater',[96] a man of exceptional evil who claimed he had not killed sufficient numbers of Jews, who disobeyed only one order – the command from Himmler telling him to cease the murders – and who charged Jewish children a half fare for the rail journey to Treblinka.[97]

[96] L. Poliakov, *Harvest of Hate: The Nazi Program for the Destruction of the Jews in Europe* (Random House Schocken, New York, NY 1988).

[97] T. Lacquer, 'Four pfennige per track km' (2004) 26(1) LRB.

This is the Eichmann who was, in fact, profoundly evil in some ordinary sense. He regretted not killing more Jews in Europe, he showed no remorse for the Holocaust and he often boasted about his important role in mass murder and deportation. In a variation on this, there are portraits of Eichmann in which he is neither banal nor ordinary but, instead, a bureaucratic genius. This is the Eichmann who had overseen the destruction of the European Jews from a relatively small office and with a relatively small staff.[98] Eichmann has been described as a clown, but he was a clown who played the violin and had read *The Critique of Pure Reason*.[99] He applied his intelligence to a life shaped by his senior role in a system of governance that sought to undo the Enlightenment project. For him, the categorical imperative was the opposite of Kant's. The idea was to avoid putting oneself in another's shoes. Perhaps Eichmann was ordinary and representative but he was representative in a particular way. He was not one of Christopher Browning's *Ordinary Men*[100] or, indeed, one of Daniel Goldhagen's *Willing Executioners*,[101] Eichmann was exceptionally powerful. *This* Eichmann is alleged to have drafted the letter sent from Goring to Heydrich on 31 July 1941 authorizing a 'final solution' to the Jewish question.[102]

Then, there is the Adolf Eichmann who perfectly captures the breakdown of a moral universe; neither better nor worse than a thousand other Nazi functionaries, he somehow belongs behind a glass booth and on trial. He is the bureaucrat in his transparent office, a petty official, a former vacuum cleaner salesman who comes to be implicated in mass criminality; the accidental *genocidaire*. This is the 'banal Eichmann' that Hannah Arendt made notorious. He was certainly ordinary enough to escape indictment at Nuremberg though this is hardly conclusive. Fritzsche and Sauckel were unexceptional individuals, too.[103] For Hannah Arendt, Eichmann was the petty bureaucrat, the clown who managed to work his way up the organisational ladder in the normal way; 'a German civil servant, absorbed in his work and getting no glory for it' (as Gerald Reitlinger put it).[104] This Eichmann is ubiquitous. This is the Eichmann

[98] Hilberg (n. 88) 150.

[99] I. Kant, *Critique of Pure Reason* (1781) (Cambridge University Press, Cambridge, 1999).

[100] C. Browning, *Ordinary Men: Reserve Police Battalion 101 and the Final Solution in Poland* (Harper Collins, New York 1992).

[101] D. Goldhagen, *Hitler's Willing Executioners: Ordinary Germans and the Holocaust* (Alfred A. Knopf, New york 1996).

[102] Hilberg (n. 88) 78.

[103] A. Neave, *Nuremberg* (Houghton and Stoughton, London 1978), p. 137.

[104] Lacquer (n. 97).

who *became* Eichmann because of his trial. Prior to the trial, there would have been very little to write about this 'obscure lieutenant-colonel'.[105] Since the trial, Eichmann has generated several biographies (the most recent of which is David Cesarani's *Eichmann: His Life and Crimes*[106]) and numerous essays and articles.

Before his trial, Eichmann was interviewed on several occasions. One of his interlocutors, an examining psychiatrist, was quizzed by the press about his views on the accused. Was he normal, they asked? He replied: 'More normal, at any rate, than I am having examined him.'[107] When we look closely at the picture of Eichmann in his bullet-proof booth, we see a third Eichmann, represented in this case not by Eichmann himself but by the stenographer sitting in front of Eichmann: he is the very image of the original, a bespectacled doppelganger. This Eichmann is, of course, the Eichmann of our nightmares. Not inhuman, he is supremely human. He is the representative *homo sapiens* – no different, in some respects, from the man sitting in front of him. He is Tojo tending his garden[108] or Hitler playing with his nieces. He is the man George Steiner describes who 'can read Goethe or Rilke in the evening … he can play Bach and Schubert and go to his day's work at Auschwitz in the morning'.[109] Only circumstances change; man remains the same.

In 1961, Adolf Eichmann, in a Jerusalem prison, awaiting his trial for crimes against the Jewish people and crimes against humanity, would not have been aware of an experiment being conducted in the United States into a behavioural phenomenon with which he came to be associated. In that year, *The New Haven Register* carried an advertisement asking for volunteers to participate in a memory experiment. These were to be paid $4 an hour to take part in a series of tests involving the application of electric shocks to a number of subjects. The volunteers were positioned in front of a fake shock machine that appeared to administer electric currents to the subjects (who, themselves, were insiders; part of the experimentation team). The electric shocks, increased in 15 volt segments reaching a maximum level of 415 volts, and were applied, in rising sequence, to 'wrong' answers given by the subject. The volunteers could hear, but not see, the subjects. The levers used to apply the shocks were marked from slight shock through severe shock to potentially

[105] Lacquer (n. 97) 7. [106] D. Cesarani, *Eichmann: His Life and Crimes* (London 2004).

[107] A. Granta, *A Literature for Politics*, Bill Buford (ed.) (Granta Books, London 1983), p. 25.

[108] T. Maga, *Judgment at Tokyo: The Japanese War Crimes Trials* (Kentucky University Press, Lexington, KY 2002), p. 49.

[109] G. Steiner, *The Death of Tragedy* (Faber, London 1961), p. 699.

fatal shock. Severe shock began at 315 volts with death or severe injury reached at the maximum of 450 volts. As the shocks reached the 300 mark, the subject would often begin crying out in pain and desperation. 65 per cent of volunteers applied the full 450 volts, often in distress themselves and often in response to insistent assertions from the experiment leaders that the experiment continue. Stanley Milgram claimed to have conducted the experiments because he was curious about whether there were sufficient numbers of people in the United States who might have been capable of running a Nazi-style *Lager* in the United States. After the experiments, he concluded, wryly, that there were enough people in New Haven, Connecticut to operate the camps.[110] The third Eichmann, then, is the most disturbing; he is unexceptional, an ordinary man receiving (and obeying) extraordinary orders.

In the end, there is an inescapable tendency to see mass criminality as an uniquely individualized expression of criminal psychopathology ('Hitler's evil mind') or a matter of socio-political joint responsibility (the failures of Versailles and the League), historical inevitability (the trajectory of modernity) or national temperament ('the German people'). The constitution of international criminal law has reflected these apparent tendencies at three different levels: in the institutional oscillations between state crime and individual responsibility, in the doctrinal ambiguities of a juridical order concerned with personal agency and collective conspiracies, and in the way the field is structured around the problem of the moral responsibility of groups and persons.

[110] T. Blass, *The Man Who Shocked the World: The Life and Legacy of Stanley Milgram* (Basic Books, New York, NY 2004).

5

A historical perspective: from collective to individual responsibility and back

ANDREA GATTINI*

I. Introductory remarks

The aim of this chapter is to outline the multifaceted and complex relations between state responsibility for grave breaches of peremptory norms of international law and individual responsibility for the same kind of crimes. In order to do so I have privileged a 'historical perspective', because it best captures my real intention, which is to show how the idea from which state responsibility originates, namely collective responsibility, although it has been superseded over the course of the centuries by more refined notions, paradoxically still lingers in concepts of both state and individual responsibility to some extent and, therefore, it can be a useful conceptual tool to better understand some of their reciprocal inferences.[1]

* Professor of International Law, University of Padua.

[1] In the last years there has been, in international legal literature, a growing attention on the complex relationship between state responsibility and the individual criminal responsibility of its organs. Cf. C. Dominicé, 'La question de la double responsibilité de l'Etat et du son agent' in E. Yakpo *et al.* (eds.), *Liber Amicorum Judge Mohammed Bedjaoui* (Brill, Leiden 1999), p. 143; P. M. Dupuy, 'International criminal responsibility of the individual and international responsibility of the state', in A. Cassese *et al.* (eds.), *The Rome Statute of the International Criminal Court: A Commentary* (vol. 2, Oxford University Press, Oxford 2002), p. 1085; A. Nollkaemper, 'Concurrence between individual responsibility and state responsibility in international law' (2002) 52 *International and Comparative Law Quarterly* 615; H. Gros Espiell, 'International responsibility of the state and individual criminal responsibility in the international protection of human rights', in M. Ragazzi (ed.), *Essays in Memory of Oscar Schachter* (Martinus Nijhoff, The Hague 2005), p. 151; A. A. C. Trindade, 'Complementarity between state responsibility and individual responsibility for grave violations of human rights: the crime of state revisited', in M. Ragazzi (ed.), *Essays in Memory of Oscar Schachter* (Martinus Nijhoff, The Hague 2005), p. 253; B. Bonafé, 'Responsabilità dello stato per fatti illeciti particolarmente gravi e esponsabilità penale dell'individuo: due approcci a confronto', in M. Spinedi *et al.* (eds.), *La codificazione della responsabilità internazionale degli Stati alla prova dei fatti* (Giuffrè, Milan 2006), p. 501.

Although my chapter will deal with some well known twentieth-century cases of state and individual responsibility for aggression, war crimes and crimes against humanity, the so-called core crimes of international law,[2] the notion of collective responsibility has been regaining the attention of doctrine also with regard to non-state entities, such as multinational companies or terrorist groups, which attests to its enduring vitality.[3] In that respect, it is a key legal response to situations of system criminality, which are characterized precisely by the collective dimension of individual criminal acts.[4]

In the following sections, I will sketch the traditional view of state responsibility before the First World War (section II), and the naissance of individual responsibility alongside state responsibility in the aftermath of the Second World War (section III). In the following sections, I will try to unearth in more detail the richness of the debate on 'collective' responsibility in postwar Germany (section IV), and show how the changes in political conditions in Germany soon made such debates inopportune (section V), as it was also made clear by the change of paradigm which the Allies used for postwar Japan (section VI). Lastly, I will focus on the somewhat contradictory signals coming from contemporary practice, from the UN and Iraqi reparations of Iraq after the Second Gulf War of 1991 (section VII) to the judicial handling of the 1992–95 Bosnian war (section VIII).

II. The tradition: international responsibility of states as 'collective' responsibility

The idea of collective responsibility is at the very bottom of state responsibility and has taken different shapes along with evolving perceptions of the political relationship between individuals and the state.

[2] See also A. Nollkaemper, 'Introduction', this volume, Chapter 1, p. 19. The present chapter, however, will not deal with some traditional concepts of the laws of war, now outlawed by humanitarian law such as collective punishments, cf. now extensively S. Darcy, *Collective Responsibility and Accountability under International Law* (Brill, Leiden 2007).

[3] For the responsibility of the first, cf., among others, M. T. Kamminga and S. Zia-Zarifi (eds.), *Liability of Multinational Corporations under International Law* (Kluwer, The Hague 2000); for the responsibility of the second, cf. J. Klabbers, '(I can't get no) recognition: subjects doctrine and the emergence of non-state actors', in J. Klabbers and J. Petman (eds.), *Essays in International Law for Koskenniemi* (Martinus Nijhoff, Leiden 2003) 35. A. Nollkaemper, 'Introduction', this volume, Chapter 1.

[4] Nollkaemper (n. 3).

In an eminently tribal state, as in the Middle Ages, it went without saying that the collectivity was responsible for the acts of any of its members. In the absolutist and patrimonial view of the state prevailing in the seventeenth century, it was clear to Grotius that the responsibility of the ruler was the responsibility of the entire nation.[5]

With time, that view lost much of its practical meaning and the grounds for claiming state responsibility became more and more abstract, as it did with the concept of state. Still, it is remarkable that, when looking for the theoretical basis of the responsibility of the state and the mechanisms for its implementation, namely the imposition of sanctions, which affected both those responsible and those who were not responsible at the same time, the criminal and the innocent, Kelsen found it in the concept of 'collective responsibility'. Being the typical form of responsibility of primitive societies, in collective responsibility Kelsen found further evidence of the presumed primitivism of international law.[6]

One could see that this latter view reached its apex, but also possibly overshot the mark in the aftermath of the First World War: Art. 281 of the Versailles Treaty, which affirmed the responsibility of Germany for the war, was not merely a technical legal device to justify the imposition of liability on Germany for the payment of reparations, as some commentators later diminutively depicted it.[7] More profoundly, it was the affirmation of what the Allied governments saw as a historical truth and a moral judgment, upon which to buttress the harshness of the ensuing sanctions. German governments and public opinion were then not completely wrong in their unanimous opposition to the solution given in Art. 281 to the *Schuldfrage,* in which they saw an unjust attempt to blame only Germans with responsibility for the war and all its consequences.[8]

[5] Cf. J. A. Hessbruegge, 'The historical development of the doctrines of attribution and due diligence in international law' (2004) 36 *New York University Journal of International Law & Politics* 276.

[6] Cf. H. Kelsen, 'Unrecht und Unrechtsfolgen' (1932) 12 *Zeitschrift für öffentliches Recht* 481; H. Kelsen, 'Collective and individual responsibility for acts of state in international law' (1948) 1 *Jewish Yearbook of International Law* 226; H. Kelsen, *Principles of International Law* (2nd ed, Holt, New York, NY 1966), p. 8.

[7] Cf. C. Bloch and P. Renouvin, 'Le Traité de Versailles et les réparations' (1931) 8 II *Revue de droit international* 375.

[8] Cf. *Mitteilungen der deutschen Gesellschaft für Völkerrecht* (1924) vol. 4 81. For an exhaustive discussion, cf. J. L. Kunz, *Die Revision der Pariser Friedensverträge* (Springer, Vienna 1932), pp. 141 *et seq.*

And yet, the Versailles Treaty simultaneously marks the first attempt to affirm a distinct responsibility of individual leaders alongside the responsibility of the state. In Art. 227, the Allied and Associated Powers 'publicly arraign[ed] Wilhelm II of Hohenzollern, formerly German emperor, for a supreme offence against international morality and the sanctity of treaties'.[9] Article 228 obliged Germany to extradite her officials responsible of war crimes on request of any Allied Power in order to be judged by their military tribunals. However, those articles were not implemented. The government of the Netherlands refused to extradite the ex-Kaiser, and the Allied Powers, after having prepared a list of 896 indictees for war crimes, did not insist on their extradition, and instead accepted that a group of forty-five be judged by the German Supreme Court in Leipzig.[10] Eventually, of the forty-five indictees, only seventeen were actually tried, and only eight very leniently sentenced. The times were obviously not yet ready to separate, for conceptual as much as for practical purposes, the responsibility of the state from that of individuals. A greater awareness in the defeated country of the importance of individual criminal responsibility may have led the Allies to reconsider their sanction policy towards Germany as a whole.

III. State responsibility and individual criminal responsibility in the aftermath of the Second World War

After the Second World War, the reasons why the former Allied Powers were not able to conclude a peace treaty with Germany are manifold and well known. The bad memories linked with the Treaty of Versailles and its application were surely one of the reasons why the Allies were reluctant to rush into a peace treaty, with Germany as well as Japan. Aware of the sheer immensity of the damages caused and of the unspeakableness of the crimes committed by individual Germans and Japanese in the name of their countries, the Allies were thinking of new avenues to attain the double goal of severely and effectively sanctioning the responsible states and making them pay for their misdeeds, but at the same time not

[9] The formulation of Art. 227 went back to a French proposal, cf. F. Larnaude and A. de la Pradelle, 'Examen de la responsabilité pénale de l´Empereur Guillaume II d´Allemagne' (1919) 46 *Journal de droit international* 131. For the German position, cf. G. Jellinek, 'Wilhelm II in den Niederlanden' (1919) 24 *Deutsche Justiz Zeitung* 42.

[10] Cf. K. Müller, 'Oktroyierte Verliererjustiz nach dem ersten Weltkrieg' (2001) 39 *Archiv des Völkerrechts* 202.

prejudicing the future of their people. So, the idea to distinguish, as much as it was possible, between the international responsibility of the state, on the one hand, to be dealt with through the traditional instruments of peace treaties, restitutions and reparations, and, on the other hand, the individual criminal responsibility of those who had to account for the commission of crimes against the peace, crimes against humanity and the gravest war crimes quickly established itself.

Yet, that dichotomy did not fully succeed, and indeed it could not succeed. It has by now become a common view that state responsibility and international individual criminal responsibility follow two different patterns, although from time to time there is a resurgence of the old idea that international criminal justice could also be seen in some way as a sanction against the state, and not only through the technicalities of attribution.[11] Briefly, state responsibility deals with the secondary rules determining the consequences of the violation of any primary rule of international law, whereas individual criminal responsibility, although itself a matter of international law, is dominated by procedural and substantive criminal law.

That is surely a classical way to depict the principles governing the two different kinds of responsibility, but their relations are multifaceted. Primary rules sometimes leave their footprint, so to speak, on the secondary ones. So, international human rights law, a sector which is here of particular relevance, focuses on the protected rights, and this aspect illuminates the secondary rules, as can be seen by the importance of the role of individual victims. International criminal law, on the contrary, focuses primarily on a list of offences, and consequently the secondary rules turn mainly around the sentencing of the perpetrator.[12] It is this

[11] Cf. R. Maison, *La responsabilité individuelle pour crime d'Etat en droit international public* (Bruylant, Brussels 2004), p. 150; cf. also P. Picone, 'Sul fondamento giuridico del Tribunale penale internazionale per la ex-Jugoslavia', in F. Lattanzi and E. Sciso (eds.), *Dai Tribunali penali internazionali ad hoc a una corte permanente* (Editoriale Scientifica, Napoli 1996), p. 65, for whom the institution of the ICTY must be seen as a 'sanction' imposed by the states acting through the Security Council, to react against the violation of *erga omnes* obligations by the parties of the Yugoslavian conflict (70). For that same reason Picone strictly distinguishes between the ICTY, as an instrument of 'interstate justice', and the ICC as an instrument exercising its punitive power against individuals.

[12] This line of reasoning is well expressed in the ICTY Trial Chamber Judgment of 22 February 2001, *Prosecutor v Kunarac*, Foca, IT-96-23 & 23/1 (2001) para. 470, in underlining the differences between international humanitarian law and human rights law: 'Human Rights Law establishes lists of protected rights, whereas international criminal law establishes lists of offences.' As is well known, the role of the victims has been

fundamental difference in perspective which explains the underlying tension, if not contradiction, in contemporary international law between some issues of state responsibility and those of individual responsibility and in international criminal law itself with regard to questions of authorship.[13]

Nevertheless, a link between the two kinds of responsibility is the collective dimension of many crimes, which calls for means in dealing with a similar collective dimension of responsibility. The centrality of this finding is not confuted by the famous passage in the Nuremberg judgment, which grounds contemporary international criminal responsibility (at p. 41): 'crimes against international law are committed by men, not by abstract entities, and only by punishing individuals who commit such crimes, can the provisions of international law be enforced.' Clapham rightly calls it 'a paradigm shift', 'a very radical moment in the history of human rights and humanitarian law'.[14] This is undoubtedly true in a way, but the question arises which individuals are we speaking of? One should not forget that the list of twenty-two defendants finally agreed upon at Nuremberg was the result of very complicated negotiations between the Allies and was inspired by the underlying idea of the maximum representation of all the different segments of German society which had underpinned the Nazi dictatorship, not just the political and military elites, but the 'cultural', economic and industrial ones as well. So, individual criminal responsibility was

neglected in the ICTY and ICTR Statutes. Rule 106 of both Tribunals ('Compensation to victims') merely provides that: '1. The Registrar shall transmit to the competent authorities of the States concerned the judgment finding the accused guilty of a crime which has caused injury to a victim. 2. Pursuant to the relevant national legislation, a victim or persons claiming through the victim may bring an action in a national court or other competent body to obtain compensation.' The ICC Statute takes into account the victims, both under the aspect of their right to participate in the proceedings (Art. 68) and to their right to reparation (Art. 75). On the multifaceted questions left opened by the Statute, and subsequent Rules of procedure and evidence, cf. G. Bitti and G. González Rivas, 'The reparations provisions for victims under the Rome Statute of the International Criminal Court', in International Bureau of the Permanent Court of Arbitration (ed.), *Redressing Injustices Through Mass Claims Processes: Innovative Responses to Unique Challenges* (Oxford University Press, Oxford 2006), p. 299; A. Gattini, 'Reparations to victims', in A. Cassese (ed.), *Oxford Companion to International Criminal Justice* (Oxford University Press, Oxford 2008).

[13] Cf. A. Marston Danner and J. S. Martinez, 'Guilty associations: joint criminal enterprise, command responsibility, and the development of international criminal law' (2005) 93 *California Law Review* 75.

[14] Cf. A. Clapham, in P. Sands (ed.), *From Nuremberg to the Hague* (Cambridge University Press, Cambridge 2002), pp. 30, 33.

understood from the beginning as a symbolic gesture that expressed the collective dimension of the crimes committed in the name and for the sake of the state.[15]

IV. In the twilight: the debate on collective responsibility and its repercussions on the solutions adopted towards Germany with regard to both state responsibility and individual criminal responsibility

From what has been said before, my point is that the debate at the end of the Second World War on the collective responsibility of 'the Germans', i.e. of the whole German nation, lingered on and influenced both responsibility tracks, that of the state and the individual. I am aware that the terrain I am moving into is a slippery one, that is where to draw the line between collective 'responsibility' and collective 'guilt'?

It has become commonplace to say that western legal tradition, imbued with legal liberalism and its focus on the individual, abhors the very concept of collective guilt. Therefore, the debate on German collective responsibility which arose at that time was soon discarded as an all too transparent attempt by the Soviet Union and some irreducible Germanophobes to impose their political draconian views on the future of the German people. However, as some recent efforts by leading US scholars in understanding and revaluating the concept of collective guilt show,[16] that debate was not just the result of political propaganda and strategy, but indeed gave voice to a genuine, deeply felt legal, even philosophical concern.

The debate was influenced early and decisively by the lectures of the German anti-Nazi philosopher Karl Jaspers. Jaspers distinguished between four different forms of guilt: criminal, moral, political, and metaphysical.[17] He maintained that only the first, embedded in the principle of legality, can be attributed to an individual and lead to criminal prosecution. The second form of guilt, moral guilt, can of course be attributed to an individual, but it does not have a legal character. As

[15] For very thought-provoking ideas on the interplay between individual and collective responsibility in international criminal justice, cf. F. Mégret, 'In defense of hybridity: towards a representational theory of international criminal justice' (2005) 38 *Cornell International Law Journal* 725.

[16] Cf. G. Fletcher, 'Liberals and romantics at war: the problem of collective guilt' (2002) 111 *Yale Law Journal* 1499.

[17] Cf. K. Jaspers, *Die Schuldfrage: ein Beitrag zur deutschen Frage* (Artemis, Zürich 1946).

opposed to the responsibility of an individual, when we come to speak of a collectivity, of a nation, only the third and the fourth categories of guilt, the political and the metaphysical can make sense, namely the 'guilt' of having been in a certain place at a certain time and not having taken up arms to overthrow the tyrant, or even more ephemerally the 'guilt' of having lived and continued to live after such an immense catastrophe. The arguments brought forward by Jaspers relating to each of the four categories are well crafted, but they are too facile, and it is no wonder that this is probably the only instance in which Hannah Arendt distanced herself from her revered mentor. It is true that under the Nazi dictatorship and during the war the vast majority of Germans personally committed no crime , but it is somehow too self-indulgent, not to say self-absolving, to maintain that for that reason they could not collectively be held morally or legally responsible.

As painful as it might sound today, in Germany there was a collective, both moral and political, responsibility. It was not just the fatal fault of the 17 million Germans who democratically voted for Hitler, the newly appointed Reich Chancellor on 5 March 1933, just eight years after the publication of *Mein Kampf*. It was the twelve long years, daily guilt of tens of millions approving fanatically what was being done to their fellow citizens of Jewish origin and to the political opponents, or of knowing about it and remaining silent, or of preferring not to ask too many questions. Nobody can expect or pretend that all Germans should have behaved as heroically as did the 437 Germans listed in the 'righteous among the nations' in the *Yad Vashem*. Nevertheless, it is not by chance that the story of the 'wives of the Rosenstrasse' in Berlin, the 'Arian' wives of Jewish German men who in 1942 publicly protested so long and so loud against the arrest and the detention of their husbands in concentration camps until they all were released, has only recently been 'rediscovered' and made public in Germany. In Nazi Germany, as at all times and in all places, what really can make the difference is always and only the degree of *Zivilcourage* of each citizen.

In my view, it is therefore interesting to trace the influence of the concept of collective responsibility, if not collective guilt, in both the solutions adopted with regard to state responsibility and individual responsibility in postwar Germany.

With regard to the first, one inevitably comes across the 2 August 1945 Potsdam Declaration of the three main Allied Powers. This document marks a dramatic climax in the history of Germany and in the consciousness of her people. Even today, there are very divergent interpretations on its legal significance.[18] My argument here is that, beyond all the criticism which can be levelled against its solutions from the perspective of today, the Potsdam agreement is still a document of the utmost importance in revealing the shared view of the Allies on the eve of the new era of the UN concerning the consequences of international responsibility for the gravest breaches of what we now call peremptory norms of international law.[19] Most telling is the caveat in the preamble that it is not the intention of the Allied Powers to 'destroy or enslave the German people', but that it is necessary to convince the German people that 'they cannot escape responsibility for what they have brought upon themselves, since their own ruthless warfare and the fanatical Nazi resistance have destroyed German economy and made chaos and suffering inevitable'.

Particularly relevant are Section IV on reparations, 'to the greatest possible extent', Section IX on territorial disposition; and Section XIII on the resettlement of persons of German origin. For each of the solutions in these sections, the question can be raised: were they stern, even particularly vicious, unacceptable sanctions, or were they an outgrowth of more traditional rules, stretched to the extreme in order to deal with the

[18] From a formal point of view, the Declaration has to be considered an executive agreement, albeit anomalous for some aspects; cf. J. A. Frowein, 'Potsdam Agreement on Germany' *Encyclopedia of Public International Law* (vol. IV Oxford University Press, Oxford), p. 141. On its content, cf. critically C. Tomuschat, 'How to make peace after war – The Potsdam Agreement of 1945 revisited' (1997) 72 *Die Friedens-Warte* 18: 'a reaction, which, notwithstanding a considerable number of well-balanced responses on individual issues (penal prosecution against the individuals responsible, governmental restructuring) proved to be blind on its part to some basic requirements of justice and humanity' 'an important historical document, but certainly not more than that'. Even more critical, R. G. Steinhardt, 'The Potsdam Accord: ex nihilo nihil fit?' (1997) 72 *Die Friedens-Warte* 29: 'the experience under the Potsdam Accord accounts for the contemporary irrelevance of its content.' Unsurprisingly, the dominant Polish legal literature adopts a more positive assessment; cf. K. Skubiszewski, 'The Great Powers and the settlement in Central Europe' (1975) 18 *Jahrbuch des Internationalen Rechts* 92; and K. Skubiszewski, 'Administration of territory and sovereignty: a comment on the Potsdam Agreement' (1985) 23 *Archiv des Völkerrechts* 31; W. Czaplinski, 'Das Potsdamer Abkommen nach 50 Jahren aus polnischer Sicht' (1997) 72 *Die Friedens-Warte* 49.

[19] This view was lucidly exposed by G. I. Tunkin in a fundamental essay published in the early 1960s in the journal directed by Ago, and which inspired Ago, some years later, to conceive the very concept of 'international crime of state', 'Alcuni nuovi problemi della responsabilità dello Stato nel diritto internazionale' (1960–62) XI (1) *Comunicazioni & Studi* 35.

enormity of the wrongs committed by Germany as a state and Germans as a nation and to guarantee that they would not happen again?

At this point I find necessary to open a brief and only apparent digression: can it be said even today that guarantees of non repetition in international law are a manifestation of a concept akin to that of 'collective responsibility' of a nation? Because of its past behaviour might a state's frontiers be revised, its citizens be resettled, its territory be demilitarized and so on? Is it perhaps the profound origins and meaning of guarantees of non-repetition, especially the risk of its being tinged with an idea of punishment that made the ILC uncertain about their insertion in the Articles on state responsibility on the very eve of their adoption?[20] A hint of the uneasiness to deal conceptually with guarantees of non repetition can be found in the reticence of the ICJ to allow them.[21] In the *Land and Maritime Border (Cameroon v Nigeria)* judgment of 10 October 2002,[22] and now in the *Genocide (Bosnia v Serbia-Montenegro)* judgment of 26 February 2007,[23] the Court resisted giving way to the request of the applicant state. Besides the circumstances of each case, the main reason might be found in the fact that it cannot be lightly presumed that a state will not comply with its most basic obligations in the future. The commission of a wrongful act, be it of the utmost gravity, cannot be taken as a grounds for stigmatising the responsible state.

Coming to the individual responsibility as envisaged in the London Statute of the Nuremberg IMT, Art. IX authorized the International Military Tribunal to declare German organizations criminal, and Art. X authorized the competent national authority of any signatory to bring individuals to trial for membership therein before national, military or

[20] It will be remembered that in the first 1996 reading, guarantees of non-repetition were listed among the different forms of satisfaction, whereas in the final articles the guarantees of non repetition prominently figure among the general principles on the content of the international responsibility of a state, 'if circumstances so require' (Art. 30b). In the commentary to the article, one can read that they 'focus on prevention rather than reparation' and they are 'future-looking'. But behind this reassuring language still lingers some doubt, since 'they are concerned with other potential breaches' (ILC Commentary to Art. 30, para. 9). Why should a state give rise to the apprehension that it would repeat its breaches, if it is not because of its historic, systemic failures?

[21] Cf. R. Higgins, 'The International Court of Justice: selected issues of state responsibility', in Ragazzi (n. 1) 280: 'The problems of jurisdiction, of quality of evidence and of sound administration of judicial proceedings suggest to this writer that assurances or guarantees should be approached with the greatest caution.'

[22] *Cameroon v Nigeria,* Land and Maritime Border (10 October 2002) para. 318.

[23] *Bosnia v Serbia,* Application of the Convention on the Prevention and Repression of the Crime of Genocide, ('*Genocide Judgment*') (26 February 2007) para. 466.

occupation courts. The rationale for such a norm was to ease the burden of proof placed upon domestic prosecutors and expedite the later prosecution of hundreds of thousands of Nazi activists.

The Nuremberg Trial against the Major Offenders declared the following organizations criminal: the Leadership Corps of the Nazi Party (*Das Korps der Politischen Leiter der Nazi-Partei*); State Secret Police (*Gestapo*); Security Service (*Sicherheitsdienst des Reichsfuehrers, SD*); Security Units (*Schutzstaffeln der NSDAP, SS*); but it refrained from declaring the Reich Cabinet, and the German General Staff and High Command (*Oberkommando der Wehrmacht, OKW*) so. This cannot be equated with an all-embracing absolution. The closing words of the judgment are remarkable in this respect, where it is said that many high military officers:

> have been responsible in large measure for the miseries and suffering that have fallen on millions of men, women and children. They have been a disgrace to the honourable profession of arms. Without their military guidance the aggressive ambitions of Hitler and his fellow Nazis would have been academic and sterile ... Many of these men have made a mockery of the soldier's oath of obedience to military orders. The truth is they actively participated in all these crimes, or sat silent and acquiescent, witnessing the commission of crimes on a scale larger and more shocking than the world has ever had the misfortune to know. This must be said.[24]

However, the Nuremberg judges sat uncomfortably with the notion of membership in criminal organizations and decided to exclude from criminal liability those who lacked awareness of an organization's criminal purposes or acts as well as those who were conscripted into such organizations, unless personally implicated in the commission of crimes (under the heading of conspiracy). The ICTY Trail Chamber in the *Tadić* case gives the following reading of the Nuremberg judgments:

> First, there is a requirement of intent, which involves awareness of the act of participation coupled with a conscious decision to participate by planning, instigating, ordering, committing or otherwise aiding and abetting in the commission of a crime. Secondly, the prosecution must prove that there was participation in that the conduct of the accused contributed to the commission of the illegal act.[25]

Interestingly, the very concept of conspiracy launched by the US experts (first by Murray Bernays, aide of the Secretary of War Stimson, and later

[24] Cf. *Trial of the Major War Criminals before the International Military Tribunal* (1 October 1946) Nuremberg 1947 vol. I 278.

[25] *Prosecutor v Tadić*, IT-94-1-T (7 May 1997) para. 674.

by Chief Public Prosecutor Robert Jackson) did not go unchallenged during the negotiations which led to the London Statute.[26] Eventually, Art. VI envisaged both conspiracy to commit a crime against the peace as a substantive crime and conspiracy or common plan to commit any of the listed crimes (i.e. also crimes against humanity and war crimes) as a form of responsibility, but the judgment narrowed significantly its scope to crimes against peace alone (eight of the twenty-two defendants were sentenced under this heading, but always together with the heading of waging an aggressive war), and did not mention either conspiracy or common plan as a liability in any of the individual convictions for crimes against humanity and war crimes.

Among the postwar national prosecutions,[27] the Supreme National Tribunal of Poland distinguished itself for prosecuting membership in criminal organizations as such, basing its jurisdiction on the Polish Decree of 31 August 1944, which, in Art. 4, specifically mentioned the Nazi Party itself as well as a criminal organization, albeit limiting liability to persons in 'leading positions'. In the *Fischer and Leist* judgment of 3 March 1947, the Supreme National Tribunal declared that the whole occupation government of the Government General of Poland was a criminal organization, thereby extending the scope of criminality to several hundred persons, from Joseph Buhler, the deputy of the Governor Hans Frank to the heads of county and town districts.[28]

Apart from this extreme instance, the other tribunals, especially British and US military courts preferred to elaborate on the notion of conspiracy, even in the trials regarding collective acts of criminality committed in concentration camps, such as the *Joseph Kramer and others* trial[29] before a British Military Court in 1945, concerning forty-five administrators and functionaries of the Bergen-Belsen concentration camp, and the *Martin Gottfried Weiss and Others* case[30] before a US military court in Dachau in 1945, concerning forty functionaries of

[26] Cf. Marston Danner and Martinez (n. 13) 113.

[27] For an accurate overview, cf. M. Lippman, 'Prosecutions of Nazi War Criminals before Post-World War II Domestic Tribunals' (1999/2000) 8 *University of Miami International & Comparative Law Review* 1.

[28] Cf. the subsequent Supreme National Tribunal judgment of 10 July 1948 in the '*Joseph Buhler* trial' in (1949) vol. XIV Law Reports of Trials of War Criminals (LRTWC), London UN War Crimes Commission 23.

[29] *Josef Kramer and others,* British Military Court sitting at Luneburg (17 November 1945) in vol. II LRTWC 1.

[30] *Martin Gottfried Weiss and others*, US General Military Government Court of the United States Zone, sitting at Dachau, (13 December 1945) in vol. IX LRTWC 5.

the Dachau concentration camp, thirty-six of whom were sentenced to death.

In conclusion, the history of Germany in the momentous months between 1945 and 1946 shows how the Allies and some of the most capable German intellectuals were genuinely trying to come to terms with the unparalleled material, institutional and moral disaster in which twelve years of Nazi rule had left Germany. However, this exceptionally fervent time was soon to allow room for policy constraints and finally to give way to the dictates of *Realpolitik*, as we will see in the next section.

V. After the storm: industrialists and soldiers in the follow-up trials before the US Military Tribunal in Nuremberg

The sheer impossibility of bringing all the individual perpetrators of justice and the political necessity of accommodating some old German potentates before the looming Cold War, led the Allies, in particular the US, to be lenient towards some groups of defendants. The trials against some industrial groups and against the OKW, and especially their aftermath, are a *Trauerspiel* of the surrender of international criminal justice on the altar of political opportunism.[31]

The *Krupp* case is very illuminating. Faced with the objection that the indictee Gustav Krupp, head of the family corporation, was unfit for trial due to senile dementia, the US Chief Prosecutor Robert Jackson unsuccessfully tried to indict Krupp's son Alfried as a substitute. The trial against Alfried Krupp began one year later before the US Military Tribunal in Nuremberg, but the momentum had passed. The verdict against Alfried Krupp reached by the Tribunal in June 1948[32] was relatively mild, because the Tribunal dismissed the charges alleging crimes against peace and conspiracy, and sentenced the defendant to twelve years' imprisonment and forfeiture of all his property, both real and personal, for plunder and for employing prisoners of war and foreign civilians under inhumane conditions in connection with the conduct

[31] Cf. M. Lippman, 'The other Nuremberg: American prosecution of Nazi war criminals in Occupied Germany' (1994) 4 *Indiana International & Comparative Law Review* 1; cf. also A. Marston Danner, 'The Nuremberg industrialist prosecutions and aggressive war' (2006) 46 *Virginia Journal of International Law* 651.

[32] Cf. *The USA v Krupp*, No. 10 Vol. IX Trials of War Criminals before the Nuremberg Military Tribunal under Control Council Law 1449.

of war. On 31 January 1951, the High Commissioner McCloy granted an amnesty to Krupp, who was released and his property restored, exactly as had already happened with Friedrich Flick a year earlier,[33] and to the thirteen *IG Farben* executives, who received sentences ranging from a year and a half up to eight years of detention for their involvement in the exploitation of forced labour in concentration camps such as Auschwitz.[34]

Nevertheless, the trials of industrialists have had a historically important legacy, which resurfaced almost fifty years later in the claims brought against German companies or their US subsidiaries before US federal courts, alleging their complicity in Nazi era crimes, above all slave labour, and against Swiss banks regarding dormant assets of Holocaust victims.[35] The first group of cases led to the dramatic, but in reality long overdue decision of the German Parliament in 2000 to establish, albeit *ex gratia* and only in order to buy 'legal peace' before US courts, a $5.2. billion fund '*Vergangenheit, Verantwortung and Zukunft*', financed half by the government and half by voluntary contributions of German firms.[36] The second group of cases was similarly extrajudicially settled, through the establishment of a fund by the concerned Swiss banks, worth $1.25 billion.[37] Here again it is striking that some authoritative commentators,[38] instead of expressing relief for the friendly settlement of this embarrassing after-effect of a tragic chapter of German history, regretted that a new promising venue of civil litigation before domestic courts for long-past systemic wrongs was 'nipped in the bud'. This criticism gives vent, even fifty years later, to a general dissatisfaction with the ways the responsibility of Germany and Germans had been disposed of as a whole after the war.

Another indicator of this critical attitude is the recent rise of civil actions against Germany for damages caused by war crimes of the *Wehrmacht* before domestic courts, in which the Greek Supreme Court

[33] Cf. *The USA v Flick*, No. 10 Vol. VI Trials of War Criminals before the Nuremberg Military Tribunal under Control Council Law 1223.

[34] Cf. *The USA v Krauch et al*, Farben Case, No. 10 Vol. VIII Trials of War Criminals before the Nuremberg Military Tribunal under Control Council Law 1205.

[35] Analogously Clapham (n. 14) 48.

[36] On the German fund, cf. R. Bank, 'The new programmes for payments to victims of national socialist injustice' (2001) 44 *German Yearbook of International Law* 307.

[37] On the Swiss fund, cf. M. J. Bazyler, 'The legality and morality of the Holocaust era settlement with the Swiss banks' (2001) 25 *Fordham Journal of International Law* 64.

[38] Cf. D. F. Vagts, 'Litigating the Nazi labor claims: the path not taken' (2002) 43 *Harvard Journal of International Law* 503.

first,[39] and the Italian Court of Cassation later[40] were all too willing to deny Germany immunity from jurisdiction because of the violation of *jus cogens* norms.

This is not the place to deal in detail with the different kinds of reparations Germany paid after the war, and the various restoration schemes developed over the years for the benefit of the persecuted groups and persons,[41] but in my view it is fair to recognise that their amount was (and actually still is, because of the ongoing character of some of these programs) quite considerable, if measured to the economic possibilities of the country, at least in the first decade after the war, and it would be ungenerous now to diminish this by using as a parameter the level of wealth the country achieved later on. It is true, however, that in general terms, not all that could and should have been done in matter both of redress and punishment of the wrongs was achieved by the restoration programs and the de-Nazification measures carried out after the war.[42]

The above lead us to the most sensitive point in sanctioning the collective responsibility of the willing bystanders, i.e. of the many people who, without having committed crimes themselves, sided with and profited from the criminal regime. The basic assumption is that liberal legalism is irreconcilable with the idea of legal sanctions against bystanders. Still there can be no genuine social reconstruction and pacification both at national and international level as long as the role of the bystanders, and their responsibility, is not properly addressed.

[39] Cf. *Prefecture of Voiotia v Federal Republic of Germany*, Greek Areios Pagos, Judgment (4 May 2000) reprinted in [2001] 49 *Nomiko Vima* 212; cf. the negative decision of the German Federal Supreme Court of 26 June 2003 (III ZR 254/98, the so-called *Distomo Massacre Case*), reprinted in English in (2003) 42 *International Legal Materials* 1030.

[40] Cf. *Ferrini v Federal Republic of Germany*, Court of Cassation, Civil Plenary Session, Judgment (11 March 2004) No. 5044, reprinted in (2004) 87 *Rivista di diritto internazionale* 539; for a critical appraisal of the judgment, cf. A. Gattini, 'War crimes and state immunity in the *Ferrini* decision' (2005) 3 *Journal of International Criminal Justice* 224; cf. the negative decision of the German Constitutional Federal Tribunal, BVerfG 2 BvR 1379/01 (28 June 2004).

[41] Cf. H. J. Brodesser *et al.* (eds.), *Wiedergutmachung in der Bundesrepublik Deutschlands* (Oldenbourg, Munich 2000); A. Gattini, *Le riparazioni di guerra nel diritto internazionale* (Cedam, Padua 2003), p. 254.

[42] For an account of the 'infinite complexities' of the denazification measures, cf. W. Friedmann, *The Allied Military Government of Germany* (Stevens, London 1947), p. 113; on the whole, cf. N. Frei, *Vergangenheitspolitik. Die Anfänge der Bundesrepublik und die NS-Vergangenheit* (Beck, Munich 1996).

This same conclusion was recently reached by Laurel Fletcher and Harvey Weinstein:[43] their work in the field demonstrates that it has not been proven that the focus of the international criminal courts on individual perpetrators leads the bystanders to undergo a process of self-reflection, leading to shame, repentance and reconciliation with the victims. A different effect is more probable, that of creating a myth of collective innocence, or even strengthening a feeling of support and identification with the prosecuted leaders.[44] To counter these risks, in cases of collective violence and mass atrocities some authors propose not to rely exclusively in the virtues of criminal justice but rather to look for some alternative collective sanctions. It is remarkable, however, that many of these supposed new and alternative instruments look very much like the old, well-known instruments for the implementation of state responsibility.[45]

VI. Making peace in the Cold War: the Allied Powers' change of paradigm with Japan

If the beginning of the Cold War marked the untimely ending of a common Allied policy towards Germany with regard to sanctions and reparations, in the case of Japan the same Cold War made such a common policy utterly impossible. Nevertheless, the case of Japan is a particularly interesting one, because it is a reminder of the fact that behind the high-sounding concept of 'international crime' and its condemnation, its concrete implementation will ultimately depend on a whole range of political considerations and decisions. A reminder that is unnecessary, if one recalls the vagaries of the international community's attitude towards

[43] Cf. L.E. Fletcher and H.M. Weinstein, 'Violence and social repair: rethinking the contribution of justice to reconciliation' (2002) 24 *Human Rights Quarterly* 573; L.E. Fletcher, 'From independence to engagement: bystanders and international criminal justice' (2005) 26 *Michigan Journal of International Law* 1013.

[44] For an appraisal of the critical reception of the Nuremberg trial in the West German legal literature and public, cf. B. Simma, 'The impact of Nuremberg and Tokyo: attempts to a comparison', in N. Ando (ed.), *Japan and International Law. Past, Present, and Future* (Kluwer, The Hague 1999), p. 59; C. Burchard, 'The Nuremberg Trial and its impact on Germany' (2006) 4 JICJ 800.

[45] Cf. the remedies proposed by M.A. Drumbl, 'Collective violence and individual punishment: the criminality of mass atrocities' (2005) 99 *Northwestern University Law Review* 576: 'disgorging the benefits of group violence, compelling community service, redistributing wealth, lustration, subjecting conflict groups to international administration, and traditional forms of state responsibility such as embargoes and trade restrictions.'

the Cambodia of the Khmer Rouge[46] or today towards Sudan because of the Darfur crisis.[47]

Using somewhat unfortunate language, the three major Allies had stated in the Potsdam Declaration with regard to Japan on 26 July 1945, that they did not intend 'that the Japanese shall be enslaved as a race or destroyed as a nation, but stern justice shall be meted out to all war criminals, including those who have visited cruelties upon our prisoners'.

Under Art. 5 of its Statute, established in January 1946 by an executive order of the Supreme Commander of the Allied Powers in Japan, General McArthur, the Tokyo Tribunal had the power 'to try and punish Far Eastern war criminals who, as individuals or as members of organizations, are charged with offences which include crimes against peace'. The Statute, however, did not foresee the possibility of declaring organizations criminal. Although Count One of the indictment in the Tokyo Tribunal embraced 'leaders, organizers, instigators or accomplices' in the conspiracy to wage a war of aggression, the Tribunal limited itself to condemning twenty-five leading officials,[48] and there was no prosecution of leading members of organizations, such as the so-called 'patriotic societies' and the *Zaibatsu*, the industrial complexes closely connected with the military and which had first made the war possible.[49]

As was the case with defeated Germany, the initial momentum to impose severe sanctions on Japan for the war unleashed by its 'violence and greed' as the Cairo Declaration of 27 November 1943 had labelled it, rapidly lapsed in face of the irreconcilable policies of the former Allies. The remarkable leniency of the San Francisco Peace Treaty, concluded under the initiative of the United States and without the participation of the Soviet Union and the People's Republic of China, is then

[46] Cf. D. Boyle 'Establishing the responsibility of the Khmer Rouge leadership for international crimes' (2002) 5 *Yearbook of International Humanitarian Law* 167; C. Etcheson, 'The politics of genocide justice in Cambodia', in C. P. R. Romano, A. Nollkaemper and J. Kleffner (eds.), *Internationalized Criminal Courts and Tribunals* (Oxford University Press, Oxford 2004), p. 181.

[47] Cf. N. Udombana, 'When neutrality is a sin: the Darfur crisis and the crisis of humanitarian intervention in Sudan' (2005) 27 *Human Rights Quarterly* 1149.

[48] For a critical assessment of the Tokyo Tribunal, cf. the interview that Cassese made to the Dutch Judge Röling, shortly before the latter's death: B. V. A. Röling and A. Cassese, *The Tokyo Tribunal and Beyond* (Polity Press, Cambridge 1993).

[49] On the measures taken by the US administration during the occupation of Japan, cf. N. Ando, *Surrender, Occupation and Private Property in International Law* (Clarendon Press, Oxford 1991).

no surprise if one considers its date, 8 September 1951, in the midst of the Korea war.[50]

Article 14 of the Treaty, having recognized that Japan's resources were not sufficient, 'if it is to maintain a viable economy, to make complete reparation for all such damage and suffering and at the same time meet its other obligations', then distinguished between the former enemies, whose territory had been occupied by Japan, and the others.[51] The latter renounced asking for reparations, except for the damages directly suffered by their citizens in Japan during the war,[52] whereas Japan was bound to initiate bilateral negotiations with regard to the former. Among these states, India, nationalist China, Laos and Cambodia eventually renounced asking for reparations. Therefore, Japan had to conclude reparations agreement only with Burma, Indonesia, South Vietnam, South Korea and the Philippines. Predictably, it was not difficult for Japan to use its incomparably greater economic resources as leverage against the four newly independent countries, by making them accept payments in kind, so as to turn its modest debt into a further opportunity for investment by its companies.[53]

VII. Back to the past: Iraq's responsibility after the Second Gulf War

The reasons for the title of this section, 'back to the past' are manifold and some of them unwittingly ironical. There is indeed a sense of utter unreality today when speaking of the legal settlement which took place only in 1991, in view of the events which have occurred in Iraq since March 2003.

After the Second Gulf War of 1991, it came as a surprise to many observers that the United Nations had opted for a traditional, in some ways even old-fashioned solution when it addressed Iraq's responsibility for having invaded Kuwait.[54] I am referring to the sanction regime in force long after the end of the hostilities and the vast programme of reparations

[50] On the negotiation of the Peace Treaty, cf. F. S. Dunn, *Peace Making and the Settlement with Japan* (Princeton University Press, Princeton, NY 1963).

[51] Article 14, para. 2, however, permitted the Allied Powers to confiscate and liquidate all public and private Japanese property on their territory.

[52] As provided for by Art. 15a of the Treaty. On 12 June 1952 an agreement was reached in Washington between Japan and twenty-six Allied Powers.

[53] For more details, cf. Gattini (n. 41) 387.

[54] Cf. A. Gattini, 'The UN Compensation Commission: old rules, new procedures on war reparations' (2002) 13 EJIL 161.

supervised by the UN Compensation Commission (UNCC).[55] Some commentators have criticized those Security Council decisions seeing in them the resurgence of the 'ghosts of Versailles'.[56] Paradoxically, there is a grain of truth in the comparison, not so much because of the sternness of the regime, but because of the stress placed on the mechanisms of state responsibility.

For all its weaknesses, the UNCC was greeted as the first attempt by the organized international community to reaffirm and to apply, in an orderly manner, the existing international rules on reparation as a consequence of a war of aggression. However, it is noteworthy that any hint of individual responsibility was carefully avoided in the settlement envisaged by the UN Security Council, to the outrage not only of Iran, but also of some US commentators.[57] There may have been many reasons for that course of conduct: the Coalition first and the Security Council later thought that the maintenance of a severe regime of state responsibility could have led to the collapse of the regime from below in a reasonable length of time, a legally more tenable and politically wiser solution than the toppling of Saddam Hussein from above, i.e. through outright military intervention, as later events have painfully demonstrated clearly enough.

However, as time revealed, it became ever more evident that the sanctions regime established by the Security Council would not attain its goal. In international legal literature some even openly challenged its legitimacy, because of its lasting negative effects on the population, such as the dramatic increase in childhood mortality.[58] A lively debate arose on the issue of the so-called 'targeted sanctions', i.e. sanctions which affect only the individuals or groups responsible and leave the rest of the population untouched.[59]

[55] Cf. sections C and D of the Security Council's Resolution 687 of 3 April 1991.

[56] Cf. E. J. Garmise, 'The Iraqi claims process and the ghosts of Versailles' (1992) 27 *New York University Journal of International Law & Policy* 840; C. P. R. Romano, 'Woe to the vanquished? A comparison of the reparations process after World War I (1914–18) and the Gulf War (1990–91)' (1997) 2 *Austrian Review of International and European Law* 361.

[57] D. D. Caron, 'Iraq and the force of law: why give a shield of immunity?' (1991) 85 AJIL 89; J. J. Paust, 'Suing Saddam: private remedies for war crimes and hostage-taking' (1991) 31 *Virginia Journal of International Law* 351; J. N. Moore, 'War crimes and the rule of law in the Gulf crisis' (1991) 31 *Virginia Journal of International Law* 403.

[58] Cf., among many others, H. C. von Sponeck, 'Sanctions and humanitarian exemptions: a practitioner's commentary' (2002) 13 EJIL 81; L. Oette, 'A decade of sanctions against Iraq: never again!' (2002) 13 EJIL 93.

[59] Cf., among many others, P. Conlon, 'The humanitarian mitigation of UN sanctions' (1996) 39 *German Yearbook of International Law* 249; S. Forlati, 'Sanzioni

On closer inspection, it does not seem that the targeted sanctions offer a self-evident alternative. While it is true that classical sanctions indiscriminately strike the responsible and the innocent, and more often than not have been proven to be inefficient, it has not yet been proven that targeted or 'smart' sanctions would do better in terms of justice and efficiency. For all their laudable concern for the plight of the innocent and suffering population under a totalitarian regime, the supporters of smart sanctions forget that a totalitarian regime cannot be reduced to a handful of leading personalities, but rather it rests upon a complex network of relations involving large sectors of the society.

The example of post-Saddam Iraq offers clear evidence of the difficulty of eradicating the Baath Party from its social, and perhaps ethnic, humus. The biased trial of the Iraqi Special Tribunal against Saddam Hussein[60] and the ugly circumstances of his execution are more redolent of vengeance by one national group against another than of a shared sense of justice and national reconciliation.

VIII. Back to the future? Individual responsibility in the ICTY trials and state responsibility in the *Genocide Case* before the ICJ

This final section is provocatively entitled 'back to the future', although with a question mark, having in mind the case of the former Yugoslavia.

The reason is that the discussion in the aftermath of the internecine Bosnian war is reminiscent in certain aspects of that following the Second World War in Germany. Of course, everyone can easily see a link in the fact that the ICTY was the first international criminal tribunal created after Nuremberg and Tokyo. But a deeper and more meaningful parallel lays, in my view, in the thought on collective responsibility

economiche e tutela umanitaria' (1997) 80 *Rivista di diritto internazionale* 705; M. Craven, 'Humanitarianism and the quest for smarter sanctions' (2002) 13 EJIL 43.

60 For an endorsement of the policy underlying the Iraqi Special tribunal, cf. J. Rabkin, 'Global criminal justice: an idea whose time has passed' (2005) 38 *Cornell International Law Journal* 776. For a more critical view, cf. F. Malekian, 'Emasculating the philosophy of international criminal justice in the Iraqi Special Tribunal' (2005) 38 *Cornell International Law Journal* 673; cf., among others, C. F. J. Doebbler and M. P. Scharf, 'Will Saddam Hussein get a fair trial?' (2005) 37 *Case Western Reserve Journal of International Law* 21; M. Bohlander, 'Can the Iraqi Special Tribunal sentence Saddam Hussein to death?' (2005) 3 JICJ 463.

applied mainly, but not only, to the Bosnian Serbs and possibly, through the mechanism of attribution, to Serbia as such.

The issue of collective responsibility has not been tackled by the ICTY, but it is perhaps not preposterous to maintain that it can be traced in the ICTY jurisprudence on Joint Criminal Enterprise (JCE). While this is not the place to go into the details of the ICTY jurisprudence on JCE from *Tadic* to the *Brdanin* case,[61] and on the subtle distinctions drawn by the Tribunal between this concept and that of aiding and abetting,[62] it is a fact that the concept of JCE, with its somewhat more liberal evidentiary standards, is particularly suitable to tackle mass atrocities, which are, as a rule, the result of a complex network of connivances. This is not by chance that the concept has been utilized widely by the ICTY Prosecutors in all those cases in which it would have been quite difficult to prove in isolation the individual responsibility of the indicted.[63]

[61] The concept of JCE has been fully articulated by the ICTY Appeals Chamber in the *Prosecutor v Tadić*, IT-94-1-A (15 July 1999) para. 227. The *actus reus* requires three elements: 'a plurality of persons', 'a common plan, design or purpose' which amounts to or involves the 'commission of a crime provided for in the Statute'. As for the *mens rea*, the criminal intent must be shared with the other members, but in a case of 'extended JCE', i.e. when the crime occurred outside the JCE's objective but nonetheless results from the JCE's execution, it suffices the *dolus eventualis*. However, later on in the *Brđanin* judgment, the Trial Chamber substantially narrowed the scope of the JCE and brought it nearer to the traditional category of conspiracy, because it demanded from the Prosecutor the proof of a direct understanding of agreement between the accused and the 'relevant physical perpetrators' (i.e. those materially committing the crime), in order to satisfy the abovementioned requirement of a 'common plan', cf. *Prosecutor v Brđanin*, IT-99-36-T (1 September 2004) para. 264. For an appraisal of the pre-*Brđanin* broad interpretation of JCE, cf. Marston, Danner and Martinez (n. 13) 107; Piacente, 'Importance of the joint criminal enterprise doctrine for the ICTY prosecutorial policy' (2004) 2 *Journal of International Criminal Justice* 446. On the *Brđanin* judgment, cf. A. O'Rourke, 'Joint criminal enterprise and Brđanin: misguided overcorrection' (2006) 47 *Harvard International Law Journal* 307, and the symposium held by the Journal of International Criminal Justice under the heading 'Guilty by association: joint criminal enterprise on trial', with a foreword by G. Sluiter, and contributions by A. Cassese, K. Gustafson, J. D. Ohlin, H. van der Wilt, K. Ambos, E. van Sliedregt, K. Hamford, cf (2007) 5 JICJ 67 *et seq*. Eventually, with judgment of 3 April 2007, the Appeals Chamber granted grounds 1 and 2 of the prosecution's appeal with regard to the questions of law presented (relating to the proper scope of the JCE doctrine), albeit without modifying Brđanin's conviction in relation thereto.

[62] The distinction was first made by the Appeals Chamber in *Prosecutor v Tadić* (n. 61) para. 229 (iv); on this issue, cf. the contribution by H. van der Wilt, 'Joint criminal enterprise and function perpetration', in the present volume, Chapter 7.

[63] It is noticeable that all three indictments against Milosevic were based on the JCE doctrine. Cf. *Prosecutor v Milosevic*, IT-02-54-T, Second Amended Indictment (22 November 2002) 6.

If this procedural course is in itself unobjectionable and to some extent the only viable one to combat impunity, the attitude which informs it, is not without risk. One such risk is to inflate the concept of 'collective' responsibility, as became apparent in the *Genocide* case (*Bosnia v Serbia*) before the ICJ.

In short, Bosnia had tried to convince the ICJ to condemn Serbia for having committed genocide in Bosnia from 1992 to 1995. In order to do this, Bosnia had to prove two conditions. The first was that genocide had been committed at all. Bosnia resolutely took the view that the ICJ should consider all the different facts and events as a single, huge whole. This first step is a quite dubious undertaking. As is well known, the ICTY found genocide had been committed only in regard to Srebrenica[64] and for all the rhetorical abilities of the counsel of Bosnia, Professor Franck,[65] it is difficult to see why an addition of crimes against humanity, as terrible as they might have been, should produce a qualitatively different result, at least in the absence of irrefutable proof of a 'mastermind plan'.[66]

Second, Bosnia had to prove that all those facts were attributable to Serbia, and here another difficult problem arises, because most of the proven crimes were committed by Bosnian Serbs not by Serbian organs. As a consequence, Bosnia had to comply with the demanding and time consuming requirement of attribution set by the ICJ in her 1986 *Nicaragua* judgment,[67] namely it had to prove that Serbia directed and controlled the acts which were supposed to constitute the crime of genocide. Here again, Bosnia did not resist the temptation of following an apparently easier, but in my view preposterous, approach of maintaining that the whole Republika Srpska was nothing else than a sum of *de facto* organs of Serbia.[68] Hence Bosnia's appeal to have Serbia condemned to pay full reparation for each and all of the horrible crimes that had happened in Bosnia from 1992 to 1995.

Before the ICJ, Bosnia's agent maintained that the sole aim of the whole action was to set the historical record straight and so to facilitate

[64] Cf. *Prosecutor v Kristic*, IT-98–33-T (2 August 2001) para. 560 and Appeals Chamber Judgment (19 April 2004) para. 23; *Prosecutor v Blagojevic and Jokic*, IT-02–60 (17 January 2005) paras. 671–677.

[65] Cf. T. M. Franck ICJ CR 2006/ 5 para. 19 *et seq*.

[66] *Genocide Judgment* (n. 23) para. 373. On the occasionally debatable handling of evidence by the ICJ, cf. A. Gattini, 'Evidentiary issues in the ICJ's *Genocide* Judgment' (2007) 5 JICJ 889.

[67] *Nicaragua v United States*, Military and Paramilitary Activities in and Against Nicaragua (1986) *ICJ Reports* 1986 para. 115.

[68] Cf. L. Condorelli, ICJ CR 2006/ 10 para. 1 *et seq*.

the reconciliation between the two countries, and between the two ethnic groups in Bosnia.[69] On the contrary, one cannot honestly help in seeing in Bosnia's submissions a dashing attempt to have the whole ethnic group of Bosnian Serbs branded with the stigma of having committed genocide, and the Republika Srpska as 'a genocidal creation' of Serbia,[70] a brand which in my view is supported neither by evidence nor by historical truth.

Of course, we would have been in a different situation, if the ICTY had previously condemned Milosevic or some other senior Serbian officials for genocide, in Srebrenica or elsewhere. In this case, through the mechanism of attribution, the issue of state responsibility would necessarily have been resolved positively, pace that doctrine which wants to limit state responsibility with regard to the Genocide Convention only to Art. I, based on the duty to prevent and to punish the commission of genocide.[71]

The core question of the complex relationship between state and individual responsibility is touched upon here, as already mentioned at the beginning of these observations. To what extent, if any, would a finding of state responsibility spill over on the individual responsibility of one or of many, and vice versa? In my view, the answer depends on the primary rule violated.[72]

Besides the crime of aggression, which in my view is still a leadership crime, so that the responsibility of an individual inevitably points to that of the state and the other way round, other crimes do not have the same structure. In particular, their commission does not necessarily imply the aggravated responsibility of the state for serious breaches of peremptory norms of international law under Art. 40 of the ILC Articles on state responsibility, para. 2 of which specifies that a breach is serious 'if it involves a gross or systematic failure by the responsible State'. Here again we encounter the underlying thought that aggravated responsibility

[69] Cf. S. Softic, ICJ CR 2006/ 2 para. 6: 'We do not entertain feelings of revenge towards the Serbs in our country. After all, they have been clearly misled by their leaders, who carried out what the Respondent initiated in the early 1990s of the past century. So, revenge is not guiding us, neither is any notion of collective guilt doing that. This case is not about blaming each and every Bosnian Serb for the acts of genocide.'

[70] Cf. M. Milanovic, 'State responsibility for genocide' (2006) 17 EJIL 589, who reports some influential voices in Bosnia claiming that the Republika Srpska is a 'genocidal creation'. It does not come as a surprise that the Republika Srpska fiercely opposed the decision of the Bosnian Presidency to pursue the case before the ICJ; cf. *Genocide Judgment* (n. 23) paras. 18 and 20.

[71] Cf. *Genocide Judgment* (n. 23) para. 155 *et seq.*, para. 179.

[72] Cf. Dupuy (n. 1) 1088.

of the state is justified only if the crime is in itself particularly heinous or, more commonly, if it forms part of a systematic failure, a failure which necessarily implies that of larger segments of the community, rather than of single individuals or organs.

Admittedly, the matter is not so clear-cut with regard to a crime like genocide, which has both to be considered 'grave' per se and which generally, if not necessarily,[73] is of a systematic nature, which presupposes at least a certain degree of collective organization often with some involvement of governmental authorities.[74] For all the differences in the structure, purposes and consequences of individual and state responsibility, it is objectively difficult to neatly separate them in the case of the commission of a crime, which from experience has brought to light the existence of a network of responsibilities at different levels. Nevertheless, it is one matter to condemn a state, through the mechanism of attribution, for a single instance of genocide, and another qualitatively quite different matter to brand it with the stigma of having committed a wholesale genocide through the (mis)deeds of an entire population for years.

In the light of the entire jurisprudence of the ICTY, I think that the ICJ was right to reject the exorbitant Bosnian claim and to stick to the only indisputable failure of Serbia to prevent the commission of the genocide of Srebrenica and diligently to prosecute those responsible of genocide such as General Mladic.[75] However, even when it found this violation, the Court decided not to award Bosnia any compensation. This last decision deserves thoughtful attention. By denying any form of reparation, other than the satisfaction of a declarative judgment, the Court probably, albeit implicitly, refused to see any systemic responsibility on the part of Serbia. This position is the opposite extreme of Bosnia's, and just as doubtful. Here the central and delicate question, addressed in this volume by Nollkaemper and van der Wilt,[76] is touched on, that is what are the ultimate objectives and the means of international law when dealing with the multifarious aspects of system responsibility.

The Court had at least three options.[77] First, it could have leaned on the opinion expressed by the counsels of both parties, that is a finding

[73] Cf. the ICTY Trial Chamber *Prosecutor v Jelisić*, IT 95–10, Judgment (15 July 1999) para. 100.

[74] Cf. Cassese (n. 1) 349; Dupuy (n. 1) 1089.

[75] *Genocide Judgment* (n. 23) operative clauses 5 and 6.

[76] Cf. A. Nollkaemper and H. van der Wilt, 'Conclusions and outlook', this volume, Chapter 15, p. 348.

[77] On the whole, cf. A. Gattini, 'Breach of the obligation to prevent and reparation thereof in the ICJ's Genocide Judgment' (2007) 18 EJIL 695.

of the ICJ would suffice to repair this kind of violation.[78] Given the importance of the matter, and the risk that Bosnia could have, as an afterthought, claimed compensation from Serbia, dragging it into a new controversy for many years, it can be understood why the Court did not follow this apparently easy path. Second, the Court could have resolved the issue in terms of causality, as in fact it did.[79] However, the solution arrived at by the Court, that the acts of genocide in and around Srebrenica would have been committed anyway, and that therefore it was impossible to measure the degree of causality due to Serbia's failure to prevent them, is not an escapable one. If it is true that the standard of international law in matters of causation by omission is extremely confused and in the end depends on the subjective approach of the judge,[80] still the Court treated a case, which itself had labelled as a case of concomitant causation through omission, as if it were a case of intervening alternative causation.

A third, more creative and forward looking approach for the ICJ would have been to award some kind of reparation of the type now called restorative justice, which would have captured the essence of Serbia's wrong, the lack of prevention and, as paradoxical as it might seem at first glance, its 'collective' dimension. One could think of the financing of programmes for the benefit of the survivors and the relatives of the victims of Srebrenica, such as measures for rehabilitation, psychotherapeutical treatments, the establishment of document centres, and various measures for honouring and keeping alive the memory of the victims.[81] Admittedly, the ICJ is inexperienced in this field, but for that matter is not very experienced in all the aspects of redress either.[82] In particular, a look at the jurisprudence of the Inter-American Court of Human Rights could have been a useful source of inspiration for the ICJ.[83]

[78] Cf. I. Brownlie (Counsel for Serbia) ICJ CR 2006/ 17, 43 para. 304; I. Pellet (Counsel for Bosnia) ICJ CR 2006/ 11, 26 para. 20.

[79] *Genocide Judgment* (n. 23) para. 462.

[80] Cf. F. Rigaux, 'International responsibility and the principle of causality', in Ragazzi (n. 1) 81.

[81] Cf. UN GA Res 60/147, 'Basic Principles and Guidelines on the Right to a Remedy and Reparation for Victims of Gross Violations of International Human Rights Law and Serious Violations of International Humanitarian Law' (16 December 2005).

[82] Cf. I. Brownlie, 'Remedies in the ICJ', in V. Lowe *et al.* (eds.), *Fifty Years of the International Court of Justice: Essays in Honour of Sir Robert Jennings* (Cambridge University Press, Cambridge 1996), p. 557.

[83] In its most recent judgments, the Inter-American Court developed innovative forms of reparations, which do not substitute the more traditional ones of compensation for damages, but take a more and more central place, alongside the guarantees of non repetition.

IX. Concluding remarks

The history of the twentieth century, and the beginning of the twenty-first, as well, has demonstrated that international law, even if it has laboriously succeeded to distinguish between state and individual responsibility, still lacks the means to satisfactorily cope with the concept of 'system' responsibility. On the one hand, this concept is difficult to harmonize with the conceptual tools of individual criminal responsibility, still in their infancy. On the other hand, when facing the complex and novel problems of system responsibility, the classical framework of state responsibility seems to revert to its 'collective responsibility' reflex, which might appear outdated, even iniquitous to some extent, and in any case too undifferentiated and lastly inadequate a conceptual tool properly to capture the peculiarity and complexity of the phenomenon of system criminality.

Just to recall a few examples, in the decision of 5 July 2006 in the *Montero-Aranguren y otros v Venezuela (Retén de Catia)* case (cf. Serie C No. 150, available at www.corteidh.or.cr/pais.cfm?id_Pais=13, accessed 10 June 2008), the Court condemned Venezuela to make, within six months, a public and solemn ceremony of atonement (*acto publico de reconocimiento de responsabilidad y pedida de esculpa*) through the highest state officials and in the presence of the relatives of the victims, at the Detention Centre at Catia, the same place where the facts giving rise to its responsibility, the extrajudicial killing of thirty-seven detainees in 1992, had happened. In the decision of 22 September 2006 in the *Goiburù y otros v Paraguay* case (cf. Serie C No. 153, available at www.corteidh.or.cr/pais.cfm?id_Pais=5, accessed 10 June 2008), concerning the *desaparecidos* of the Operation Condor in Paraguay in the 1970s, the Court took notice of various measures already taken by Paraguay, among which were the establishment of a Commission for Truth and Justice, the establishment of a Documentation and Archive Centre denominated 'Archivio del terror', the naming of a public square to the memory of the desaparecidos, and indicated a whole series of measures, such as the therapeutical treatment of relatives of the victims, the construction of monuments and public ceremonies of excuses, alongside more general and wider ranging measures such as the dissemination of a human rights culture in schools and institutions, and changes in the criminal code.

6

Command responsibility and *Organisationsherrschaft*: ways of attributing international crimes to the 'most responsible'

KAI AMBOS*

I. Introductory remarks

The increasing trend to prosecute and punish international crimes and criminals, to fight against the widespread impunity for gross violations of human rights, with the means of (international) criminal law (see para. 4 of the preamble of the ICC Statute) is certainly to be welcomed and has received broad support in the academic literature, including by this author.[1] At the same time, however, one must not lose sight of the fundamental principles of criminal law which are the product of centuries' long fights for fairness and the rule of law and which must not be ignored by the international criminal tribunals, especially the International Criminal Court (hereinafter 'ICC').

Indeed, from a national criminal law perspective, rooted in the tradition of enlightenment, there exists a tension between International Criminal Law (hereinafter ICL)/international criminal jurisdiction and national criminal law/domestic jurisdictions at least in two respects. On the one hand, the increasing trend to criminalization, especially in its extreme form promoted by certain NGOs as prosecution and punishment at whatever cost, often conflicts with the traditional criminal law

* Professor of Criminal Law, Criminal Procedure, Comparative Law and International Criminal Law at the Georg-August Universität Göttingen; Head of the Department of Foreign and International Criminal Law of the Institute of Criminal Law and Criminal Justice; Judge at the State Court (*Landgericht*) Göttingen.

I am grateful to Ousman Njikam and Stefanie Bock, both research assistants in my department, for their help in preparing this final version.

[1] K. Ambos, *Straflosigkeit von Menschenrechtsverletzungen, Zur "impunidad" in südamerikanischen Staaten aus völkerstrafrechtlicher Sicht* (Max Planck Institute, Freiburg 1997); *Impunidad y Derecho Penal Internacional* (2nd ed, Ad Hoc, Buenos Aires 1999).

principles grounded in the rule of law (*Rechtsstaat*).[2] To a lesser extent, the criminalization efforts at the international level may conflict with decriminalization efforts at the national level, either by a reduction of the substantive criminal law (downgrading criminal offences to mere administrative infringements of the law) or by procedural means using the well-known techniques of procedural discretion, abbreviations of criminal proceedings or various forms of negotiations (guilty plea, *conformidad*, *pattagamiento*, *transactie*, etc.).[3] On the other hand, the relationship between the system (criminality) and the individual (criminality) is not free from doubt. While it is clear that ICL is concerned with macro-criminality in the sense of Herbert Jägers' fundamental study[4] and that domestic criminal law is, normally, concerned with ordinary and individual criminality, the boundaries between the system and the individual level are blurred. While criminal law, at whatever level and in whatever form, always goes after the individual perpetrator, it is clear that ICL cannot do without investigating and understanding the political, social, economic and cultural framework and background of the crimes (the 'crime base') and thus goes well beyond the establishment of mere individual responsibility. This is all the more true if we take into account that current practice in ICL concentrates increasingly, as a matter of law or fact, on the top or high-level perpetrators and leaves the mid- or low-level perpetrators to the domestic jurisdictions.[5] The focus on the top necessarily leads to an

[2] For a radical critique in this respect with regard to Latin America, see D. Pastor, 'La deriva neopunitivista de organismos y activistas como causa del desprestigio actual de los derechos humanos', Nueva Doctrina Penal (Buenos Aires, Ediciones del Puerto 2005 A) 73 *et seq*.

[3] See on the increasing trend against mandatory prosecution (principle of legality in its procedural form) recently Jehle and Wade (eds.), *Coping with Overloaded Criminal Justice Systems: the Rise of Prosecutorial Power Across Europe* (Springer, Berlin 2006).

[4] H. Jäger, *Makrokriminalität. Studien zur Kriminologie kollektiver Gewalt* (Suhrkamp, Frankfurt 1989).

[5] Cf. ICC, Office of the Prosecutor ('OTP'), Paper on some policy issues before the Office of the Prosecutor (September 2003) www.icc-cpi.int/library/organs/otp/030905_Policy_Paper.pdf 3, 7, accessed 2 July 2008 ('focus … on those who bear the greatest responsibility'; more recently OTP, Fourth Report of the Prosecutor of the International Criminal Court, to the Security Council pursuant to UNSC 1593 (2005) (14 December 2006) www.icc-cpi.int/library/organs/otp/OTP_ReportUNSC4-Darfur_English.pdf 4 accessed 2 July 2008. For Pre-Trial Chamber I this *ratione personae* limitation is also ensured by the gravity threshold of Art. 17(1)(d) (situation in the DRC in the case of the *Prosecutor v Thomas Lubanga Dyilo*, Decision concerning PTC I's Decision of 10 February 2006 and the Incorporation of Documents into the Record of the Case against Mr Thomas Lubanga Dyilo, ICC-01/04–01/06 (24 February 2006) para. 50: 'intended to

inquiry into the criminal structures they represent. In this sense, it also seems clear that the system and individual level are not mutually exclusive but rather complement each other; a one-sided focus on one or the other would not fully take into account the complexities of macro criminality. For the analysis of individual criminal responsibility, this means that one should focus on the rules of imputation or attribution for the top perpetrators, the intellectual mastermind, the 'man in the background', i.e. the people running the criminal organization or enterprise responsible for the atrocities.[6] This brings us to the three possible forms of attribution which may be applied alternatively or cumulatively: joint criminal enterprise ('JCE'); command responsibility; and control/domination of the act by virtue of a hierarchical organization (hereinafter: *Organisationsherrschaft* or 'domination by virtue of an organization').[7] As the first one is the object of another study in this book, by Harmen van de Wilt, I will focus on command responsibility (in section II) and *Organisationsherrschaft* (section IV) and treat JCE only in relation to the former (section III).[8]

II. Command responsibility

1. *The basics*

Modern case law lists *three requirements* for the responsibility of the superior:[9]

ensure that the Court initiates cases only against the most senior leaders as being the most responsible').

6 For the purpose of imputation in criminal law the 'man' or people in the background are always natural, not juridical persons. This does not deny that system criminality, as defined in the introductory chapter of this book, refers to situations where collective entities order or encourage, or permit or tolerate the commission of international crimes. This collective element precisely concerns the system level of macro criminality and explains the existence of a collective or context element in international crimes.

7 It is difficult to find a precise translation of the German term '*Organisationsherrschaft*'; for the substance of the concept the reader should turn to section IV below.

8 For my view on JCE, see 'Joint criminal enterprise and command responsibility' (2007) 5 JICJ 159–83 and *Internationales Strafrecht* (Beck, München 2006), § 7 marginal numbers (mn) 19 *et seq.*

9 *Prosecutor v Delalic et al.*, IT-96–21, Judgment, Trial Chamber (16 November 1998) para. 346. See also the following ICTY Judgments: *Prosecutor v Aleksovski*, IT-95–14/1, Judgment, Trial Chamber (25 June 1999) para. 69 *et seq.*; concurring Appeals Chamber (24 March 2000) paras. 69–77; *Prosecutor v Blaskić*, IT-95–14, Judgment, Trial Chamber (3 March 2000) para. 289 *et seq.* (294); concurring Appeals Chamber (29 July 2004) para. 484; *Prosecutor v Kordić and Čerkez*, IT-95–14/2, Judgment, Trial Chamber

1. the existence of a superior-subordinate relationship;
2. the superior's failure to take the necessary and reasonable measures to prevent the criminal act of his subordinates or punish them;
3. the superior's knowledge or having reason to know that a criminal act was about to be committed or had been committed.

As a fourth element one may consider the principal crime(s) to be committed by the subordinates,[10] yet this is rather an 'external' requirement, flowing quite logically from the conceptual structure of command responsibility.[11] Possibly the most important (objective) requirement is implicit in the first requirement, namely the material (factual) ability to exercise sufficient *control* over the subordinates so as to prevent them from committing crimes. In *Kayishema/Ruzindana* this ability was called 'the touchstone' of the doctrine, 'inherently linked with the factual situation' in the concrete case.[12] The third requirement, referring to the *mens rea*, can be subdivided into two different *subjective thresholds*: either the

(26 February 2001) para. 401 *et seq.*; partly reversed by Appeals Chamber (17 December 2004) but no change with regard to the requirements for superior/command responsibility, see *ibid.*, para. 827; *Prosecutor v Brđanin*, IT-99–36, Judgment, Trial Chamber II (1 September 2004) para. 275; *Prosecutor v Strugar*, IT-01–42 Judgment, Trial Chamber II (31 January 2005) para. 358; *Prosecutor v Halilović*, IT-01–48, Judgment, Trial Chamber (16 November 2005) para. 55 *et seq.* (confirmed by the App. Ch. (16 October 2007); *Prosecutor v Limaj et al.*, IT-03–66, Judgment, Trial Chamber (30 November 2005) para. 520 *et seq.*; *Prosecutor v Hadzihasanovic/Kubura*, IT-01–47-T, Judgment, Trial Chamber (15 March 2006) para. 76 *et seq.*; *Prosecutor v Oric*, IT-03–68-T, Judgment, Trial Chamber II (30 June 2006) para. 294 (confirmed by the App. Ch. (3 July 2008) para. 18); *Prosecutor v Mrksic/Radic/Sljivancanin*, IT-95–13/1, Judgment, Trial Chamber II (27 September 2007) para. 558; *Prosecutor v Boskoski/Tarculovski*, IT-04-82-T, Judgment, Trial Chamber II (10 July 2008) para. 406, *Prosecutor v Delic*, IT-04-83-T, Judgment, Trial Chamber I (15 September 2008) para. 56.

For the ICTR: *Prosecutor v Akayesu*, ICTR-96–4, Judgment, Trial Chamber (2 September 1998) para. 486 *et seq.*; *Prosecutor v Kayishema and Ruzindana*, ICTR-95–1; ICTR-96–10, Judgment, Trial Chamber II (21 May 1999) paras. 208–31; *Prosecutor v Rutaganda*, ICTR-96–3, Judgment, Trial Chamber I (6 December 1999) para. 31 *et seq.*; *Prosecutor v Bagilishema*, ICTR-95–1A, Judgment, Trial Chamber I (7 June 2001) para. 38; *Prosecutor v Kajelijeli*, ICTR-98–44A, Judgment, Trial Chamber II (1 December 2003) paras. 754–82 (772); *Prosecutor v Semanza*, ICTR-97–20, Judgment, Trial Chamber III (15 May 2003) paras. 375–407.

[10] *Prosecutor v Oric*, IT-03–68-T, Judgment, Trial Chamber (30 June 2006) para. 294

[11] See also *Oric* Trial Judgment (n. 10) para. 295: 'so obvious that there is hardly the need of it being explicitly stated.'

[12] *Kayishema and Ruzindana* Trial Judgment (n. 9) para. 229 *et seq.* Concurring A. M. Danner and J. S. Martinez, 'Guilty associations: joint criminal enterprise, command responsibility, and the development of international criminal law' (2005) 93 *California Law Review* 122, 130; B. L. Bonafé, 'Finding a proper role for command responsibility' (2007) 5 JICJ 608 *et seq.*

superior must have actual *knowledge* with regard to the crimes; or he must possess *information* of a nature which would put him on notice of the risk of such crimes by indicating the need for additional investigation in order to ascertain whether they were committed or were about to be committed.[13] It follows that ignorance with regard to the commission of crimes cannot be held against the superior if he/she has properly fulfilled his/her duties of supervision (in particular, did not ignore information which indicated the commission of crimes) but still did not find out about the crimes committed by the subordinates.

2. *Doctrinal considerations*

The doctrinal analysis of a legal concept so complex as command responsibility is not a purpose *per se* or, as the French would say, *l'art pour l'art*. It is important to understand the concept fully, with a particular view to its theoretical justification and practical consequences. Article 28 of the ICC Statute, the most advanced codification of the command responsibility doctrine, can be characterized as a genuine offence or *separate crime of omission* (*echtes Unterlassungsdelikt*), not an improper form of omission in the sense of a *commission par omission*.[14] Although, in structural terms, the superior is to be blamed for his/her improper supervision (a 'neglect of duty'),[15] he/she is not only punished for this reason but also for the crimes of the subordinates. As a result, the concept creates, on the one hand, *direct* liability for the lack of supervision, and, on the other, *indirect* liability for the criminal acts of others (the subordinates), thereby producing a kind of *vicarious liability*.[16] The liability for the failure to

[13] This standard was established for the first time in *Delalic et al.* Trial Judgment (n. 9) para. 383; it was most recently confirmed in *Prosecutor v Hadzihasanovic/Kubura*, IT-01-47, Judgment, Appeals Chamber (21 April 2008) paras. 26 *et seq.*

[14] See, for an explanation, K. Ambos, 'Superior responsibility', in A. Cassese, P. Gaeta and J. Jones (eds.), *The Rome Statute of the ICC: A commentary* (vol. I, Oxford University Press, Oxford 2002), pp. 850–1.

[15] See, most recently, *Oric* Trial Judgment (n. 10) para. 293; B. Burghardt, *Die Vorgesetztenverantwortlichkeit im völkerrechtlichen Straftatsystem* (BWV, Berlin 2008), pp. 261 *et seq.*, 461, 464; R. Kolb, 'Droit international pénal', in R. Kolb (ed.), *Droit international pénal* (Helbing Lichtenhahn, Bâle 2008), p. 185.

[16] For the similarity to the employer's criminal responsibility see Ambos (n. 14) 844 *et seq.*; also E. van Sliedregt, *The Criminal Responsibility of Individuals for Violation of International Humanitarian Law* (TMC Asser Press, The Hague 2003), p. 352; C. Meloni, 'Command responsibility: mode of liability for the crimes of subordinates or separate offence of the superior?' (2007) 5 JICJ 628 *et seq.* On the '*objet de la responsabilité du supérieur*' see also *Hadzihasanovic* Trial Judgment (n. 9) para. 67 *et seq.* (69). For an

intervene is put on an equal footing with (accomplice) liability for not adequately supervising the subordinates and not reporting their crimes. In fact, recent case law takes the position that the superior is charged with his failure to comply with the duty of supervision[17] but this responsibility still seems to be understood as a direct one (as a principal) instead of downgrading it to accomplice liability. This is but one of the problems of the doctrine with regard to the principle of culpability.[18]

Responsibility for omission presupposes a *duty to act* of a person with a specific position of a 'guarantor' (*Garantenstellung und – pflicht*). This duty justifies the moral equivalence between the failure to prevent harm and the active causation of harm. As to command responsibility, it is supported by case law, scholarly writings and now, with Article 28 of the ICC Statute, regulated by statute. In essence, the status of the superior as a guarantor flows from his/her responsibility for a certain area of competence and certain subordinates (see Article 1 of the Hague Convention of 1907 and Article 4(A)(2) of the Geneva Convention III of 1949). The superior possesses the status of a *supervising guarantor* with duties to observance and control vis-à-vis his/her subordinates who constitute a potential source of danger or risk.[19] These duties are defined in Article 87

innovative distinction between four forms of superior responsibility (knowledge superior responsibility before the fact, knowledge superior responsibility after the fact; lack-of-knowledge superior responsibility before the fact, lack-of-knowledge superior responsibility after the fact) with different liability with regard to the conduct of the subordinates and the result produced by this conduct recently, V. Nerlich, 'Superior responsibility under Art 28 ICC Statute: for what exactly is the superior held responsible?' (2007) 5 JICJ 667–8 and *passim*.

[17] *Prosecutor v Krnojelac*, IT-97–25, Judgment, Appeals Chamber (17 September 2003) para. 171: 'It cannot be overemphasized that, where superior responsibility is concerned, an accused is not charged with the crimes of his subordinates but with his failure to carry out his duty to exercise control.'

[18] For this reason the German International Criminal Law Code (*Völkerstrafgesetzbuch*, Bundesgesetzblatt 2002 I 2254; for an English translation see http://jura.uni-goettingen.de/k.ambos/Forschung/laufende_Projekte_Translation.html, accessed 22 March 2007) distinguishes between liability as a *perpetrator* (principal) for the failure to prevent the subordinates' crimes (section 4) and *accomplice liability* for the (intentional or negligent) failure to properly supervise the subordinates (section 13) and to report the crimes (section 14); concurring A. Cassese, *International Criminal Law* (2nd edn, Oxford University Press, Oxford 2008), pp. 244–47; Meloni (n. 16) 637 with n. 108.

[19] Cf. T. Weigend, '*Bemerkungen zur Vorgesetzenverantwortlichkeit im Völkerstrafrecht*' (2004) 116 ZStW 1004, 1013. See also Burghardt (n. 15) 186 *et seq.*, 192; H. Olásolo, *Unlawful Attacks in Combat Situations* (Martinus Nijhoff, Leiden 2008), p. 193. According to O. Triffterer, 'Command responsibility' – *crimen sui generis* or participation 'as otherwise provided' in Art. 28 ICC Statute in J. Arnold *et al.* (eds.), *Festschrift für Albin Eser* (Beck, München 2005), p. 910, the duty is based on the requirement of effective control.

of the Additional Protocol I to the Geneva Conventions of 1977 ('AP I') in relation with Article 43(1) AP I. Accordingly, military commanders are obliged to prevent, suppress and report breaches of the Conventions and AP I by members of their armed forces and other persons under their control (Article 87(1) AP I). In a way, one can speak of a legal or positive duty to act, since the duty to act is based on a positive norm of treaty law which, in addition, is regarded as customary law. This general duty to act is complemented by the various specific rules of positive conduct as laid down in the AP I.[20] Although these rules were initially addressed only to state parties, they have always served as conduct rules for individuals and for prosecution of individual violators;[21] in any case, they must now be considered the basis of rules of responsibility for an individual's failure to act, since the doctrine of superior responsibility and the major part of the offences established by the Geneva law (including AP I) have been 'individualized' by the ICC Statute and by national implementation laws.

The minimum requirement of command responsibility is that the superior concerned have *command*,[22] based on a *de iure* or *de facto* position of superiority.[23] A superior with command and authority normally *controls* his/her subordinates, but this control (command, authority) has to be '*effective*'.[24] This is not a mechanical, naturalistic but a highly normative standard.[25] For the control requirement is an element

[20] J. de Preux, 'Commentary on Articles 86 and 87 of Protocol Additional I', in Y. Sandoz, C. Swinarski and B. Zimmermann (eds.), *Commentary on the Additional Protocols of 8 June 1988 to the Geneva Conventions of 12 August 1949* (Nijhoff, Geneva 1986) mn 3536; Burghardt (n. 15) 187 *et seq.*

[21] Cf. C. Greenwood in D. Fleck (ed.), *The Handbook of International Humanitarian Law* (2nd edn, Oxford University Press, Oxford 2008) mn 134.

[22] On the sources of *de iure* command, see I. Bantekas, 'The contemporary law of superior responsibility' (1999) 93 AJIL 578–9. For a detailed analysis of the *de facto* command and its preconditions, see Burghardt (n. 15) 108 *et seq.*, 152 *et seq.*

[23] Most recently, *Oric* Trial Judgment (n. 10) para. 309; *Mrksic* Trial Judgment (n. 9) para. 560; *Prosecutor v Karera*, ICTR-01-74, Judgment, Trial Chamber I (7 December 2007) para. 564.

[24] *Delalic* Trial Judgment (n. 9) para. 378; concurring Judgment, *Delalic et al.*, IT-96-21, Judgment, Appeals Chamber (20 February 2002) para. 346; *Aleksovski* Trial Judgment (n. 9) para. 76; *Blaskic* Trial Judgment (n. 9) paras. 301, 335; *Bradjanin* Trial Judgment (n. 9) para. 276; *Oric* Trial Judgment (n. 10) para. 311; *Mrksic* Trial Judgment (n. 9) para. 560; *Strugar* Trial Judgment (n. 9) para. 362; *Karera* Trial Judgment (n. 23) para. 564; *Hadzihasanovic* Appeals Judgment (n. 13) para. 21. See also I. Bantekas (n. 22) 580; M. Osiel, 'Modes of participation in mass atrocity' (2005) 39 *Cornell International Law Journal* 795–6; M. Osiel, 'The banality of the good: aligning incentives against mass atrocity' (2005) 105 *Columbia Law Review* 1774 *et seq.*; Olásolo (n. 19) 190 *et seq.* See also the critical overview of the ICTY case law by Burghard (n. 15) 156 *et seq.*, 181 *et seq.*

[25] See also Osiel (n. 24) (*Columbia Law Review*) 1779.

of the objective imputation of the crimes to the superior and modern theories understand this imputation normatively.[26]

While it is clear that the form of control may differ according to the position of the superior,[27] the standard must be concretely determined on a case-by-case basis. In fact, the case law has developed certain criteria that indicate to some extent the degree of control necessary, for example the power to issue orders or to take disciplinary action.[28] Yet fine points are controversial: for example, whether a direct control of subordinates is necessary or whether this control can be mediated by other superiors/subordinates and to what extent the superior must be able to identify the subordinates.[29] In any case, the superior's liability for her omission stands and falls – on an objective level – with her effective authority and control: the possibility of control forms the legal and legitimate basis of the superior's responsibility; it justifies her duty of intervention. Article 28 of the ICC Statute requires that the crimes of the subordinates be 'a *result*' of the superior's 'failure to exercise control properly', i.e. – setting aside the ICTY case law[30] – a *causal relationship* between the superior's failure and the subordinate's commission of crimes must exist. The causality requirement also follows from the fact that the underlying crimes of the subordinates constitute the point of reference of the superior's failure of supervision, i.e. the occurrence of the crimes was 'caused' by the failure of supervision.[31]

The superior must take the necessary and reasonable measures to *prevent* the criminal acts of his subordinates *or punish* them. These are two distinct duties, the former being the primary one with respect to future crimes and the latter being subsidiary with respect to past crimes.[32] The

[26] See, for the development from *imputatio facti* to normative imputation, K. Ambos, *Der Allgemeine Teil des Völkerstrafrechts* (Duncker und Humboldt, Berlin reprint 2004), p. 557 *et seq.*; K. Ambos, *La Parte General del Derecho Penal Internacional* (Temis, Bogotá 2006), p. 143 *et seq.*

[27] See Osiel (n. 24) (*Cornell International Law Journal*) 796.

[28] For a summary of the case law, see *Oric* Trial Judgment (n. 10) para. 312.

[29] For a broad interpretation on both points, see *Oric* Trial Judgment (n. 10) para. 311. The defence in this case required the 'identification of the person(s) who committed the crimes' (quoted in (n. 10) para. 315).

[30] See recently, with further references, *Oric* Trial Judgment (n. 10) para. 338. See also the critical analysis by Burghardt (n. 15) 206 *et seq.*

[31] Osiel (n. 24) (Columbia Law Review) 1779 *et seq.*; Olásolo (n. 19) 190; see also Meloni (n. 16) 629–30; Nerlich (n. 16) 673, arguing for a risk-increase-standard (following Ambos (n. 14) 860); Kolb (n. 15) 189. See also the different approach adopted by Burghardt (n. 15) 215 *et seq.* (219), 225, 261 *et seq.*, 405, 463 *et seq.*

[32] *Oric* Trial Judgment (n. 10) para. 326, with further references to the case law.

duty is triggered by the awareness of the crimes[33] or reasonable suspicion as to the commission of past crimes.[34] The type of countermeasure depends on the circumstances of each case, criteria being, for example, the degree of effective control, the gravity of the crime, etc.[35] Concrete measures include giving special orders for seeking compliance with the law of war, investigating alleged crimes, protesting against criminal action, reporting to competent authorities, etc.[36] While with regard to the duty to *prevent* (future) crimes, the commander must be in control at the moment of the possible commission (principle of coincidence) – otherwise he will not be able to prevent them – the duty to *punish* also arises for earlier crimes, i.e., crimes committed under the former commander but subsequently known to his successor who therefore has the duty to punish the subordinates.[37] As the duty to punish is a distinct and independent duty which operates *ex post* – i.e. after the subordinates' crimes but at a moment when the new commander is already in charge – it does not make sense, contrary to the Appeals Chamber's view,[38] to apply the coincidence principle to this duty. In addition, this would have the consequence that these crimes remain unpunished, i.e. the subordinates would benefit from the former superior's failure to supervise them adequately.

The nature or scope of the *crimes of the subordinates* is controversial. The Oric Trial Chamber, relying on a former decision,[39] recently argued for a broad liability of the superior with regard to all acts or omissions of the subordinates, be it direct acts (e.g. torture, maltreatment), forms of participation (instigating, aiding or abetting) or omissions[40] with regard to inchoate or completed crimes.[41] The Chamber justifies this broad liability with the purpose of superior responsibility which is to impose on commanders an affirmative duty 'to ensure that subordinates do not violate international humanitarian law, either by harmful acts or by omitting a protective duty'.[42] As to the omission situation the Chamber refers

[33] *Oric* Trial Judgment (n. 10) para. 328. [34] *Oric* Trial Judgment (n. 10) para. 336.
[35] *Oric* Trial Judgment (n. 10) paras. 329–30. [36] *Oric* Trial Judgment (n. 10) para. 331.
[37] *Oric* Trial Judgment (n. 10) paras. 327, 335.
[38] *Hadzihasanovic*, Jurisdiction Appeal Decision para. 37 *et seq.*, 51.
[39] *Prosecutor v Boskoski and Tarculovski*, Decision on Prosecution's motion to amend the indictment, IT-04-82-PT (26 May 2006) paras. 18 *et seq.*
[40] *Oric* Trial Judgment (n. 10) para. 298 *et seq.*
[41] *Oric* Trial Judgment (n. 10) paras. 328, 334 with further references to the inconsistent case law. The judgment was, however, reversed since the T. ch. failed to resolve the issue of whether *Oric*'s subordinate incurred criminal responsibility, *Oric* Appeals Judgment (n. 9) paras. 36 *et seq.* (47).
[42] *Oric* Trial Judgment (n. 10) para. 300.

to cases where the subordinates 'are under a protective duty to shield certain persons from being injured, as in the case of detainees kept in custody'. If these persons are injured due to a failure of protection by these subordinates, their superior incurs responsibility for these culpable omissions.[43] The approach of the Chamber is not free from doubt.[44] First, it is questionable whether a 'possibility of a different interpretation'[45] with regard to the meaning of 'committed' in Art. 7(3) of the ICTY Statute (or, *mutatis mutandi*, in Art. 28 ICC Statute) can support the Chamber's extensive interpretation to the detriment of the accused. This interpretation may conflict with the principle of legality, in particular in its form of *nullum crimen sine lege stricta* (prohibition of analogy), since it entails a broadening of the scope of the liability of the superior which is not clearly covered by the wording of Art. 7(3). On the contrary, a closer look at the meaning of committed as a form of individual criminal responsibility in Art. 7 of the ICTY Statute shows that committed is understood as a form of direct perpetration besides other forms of participation listed as 'planned, instigated, ordered… or *otherwise* aided and abetted' in Art. 7(1); even if one construes 'committed' as including indirect perpetration (through another person)[46] the wording clearly indicates that aiding and abetting is not covered by 'committed'. Article 25(3) of the ICC Statute similarly conceives committing a crime as a form of direct (co) perpetration or perpetration through another person (sub-para. (a)) to be distinguished from other forms of participation such as 'orders, solicits or induces' (sub-para. (b)) or 'aids, abets or otherwise assists' (sub-para. (c)). In addition, in the ICTY's case law the term 'committing' has been construed as meaning 'physically perpetrating a crime or engendering a culpable omission'.[47] The relatively clear wording of Art. 7(3) regarding the scope of the crimes to be 'committed' by the subordinates cannot be outweighed by a teleological interpretation, invoking an alleged purpose of the command responsibility doctrine. Even if one accepted the purpose argument as such, assuming, for the sake of argument, that the literal

[43] *Oric* Trial Judgment (n. 10) para. 305.

[44] See also the Appeals Brief by V. Vidovic and J. Jones, filed on 16 October 2006, para. 340 *et seq*.

[45] *Oric* Trial Judgment (n. 10) para. 299.

[46] See nn. 85 *et seq*. below and main text.

[47] *Prosecutor v Tadic*, IT-94-1, Judgment, Appeals Chamber (15 July 1999) para. 188; *Prosecutor v Kunarac/Kovac*, IT-96-23-T & IT-96-23/1-T, Judgment, Trial Chamber (22 February 2001) para. 390; *Prosecutor v Krstić*, IT-98-33, Judgment, Trial Chamber (2 August 2001) para. 601; *Prosecutor v Kvočka et al.*, IT-98-30/1, Judgment, Trial Chamber (2 November 2001) para. 243.

interpretation is inconclusive, it is highly dubious if such a broad purpose can be read into the command responsibility doctrine. It would convert a military commander into a quasi-policeman with a general responsibility for law and order in the zone under his command and it would find little support in state practice. Thus, in the end it would be counterproductive, since states, especially the ones engaged in armed conflicts all over the world, would refrain from applying this concept in their military law and practice.

Article 28 has a peculiar structure in that it extends the superior's *mens rea,* beyond his or her own failure to supervise, to the concrete acts of the subordinates.[48] The degree of *mens rea* required is, apart from awareness of the aforementioned effective control[49] and knowledge explicitly mentioned in Art. 7(3) ICTY, Art. 6(3) ICTR and Art. 28(a)(i), (b)(i) ICC Statute, *conscious negligence or advertent recklessness.* This already follows from the wording of Art. 86(2) AP I ('had information which should have enabled them to conclude') which has been correctly interpreted as *conscious ignorance* in the sense of *wilful blindness.*[50] Similarly, the 'should have known' and 'consciously disregarded' standards of Art. 28(1)(a) and (2)(a) require, on the one hand, neither awareness, nor suffices, on the other, the imputation of knowledge on the basis of purely objective facts. In essence, the superior must possess *information* that enables him or her to conclude that the subordinates are committing crimes[51] or at least indicates the need for additional investigation in order to ascertain the commission of offences,[52] i.e. the superior must, in the sense of the ICTY/ICTR case law,[53] have reason to know. In other words, he should have known and the reason-to-know

[48] On the issue of the commission of (subordinates') crimes of intent by negligence, see already Ambos (n. 14) 852–3; see also Nerlich (n. 16) 676, 680, 682 arguing for a parallel structure of liability between the superior and the subordinates on the basis of a distinction between the subordinate's conduct ('base crime') and the result produced by this conduct.

[49] For this additional requirement correctly, *Oric* Trial Judgment (n. 10) para. 316.

[50] J. de Preux, 'Commentary on Articles 86 and 87 of Protocol Additional I' in Y. Sandoz, C. Swinarski and B. Zimmermann (eds.), *Commentary on the Additional Protocols of 8 June 1988 to the Geneva Conventions of 12 August 1949* (Martinus Nijhoff, Geneva 1986) mn 3545–46.

[51] See Ambos (n. 14) 868–7, and 870 with further references. Confirmed recently by *Oric* Trial Judgment (n. 10) para. 321.

[52] Cf. (n. 13) and *Oric* Trial Judgment (n. 10) para. 322 with further references to the abundant case law and examples of such information in para. 323.

[53] See n. 9 above with main text.

standards are, in substance, identical.[54] There is, however, a difference between the standards applicable to a military and a civilian superior but it is only one of degree: while the military superior must take any information seriously, the civilian one must only react to information which 'clearly' indicates the commission of crimes;[55] this latter standard is one of conscious negligence or recklessness (as more clearly expressed by the French version of Art. 28(b)(i) ICC Statute: '*delibérément negligé de tenir compte d'informations qui l'indiquaient clairement*'),[56] yet the former one requires – contrary to the interpretation given by the case law[57] – less, i.e. any form of negligence, including an unconscious one.

III. Command responsibility and JCE compared

As an analysis of JCE and command responsibility shows, the two doctrines differ fundamentally in their conceptual structure. The most striking difference is possibly that JCE requires a *positive act* or contribution to the enterprise while for command responsibility an *omission* suffices. From this perspective the doctrines seem to be mutually exclusive: either a person contributes to a criminal result by a positive act or omits to prevent a criminal result from happening. Both at the same time seem, at first sight, to be logically impossible. However, a closer look reveals that in the context of macro-criminality where criminal conduct develops over different time periods and in different geographical locations there may be cases in which the superior actively participates in a JCE and simultaneously omits to intervene in the execution of the crimes committed by the subordinates within the framework of this JCE.

Another important difference between command responsibility and JCE lies in the fact that the former requires, *per definitionem*, a superior and subordinates, i.e. a *hierarchical, vertical relationship* between the person whose duty it is to supervise and the ones who directly commit the

[54] See already Ambos (n. 14) 864; concurring U. Roßkopf, *Die innere Tatseite des Völkerrechtsverbrechens* (Berliner Wissenschafts-Verlag, Berlin 2007), p. 174.

[55] For a higher threshold for a superior 'exercising more informal types of authority', see also *Oric* Trial Judgment (n. 10) para. 320.

[56] For a detailed analysis, see Ambos (n. 14) 863 *et seq.*; recently Meloni (n. 16) 634. It goes too far, however, to read into the should have known a 'duty of knowledge' standard and justify this strict standard with retributive and utilitarian arguments (J.S. Martinez, 'Understanding mens rea in command responsibility: from Yamashita to Blaskic and beyond' (2007) 5 JICJ 660 *et seq.*; convincingly against this standard see Bonafé (n. 12) 606–7.

[57] *Prosecutor v Bagilishema*, Judgment (Reasons), Appeals Chamber (3 July 2002) para. 35; concurring *Blaskić* Appeals Judgment (n. 9) para. 63.

crimes to be prevented by the supervisor. By contrast, the members of a JCE, at least of a JCE I understood as co-perpetration, normally belong to the same hierarchical level and operate in a *coordinated, horizontal way.*[58] In this sense, neither 'any showing of superior responsibility'[59] nor the 'position of a political leader' is required.[60] As a rule, JCE requires 'a minimum of coordination' and this minimum is 'represented as a horizontal expression of will' which binds the participants together.[61] However, the amplitude and elasticity of the doctrine allows for informal networks and loose relationships and as such stretches well beyond command responsibility.[62] A third difference refers to the *mental object* of JCE and command responsibility. By JCE I, the participant shares the intent of the other participants, i.e. the common *mens rea* refers to the commission of specific crimes and to the ultimate objective or goal of the enterprise; in the other categories, especially JCE III, the participant must, at least, be aware of the common objective or purpose and of the (objective) foresee ability of the commission of certain crimes. In contrast, in the case of command responsibility, the main object of the offence is the superior's failure to properly supervise and, consequently, his/her *mens rea* needs to extend to this failure but not (necessarily) to the crimes committed by the subordinates.

Despite these (and other) conceptual differences, the two doctrines are sometimes *simultaneously applied* in the case law.[63] A prerequisite for this simultaneous application is that the accused possesses a certain rank in the hierarchy of the criminal apparatus. In other words, the simultaneous application of both doctrines presupposes that *hierarchical differences* between members of a given criminal enterprise exist. Thus, the structural difference between JCE and command responsibility mentioned above – hierarchy versus coordination – loses importance. In fact, this difference is only valid with regard to JCE I, understood as a form of co-perpetration and as such typically characterized by a horizontal relationship between the co-perpetrators. In contrast, in cases of JCE II or III, a middle or high ranking superior may support or further a criminal enterprise and at the same time fail to control his criminal

[58] See on this structural difference, also Osiel (n. 24) (*Cornell International Law Journal*) 797 and Osiel (n. 24) (*Columbia Law Review*) 1769 *et seq.*

[59] *Prosecutor v Kvočka et al.*, IT-98–30/1, Judgment, Appeals Chamber (28 February 2005) para. 104.

[60] *Prosectuor v Babić*, IT-03–72, Sentencing Judgment, Trial Chamber (29 June 2004) para. 60.

[61] *Perreira*, Judgment, East Timor Special Panel for Serious Crimes (27 April 2005) 19–20, available at www.jsmp.minihub.org/Court%20Monitoring/spsccaseinformation2003.htm, accessed 2 July 2008.

[62] Osiel (n. 24) (*Columbia Law Review*) 1786 *et seq.*

[63] Ambos (n. 8) 162 *et seq.*

subordinates. This also shows that the antagonism between a positive act and an omission, indicated above, does only apply, strictly speaking, to single crimes but not to collective commissions. Collective JCE (II or III) is characterized by the interaction of various persons at different hierarchical levels.[64] The prosecution benefits from the *evidentiary advantages* of both doctrines: instead of proving a direct commission of crimes by the superior, it suffices to prove a crime base or pattern of commission and link the superior to it.[65] The structural similarity between JCE III and command responsibility becomes obvious with regard to the *mental state* necessary for conviction: both doctrines enable the Prosecution to downgrade the specific intent (in genocide) to a lower mental state, either foresee ability (JCE III) or negligence (command responsibility). The *Milošević* Trial Chamber extended this approach, developed by the *Brdanin* Appeals Chamber with regard to JCE III, to command responsibility.[66] Similarly, the *Krstić* Trial Chamber, with regard to command responsibility, only required that the accused 'had been aware of the genocidal objectives' of the main perpetrators.[67] This means that both a participant in a JCE III and a commander in the sense of Art. 7(3) ICTY Statute can be held responsible for genocide without having the specific genocidal intent themselves; mere knowledge of the *dolus specialis* of the actual *genocidaires* would be sufficient. This, again, shows that the common ground of JCE and command responsibility is the need or desire to overcome evidentiary problems,[68] in the case of genocide typically

[64] Similarly, V. Haan, 'The development of the concept of JCE at the ICTY' (2005) 5 ICLR 196, considering that most cases before the ICTY are of this nature.

[65] About the advantages of the Prosecution, see also K. Gustafson, 'The requirement of an "express agreement" for joint criminal enterprise liability' (2007) 5 JICJ 137: 'ability to connect a defendant, who did not physically perpetrate certain crimes, to these crimes by encompassing the defendant and the perpetrators within a single common criminal group.' The whole argument of this author is directed towards a successful prosecution and, consequently, conviction of the suspects, see also p. 158: 'If the Trial Chamber's conclusions … are upheld, the prosecution is unlikely to be successful.'

[66] *Prosecutor v Brdanin*, Decision on Interlocutory Appeals, Appeals Chamber (19 March 2004) para. 6; *Prosecutor v Milošević*, IT-02–54, Decision on Motion for Judgment of Acquittal, Trial Chamber (16 June 2004) paras. 291, 292, 300. On this issue, see more detailed Ambos (n. 8) 175–6, 181.

[67] *Krstić* Trial Judgment (n. 47) para. 648; contrary the Appeals Chamber, IT-98–33-A (19 April 2004) para. 134: 'Krstić was aware of the intent to commit genocide on the part of some members of the VRS Main Staff… This knowledge on his part alone cannot support an inference of genocidal intent.' Thus, the Chamber (para. 135 *et seq.*) only convicted Krstic of aiding and abetting genocide for which awareness of the genocidal intent is sufficient (para 140: 'knowing the intent behind the crime').

[68] In a similar vein, Danner and Martinez (n. 12) 152.

represented by the high threshold of a special, ulterior intent. Yet, such an approach, in the final result, means that a superior is, on the basis of JCE or command responsibility, no longer punished as a (co-)perpetrator but only as a mere aider or abettor, since only in this case could knowledge with regard to a specific intent crime – instead of specific intent on the part of the perpetrator himself – be considered sufficient.[69]

As to the future case law of the ICC, it is important to note that command responsibility is clearly provided for in Art. 28 ICC Statute while JCE is not explicitly contained in Art. 25 ICC Statute. As has been explained elsewhere,[70] while JCE I and II, understood as co-perpetration, may be contained in Art. 25(3)(a) ICC Statute,[71] the same cannot be said for JCE III with regard to Art. 25(3)(d) ICC Statute. Although it may be possible to include JCE III in Art. 25(3)(d)(i) given that the volitional element of this subparagraph ('aim of furthering the criminal activity') is not incompatible with the cognitive standard of foreseeability,[72] in any case the contribution to the collective crime must be 'intentional' (Art. 25(3)(d) clause 1) and this requires more than mere foreseeability;[73]

[69] See already K. Ambos, 'Some preliminary reflections on the *mens rea* requirements of the crimes of the ICC Statute and of the elements of crimes', in L. C. Vohrah *et al.* (eds.), *Man's Inhumanity to Man: Essays in Honour of Antonio Cassese* (Kluwer, The Hague 2003), pp. 23–4.

[70] Ambos (n. 8) 172–3.

[71] The ICC Pre-Trial Chamber apparently takes a different view, see Decision on the Confirmation of Charges, *Prosecutor v Thomas Lubanga Dyilo,* ICC-01/04-01/06-803, Pre-Trial Chamber I (29 January 2007) para. 323: 'the concept of co-perpetration pursuant to Article 25(3)(a) of the Statute differs from that of co-perpetration based on the existence of a joint criminal enterprise.' The Chamber understands JCE as co-perpetration in a subjective sense focusing on the mental state with which the participant makes his contribution (para. 329).

[72] In this sense, J. D. Ohlin, 'Three conceptual problems with the doctrine of Joint Criminal Enterprise' (2007) 5 JICJ 85. van Sliedregt (n. 108) discusses whether JCE II could be included in Art. 25(d)(ii) with regard to the participants belonging to the medium level of the organization if they knew of the system of mistreatment.

[73] The counter-argument by A. Cassese, 'The proper limits of individual responsibility under the doctrine of joint criminal enterprise' (2007) 5 JICJ 132, based on an extensive interpretation of the term 'intentional' ('requiring that the intent be referred to the common criminal plan, and, as such, may also embrace acts performed by one of the participants outside that criminal plan') conflicts with the principle of legality, in particular with the prohibition of analogy provided for in Art. 22(2) ICC Statute. Even more obvious is a violation of the principle if one extends the term 'knowledge' in Art. 25(3)(d)(ii) to 'foresight and voluntary taking of a risk'. The apparent contradiction between 'intention' and 'foreseeability' can only be resolved if one distinguishes between the object of reference of the intention required in Art. 25(3)(d): while the concrete contribution of the participant to the collective crime may be intentional, he or she is not acting intentionally with regard to the excessive acts of the members of the group or JCE but these would only be 'foreseeable' to her.

in addition, given the similarity between the responsibility based on JCE III and '*conspiracy*', the inclusion of the former in Art. 25(3)(d) could hardly be reconciled with the will of the ICC Statute's drafter who wanted to exclude conspiracy liability from the Statute.

IV. The doctrine of *Organisationsherrschaft* as an alternative form of attribution

Apart from JCE and command responsibility, the theory of *control/domination of the act by virtue of a hierarchical organization* (*Organisationsherrschaft*),[74] pursues the same objective of linking superiors to crimes committed on their behalf.[75] The notion underpinning this approach is that principals to a crime are not limited to those who physically carry out the objective elements of the offence, but also include those who, in spite of being away from the scene of the crime, control or mastermind its commission because they decide whether and sometimes even how the offence will be committed.[76] Accordingly, the 'man in the background' dominates the direct perpetrators by means of an organizational apparatus of hierarchical power. Thus, the theory is based on a concept of *control or domination of the act* (*Tatherrschaft*),[77] recently

[74] See the fundamental work of C. Roxin, *Täterschaft und Tatherrschaft* (8th edn, De Gruyter, Berlin 2006), pp. 242–52, 704–17; see also Ambos (n. 26) 590 *et seq.* (*Allgemeine Teil),* 216 *et seq.* (*Parte General)* with references on the recent (critical) discussion; see also Ambos, *Internationales Strafrecht* (2nd edn, Beck, Munich 2008) § 7 mn 29 *et seq.*; H. Radtke, Mittelbare Täterschaft kraft *Organisationsherrschaft* im nationalen und internationalen Strafrecht (2006) GA 350 *et seq.*; J. Schlösser, Organisationsherrschaft durch Tun und Unterlassen (2006) GA 161 *et seq.*; J. Wessels and W. Beulke, *Strafrecht Allgemeiner Teil* (37th edn, Müller, Heidelberg 2007) 193 *et seq.* For a good explanation in English, see Osiel (n. 24) (*Columbia Law Review*) 1829 *et seq.*

[75] See also E. van Sliedregt, 'Joint criminal enterprise as a pathway to convicting individuals for genocide' (2007) 5 JICJ 207, acknowledging that 'indirect perpetration would offer an escape from the restraints that a purpose-based approach to genocidal intent and principles of derivative liability would impose on prosecution the mastermind'. About the Dutch concept of 'functional perpetration' as another alternative of imputation, see H. van der Wilt, 'Joint criminal enterprise: possibilities and limitations' (2007) 5 JICJ 102 *et seq.*

[76] Cf. *Prosecutor v Lubanga* (n. 71) para. 330.

[77] M.D. Dubber, 'Criminalizing complicity' (2007) 5 JICJ 982 translates it as 'dominion over the act'. His criticism of this concept, partly based on a comparison with the common law concept of 'presence' (Dubber, 983, 1001), however, does not sufficiently account for the fact that C. Roxin himself considers it only as an 'open notion' (Roxin (n. 74) 122 *et seq.*, 282 *et seq.*) and thus merely a normative starting point to develop the forms of perpetration more concretely (cf. Ambos (n. 26) 546 *et seq.*).

recognized by the ICC Pre-Trial Chamber.[78] It is a form of perpetration by means and as such recognized in Art. 25(3)(a) 3rd alternative ('through another person').[79] It has been applied in various national proceedings (Eichmann,[80] Argentinean Generals,[81] East German border killings[82])[83] and may be identified in the Nuremberg *Justice* case.[84] At the ICC, the Katanga Pre-Trial Chamber now develops this control over the crime approach even further.[84a] In fact, unlike JCE, it finds a legal basis in the term 'committed' in Art. 7(1) ICTY Statute, since 'commission' in this sense means that a person 'participated, physically or otherwise directly or *indirectly*, in the material elements of the crime charged through positive acts or, based on a duty to act, omissions, whether individually or

[78] See *Prosecutor v Lubanga* (n. 71) para. 322, where the co-perpetration in the sense of Art. 25(3)(a) ICC Statute is characterized by the 'joint control over the crime as a result of the essential contribution' (para. 322), and based on the 'concept of control over the crime' (para. 338). But see also the recent criticism against the doctrine of *Tatherrschaft* in Germany: E.-J. Lampe, 'Tätersysteme: Spuren und Strukturen' (2007) 119 ZStW 475 *et seq.*; V. Haas, 'Kritik der Tatherrschaftslehre' (2007) 119 ZStW 523 *et seq.*

[79] Concurring G. Werle, *Principles of International Criminal Law* (TMC Asser Press, The Hague 2005), p. 124 with n. 196; G. Werle, 'Individual criminal responsibility in art 25 ICC Statute' (2007) 5 JICJ 963–4.

[80] Jerusalem District Court (12 December 1961) 36 ILR 236–37 para. 197.

[81] Cámara Nacional de Apelaciones en lo Criminal y Correccional de la Capital (9 December 1985) 309-I/II Coleccion Oficial de Fallos de la Corte Suprema de Justicia de la Nacion ('Fallos') 1601–2.

[82] BGHSt 40, 218 (Official collection of the Supreme Court judgments in criminal matters) 236 *et seq.* = BGH (1994) NJW 2703; for the subsequent case law see BGHSt 45, 270, 296; BGHSt 48, 331; BGHSt 49, 147; BGH, (2004) NStZ 457, 458 and NStZ 2008, 89.

[83] See also the case law in Chile (*Letelier/Mofitt, Juez de Instrucción Bañados* (12 November 1993) Fallos del Mes, año XXXV, noviembre 1993, edición suplementaria; CSJ, 30 May and 6 June 1995), Colombia (Corte Suprema de Justicia, Sala Penal, casación n° 23825 del 7 de marzo de 2007, *Magistrado Ponente Javier Zapata Ortiz*) and Peru (Sala Penal Nacional, caso *Abimael Guzmán Reinoso et al.*, sentencia del 13 de octubre de 2006, expediente acumulado 560-03). See also K. Ambos, 'Individual criminal responsibility in international criminal law: a jurisprudential analysis – from Nuremberg to the Hague', in G. K. McDonald and O. Swaak-Goldmann (eds.), *Substantive and Procedural Aspects of International Criminal Law: The Experience of International and National Courts, vol. I, Commentary* (Kluwer, The Hague 2000), pp. 1-31. For a recent comparative analysis see K. Ambos (ed.), *Imputación de crímienes de los subordinados al dirigente* (Temis, Bogotá 2008) with reports on Argentina, Chile, Colombia, Germany, Peru and Spain.

[84] *US v Altstoetter et al.* (*Justice Trial*), Judgment, US Military Tribunal sitting at Nuremberg (4 December 1947) in Trials of War Criminals (US-GPO, 1947) 985: 'conscious participation in a nationwide government-*organized system* of cruelty and injustice' (emphasis added).

[84a] *Prosecutor v Katanga and Ngudjolo Chui*, Decision on the confirmation of charges, Case No. ICC-011 04-01107, 30 Sept. 2008, para. 480 *et seq.*

jointly with others'.[85] This includes, as indirect commission, perpetration by means[86] and as such *Organisationsherrschaft*. Clearly, the key issue of this doctrine is whether the mastermind is able to exercise effective *control* over the direct perpetrators by means of the organizational apparatus created and dominated by him. Yet, while the 'man in the background' will hardly be able to completely control the responsible perpetrators, this lack of control may be compensated by the control of the apparatus, which produces an unlimited number of potential willing executors. In other words, although direct perpetrators acting with full criminal responsibility cannot be considered mere 'interchangeable mediators of the act' (*fungible Tatmittler*) as such, the 'system' provides for a practically unlimited number of replacements and thereby for a high degree of flexibility as far as the personnel necessary to commit the crimes is concerned. While such a concept of control rests on the assumption that the apparatus functions hierarchically from top to bottom and one may question the applicability of this assumption to all kinds of criminal organizations,[87] a too naturalistic or mechanical perspective distorts the *normative basis* of this theory. Still, the doctrine requires further elaboration and I will therefore deal with two fundamental questions in this regard: the tension between the domination of the organization and the liberty of the immediate or direct perpetrator (below, section 1) and the delimitation of (indirect) perpetration through another person and co-perpetration along levels of hierarchy (below, section 2).

1. *Domination of the organization versus freedom of the immediate perpetrator*

According to the doctrine of *Organisationsherrschaft* the immediate perpetrators are nothing more than interchangeable cogs in the machine of the organizational apparatus of hierarchical power. Their interchangeability makes the apparent freedom of the immediate perpetrator a naturalistic date which from a normative perspective is of no importance. For it does not matter who executes the act but only that it is executed at all. For

[85] *Stakić* Trial Judgment, IT-97–24-T (31 July 2003) para. 439 (emphasis added).

[86] *Stakić* Trial Judgment (n. 85) para. 439 with n. 942, para. 741. See on *Stakić*, Haan (n. 64) 197; H. Olásolo and C. Pérez, 'The notion of control of the crime and its application by the ICTY in the Stakic case' (2004) 4 ICLR 475 *et seq.* (478–9).

[87] Critical Osiel (n. 24) (*Columbia Law Review*) 1833 *et seq.*, 1861, arguing for an application of *Organisationsherrschaft* only to relax the effective control requirement of command responsibility.

the man in the background who gives the order to execute certain acts it is of no interest who complies with his orders but only that it is complied with at all. Thus, the former Chilean dictator *Pinochet* stated with regard to his giving orders to Manuel *Contreras,* the former Chilean chief of the secret police DINA:

> there are many things I ordered him to do, but which things? I had to exercise power. But I could never say that I was actually running DINA. [They] were under the orders, under the supervision of all of the junta, the four members of the junta ... And I would like you to understand the following. The chief of the army always asks 'What are you going to do?' The question of '*How*', 'how am I going to do it?' is a question for the chief of intelligence rather than the Chief of the Army. This is what civilians ... don't understand.[88]

Thus, it is irrelevant 'how' and 'by whom' the order will be executed if only the mastermind can be sure that it will be executed by someone somehow. The automatic functioning of the apparatus accounts for the domination of the immediate perpetration and, apparently, over the immediate perpetrators too. Their secondary perpetration remains morally indifferent.[89] Certainly, the whole idea of a domination or control of the act by virtue of a hierarchical organization stands and falls with criterion of interchangeablility (*Fungibilität*). For if one assumes that the man in the background cannot rely any more on the automatic execution of his orders then his domination over the act would fail in the face of this insecurity and the freedom of the immediate perpetrator would prevail. A domination of his act could in such a situation only exist if the immediate perpetrator were coerced by the superior or involved in a mistake and therefore could be concretely dominated. On the other hand, the dependence of the *Organisationsherrschaft* on the interchangeability criterion of means that the domination is only lacking if one could disprove the interchangeable nature of the direct perpetrator in a concrete case. That is, first, an empirical problem, namely whether one could really assume that in all cases, in which the act was committed within an organized apparatus, the direct perpetrator was interchangeable. Given the high specialization within modern repression apparatus and special tasks assigned

[88] Pinochet's interview, *The Pinochet fact file,* Daily Telegraph, 19 July 1999.

[89] Cf. H.-G. Soeffner, 'Individuelle Macht und Ohnmacht in formalen Organisationen', in K. Amelung (ed.), *Individuelle Verantwortung und Beteiligungsverhältnisse bei Straftaten in bürokratischen Organisationen des Staates, der Wirtschaft und der Gesellschaft* (Pro-Universitate, Sinzheim 2000), p. 28. In formal organizations, acts committed by the perpetrator appear to him to be neither good nor bad.

to the 'specialists' it cannot be ruled out that a certain task can only be carried out by a specialist.[90] Nor can it be taken for granted that the apparatus possesses a sufficient number of specialists so that they are all easily and immediately replaceable. Thus the interchangeability criterion cannot pretend to have general validity; in fact, only one case to the contrary, i.e. a specialist is refusing to comply with an order and cannot be replaced, disproves the general validity of the principle.

In addition, the interchangeability of the immediate perpetrator can only explain domination in a general sense but not in the concrete situation of execution of the act. While the man in the background may well dominate the organization he does not directly dominate those who concretely have to execute the act. If, for example, a border guard or a whole border patrol at the East German border had refused to shoot at a refugee, there would not have been other guards immediately available to hinder *this* refugee from jumping over the wall. Indeed, his escape would have been successful and the concrete control of the executors of the orders of the organization's command would have failed.[91] Or take the often-quoted case of the KGB secret agent *Stachynski* who, on orders from Moscow,

[90] One thinks of the practice of Chilean torture techniques, which are referred to several times in the Spanish investigatory documents in the criminal proceedings against Pinochet (cf. H. Ahlbrecht and K. Ambos (eds.), *Der Fall Pinochet(s): Auslieferung wegen Staatsverstärkter Kriminalität?* (Nomos-Verl.-Ges., Baden-Baden 1999), p. 54 *et seq.* and *passim*). The 'specialist argument' was already made earlier by F.-C. Schröder, *Der Täter hinter dem Täter. Ein Beitrag zu Lehre von der mittelbaren Täterschaft* (Duncker und Humblot, Berlin 1965), p. 168; see also G. Freund, *Strafrecht, Allgemeiner Teil. Personale Straftatlehre.* (Springer, Berlin 1998) § 10, mn 92.

[91] Cf. R. D. Herzberg, 'Mittelbare Täterschaft und Anstiftung in formalen Organisationen,' in Amelung (n. 89) 37 *et seq.*; for further critique, see U. Murmann, 'Tatherrschaft und Weisungsmacht' (1996) GA 273, to whom Herzberg expressly refers; J. Renzikowski, *Restriktiver Täterbegriff und fahrlässige Beteiligung* (Mohr Siebeck, Tübingen 1997), p. 89; T. Rotsch, 'Die Rechtsfigur des Täters hinter dem Täter bei der Begehung von Straftaten im Rahmen organisatorischer Machtapparate und ihre Übertragbarkeit auf wirtschaftliche Organisationsstrukturen' (1998) NStZ 493; T. Rotsch, 'Unternehmen, Umwelt und Strafrecht – Ätiologie einer Misere. Teil 1' (1999) *wistra* 327; T. Rotsch 'Tatherrschaft kraft Organisationsherrschaft?' (2000) 112 ZStW 526 *et seq.* (528), 536, 552, 561; S. K. Hoyer in *Systematischer Kommentar* (ed. 2000) § 25 mn. 90; J. Brammsen, 'Unterlassungshaftung in formalen Organisationen', in Amelung (n. 89) 142; B. M. Hilgers, *Verantwortlichkeit von Führungskräften in Unternehmen für Handlungen ihrer Mitarbeiter* (Edition Iuscrim, Freiburg 2000), p. 132 *et seq.*; G. Heine, 'Täterschaft und Teilnahme in staatlichen Machtapparaten' (2000) JZ 925; K. Rogall, 'Bewältigung von Systemkriminalität', in C. Roxin and G. Widmaier (eds.), *50 Jahre Bundesgerichtshof, Festgabe aus der Wissenschaft, Band IV, Strafrecht, Strafprozessrecht* (Beck, Munich 2000), p. 425 *et seq.*; for a concrete view, see also H. Plasencia and J. Ulises, *La autoria mediata en Derecho Penal* (Comares, Granada 1996), p. 275.

killed a soviet dissident in West Germany. If he had refused to carry out the execution order no replacement would have arrived immediately but at most later and maybe too late to still comply with the order. Thus, from this concrete perspective it is difficult to say that Stachynski was only a replaceable cog in the machinery of the Soviet totalitarian apparatus.[92] Similarly, imagine that a torturer, contrary to orders from the highest authorities, abstains from using torture. A domination of the concrete act of torture from the organization's top level could in this case only exist if the acts of torture could immediately be commenced or continued notwithstanding the disobedience of the original torturer. These examples could be continued indefinitely. While they are certainly not identical with regard to the consequences of the non-execution of the order – in the border case it cannot be restored any more, since the refugee has made it to the west, in the other cases the order may be executed later – they all make clear that the domination of the *concrete* act is predicated upon the *immediate* interchangeability of the direct perpetrators. They further show that interchangeability rarely exists in concrete cases, rather it may, from an empirical perspective, be rejected with sound arguments.

The problematic nature of the interchangeability criterion is even more clearly seen with regard to the responsibility of persons who do not directly belong to the top level of the organisation such as for example mid-ranking bureaucrats (*Schreibtischtäter*) as Adolf Eichmann. If these persons are really indispensable for the fulfilment of the whole criminal plan, one can hardly assume that *they* are interchangeable in relation to their superior. Thus, one faces here a double problem: on the one hand, the interchangeability of these persons is necessary too in order to justify their actual control by the organisation's top level by virtue of the doctrine of *Organisationsherrschaft*; on the other hand, this assumption of their interchangeability would contradict the possibility of their own organizational control over the immediate perpetrators and therefore their indirect responsibility on the basis of a perpetration by means. A similar argument can be made with regard to *Höß*, the commander of the Auschwitz concentration camp.[93] He too could decide on the life and death of thousands of persons, and had at his disposal his subordinate camp personnel. However, also in this case, much speaks for a precise

[92] Cf. also G. Jakobs, *Strafrecht, Allgemeiner Teil, Die Grundlagen und die Zurechnungslehre, Studienausgabe* (2nd edn, de Gruyter, Berlin 1993) 21/103, mn. 190; see also Herzberg (n. 91) 38.

[93] Cf. also Herzberg (n. 91) 38 *et seq.*

allocation of responsibilities or tasks within the camp and thus against the smooth interchangeability of the direct perpetrators in the concrete situation of commission. This case indicates a deficit of the doctrine *Organisationsherrschaft*, i.e. that it has so far not clearly distinguished between the areas of responsibility and the levels of hierarchy, that is, it has not satisfactorily settled up to which level of command one could really assume that there is a factual control over the organisation. We will return to this question below (section 2).

What results from all of this is the fact that the leadership of the criminal organization can only be sure that the apparatus as such (in one way or the other) carries on with its work and the next order gets carried out smoothly by the in-the-meantime replaced executor. Thus, the interchangeability is generally not possible simultaneously, but rather *subsequently*.[94] In Hernández Plasencia's words: 'the quality of injury caused by the conduct of the person in front is not controlled by the men in the background.'[95] The interchangeability criterion thus becomes – put in relative terms – a 'requirement of personal mobility': 'The control of the act by virtue of a hierarchical organisation is bound by the fact that the order for the commission of the criminal act is issued within a hierarchy, which in the case of a *timely* refusal would *normally* immediately have a replacement at its disposal.'[96] One could only argue that the man in front increases the chances of succeeding in accordance with an 'incomplete interchangeability', the *Organisationsherrschaft* thus becomes a control of the substitute or replacing cause (*Ersatzursachenherrschaft*).[97] Yet, in such a weakened form, the interchangeability criterion can no longer serve as foundation of the control or domination over the act by the men in the background issuing orders.

From all this it follows that the criterion of interchangeability proves, from an empirical point of view, unsuitable to convincingly explain the doctrine of *Organisationsherrschaft*. This doctrine can only be explained with a normative theory and such a theory has been presented by Uwe Murmann.[98] In the result, Murmann transfers the structure of offences

[94] Cf. Jakobs (n. 92) fn. 190; see also Herzberg (n. 91) 38.

[95] Plasencia (n. 91) 275 (translated by the author): 'la cualidad lesiva del comportamiento del sujeto de delante no es dominada por los sujetos de atrás.'

[96] See Herzberg (n. 91) 58 *et seq.* (translated from German).

[97] S.K. Hoyer (n. 91) § 25 mn. 90.

[98] Cf. U. Murmann, *Die Nebentäterschaft im Strafrecht: ein Beitrag zu einer personalen Tatherrschaftslehre* (Duncker & Humblot, Berlin 1993), p. 60 *et seq.*, 181 *et seq.*; U. Murmann, *Tatherrschaft und Weisungsmacht* (1996) GA 275 *et seq.*, 278 with reference to Jakobs (n. 92). Murmann's conception takes as a starting point Zaczyk's doctrine of

requiring a certain position of duty on the part of the perpetrator (*Pflichtdelikte*) to the doctrine of control over the act and invokes a material concept of freedom. Thus the state appears – as guarantor of basic rights with a resulting duty to protect – in a specific *position of responsibility* vis-à-vis its citizens and has a specific *power of violation* (*Verletzungsmacht*)[99] towards them. The state breaches its duty to protect by illegally ordering the mediator of the act to injure a particular person. The relationship of dependence between the citizens and the state is at the same time comparable with the guarantor position in crimes of omission. The guarantor is in this case equally liable since he breaches the particular duty to protect which results from his position as guarantor. In the case of illegal state orders, the – at least from a normative perspective – dependence of the citizen on the state establishes the *state's control over the act*. The state exercises this control by ordering the mediator of the act, a citizen, to injure the victim, another citizen. Thus, two legal relationships are concerned: the relationship of recognition between the state and the citizen, characterized by particular duties, as well as the general relationship of recognition among the citizens themselves. The state's control over the act, more precisely the control by the state's top level and most responsible, depicts itself as '*control over the quality of the relationship*',[100] namely the *relationship of recognition* between the state and its citizens.[101] In *this* relationship, thus, the special duty of the state vis-à-vis its citizens, deduced from the doctrine of the *Pflichtdelikte*, is crucial; while in the other relationship among the citizens themselves – *in concreto* between the perpetrator who executed the order and the victim – the violation caused by the direct invasion in the freedom of others (*fremde Freiheit*) is crucial. Thus, both legal relationships are violated. For if one tries to attribute the victim's injury to the leaders of the state organization, one cannot only

personal freedom (*Das Unrecht der versuchten Tat* (Duncker & Humblot, Berlin 1989), p. 128 *et seq.* (1939), p. 194 *et seq.*) This in turn is based on the conception of *Kant* and *Fichte*. Accordingly, its legal foundation lies in a mutual recognition of individuals as autonomous reasonable persons. This *relationship of recognition* which is at the same time a legal relationship is realized through mutual, practically correct behaviour and thus guarantees the freedom of all persons (pp. 165, 193 and 326). I have earlier rejected Murmann's view on the basis of a too factual-instrumental view of things (see K. Ambos, *Tatherrschaft durch Willensherrschaft kraft organisatorischer Machtapparate. Eine kritische Bestandsaufnahme und weiterführende Ansätze* (1998) GA 230 *et seq.*; also see in this respect Rotsch (n. 91) 493).

[99] In favour of *Macht* (power) instead of *Herrschaft* (domination, control) also Lampe (n. 78) 481 *et seq.*

[100] Murmann, *Nebentäterschaft* (n. 98) 181; Murmann (GA) (n. 98) 276.

[101] Murmann, (*Nebentäterschaft*) (n. 98) 168 *et seq.*

consider the relationship between the leaders and the mediator of the act, but one must also take into account the victim – by way of the general relationship of recognition among the citizens themselves. Thus, the special state's duty vis-à-vis its citizens – which compels it to protect them and prohibits it from harming them and which, at the same time, entails a particular power to violate (*Verletzungsmacht*) within this relationship – provides in all those cases a normative foundation of the control over the act where the notion of interchangeability must fail for empirical reasons. With this approach the *Organisationsherrschaftslehre* is not abandoned but reinforced by normative, value-based considerations.

The normative explanation set out does not, however, substitute, but complements the factual perspective. For as little as a mere factual perspective can contribute to explain convincingly the *Organisationsherrschaft* a mere normative perspective is unable to identify concrete situations of *Organisationsherrschaft*. This becomes clear with a practical case by case approach. Take, for example, the opening decision by the Spanish investigating judge *Baltasar Garzón* of 10 December 1998 in the investigation no. 19/97 against Augusto Pinochet:

> Augusto Pinochet Ugarte is presumed to be the head of this terrifying organization, he, though he may not [with his own hands] have been involved in the actual execution of the acts, devised the plan and financed it with public funds …
> Augusto Pinochet's presumed involvement as an *instigator* is clear …;
> (a) The involvement is direct and is exercised through particular persons. As a head of state and President he had the possibility to immediately stop the chain of events, but he instead encouraged it by giving the relevant orders; sometimes he even exercised *absolute control* over the direct execution of acts through the leadership of the DINA;[102]
>
> …
>
> (g) [The involvement] is *followed by the execution* of the agreed crimes …
> Pinochet developed as *head* of the provisional criminal plan … a number of necessary, indispensable and essential acts, without which the acts would not have been able to be committed and pursued; the execution of the acts was based on the previous arranged plan according to which all persons involved exercise particular 'roles and functions' and [therefore] in accordance with the 'scarce goods theory' were hardly replaceable. As a result all members of the Junta, the military officers involved, especially the secret service or those who directly executed orders coming from the high level of the hierarchy should be

[102] *Dirección de Inteligencia Nacional,* Chilean Secret Police.

> characterized as *co-perpetrators.* Clearly, this characterization is also inevitable for Pinochet himself....[103]

Apart from the controversial legal evaluation which is apparently based on *Gimbernats* doctrine of the *scarce goods* (*bienes escasos*)[104] and which results – if one wants to resolve the contradiction of a coincidence between instigation and co-perpetration – in an instigation by various co-perpetrators, the quoted passage clearly indicates that an accurate legal evaluation must first of all be preceded by a factual analysis of the persons involved and their relationships. The facts of the case, once established, form the basis of the legal evaluation and this – universally accepted – self-evident truth is a decisive argument in favour of a predominantly factual perspective, which eventually may be complemented and reinforced by a normative, value-based reasoning. With regard to Pinochet's criminal liability, on the basis of the available facts, arguments amounting to an indirect perpetration based on the doctrine of *Organisationsherrschaft* can certainly be found: Pinochet is presumed not only to have given criminal orders, but sometimes even to have – 'with absolute control' over the act – controlled the direct execution of these orders; the agreed crimes were executed without a second thought; Pinochet was the 'head' of the criminal plan.

All this also demonstrates that the control of the act (*Tatherrschaft*) is not only, contrary to *Jakobs*,[105] a legal or normative phenomenon but above all a factual one. This is also demonstrated by the fact that the criterion of interchangeability is problematic in particular from an empirical perspective. For this very reason the normative explanation or foundation of the *Organisationsherrschaft* set out here is indispensable.

2. *Delimitating (indirect) perpetration through another person and co-perpetration along levels of hierarchy*

The doctrine has not really looked into the issue of up to what level of hierarchy one can assume the existence of the man in the background's

[103] In Ahlbrecht and Ambos (n. 90) 136 *et seq.* (retranslation from German; footnotes omitted and emphases added).

[104] Cf. E. Gimbernat, *Autor y complice en Derecho Penal* (Universidad Madrid, 1966), p. 151 *et seq.*, p. 194 *et seq.*; E. Gimbernat, 'Gedanken zum Täterbegriff und zur Teilnahmelehre' (1968) ZStW 930–1.

[105] G. Jakobs, 'Mittelbare Täterschaft der Mitglieder des Nationalen Verteidigungsrats' (1995) NStZ 27.

control of the act by virtue of a hierarchical organization.[106] The German case law applies Roxin's theory also to defendants who do not belong to the leadership of the organization.[107] The courts repeat over and over again the well-known formula according to which the control of the act exists if the man in the background 'through the structures of the organization makes use of certain basic conditions which make sure that his contribution produces a certain change of events'.[108] According to this case law, even a West German citizen who, by denouncing a former East German citizen's plan to escape caused his illegal arrest, could be sentenced for indirect responsibility for wrongful deprivation of personal liberty, 'especially if the perpetrator consciously uses an illegally acting state apparatus in pursuit of his own goals'.[109] This begs the question how an ordinary citizen could ever be able to control a (foreign) state apparatus. The *Organisationsherrschaft* does not even depend on the defendant's membership in the respective organization.[110] Yet, one can hardly claim that a judge, security agent or police officer who may all have concretely executed the illegal arrest are mere replaceable cogs in the machinery of the respective (foreign) state apparatus.

The Eichmann case is also worthwhile mentioning in this context. *Roxin* considered Eichmann as an indirect perpetrator, arguing that he was not only a mere executor of orders but at the same time a superior with regard to the persons assigned to him as subordinates, 'so that the criteria which render his men in the background indirect perpetrators also apply to him'.[111] However, while Eichmann's responsibility as a perpetrator is beyond doubt,[112] the type of perpetration is by no means clear. As is known, the Jerusalem district court itself sentenced Eichmann as a

[106] For critique, see Jakobs (n. 92) 21/103 n. 190. See also H. Vest, 'Humanitätsverbrechen – Herausforderung für das Indivdualstrafrecht' (2001) ZStW 493 *et seq.*; H. Vest, *Genozid durch organisatorische Machtapparate* (Nomos, Baden-Baden 2002), p. 230 *et seq.* and *passim*.

[107] Ambos (n. 26) 243.

[108] BGHSt 40, 218 (236: 'durch Organisationsstrukturen bestimmte Rahmenbedingungen ausnutzt, innerhalb derer sein Tatbeitrag regelhafte Abläufe auslöst').

[109] BGHSt 42, 275 (278).

[110] Cf. in this respect the accurate critique from J. Arnold, 'Rechtsbeugung von Richtern und Staatsanwälten der DDR im "Fall Robert Havemann"?' (1999) NJ 289–90 with regard to Havemann Judgment of the BGH (10 December 1998) by which the doctrine of *Organisationsherrschaft* was implicitly introduced in the cases of the perversion of (the course of) justice.

[111] Roxin (n. 74) (249) 246 *et seq.* (246) [translation from German] C. Roxin, *Straftaten im Rahmen organisatorischer Machtapparate,* (1963) GA 201 *et seq.*

[112] Ambos (n. 26) 549, 554.

co-perpetrator.[113] I expressed some doubts as to Eichmann's responsibility on the basis of the *Organistationsherrschaft* in an earlier paper,[114] but it still seems correct to me that, with the Eichmann case, the possibility of an *Organisationsherrschaft* at different hierarchical stages has been recognized and that this control itself grows and accumulates with increasing power of decision-making and the availability of personnel resources.[115] Against the background of the expansion of the doctrine of *Organisationsherrschaft* in the German case law, it seems more than ever necessary, however, to distinguish clearly between the leadership level in a criminal organization and the level below the leadership of medium, albeit important participants in the criminal enterprise. On closer examination, one can hardly deny the fact that absolute control *through* and/or *over* an organizational apparatus of hierarchical power can only be exercised at the leadership level, i.e. at the level of the formally constituted National Defense Council, *junta* or merely as a government.[116] In addition, this institution or organ represents the state in a particular way and as such bears the overall responsibility for possible violations of the fundamental rights of the citizen. All other power is derived from this highest authority and thus in its exercise attributable to the state leadership. Only its power and authority can neither be blocked nor disturbed in any way from above. In contrast, such a 'disturbance' is possible in the case of a high- or mid-level civil servant like Eichmann: his orders to transport the Jews to the concentration camps could at any moment have been reversed or cancelled by his superiors. Equally, his authority of issuing orders to the direct perpetrators could have been overturned by his superiors, for ultimately the direct perpetrators had to respond not to Eichmann or his level of responsibility but to the NS-leadership. A similar argument can be made with regard to the abovementioned SS-Commander *Höß*.[117] He too was neither – 'downwards' – the sole person responsible for the events nor – 'upwards' – completely independent. The lack of control of participants who do not belong to the leadership level, although they have a considerable power of decision-making and therefore belong to the higher level, can also be seen in the following statement of the already mentioned Manuel Contreras, who was the head of the secret police DINA and a direct subordinate of Augusto Pinochet:

[113] Cf. Ambos (n. 26) 185: 'his responsibility is that of a principle offender, who acted together with others in committing the entire crime.'

[114] Ambos (n. 26) 236 *et seq.* [115] Ambos (n. 26) 237, 238.

[116] See H. Vest, *Humanitätsverbrechen – Herausforderung für das Individualstrafrecht?* (2001) 13 ZStW 493 *et seq.*

[117] Cf. n. 93 above and corresponding text.

> the exercise of full command (*mando pleno*) in a military institution does not mean being independent, since all commanders have a higher commander on whom they depend, to whom they constantly have to give account on the execution of their task and orders received. In my particular case, this [higher commander] was the President of the Republic and this is why I say that I did not have command over myself and that every task I executed always had to have come from the President of the Republic.[118]

From all this it follows that the doctrine of *Organisationsherrschaft* can only convincingly be applied to men in the background, whose orders and instructions cannot without any further ado be revoked or cancelled, i.e. those who, in this sense, can rule and control without any interference (from above). This is only the case for the leadership level of the formally established government and, in exceptional cases, also for the top hierarchy of the military and police forces. Obviously, their ability to exercise *Organisationsherrschaft* is furthermore to be assumed when they are ruling themselves or belong to the government. In contrast, perpetrators who do not belong to the leadership but only to the mid-level of the organization exercise at the most control with regard to *their* subordinates *within* the apparatus.[119] Thus they do not exercise control over the whole apparatus but rather, at the most, over *a part* of it. In any case, this partial control justifies considering them as indirect perpetrators with regard to the events which took place under their control. At the same time, their dependence on the leadership of the organization militates against a responsibility as indirect perpetrators for the overall chain of events and for a responsibility as *co-perpetrators* on the basis of the functional division of labour. Without such a division of labor the 'final solution' (*Endlösung*) of the Nazis could not have been achieved. Equally, the extermination machinery of a concentration camp such as Auschwitz, personally arranged and supervised by camp commander Höß, could not have functioned so efficiently. The common arguments against co-perpetration within the framework of formal organizations, eloquently presented by *Roxin*,[120] do not lead to another result. First, as to the joint decision or common plan to carry out the acts it suffices to assume an informal consensus or agreement of the persons

[118] Quoted from the abovementioned Spanish decision to formally opening the investigation statement in the Pinochet proceedings (n. 90) 124.

[119] Cf. also Vest (n. 116) 493 *et seq.*

[120] C. Roxin, *Probleme von Täterschaft und Teilnahme bei der organisierten Kriminalität*, in E. Samson *et al.* (eds.), *Festschrift für Gerald Grünwald zum 70. Geburtstag* (Nomos-Verl.-Ges., Baden-Baden 1999), p. 552 *et seq.*; also G. Küpper, *Zur Abgrenzung der Täterschaftsformen* (1998) GA 524.

involved.[121] While *Roxin* is right, in that the superior giving orders and the subordinate executing these orders do within the framework of an organizational criminal apparatus, as a rule, neither know each other nor take a joint decision, this is not the decisive issue. For an informal agreement it suffices that the direct perpetrator makes clear through his belonging to the criminal organization that he agrees with the superior as to the organization's policies. This agreement manifests itself implicitly by the execution of the act.[122]

The commission by co-perpetration is, as explained elsewhere,[123] not to be strictly interpreted as excluding any *acts of preparation*. Even the gang leader, to take a classical example from ordinary criminality, 'does not dirty his hands but makes use of executors'.[124] A functional control over the act means nothing else than a division of labour of the persons involved. This division in such a case consists of the mastermind's ordering, preparing and planning of the act and the subordinates executing it. Both contributions are indispensable for the commission of the crime, superior and subordinate control the act equally.[125] Furthermore, it is important to consider the fact that it lies in the logic of a functional control over an act that by an increase in the number of persons involved the individual contributions to the act lose importance without necessarily leading to a predominance by the other persons involved.

Last but not least, the argument of a *structural difference* between the *vertical* indirect perpetration and the *horizontal* co-perpetration is equally not decisive. While it cannot be denied that this difference exists in principle,[126] it is only of a structural nature and as such does not permit a reliable delimitation in the borderline cases of macro criminality discussed here. In fact, it is valid in our context as an argument for indirect perpetration only in those cases in which the vertical relationship between the man in the background and the mediator of the act is not overlapped or disturbed by the existence of a further relationship of dependence of the man in the background. The gist of the question of the

[121] Cf. Ambos (n. 26) 558.

[122] Also see Plasencia (n. 91) 266: 'El acuerdo comun … puede producirse a través de actos *concluyentes*' (emphasis added).

[123] Cf. Ambos (n. 26) 565 *et seq.*

[124] Roxin (n. 120) 553.

[125] Against C. Roxin's strict view, see also F. J. Muñoz Conde, Problemas de autoría y participación en la criminalidad organizada', in J. C. Ferré and E. Anarte (eds.), *Delincuencia organizada* (Universidad de Huelva, Huelva 1999), p. 155 *et seq.*, who for this reason advocates for indirect perpetration of non-state organisations (see also Ferré and Anarte, (2000) 6 *Revista Penal* 113; Festschrift Roxin [2001], p. 622 *et seq.*).

[126] Cf. Ambos (n. 26) 567, 569.

delimitation between indirect perpetration and co-perpetration in case of mid- and low-level members of the hierarchy is whether one is rather ready to accept a deficiency in control by the superior or a deficit in the equal ranking or footing of the participants. Given that control or domination is the solely decisive criterion for indirect perpetration, deficiencies or doubts cannot be accepted; in contrast the criterion of an equal ranking and timing of the co-perpetrators must not be interpreted too strictly. Indeed, the classical case of the gang leader makes it clear that a hierarchical relationship between the persons involved may also exist in the case of co-perpetration.[127]

V. Conclusion

The analysis shows that there are three forms or possibilities to impute or attribute international crimes to the top level perpetrators. One of them, *command responsibility*, is explicitly recognized in the statutes of the International Criminal Tribunals, in particular and most detailed by Art. 28 of the ICC Statute. The other two, *joint criminal enterprise* and *Organisationsherrschaft*, can be grounded, at least in their basic form (JCE I) or doctrinal foundation (control of the act), on positive international criminal law (e.g. Art. 25(3)(a) ICC Statute) and have been recognized more (JCE) or less (*Organisationsherrschaft*) by comparative and international case law. As to the – internationally emerging – doctrine of *Organisationsherrschaft*, in essence, it comes down to the question of the liberty of the direct perpetrator operating in a hierarchical organization vis-à-vis the top executive(s) of this organization. In any case, only very few persons command the control necessary to replace immediately one (failing) executor by another, namely only those who belong to the leadership of the criminal organization or who at least control a part of the organization and are, therefore, able to dominate the unfolding of the criminal plan undisturbed by other members of the organization. Although these persons are generally far away from the actual execution of the criminal acts and are therefore normally considered indirect perpetrators or even accessories,[128] they are in fact, from

[127] See also Plasencia (n. 91) 267.

[128] See e.g. Osiel (n. 24) (*Cornell International Law Journal*) 807 who, however, apparently fails to grasp the different forms of participation provided for by the differentiated concept of perpetration according to which *Organisationsherrschaft* is more than mere accessorship. Further, it is misleading to state that prosecutions in Latin America ((n. 24) 808) 'rely heavily on ... superior responsibility'. The truth is that most prosecutions invoke

a normative perspective, the main perpetrators while the executors are merely accessories or accomplices in the implementation of the criminal, collective enterprise.[129]

Thus, ultimately, the doctrine of *Organisationsherrschaft* confirms what has been identified as the underlying rationales of JCE and also command responsibility. First, the traditional system of individual attribution of responsibility, as applied for ordinary criminality characterized by the individual commission of single crimes, must be adapted to the needs of ICL aiming at the development of a *mixed system of individual-collective responsibility* in which the criminal enterprise or organization as a whole serves as the entity upon which attribution of criminal responsibility is based. The doctrine has called this a *Zurechnungsprinzip Gesamttat*,[130] i.e. a principle or theory of attribution according to which the 'global act' (the criminal enterprise) constitutes the central object of attribution. In a way, such a doctrine brings together all the theories discussed in this paper and proves the central point of the JCE doctrine, i.e. to take the *criminal enterprise as the starting point of attribution* in international criminal law. Secondly, all the doctrines discussed here have the common aim of attributing the individual crimes committed within the framework of the system, organization or enterprise to its *leadership*, to its 'masterminds', leaving the destiny of low-level executors and mid-level officials in the hands of the national criminal justice systems. Last, but not least, the criminal responsibility of leaders presupposes a kind of (*normative*) *control* over the acts imputed to them and a mental state linking them to these acts, thereby complying with the principle of *culpability*.

Roxin's theory, especially the *Organisationsherrschaftslehre,* since it can be based on the general rules of perpetration by means (*autoría mediata*) which are unlike the command responsibility doctrine well recognized in civil law systems (as in Latin American). Finally, the fine distinctions between modes of participation discussed in a differentiated system of perpetration as the German or Spanish one demonstrate that 'simplicity' is not, as suggested by Osiel (n. 24) (Columbia Law Review) 1753, the preferred option for criminal law doctrine, at least not for that of the core civil law countries.

129 Cf. Vest (n. 116) 220, 249.

130 On this new concept of attribution for collective criminality, see the fundamental work of F. Dencker, *Kausalität und Gesamttat* (Duncker & Humblot, Berlin 1996), pp. 125 *et seq.*, 152 *et seq.*, 229, 253 *et seq.* and *passim*. The concept was further elaborated by Vest (n. 116) 214 *et seq.*, 236 *et seq.*, 303, 304 *et seq.*, 359 *et seq.*

7

Joint criminal enterprise and functional perpetration

HARMEN VAN DER WILT*

I. Introduction

The joint criminal enterprise doctrine (hereafter JCE) has made quite an impressive appearance on the stage of the International Criminal Tribunal for the Former Yugoslavia. Raised from the ashes of Nuremberg conspiracy law, the doctrine has been enthusiastically embraced by the Tribunal, which has polished the doctrine in order both to meet the principles of criminal law and to face the complexities of international crimes.

The gist of the doctrine is to nail persons who joined forces for a common purpose to commit (international) crimes and contributed to this aim, although they did not physically perpetrate those crimes. The doctrine connotes group responsibility. However, mere membership does not suffice to incur criminal responsibility, as the ICTY has emphasized correctly.

In the *Tadić* case, the Appeals Chamber of the ICTY has tried to refine and diversify the doctrine, identifying no fewer than three versions.[1] Whereas the requirements as to the *actus reus* are basically the same – a plurality of persons, membership of this group and an unarticulated 'contribution' – they differ in the *mens rea*. The first, relatively straightforward and unproblematic form (JCE (I)) implies that all group members share the common intent to commit certain crimes which actually materialize. The second form (JCE (II)), which has been called the 'systemic variant', covers participation in a repressive system in the context of which multiple crimes are committed on a structural basis and has been applied in the so-called 'concentration camp' cases. The *mens*

* Harmen van der Wilt is Professor of International Criminal Law at the University of Amsterdam and Research Fellow of the Amsterdam Center for International Law.

[1] *Prosecutor v Dusco Tadić* IT-94-1-A, Judgment, Appeals Chamber (15 July 1999) paras. 185–234.

rea requirement entails that the accused possessed positive knowledge of the system of repression – i.e. a common purpose to maltreat the inmates – and had the intent to further this aim. The position of the accused within the hierarchy of the organization serves as refutable evidence of both his *actus reus* and his *mens rea*. The third and most contested variant (JCE (III)) refers to a situation where all group members share a common purpose, but one of them jumps out of line and commits a crime which has initially not been envisaged. All members nevertheless incur criminal responsibility, if this crime was a natural and foreseeable consequence of the common plan and they recklessly took the risk, rather than withdrawing.[2]

Joint criminal enterprise liability as such does not feature in the provisions on criminal responsibility in the Statutes of the ICTY and ICTR (Articles 7 and 6, respectively). However, as the Appeals Chamber held in the *Tadić* case, these provisions are not meant to be exhaustive. Article 7 implicitly refers to participation in a group with a common purpose to commit international crimes.[3] Whether Article 25, section 3(d) of the Rome Statute covers all the variants of JCE is a matter of controversy.[4] As Article 30 of the Statute mentions intent and knowledge as the requisite *mens rea*, while for JCE (III) *dolus eventualis* in respect of the crimes suffices, one could make the convincing argument that at least JCE (III) is outside the ambit of the provision.[5]

The attractiveness of the JCE doctrine rests on its capacity to serve as a double-edged sword. From a criminal law point of view, it extends

2 *Prosecutor v Dusco Tadić* (n. 1) para. 204.

3 *Prosecutor v Dusco Tadić* (n. 1) para. 190: '[the Statute] does not exclude those modes of participating in the commission of crimes which occur where several persons having a common purpose embark on criminal activity that is then carried out either jointly or by some members of this plurality of persons.'

4 Article 25(3)(d) reads: 'In accordance with this Statute, a person shall be criminally responsible and liable for punishment for a crime within the jurisdiction of the Court if that person:

...

(d) In any other way contributes to the commission or attempted commission of such a crime by a group of persons acting with a common purpose. Such contribution shall be intentional and shall either:

(i) Be made with the aim of furthering the criminal activity or criminal purpose of the group. Where such activity or purpose involves the commission of a crime within the jurisdiction of the Court; or

(ii) Be made in the knowledge of the intention of the group to commit the crime.

5 E. van Sliedregt, *The Criminal Responsibility of Individuals for Violations of International Humanitarian Law* (TMC Asser Press, The Hague 2003), p. 356.

criminal liability by linking crimes to several persons and, conversely, connecting persons with distinct crimes. But it has a more hermeneutic quality as well, portraying the interaction and cooperation between members of a group or organization and showing the dynamics of collective action without which, according to many, international crimes cannot be properly understood. Gradually, the JCE doctrine has emerged as a 'jack of all trades', coping with mob violence, providing for extensive criminal responsibility for political and military leaders and addressing the responsibility of those who are involved in criminal organizations such as detention camps.[6]

The present author, though acknowledging the potential of JCE doctrine, has criticized in recent publications its broad application.[7] Essentially, my apprehensions boil down to a profound doubt whether the criminal law functions of the doctrine can be reconciled with its hermeneutic or narrative aspirations. This point of view will be further elaborated in this chapter. Part II will address the legal nature of the JCE doctrine and will trace its pedigree. Part III will highlight the sociological and psychological aspects of system criminality, in order to appraise the applicability of JCE liability in such a context. Part IV will discuss the recent efforts in case law of (mainly) the ICTY to gear the doctrine to enterprises of a vast scope. In part V, I will propose and discuss some alternative concepts of criminal responsibility which might be suitable to tackle collective criminality. The concluding section will address the question whether the JCE doctrine has still some limited but useful functions to serve.

II. JCE: its legal pedigree and further developments of the concept

Criminal law stresses the value of individual guilt and personal fault. Those specific features hamper its capacity to address system criminality which connotes collective agency. It is no secret that the Nuremberg Tribunal wrestled with this problem. The Tribunal invoked two legal concepts in particular – conspiracy and membership of a criminal organization – in

[6] van Sliedregt (n. 5) 353–8.

[7] H. van der Wilt, *Het Kwaad in Functie* ('Evil in Function'), inaugural address (Amsterdam 2005); H. van der Wilt, 'Joint criminal enterprise: its possibilities and limitations' (2007) 5 I JICJ 91–108; H. van der Wilt 'Commentary on *Prosecutor v Milutinović, Šainović and Ojdanić*, Decision on Dragoljub Ojdanić's Motion Challenging Jurisdiction – Joint Criminal Enterprise', IT-99-37-AR72 (21 May 2003) in A. Klip and G. Sluiter (eds.) *Annotated Leading Cases* (vol. XIV, Intersentia, Antwerp/Groningen/Oxford/Vienna 2008, 115–122). The present article draws partly on these previous publications.

order to sustain the criminal responsibility of the top of the Nazi hierarchy and the rank and file respectively. Now conspiracy in its archetypal form is an inchoate crime which requires an agreement between the parties.[8] In this restricted meaning, the concept was only recognized and applied by the Nuremberg Tribunal in respect of crimes against peace. The content of conspiracy, however, has expanded over time, covering not only single agreements, but also sustaining the individual responsibility of scores of individuals who were only loosely connected *inter se* or indirectly implicated in the (commission of) crimes. This perversion of the initial concept of conspiracy, in which people incurred criminal responsibility for all crimes ensuing from a conspiracy, without need to prove that they had knowledge of those crimes, or their co-perpetrators, derived from the infamous *Pinkerton* case.[9] The Nuremberg Tribunal did not shy away from applying conspiracy in this wider sense in respect of war crimes and crimes against humanity as well. For want of a better term, this concept has been named 'complicity-conspiracy', which at least adequately captures the flawed theory that conspiracy is equivalent in law to aiding and abetting.[10]

From the perspective of the principle of individual guilt, criminal responsibility for mere membership of an organization was equally questionable.[11] Although the Nuremberg Tribunal has succeeded in mitigating its harshest effects – by adding two further conditions: that the accused had to be aware of the criminal aims of the organisation; and that he could plead innocence in case of conscription – the construction remains a suspicious example of collective criminal responsibility, as it negates the importance of contributory fault.

Have the Tribunals succeeded in avoiding the pitfalls of collective responsibility? In some cases, the ICTY has taken great pain to show that the JCE doctrine does not equate to 'conspiracy', nor mere membership of a criminal organization. In a separate opinion to the *Ojdanić* case, Judge Hunt emphasized that, whereas 'conspiracy' is a separate crime of an inchoate nature which is completed as soon as the conspirators have reached an agreement, joint criminal enterprise liability requires concrete

[8] A. Ashworth, *Principles of Criminal Law* (3rd edn, Oxford Unviersity Press, Oxford 1999), p. 476: 'Agreement is the basic element in conspiracy. The idea of an agreement seems to involve a meeting of minds, and there is no need for a physical meeting of the persons involved so long as they reach a mutual understanding of what is to be done.'

[9] *Pinkerton v United States*, 328 US 640.

[10] Compare van Sliedregt (n. 5) 354 and S. Pomorski, 'Conspiracy and criminal organisation', in G. Ginsburg and V. N. Kudriavtsev (eds.), *The Nuremberg Trial and International Law* (Martinus Nijhoff, Dordrecht 1990), p. 224.

[11] On this topic: N. Jørgensen, 'Criminality of organizations under international law', this volume, Chapter 9.

crimes to be committed and a material contribution of the accused.[12] This final condition already shows that mere membership of a criminal group would never suffice for imputing crimes, committed by a group, to all of its members. Judge Hunt's reading of the doctrine suggests that JCE liability is equivalent to conspiracy plus an additional element: an overt act and a contribution by the person who stands trial.[13]

Whereas an agreement is the essential element in the pristine concept of 'conspiracy', the Appeals Chamber of the ICTY explicitly denied that in JCE (II) – the concentration camp cases – an agreement between the members of the criminal organization was necessary.[14] In its legal assessment of a vast joint criminal enterprise, linking the perpetrators of war crimes with the political top figures, the Trial Chamber in the *Brđanin* case again acknowledged the connection between the JCE doctrine and conspiracy.[15] Postulating an explicit agreement between the perpetrators (or accomplices) as a necessary element of JCE responsibility, the Trial Chamber concluded that

> joint criminal enterprise is not an appropriate mode of liability to describe the individual criminal responsibility of the Accused, given the extraordinary broad nature of this case, when the Prosecution seeks to include within a joint criminal enterprise a person as remote from the commission of the crimes charged in the Indictment as the Accused.[16]

The judgment of the Trial Chamber in *Brđanin* exemplifies a principled criminal law approach. In the concept of conspiracy an agreement between the partners in crime is an essential element as it compensates for the withering of the *actus reus*. If one were to flout the interactive dimension of a conspiracy, both constitutive elements of criminal law – *actus reus* and *mens rea* – would fall short of accepted requirements.

[12] Separate Opinion of Judge Hunt to *Prosecutor v Milutinović, Šainović & Ojdanić*, Decision on Dragoljub Ojdanić's Motion Challenging Jurisdiction – Joint Criminal Enterprise, IT-99–37-AR72 (21 May 2003) para. 23.

[13] In a similar vein: A. Zahar and G. Sluiter, *International Criminal Law: A Critical Introduction* (Oxford University Press, Oxford 2007), p. 243, who provide an excellent analysis of the JCE doctrine.

[14] *Prosecutor v Krnojelac*, IT-97–25-A, Judgment (17 September 2003) para. 97. This point of view was confirmed in *Prosecutor v Kvočka et al.*, IT-98–30/1 Judgment, Appeals Chamber (28 February 2005) paras. 118, 119.

[15] *Prosecutor v Brđanin*, IT-99–36-T, Judgment, Trial Chamber I (1 September 2004).

[16] *Prosecutor v Brđanin* (n. 15) para. 355.

The judgment has been severely criticized for being too cautious by Gustafson.[17] She argues that the political and military leadership may be loosely connected to the physical perpetrators by interlinking JCEs. Although the present author finds these proposals ingenious, he would like to point out the obvious danger of overstretching the limits of criminal responsibility and mutilation of the doctrine.

On appeal, the Trial Chamber's opinions on the limits of JCE were reversed on all points.[18] First, the Appeals Chamber denied that the persons who actually carried out the *actus reus* of a particular crime within the scope of the common purpose (the 'principal perpetrators') had to be members of the JCE. They did not even have to share the 'common purpose', provided that some link with the JCE was demonstrated by their being used as 'tools' by the members of the joint criminal enterprise.[19] A logical inference from the previous position was that, contrary to the point of view as expressed by the Trial Chamber, JCE responsibility did not require an understanding or an agreement to commit (a) crime(s) between the remote offender and the physical perpetrators.[20] Finally, this broad interpretation of JCE responsibility paved the way for the acceptance of large-scale cases in which the plan encompassed a 'nation wide government-organized system of cruelty and injustice'.[21] The Appeals Chamber did not share the opinion of the accused that 'attaching JCE liability to an individual who is structurally remote from the crime increases the possibility of the individual being made guilty by "mere association"' and added that it was not a legal requirement that the mode of liability of JCE should only be applied to small-sized cases.[22]

Although one has to admit that the arguments of the Appeals Chamber reveal inner consistency, in the opinion of the author the Chamber has largely lost sight of the element of synergy between the participants in a joint criminal enterprise.[23]

The partly contradictory judgments of the ICTY add to the confusion and hamper any attempt to understand the nature of joint criminal

[17] K. Gustafson, 'The requirement of an "express agreement" for joint criminal enterprise liability: a critique of *Brđanin*' (2007) 5 I JICJ 134–58.

[18] *Prosecutor v Brđanin*, IT-99-36-A, Judgment (3 April 2007).

[19] *Prosecutor v Brđanin* (n. 18) paras. 410–14.

[20] *Prosecutor v Brđanin* (n. 18) paras. 415–19.

[21] The Appeals Chamber quoted with approval the opinion of the ICTR Appeals Chamber in the *Rwamakuba*-case, *Prosecutor v Brđanin* (n. 18) para. 423.

[22] *Prosecutor v Brđanin* (n. 18) paras. 424 and 425.

[23] For similar criticism, compare the contribution of E. van Sliedregt, 'System criminality at the ICTY', this volume, Chapter 8.

enterprise liability. In the view of the present author, the JCE doctrine, like its predecessor, complicity-conspiracy, has a mixed pedigree, combining complicity law with conspiracy law.[24] The danger looms that, in this 'mixture', the basic elements of both bodies of criminal law – substantial contribution for accomplices, mutual agreement for conspirators – may evaporate. In the case law of the ICTY and – to a lesser extent – the ICTR, the joint criminal enterprise has served as a vehicle to aggregate persons who are somehow related to international crimes, without much heed being paid to the question how they exactly contributed to the crimes or whether they had at least a silent understanding.

The *Kvočka* judgment provides a classic example.[25] Mr Kvočka, a policeman who stood trial on the basis of JCE (II) for his involvement in the repressive system of Omarska's concentration camp, was accused of 'having played a key role in the administration and functioning of the camp as Željko Meakic's deputy and as an experienced police officer'. The Trial Chamber added that 'Kvočka's continued participation in the Omarska camp sent a message of approval to other participants in the camp's operation, specifically guards in a subordinate position to him, and was a condonation of the abuses and deplorable conditions there'.[26] The evidence in respect of Kvočka's *actus reus* and *mens rea* is not overwhelming. The judgment nowhere indicates that Kvočka was involved in the commission of crimes, nor is it clear how his activities *directly* advanced the criminal purpose of the repressive system. Proof of his interactions and agreements with physical perpetrators might have sustained a finding of guilt and complicity, but such proof was explicitly renounced. The Trial Chamber's final judgment, in which Kvočka was held responsible for participation in a *joint* criminal enterprise or a *common* purpose, seems far fetched on the basis of the available evidence. The situation is aggravated by the fact that Kvočka was not held criminally responsible for his membership of a criminal organization, but for the crimes themselves.[27]

[24] On the latter, see the excellent article of A. M. Danner and J. S. Martinez, 'Guilty associations: joint criminal enterprise, command responsibility and the development of international criminal law' (2005) 93 *California Law Review* 75; the authors assert, contrary to the Appeals Chamber's view, that 'joint criminal enterprise is historically and conceptually related both to conspiracy and to the prosecution of criminal organisations' (110).

[25] *Prosecutor v Kvočka et al.*, IT-98–30/1-T, Judgment (2 November 2001).

[26] *Prosecutor v Kvočka et al.* (n. 25) paras. 405 and 406.

[27] Referring to the *Einsatzgruppen* case, the Trial Chamber suggested a useful distinction between significant and insignificant contributions to the joint criminal enterprise, indicating that 'aiding and abetting' a JCE was a possible option (*Prosecutor v Kvočka et al.* (n. 25) paras. 281, 282). On appeal, however, this refinement was dismissed as a

It is remarkable that the JCE doctrine has been criticized within the circles of the ICTY itself. In the *Stakić* case, the Trial Chamber argued that more direct references to 'commission' in its traditional sense should prevail over application of the JCE doctrine.[28] The Trial Chamber reasoned that Stakić's participation in offences committed in Prijedor Municipality could best be qualified as 'co-perpetration' and proceeded by identifying and discussing the elements of this mode of responsibility.[29] There had been an agreement, or at least a silent understanding, between Stakić and police and armed Serbs to take over power in the municipality, an event which preceded ethnic cleansing.[30] They had acted in concert and each co-perpetrator had control over the criminal conduct, in the sense that they had the power to frustrate the venture by breaking off.[31] As Dr Stakić's contribution to and position in the criminal conduct perfectly matched the archetypical co-perpetrator, there was no need to have recourse to the JCE doctrine.

Even more outspoken in his rejection of the JCE doctrine was Judge Per-Johan Lindholm in his dissenting opinion in the *Simić* case.[32] The judge boldly dissociated himself from the doctrine of joint criminal enterprise, in the case under scrutiny and in general, and shared the Trial Chamber's preference for co-perpetration in the *Stakić* case.

However, the rebellion against the JCE turned out to be short-lived, as the Appeals Chamber found the Trial Chamber in error 'in employing a mode of liability which is not valid law within the jurisdiction of this Tribunal' and restored the JCE doctrine.[33]

Undoubtedly, the discussion on the proper relationship between JCE and co-perpetration will resurge in the case law of the ICC, as the Rome Statute explicitly acknowledges co-perpetration as a mode of liability.[34] It

categorical mistake, as the Trial Chamber apparently confused JCE 'as a means to commit a crime with the crime itself', *Prosecutor v Kvočka*, IT-98–30/1, Judgment, Appeals Chamber (28 February 2005) para. 91.

28 *Prosecutor v Stakić*, IT-97–24-T, Judgment (31 July 2003) para. 438.

29 *Prosecutor v Stakić* (n. 28) 468.

30 *Prosecutor v Stakić* (n. 28) paras. 472–7.

31 *Prosecutor v Stakić* (n. 28) paras 478–91.

32 Separate and partly dissenting opinion of Judge Per-Johan Lindholm, *Prosecutor v Simić, Tadić and Zarić*, IT-95–9-T (17 October 2003) paras. 1–5.

33 *Prosecutor v Stakić*, IT-97–24-A, Judgment (22 March 2006) para 62.

34 In the *Lubanga* case the ICC's Pre-Trial Chamber rejected the suggestion that the phrasing of Article 25(3)(a) ('commits such a crime … jointly with another') included JCE. As Lubanga was charged with co-perpetrating the enlisting and conscription of child soldiers, the whole JCE-doctrine was largely left aside. *Prosecutor v Lubanga*, Decision on Confirmation of the Charges, ICC 01/04-01/06, PTC 1 (29 January 2007), §§ 325–41. Weigend predicts that 'JCE will not play the dominating role in the ICC that it has

is questionable, however, whether the efforts to understand system criminality will gain much by the application of co-perpetration, as the concept emerges from the cradle of individualistic criminal law and is poorly equipped to grasp the collective dimension of international crimes.

The mid-term conclusion must be that the ICTY has been quite ambiguous as to the required elements of JCE, both in respect of the contribution and the interaction between the members. This vagueness arguably falls short of the exacting demands of criminal law. According to the present author, these vacillations reflect a lasting dilemma. Either one doggedly sticks to the basic tenets of the doctrine – as the Trial Chamber did in *Brđanin* – or one moulds the doctrine of JCE to fit reality. The *Brđanin* approach limits the scope of application, probably to situations of gang crime or mob violence. The result jettisons the narrative or hermeneutic function of the doctrine; that of portraying the collective dimension of international crimes and the complex organizational structure responsible for their commission. The alternative approach, however, creates a shape-shifting concept of JCE, made to measure depending on the changing facts of each case. This jeopardizes legal integrity, by sacrificing the principle at the core of all criminal justice systems: *nullum crimen sine lege,* which guards against the overbroad attribution of criminal responsibility.

This dilemma cannot be solved within the context of the doctrine itself. The central hypothesis is that the JCE doctrine does not dovetail with the grim reality of modern state bureaucracies or large organizations that engage in international crimes. This hypothesis will be elaborated in the next section.

III. Incongruities between the joint criminal enterprise doctrine and system criminality

The poor performance of the JCE doctrine in establishing and justifying the criminal responsibility of participants in larger groups and organizations has a more profound cause. System criminality requires meticulous planning, preparation and organization. In this respect, modern bureaucracy can obviously serve useful functions. But apart from these technological and organizational aspects, the bureaucratic model has a deeper psychological impact. In her account of the Eichmann trial, Hannah Arendt raises the pivotal question how the perpetrators of the *Endlösung* overcame 'their animal pity by which all normal men are affected in the

assumed in the jurisprudence of the ICTY,' Th. Weigend, 'Intent, Mistake of Law and Co-perpetration in the *Lubanga* Decision on Confirmation of Charges' (2008) 6 JICJ 478.

presence of human suffering'.[35] In his *Modernity and the Holocaust*, the Polish sociologist Zygmunt Bauman ventures to give an answer, where he points at a conspicuous feature of modern bureaucracies 'to dissociate evil from human motives'.[36] In the bureaucratic model, the activities are fragmented and subdivided in order to conceal the visible end result from those who perform them. Bauman suggests that, when bureaucracies engage in heinous crimes, this process of dissociation is done on purpose, to nip all qualms of conscience in the bud:

> The use of violence is most efficient and most cost-effective when the means are subjected to solely instrumental-rational criteria, and thus dissociated from moral evaluation of the ends.[37]

Functionaries derive their satisfaction from – and are rewarded for – the *progress* of their work and not from what they ultimately achieve. The focus on technological accomplishments distracts the attention from the true impact of one's activities that might prompt the functionary to recoil in horror.[38]

Detachment and dissociation in a hierarchical division of labour will imply difficulties in imagining the effects of one's conduct, but the effects of distance reach a dramatic apex when such a division becomes functional:

> Now it is not just the lack of direct, personal experience of the actual execution of the task to which successive commands contribute their share, but also the lack of similarity between the task at hand and the task of the office as a whole (one is not a miniature version, or an icon, of the other), which distances the contributor from the job performed by the bureaucracy of which he is a part.[39]

Of course, Bauman does not deny that international crimes require extensive preparation, planning and organization, but he only contends that this common plan is not divulged to most of the functionaries who are involved in the enterprise. Moreover, he suggests that modern bureaucracies thrive on 'anonymity' and that their functionaries do not communicate:

[35] H. Arendt, *Eichmann in Jerusalem: A Report on the Banality of Evil* (Viking Press, London/New York 1964), p. 106.

[36] Z. Bauman, *Modernity and the Holocaust* (Cambridge University Press, Cambridge 1989), p. 41.

[37] Bauman (n. 36) 98.

[38] Most illuminating in this respect is Hannah Arendt's comment on Eichmann's reaction when he was confronted with the practical effects of his decisions: 'He had seen the places to which the shipments were directed, and he had been shocked out of his wits.' Arendt (n. 35) 90.

[39] Bauman (n. 36) 99, 100.

> By itself, the function is devoid of meaning, and the meaning which is eventually bestowed on it is in no way pre-empted by the actions of its perpetrators. It will be 'the others' (*in most cases anonymous and out of reach*) who will some time, somewhere, decide that meaning.[40]

By now, the abyss between joint criminal enterprise doctrine and the modern criminal bureaucracy becomes strikingly clear. Bauman's functionaries and Arendt's *Schreibtishmörder* did contribute to heinous crimes; there is no mistake about that. But their share in the atrocities was often elusive and did not mirror the crimes themselves. Besides, the fragmentation of labour was conducive to lines of communication becoming more diffuse or even entirely obliterated. If one seeks to squeeze such persons into the pattern of a joint criminal enterprise, one must be prepared to stretch the concept to its outer limits or even relinquish its most conspicuous elements completely.

The Norwegian scholar Arne Johan Vetlesen has challenged the Bauman/Arendt thesis on modern bureaucracy and systematic criminality for being too rigid and distorting reality.[41] His criticism is twofold. For one thing, Bauman and Arendt have over-accentuated the picture of the detached and remote bureaucrat who had no personal resentment or motive in exercising his contribution to the *Endlösung*. The Eichmann-like figures are countered by numerous examples of all too willing executioners who displayed a brand of avid anti-Semitism and had fully internalized a structure of beliefs or *Weltanschauung*.[42] Secondly, and more to the point, Bauman's (and Arendt's) analysis does not comport with the practice of ethnic cleansing in the former Yugoslavia. Building on the profound cultural/sociological and psychological research of Alford, Girard and Melanie Klein, Vetlesen explains how ethnic cleansing emerged from identity politics.[43] The specific political constellation in the aftermath of the fragmentation of Yugoslavia, in combination with the universal process of globalism, created an atmosphere of existential anxiety and produced, as a backlash, the merging of individual and collective identity:

[40] Bauman (n. 33) 100 (emphasis added).

[41] A. J. Vetlesen, *Evil and Human Agency. Understanding Collective Evildoing* (Cambridge University Press, Cambridge 2005).

[42] Vetlesen (n. 41) 31/32; obviously, Vetlesen's arguments draw upon the work of D. J. Goldhagen, *Hitler's Willing Executioners: Ordinary Germans and the Holocaust* (Knopf, New York 1996) and C. Browning, *Ordinary Men: Reserve Police Battalion 101 and the Final Solution in Poland* (Harper Collins, New York 1992).

[43] Vetlesen (n. 41) 159–61.

> The individual's future was made one with the future and destiny of his group; and this future and issue was made into *the* issue of identity in such an existentially dramatized manner that *the identity issue became identical with the issue of sheer survival: when identity is endangered*, ultimately life itself is.[44]

Identity politics turned out to be a lasting project and a precarious one indeed, as the risk of contamination was always imminent, precisely because the cultural and ethnic distinctions were slight:

> The 'otherness' of the enemy needs to be asserted, nay displayed and quasi proven more vehemently in cases where at the start the differences between 'us' and 'them' are hard to spot.[45]

This explains why the neighbour became the prime target, the 'surrogate victim' of a ritual of purification.[46] Radically different from the assumptions of Arendt and Bauman, ethnic cleansing thrives on proximity, rather than on 'distantiation'.[47] Ethnic cleansing was a diabolic device to perpetuate the stain and to prevent the prospect of forgiving and reconciliation:

> The closer the perpetrator to the victim – in terms of kinship, friendship; a shared place, a shared past – the deeper and more lasting will be the psychological and emotional impact of the assault on the relationship between the two parties. Chances are that their relationship will be shattered forever. For these reasons alone, 'ethnic cleansing' is a particularly subtle and cruel form of evil.[48]

Vetlesen's 'proximity thesis', however, does not only permeate the relationship between perpetrator and victim. It also highlights the close ties between the perpetrators *inter se*, who seek to forge intimate relations between themselves, in an attempt – again – to confirm their common identity and to conceal their individual guilt by submerging into the collective. Ethnic cleansing creates – in Vetlesen's terminology – 'a sisterhood of shame and a brotherhood of guilt'.[49] With approval Vetlesen

[44] Vetlesen (n. 41) 187 (emphasis in original). [45] Vetlesen (n. 41) 191.

[46] Vetlesen (n. 40) 188, quoting R. Girard, *The Violence and the Sacred* (Grasset, Paris 1972) p. 278: 'the surrogate victim is fundamentally a member of the community, a neighbour of those destined to kill him.'

[47] Vetlesen (n. 41) 194: 'My claim is that "ethnic cleansing", by contrast, seizes upon and *maintains* existing conditions of proximity between perpetrator and victim and in fact *creates such conditions if they are not present and prolongs them as a matter of principle whenever they seem to wane.*' (emphasis in original).

[48] Vetlesen (n. 41) 207. [49] Vetlesen (n. 41) 207.

quotes Bauman, who contends that 'the community born of the initiatory crime remains the only refuge for the perpetrators', adding that:

> such individuals are glued together by joint vested interest in contesting the criminal and punishable nature of their crime. The best way to meet these conditions is not to allow the spilt blood to dry up: to (periodically or continually) refresh the memory of crime and the fear of punishment by topping the old crimes with new ones.[50]

Vetlesen's observations are a useful qualification of the Bauman/Arendt thesis and remind us that the dark side of life is too diverse to be straight-jacketed in a single sociological or philosophical theory. His findings point out that gang crime in the Balkans was rampant and suggest that the JCE doctrine may serve a useful function in case of mob violence. I will return to this topic in the final paragraph of this contribution. The litmus test, however, is whether JCE doctrine, on further scrutiny and different from our assumptions, would also be applicable in large-scale cases. After all, I have tried to demonstrate in the previous paragraph that the urge to combine the political/military leadership with the 'rank and file' in one large JCE is the major flaw in the doctrine, in view of the considerable physical and mental distance between these actors. Did the conflict in the Balkans, as analyzed by Vetlesen, breed closer relations between the higher echelons and the physical perpetrators and were the first mentioned more personally involved in the atrocities than in Bauman's anonymous bureaucracies? Vetlesen's own point of view in this matter is not entirely clear, although he certainly suggests that the protagonists were inspired by different motives.[51] As will be demonstrated in the next paragraph, however, Trial Chambers of the ICTY in recent decisions have made ardent efforts to show the synergy between the political hierarchy and the executioners, in order to buttress their preference for large scale JCEs.

IV. Putting the JCE doctrine to the test: some recent developments in the case law of the ICTY

One of the recurrently contested issues in recent case law concerns the scale of the joint criminal enterprise. In the *Kvočka* case, the Trial

[50] Vetlesen (n. 41) 195, 196, quoting Z. Bauman, *Liquid Modernity* (Oxford University Press, Oxford 2000), p. 20.

[51] Vetlesen (n. 41) 191, 192: 'I note that, though undoubtedly highly ideological from above (meaning top-down), the genocide that took place in the former Yugoslavia was highly personalized on the ground.'

Chamber suggested that a joint criminal enterprise might encompass the entire Nazi regime, which could be 'chopped up' in smaller subsidiaries, harbouring more particular criminal goals.[52] With apparent approval, the Trial Chamber quoted a judgment by a US Federal court, holding that federal drug laws provide that 'the relationship requirement for showing a common criminal enterprise is flexible, such that a defendant's relationship with other individuals need not exist at the same moment, those individuals need not have a relationship with one another and they may have different roles in the criminal enterprise.'[53]

In the *Krnojelac* case the Appeals Chamber expressed some scepticism in respect of such a broad understanding of the concept. The prosecution denied that, under the doctrine, the offenders should have a common state of mind and gave, as an illustration, the example of high-level political and military leaders who, from a distant location, plan the widespread destruction of civilian buildings (hospitals and schools) in a particular area in order to demoralize the enemy without the soldiers responsible for carrying out the attacks sharing the objective in question or even knowing the nature of the relevant targets. The Appeals Chamber disagreed with the Prosecution's position and pointed out that 'the example given by the Prosecution in support of its argument on this point appears more relevant to the planning of a crime under Article 7(1) of the Statute than to a joint criminal enterprise'.[54]

Apparently encouraged by the outcome of the *Brđanin* judgment, the appellant in the *Karemera* case chose a frontal confrontation by arguing that the Tribunal lacked jurisdiction to convict an accused pursuant to the third category of joint criminal enterprise for crimes committed by fellow participants in a JCE of 'vast scope'. Moreover, the appellant continued, the Tribunal lacked jurisdiction to consider third category JCE liability when there is no 'direct relationship' alleged between the accused and the physical perpetrators of the crime.[55] Obviously, both arguments

[52] *Prosecutor v Kvočka et al.*, IT-98–30/1-T, Judgment (2 November 2001) para. 307; a similar broad understanding of joint criminal enterprise was exhibited by the Appeals Chamber in the ICTR case of *Rwamakuba* (*Prosecutor v Rwamakuba*, Decision on Interlocutory Appeal Regarding Application of Joint Criminal Enterprise to the Crime of Genocide, ICTR-98–44G, Appeals Chamber (22 October 2004) para. 25): 'liability for participation in a criminal plan is as wide as the plan itself, even if the plan amounts to a "nation wide government-organized system of cruelty and injustice".'

[53] *US v Long*, 190 F.3d 471, 474 (6th Cir. 1999), quoted in *Prosecutor v Kvočka et al.* (n. 52) para. 311.

[54] *Prosecutor v Krnojelac*, IT-97–25-A, Judgment (17 September 2003) paras. 83 and 84.

[55] *Prosecutor v Édouard Karemera et al.*, Decision on Jurisdictional Appeals: Joint Criminal Enterprise, ICTR-98–44-AR72.5, ICTR-98–44-AR72.6 (12 April 2006) para. 2.

are strongly interrelated. The appellant suggests that communication and agreements between the participants are severely inhibited by the sheer size of the enterprise, a line of reasoning which is reminiscent of the *Brđanin* judgment. However, the Appeals Chamber did not buy the appellant's sweeping statement. Rehearsing the opinion of the Appeals Chamber in other cases, it considered that international customary law did not restrict the application of the JCE doctrine to enterprises of limited size or geographical scope. Nevertheless, in a way the Appeals Chamber recognized the concerns of the appellant by adding that the large scale of the JCE might affect the foreseeability of certain crimes.[56]

The approach of the Appeals Chamber is interesting. Although it does not directly address the issue of (lack of) communication between the participants, it implicitly suggests that establishing criminal liability on the basis of JCE doctrine may run astray, when participants, due to its large scope, are ignorant of each others' contributions or even existence.[57] After all, in such cases the risk of being unaware of sudden unpredictable developments and excesses augments to a considerable extent.

In the *Krajišnik* case the accused advanced similar arguments as had been brought forward by the defence in the *Karemera* case. As might have been expected, the line of reasoning was rejected by the Trial Chamber. The fact that the accused was structurally remote from the commission of the crimes charged in the indictment did not exclude the application of JCE (III). On the contrary, as the Trial Chamber observed: 'far from being inappropriate, JCE is well suited to cases such as the present one, in which numerous persons are all said to be concerned with the commission of a large number of crimes.'[58] Nevertheless, the Trial Chamber qualified this opinion by holding that: 'the persons in a criminal enterprise must be shown to act together, or in concert with each other, in the implementation of a common objective, if they are to share responsibility

[56] *Prosecutor v Karemera* (n. 55) para. 17.

[57] The problem of lack of communication in vast enterprises – in view of the assessment of 'common purpose' – is also acknowledged by M. Osiel in his outstanding contribution 'The banality of good: aligning incentives against mass atrocity' (2005) 105 *Columbia Law Review* 1751, 1800: 'Even acting in perfectly good conscience, prosecutors do not currently have any clear criteria for defining the enterprise and its membership. This is especially true as they move beyond the simplest case of those working together in a particular detention camp, interacting regularly face to face. The problem becomes perhaps most acute when prosecution moves to those involved at the very highest level of policymaking, working in the nation's capital, at great distance from subordinates in the hinterlands, *with whom they never communicate*.' (emphasis added).

[58] *Prosecutor v Krajišnik*, Judgment, IT-00–39/40 (27 September 2006) para. 876.

for the crimes committed through the JCE.' This would meet the concerns of the Trial Chamber in the *Brđanin* case.[59] The Trial Chamber took great pains to investigate the involvement of the accused in the policy of ethnic cleansing and the ensuing crimes. As President of the Bosnian-Serb Assembly, Mr Krajišnik occupied a pivotal position in the Bosnian-Serb leadership. He co-acted with other leaders, such as Radovan Karadžić and Biljana Plavšić, in order to draft and enact a twofold policy. First, the Serbs should be separated from the Croats and the Moslems, as living together had become quite impossible. Next, the Serbs were to claim their historical birthright to the grounds and regions where they occupied the majority, which was obviously a self-fulfilling prophecy, as the Bosnian Serb (para)military had evicted and deported the enemy civilians themselves. The Trial Chamber noticed the dangerous rhetoric, employed by the Bosnian-Serb leadership, in which Muslims were denounced as fascists, creating a climate of fear and conducive to violence and the commission of serious crimes.[60]

The accused did not only know, but actively supported arming activities,[61] take-over operations,[62] crimes related to the attacks, such as, for instance, the shelling of Sarajevo,[63] population expulsions[64] and detention of civilians.[65] He was aware of and applauded the involvement of paramilitary groups, like the infamous Tigers of Arkan.[66] Particularly telling are the Trial Chamber's observations on the accused's style of leadership. Mr Krajišnik was not the hierarchically isolated bureaucrat he pretended to be. He and Radovan Karadžić 'intervened and exerted direct influence at all levels of Bosnian-Serb affairs, including military operation'.[67] His was 'an unencumbered style of leadership that cut straight to the source and displayed little patience for lines of reporting'.[68] The Bosnian Serb leadership had regular meetings with local authorities and representatives to discuss political and strategic military matters which seems to corroborate Karadžić's boasting that he and the accused 'were no ivory-tower politicians, but travelled the

[59] *Prosecutor v Krajišnik* (n. 58) para. 884.
[60] *Prosecutor v Krajišnik* (n. 58) paras. 921–24.
[61] *Prosecutor v Krajišnik* (n. 58) paras. 925–34.
[62] *Prosecutor v Krajišnik* (n. 58) paras. 935–49.
[63] *Prosecutor v Krajišnik* (n. 58) paras. 950–74.
[64] *Prosecutor v Krajišnik* (n. 58) paras. 1021–34.
[65] *Prosecutor v Krajišnik* (n. 58) paras. 1035–64.
[66] *Prosecutor v Krajišnik* (n. 58) paras. 975–86.
[67] *Prosecutor v Krajišnik* (n. 58) para. 987.
[68] *Prosecutor v Krajišnik* (n. 58) para. 991.

land learning the facts and conferring with and counselling Bosnian Serb leaders on the ground'.[69]

Summarizing the findings and addressing the question whether the accused would incur criminal liability because of his participation in a joint criminal enterprise, the Trial Chamber inquired whether he satisfied the three conditions for JCE (III):

1. *A plurality of persons.* The Trial Chamber concluded that the JCE comprised a large number of persons, including the Pale-based leadership and the rank and file which consisted of local politicians, military and police commanders, paramilitary leaders and others. The accused was sufficiently connected and concerned with the physical perpetrators, or those who procured other persons to do so.[70]
2. *Common objective.* Initially, the common objective was the removal of Bosnian Muslims and Bosnian Croats from large areas of Bosnia-Herzegovina which inevitably entailed the crimes of deportation and forced transfer of these people. Gradually, the JCE members accepted that other crimes, like illegal detention, inhumane treatment, rapes and killings were instrumental in accomplishing this goal. The acceptance of this greater range of criminal means implied an adaptation of the prior common objective which induced the JCE (III) to transform into a JCE (I). After all, it would be hard to sustain that these crimes were only predictable outcomes of the general policy; they were part and parcel of the common intent.[71]
3. *Contribution.* The main contribution of Mr Krajišnik consisted of his efforts to establish and perpetuate the SDS party and state structures that were instrumental to the commission of the crimes. 'He also deployed his political skills both locally and internationally to facilitate the implementation of the JCE's common objective through the crimes envisaged by that objective.'[72]

I have dwelled upon this judgment, because, in my opinion and to the best of my knowledge, it exemplifies the strongest and most profound effort to come to terms with the intricate problem of applying the JCE doctrine to vast enterprises. Obviously, the most conspicuous asset is that the Trial Chamber takes the requirement of 'concerted action' seriously. Another of its qualities is that the Trial Chamber shows a fine understanding of the

[69] *Prosecutor v Krajišnik* (n. 58) para. 1014.
[70] *Prosecutor v Krajišnik* (n. 58) paras. 1086, 1087.
[71] *Prosecutor v Krajišnik* (n. 58) para. 1118.
[72] *Prosecutor v Krajišnik* (n. 58) para. 1120.

fact that objectives and purposes are not static, but may change over time, affecting the character of the JCE and the nature of its members' criminal responsibility.

Should I then qualify – or even renounce – my former statement that the JCE doctrine is not easily applicable to sustain criminal liability for political and military leaders in a vast enterprise? Not necessarily. Although the legal findings in this judgment are razor sharp they are not matched by the evidence, which is sometimes less strong or even disappointing. In spite of the sincere efforts of the Trial Chamber to prove direct contacts between the accused and the rank and file – which indeed produce some interesting examples – the evidence of concerted action in respect of more specific crimes is less convincing. Two examples may suffice. From the fact that the accused had been *informed* about irregularities in detention facilities, the Trial Chamber derives that he was both *involved* in the maintenance of detention centres and aware of inhumane treatment.[73] Furthermore, Mr Krajišnik's belligerent language towards the Muslims and Croats and his unrelenting insistence on the need for 'ethnic division on the ground' will certainly have been conducive to violence and crimes against civilian enemies, but are still rather remote from the commission of specific crimes.

The general picture that emerges is one of *indirect* and *remote* involvement.[74] Mr Krajišnik created the political climate in which violent crimes could prosper. He ripened the minds of his fellow Bosnian Serbs, instilling them with fear and hatred of Bosnian Moslems and Bosnian Croats, so that they would easily indulge in war crimes and crimes against humanity. He must have understood, if not intended, that his policy of ethnic division could only be accomplished through large-scale violence and crimes and that he had incontrovertibly acted closely together with others to reach his political goals.

In view of these findings, it seems obvious that Krajišnik should incur criminal responsibility for the atrocities, but *not* on the basis of joint criminal enterprise liability. These observations raise the question whether other concepts of perpetration and participation would not have been more appropriate to sustain the criminal responsibility of the accused.

[73] *Prosecutor v Krajišnik* (n. 58) para. 1047.

[74] In the same vein: Zahar and Sluiter (n. 13) 221: ' "Leadership cases", such as the ICTY's *Krajišnik* case, are all about the responsibility of a person far removed from the crimes on the ground.'

V. In search of alternatives

The question to be explored is whether the presumed inadequacy of the JCE doctrine to fully grasp the nature of collective criminality is exemplary for criminal legal concepts as a whole. The present author is not of this opinion. The statutes of the *ad hoc* Tribunals for the Former Yugoslavia and Rwanda display a host of modes of participation which forge more direct links between high-level military or politicians and physical perpetrators or specific crimes. Simultaneously, they suggest the collective dimension and the complex organization, required for the commission of international crimes. Suffice to mention here 'planning', 'instigation' and 'ordering', as incorporated in Article 7(1) of the Statute of the ICTY, respectively Article 6(1) of the Statute of the ICTR. Van Sliedregt presents 'perpetration by means (of another person)', which is incorporated in Article 25, section 3(a) of the Rome Statute, as the concept *par excellence* to frame the instigators on macro level.[75]

Closely connected to 'perpetration by means' are the legal concepts of 'functional perpetration' and *Organisationsherrschaft*, which have been developed in Dutch and German law respectively.[76] The Dutch concept has come to fruition in the realm of economic crime and is predicated on the notion that those who in a functional capacity 'effectuate' crimes would qualify to incur criminal responsibility, rather than those who, usually as subordinates or employees, carry out instructions or orders. In Dutch criminal law the concept has been refined in case law. The lower limit for criminal responsibility requires that the accused accepted the crimes as part of the normal course of events, which obviously implies that he or she was aware that these crimes or similar ones occurred. Furthermore, he or she should have had some measure of control on their occurrence, in the sense that it was in his or her power whether the crimes were committed or not.[77]

[75] van Sliedregt (n. 5) 360.

[76] Compare on the Dutch concept of 'functional perpetration': A.M. van Woensel, *In de daderstand verheven; Beschouwingen over functioneel daderschap in het Nederlandse strafrecht* ('Elevated to Perpetration; Reflections on Functional Perpetration in Dutch Criminal Law') (Gouda Quint, Arnhem 1993); on *Organisationsherrschaft*: C. Roxin, *Täterschaft und Tatherrschaft* (6th edn, Walter de Gruyter, Berlin/New York 1994), pp. 248–52 and K. Ambos, 'Command responsibility and *organisationsherrschaft*: ways of attributing international crimes to the "most responsible"', this volume, Chapter 6. By the same author: K. Ambos, 'Joint criminal enterprise and command responsibility' (2007) 5 I JICJ 179–83 and K. Ambos, *Der Allgemeine Teil des Völkerstrafrechts: Ansätze einer Dogmatisierung* (Duncker & Humblot, Berlin 2003), pp. 590–4.

[77] Supreme Court, 23 February 1954, NJ 378.

In Dutch criminal law doctrine, there has been some reluctance to accept the viability of the concept beyond the realm of economic crime. Recently, however, some writers, including the present author, have admitted that the concept may serve useful purposes in addressing system criminality.[78] In his major textbook on substantive criminal law in the Netherlands, De Hullu argues that the question whether the concept of functional perpetration is an appropriate tool to attribute criminal responsibility depends on the factual context in which the crime has been committed, especially whether an organization displaying hierarchical features and distinctions between organizers and executioners has been involved in the crimes. He explicitly mentions campaigns of strategic rape in the former Yugoslavia as an illuminating example.[79]

The German legal concept of *Organisationsherrschaft* essentially conveys the idea that political or military leaders at the apex of the state power apparatus may take advantage of their dominant position to procure others to commit (international) crimes.[80] The control over the physical perpetrators is not exercised directly, but rather by virtue of the organization which serves the *auctor intellectualis* as an instrument.[81] A characteristic feature of this legal doctrine of criminal responsibility is that the physical perpetrators are dispensable, as the leaders can recruit from a sheer inexhaustible supply.[82] Some German scholars have openly propagated the concept of *Organisationsherrschaft* as a splendid instrument to confront the complexities in assessing criminal responsibility of political and military leaders for system criminality.[83]

[78] T. J. Noyon, G. E. Langemeyer and J. Remmelink (eds.), *Het Wetboek van Strafrecht, losbladig commentaar* ('The Penal Code: A Loose-leaf Commentary) (Kluwer, Deventer 2005) Part I, Entry 19 to Art. 47 Dutch Penal Code; van der Wilt (n. 7) (2005) 20–5.

[79] J. De Hullu, *Materieel strafrecht; over algemene leerstukken van strafrechtelijke aansprakelijkheid naar Nederlands recht* ('Substantive Criminal Law: On General Doctrines of Criminal Responsibility in Dutch Law') (Kluwer, Deventer 2000), p. 153.

[80] Roxin (n. 76) 248: '*Wer in einen Organisationsapparat an irgendeiner Stelle in der Weise eingeschaltet ist, daß er ihm untergebenen Personen Befehle erteilen kann, ist kraft der ihm zukommenden Willensherrschaft mittelbarer Täter, wenn er seine Befugnisse zur Durchführung strafbarer Handlungen einsetst.*'

[81] Ambos (n. 76) 181–3.

[82] Roxin (n. 76) 250: '*Wenn ein Apparat so aufgebaut ist, läßt sich das die Organisationsherrschaft kennzeichnende Kriterium auch hier aufweisen: Das vom Hintermann in Gang gesetzte Unternehmen wird unabhängig von der Person des Ausführenden verwirklicht.*'

[83] Cf. H. Vest, 'Humanitätsverbrechen – Herausforderung für das Individualstrafrecht?' ('International Crimes: A Challenge for Individual Criminal Responsibility?') (2002) 3 113 ZStW 493 and Roxin (n. 76) 242–52; Osiel (n. 57) 1831–3 is interested in the concept of *Organisationsherrschaft*. Nevertheless, he comments that the concept is predicated on

The concepts of functional perpetration and *Organisationsherrschaft* are not entirely interchangeable. Whereas *Organisationsherrschaft* focuses on the apparatus which enables the remote offender to steer the actual perpetrators, functional perpetration has a broader field of application in criminal law, as it puts emphasis on the position of the 'man at the top', rather than on the specific features of the organization. Whatever their differences may be, both concepts offer a number of interesting opportunities in capturing the essence of collective responsibility in system criminality. First, they enable courts to 'pierce the functional veil'. The contentions of Eichmann's counsel, Dr Servatius, that his client was nothing more than a cog in the machine, are well known. He had not physically perpetrated the atrocities. His activities had the outward appearance of legality and he had merely obeyed orders. Besides, he could not have prevented the hideous crimes, because if he had stepped down, others would have gladly replaced him.[84] In this way, Eichmann's function served him as a cloak to ward off criminal responsibility. By taking someone's function as point of departure for the assessment of his or her guilt, the concept of functional perpetration converts the protective shield into an offensive weapon. Large bureaucracies which engage in system criminality need unquestioning and dedicated functionaries. The individuals may be dispensable, but the functions are certainly not.[85] In other words, the functionaries are pivotal to the working and success of the system. The concept of functional perpetration and *Organisationsherrschaft* shed a light on the way the accused is related to specific crimes and thus contribute in elucidating *actus reus*. Moreover, these concepts have a strong moral appeal. The criminal trial should transform the 'cogs in the machine' back into human beings.[86] Once the accused has made the decision to identify him- or herself completely with a devious system and squander his or her

Max Weber's famous ideal type of modern bureaucracy with its 'rational orderliness, desensitized precision and efficiency'. It would not dovetail with the modern 'more informal, unsystematic, and decentralized dimensions of mass atrocity' (1834). These antagonisms echo the discussion in § 3.

84 On the 'cog in the machine' argument, see Roxin (n. 76) 246, who quotes parts of Servatius' closing statement. On the legal justifications, see Arendt (n. 34) 135–50.

85 Arendt (n. 35) 289 acutely comments: 'If the defendant excuses himself on the ground that he acted not as a man but as a mere functionary whose functions could just as easily have been carried out by anyone else, it is as if a criminal pointed to the statistics of a crime – which set forth that so-and-so many crimes per day are committed in such-and-such a place – and declared that he only did what was statistically expected, that it was mere accident that he did it and not somebody else, since after all somebody had to do it.'

86 Arendt (n. 35) 289.

humanity to this purpose, it seems appropriate to tackle the accused on this one-dimensional capacity.

Finally, the concepts serve to portray the collective dimension of collective criminality. As has been observed before, international crimes are by definition committed by a collective within a system of injustice. The coherence in policy and purpose may not always be visible for those who are involved in the system, but it cannot be denied that the success of the system depends on those elements.[87] The concepts of functional perpetration and *Organisationsherrschaft* enable courts to disentangle complex structural relationships and to identify precisely each contribution to the repressive system. They recognize that functionaries and their contributions are interrelated and may thus be helpful in obtaining a comprehensive picture of system criminality, which is arguably one of the major goals of international criminal law enforcement.

It stands to reason that courts should carefully distinguish between different kinds of functional perpetrators. They should establish responsibility and mete out punishment in accordance with each position and characteristic contribution. After all, system criminality hosts a wide variety of functional perpetrators: the bookkeeper who makes up the list of families eligible for being evicted from their homes; the doctor in a detention camp who approves and selects the 'patients' qualifying for medical experiments; the propagandist who constantly bangs the drums of historical deprecation and in no uncertain terms calls for revenge. Such functional activities give a clue as to how these people are related to the crimes. The political and military leaders who stand trial in their capacity as head of state, member of government or head of the secret police, on the other hand, do not *only* incur criminal responsibility for the international crimes, but are also accountable for employing the system or organization for this very purpose.[88] The concepts of functional perpetration and *Organisationsherrschaft* are perfectly capable of serving as tools in the hands of courts to make such refined distinctions.

[87] Compare again Arendt (n. 35) 289: 'Of course it is important to the political and social sciences that the essence of totalitarian government, and perhaps the nature of every bureaucracy, is to make functionaries and mere cogs in the administrative machinery out of men, and thus to dehumanise them.'

[88] Vest (n. 83) 494 makes a useful distinction between '*Organisationsherrschaft innerhalb des Apparates*' (control over the organization within the state system) and '*Organisationsherrschaft über den Apparat*' (control over the whole state system: '*Sie steuern "nur" ein Teilgeshehen, indem – und solange – sie das Funktionieren der Institution modifizieren*'. ('They, i.e. the lower- and mid-level functionaries only govern or control part of the events in so far – and as long – as they modify the functioning of the institute'.)

The question is whether the concepts of functional perpetration and *Organisationsherrschaft* could be incorporated into international criminal law. There are some signs that point in this direction. For one thing, a species of functional perpetration surfaces in the concept of 'superior responsibility' which, after all, links up with the function of a military or civil commander. Furthermore, the identification of functionaries in a system of repression, such as a concentration camp, shows that functional capacity is considered an important element for the establishment of criminal responsibility. Their position should, however, not be considered as a sufficient condition for their criminal participation in a JCE, but rather as a starting point for an inquiry into their involvement in specific crimes.

Finally, and perhaps most interestingly, one could advance the argument that 'functional perpetration' and *Organisationsherrschaft* are implicit in some concepts of criminal responsibility which are recognised in the Statutes.[89] The organs of the ICTY have made some pronouncements which seem to corroborate this point of view. In the *Krajišnik* case, the prosecution itself has made the interesting suggestion that the physical perpetrators might be qualified as *instruments* of the political and military leadership.[90] This obviously reminds us of the legal construct of *perpetration by means*, which does not feature in the Statute of the ICTY, but which has been incorporated in Article 25 of the Rome Statute. From a continental law perspective, the involvement of the leadership is a prime example of functional perpetration or *Organisationsherrshaft*. It was the position and function of Krajišnik within the political hierarchy which enabled him to draft the general policy, to direct and steer local leaders and to leave the dirty work to the rank and file.

In the *Stakić* case the Trial Chamber, anticipating Article 25 of the Rome Statute, emphasized that 'commission' encompassed *indirect* commission as well.[91] Such findings confirm the impression that 'functional perpetration' and *Organisationsherrshaft* do not introduce entirely new forms of responsibility – which would arguably militate against the

[89] In this vein. Ambos (n. 76) 181, 182: 'This theory (i.e. *Organisationsherrschaft*) is a form of perpetration by means, recognized in Art. 25(3)(a) 3rd alternative ("through another person"), according to which the "man in the background" dominates the direct perpetrators by means of an organizational apparatus of hierarchical power.' Similarly, though slightly more hesitant: G. Werle, *Principles of International Criminal Law* (Asser Press, The Hague 2005), p. 124.

[90] *Prosecutor v Krajišnik* (n. 58) para. 1080.

[91] *Prosecutor v Stakić*, IT-97–24, Judgment (31 July 2003) para. 439.

nullum crimen-principle – but rather are tools to interpret existing modes of criminal responsibility.[92]

VI. The JCE doctrine revisited

The major conclusion of this chapter is that JCE doctrine is inadequate to sustain the criminal responsibility of all persons who are somehow involved in a vast enterprise that engages in system criminality. The original doctrine provides a number of safeguards in respect of contribution and concerted action. The reality of system criminality, however, forces courts to relax or even outright relinquish such criminal law requirements, as soon as they try to squeeze all 'participants' – however remote – in the straightjacket of a joint criminal enterprise. The result is a contrived distortion of the initial concept, which arguably falls short of the demands of criminal law.

The final question which needs to be addressed is whether the JCE doctrine still serves a number of useful purposes. The present author is convinced that it does. For one thing, the doctrine has been mobilized in order to extend criminal responsibility over those members of a criminal group which could not be held accountable on the basis of other concepts of criminal responsibility. In case of mob violence, such an extension may be warranted, because group processes unchain a specific dynamic. Group crimes are committed by virtue of a common effort in which each and every contribution counts, as each member is fortified and feels comforted by the presence of others. Criminal responsibility is largely predicated on the reproach that the accused has not dissociated himself from the group, although – admittedly – it may not always be easy to leave a group, once one has joined its ranks. The strong element in the JCE doctrine is that it assumes that the members, by entering into a prior agreement, have proved to be psychologically capable and prepared to commit those crimes. It suggests that they have incapacitated themselves to withdraw and therefore have only themselves to blame for this predicament. This is precisely the reason why a prior agreement is such a crucial element, because it is the essential link that binds the group members together.

92 Compare E. J. Lampe, '*Systemunrecht und Unrechtssysteme*' ('System injustice and unjust systems') (1994) 106 ZStW 743, who points at the German legal figure of the *Hintermann* (comparable to 'perpetration by means') and comments: '*Denn dem hierarchischen Aufbau totalitärer Unrechtssysteme entspricht die Rechtsfigur eines "Täters hinter dem Täter" besser*'.

The second function of the JCE is a symbolic one. Although functionaries in modern bureaucracies often work in relative isolation and are not connected to the physical perpetrators, it cannot be denied that, at the highest level, political and military leaders often closely cooperate and conspire. The JCE doctrine may not be necessary to *establish* their criminal responsibility for 'policy' crimes, but it is certainly a most appropriate concept to *express* the common plight. This symbolic function should not be underestimated. Criminal law's natural proclivity is to focus on personal fault and individual guilt. Such an approach is generally to be applauded, also as it prevents culprits from hiding behind 'Acts of states' and thus declining any personal responsibility. However, a one-sided emphasis on personal guilt may obscure the collective dimension of system criminality.

The *Krajišnik* case provides a good example. Obviously, the policy-oriented, scheming disposition of the accused evokes the legal concept of *planning*. The Trial Chamber might have followed the suggestions of the Appeals Chamber in the *Krnojelac* case by holding the accused responsible for planning in conjunction with others. A more limited 'core' JCE might encompass the Pale-based leadership who would incur criminal responsibility on the basis of the Joint Criminal Enterprise doctrine not for the actual commission of the crimes, but for the *planning* of these crimes. Krajišnik and the other members of this JCE could be linked to the specific crimes and the physical perpetrators by means of the concepts of 'functional perpetration', *Organisationsherrschaft* or 'perpetration by means'. The combination of several concepts of criminal responsibility in this way serves to fine tune the contribution and position of senior leaders with their criminal guilt, while it succeeds in reflecting the character of system criminality.

8

System criminality at the ICTY

ELIES VAN SLIEDREGT*

I. Introduction

Violations of international humanitarian law connote what Röling called 'system criminality'.[1] Indeed, almost by nature, genocide, crimes against humanity, and war crimes occur on a mass scale or in the context of systemic violence. System criminality very often concerns a plurality of offenders, particularly in carrying out the crimes. It further presupposes an *auctor intellectualis* pulling the strings. This can be one person, but also a group of people gathered together in a political or military structure.

The concept of individual criminal responsibility in international criminal law comes with a certain 'flavour'. System criminality engenders system responsibility. System responsibility borders on collective responsibility. This is evidenced by Bernays' collective criminality theory applied in Nuremberg.[2] System criminality can put pressure on the principle of individual criminal responsibility and can make it expand beyond the limit of personal culpability.

In this chapter I will argue that the way the ICTY has dealt with system criminality is unsatisfactory from a conceptual and legality point of view. My focus will be on two legal concepts, or modes of liability, superior responsibility and joint criminal enterprise. Describing the development of these two concepts in the case law of the *ad hoc* Tribunals, it becomes clear that the concepts are not the most obvious basis of liability for those in the higher echelons of government. This has lead to expanding the limit of, or reconceptualizing these modes of liability. In particular, JCE seems

* Professor of Criminal Law, VU University Amsterdam.

[1] B. V. A. Röling, 'Aspects of the criminal responsibility for violations of the laws of war', in A. Cassese (ed.), *The New Humanitarian Law of Armed Conflict* (Editoriale Scientifica, Napoli 1979), p. 203; see also A. Nollkaemper, 'Introduction', this volume, Chapter 1.

[2] See B. F. Smith, *Reaching Judgment at Nuremberg* (Basic Books Publishers, New York 1977), pp. 33–7.

to be a concept with ever expanding boundaries. In this chapter, superior responsibility will be discussed in section II and JCE in section III. In each section the development of the concept in case law will be described and its role in prosecuting system criminality is examined. In section IV the relationship between those on the ground and those at leadership level will be analysed. Section V will contain concluding observations.

II. Superior responsibility

The landmark case at the ICTY on superior responsibility is undoubtedly the case of *Mucic et al.*, also referred to as the *Čelebići* case, after the camp where the crimes were committed. Two of the accused, Delić and Landzo, in their respective positions as deputy commander and guard, were found guilty of being personally responsible for their direct participation in the crimes against detainees. However, Mucić, the commander of the camp, was found guilty of crimes committed by his subordinates by virtue of his position as a *de facto* superior of the camp. The judgment in the *Čelebići* case was the first solid decision on superior responsibility by an international tribunal after Nuremberg and Tokyo.[3] It was also the first superior responsibility case before the ICTY. Until then, the accused were charged and convicted for direct participation under Article 7(1) of the Statute. The Trial Chamber in *Čelebići* formulated three criteria that should be met before anyone can be held liable as a superior under Article 7(3) of the Statute.[4] These criteria reflect the three aspects of the concept of superior responsibility established in post-Second World War case law. Proof is required:

(1) of the existence of a superior-subordinate relationship;
(2) that the superior knew or had reason to know that the criminal act was about to be or had been committed; and

[3] For comments on the *Čelebići* case, see I. Bantekas, 'The contemporary law of superior responsibility' (1999) 93 AJIL 573–95; M. R. Lippman, 'The evolution and scope of command responsibility' (2000) 13 LJIL 139; commentary on the *Čelebići* judgment by H. van der Wilt, in A. Klip and G. Sluiter (eds.), *Annotated Leading Cases of International Criminal Tribunals, vol 3, The International Criminal Tribunal for the Former Yugoslavia 1997–1999* (Intersentia, Antwerp-Groningen and Oxford 2001), pp. 669–83.

[4] Article 7(3) ICTY Statute reads: 'The fact that any of the acts referred to in articles 2 to 5 of the present Statute was committed by a subordinate does not relieve his superior of criminal responsibility if he knew or had reason to know that the subordinate was about to commit such acts or had done so and the superior failed to take the necessary and reasonable measures to prevent such acts or to punish the perpetrators thereof.'

(3) that the superior failed to take the necessary and reasonable measures to prevent the criminal act or to punish the perpetrator thereof.[5]

As the *Čelebići* Trial Chamber's findings on the scope and content of superior responsibility have been endorsed on appeal and repeatedly confirmed by ICTY and ICTR Trial Chambers, the groundwork and underlying principles of this doctrine seem settled in the Tribunals' case law.

1. *Superior responsibility beyond the* Čelebići *case*

In the judgments that followed the *Čelebići* judgment, the doctrine of superior responsibility has been further developed and clarified. On three points the concept has been elaborated: (1) the scope and nature of the concept of superior responsibility; (2) the superior-subordinate relationship; and (3) the 'had reason to know' standard.

a. Scope, nature and punishment

Superior responsibility does not extend to acts committed by subordinates *before* the assumption of command. This was determined by the ICTY Appeals Chamber in an interlocutory appeal on jurisdiction in the *Hadžihasanović and Kubura* case. Commander Kubura, who had taken up the position as commander on 1 April 1992, was not criminally liable for crimes committed by subordinates in January 1992.[6] The Appeals Chamber held that it follows from the doctrine of superior responsibility that a superior-subordinate relationship should exist *at the time of the offence* for the superior to be held liable.[7] This ensures that there is a close link between superiors and subordinates, which makes the concept difficult to apply to situations of system criminality where those at leadership level are far removed from those on the ground, at 'execution level'.[8]

[5] *Prosecutor v Delalić et al.*, IT-96–21-T, Judgment, para. 346, confirmed in appeal; *Prosecutor v Delalić et al.*, IT-96–21-A, Judgment, Appeals Chamber (20 February 2001) paras. 189–98, 225–6, 238–9, 256, 263. The principles developed in *Čelebići* were reiterated and endorsed in the *Aleksovski* Judgment, and confirmed in the *Aleksovski* Appeal Judgment, see *Prosecutor v Zlatko Aleksovski*, IT-95–14/1-A (24 March 2000) para. 72.

[6] *Prosecutor v Hadžihasanović*, Decision on Joint Challenge to Jurisdiction, IT-01–47-AR72 (16 July 2003).

[7] It is worth noting that Art. 28 of the ICC Statute – the most recent provision on superior responsibility – requires that 'subordinate crimes' are *a result of* a superior's failure to exercise control properly thus ruling out superior responsibility for past crimes.

[8] Recently, a majority of the Appeals Chamber in *Orić* expressed discontent with the *Hadžihasanović and Kubura* jurisdiction decision. In one declaration and two partially dissenting opinions three judges declare that they think previous crimes should be

Another important finding concerns the nature of superior responsibility. In *Halilović* the Trial Chamber held that under the doctrine of superior responsibility, superiors are not indirectly liable for the crimes of their subordinates. The clause 'for the acts of his subordinates' in Article 7(3) '[d]oes not mean that the commander shares the same responsibility as the subordinates who committed the crimes, but rather that….the commander should bear responsibility for his failure to act'.[9] The Trial Chamber in the *Hadžihasanović and Kubura* case endorsed this finding. The judges in this case found the two accused guilty solely on the basis of superior responsibility. In determining the sentence, the Trial Chamber held that superior responsibility pursuant to Article 7(3) ICTY St is a *sui generis* responsibility, distinct from that defined in Article 7(1)ICTY St. A superior who has failed in his obligation to ensure that his troops respect international humanitarian law is held criminally responsible for his *own* omissions, rather than for the crimes resulting from them.[10] A superior who is found guilty solely on the basis of superior responsibility did not participate in the commission of the material elements of the subordinates' crimes and lacked the requisite intent in respect of these crimes. Hence, such responsibility carries a lower sentence than if the superior was found to have participated in a crime pursuant to Article 7(1) ICTY St. The findings of the *Hadžihasanović and Kubura* Trial Chamber on the nature of superior responsibility were left undisturbed on appeal.[11]

b. Superior-subordinate relationship

In at least two cases before the ICTY the question arose whether a superior can be held responsible for acts of 'unidentified' subordinates. The Trial Chamber in *Hadžihasanović and Kubura* held that, to establish the existence of a superior-subordinate relationship, it is important to be able to identify the alleged perpetrators. This does not mean that the perpetrator needs to be identified exactly. It is sufficient to specify to which

attributable to the superior who assumes command after crimes have been committed and he/she has been made aware of such crimes. See *Prosecutor v Orić*, IT-03-68-A (3 July 2008).

9 *Prosecutor v Halilovic*, IT-01–48-T, Judgment (16 November 2005) para. 54. See also Appeals Chamber in Krnojelac: 'It cannot be overemphasised that, where responsibility is concerned, an accused is not charged with the crimes of his subordinates but with his failure to carry out his duty as a superior to exercise control.' *Prosecutor v Krnojelac*, IT-97–25-A, Judgment (17 September 2003) para. 171.

10 See also *Orić* Trial Judgment (n. 8) para. 317, where the findings of the *Hadžihasanović* Trial Chamber on this point were endorsed.

11 *Prosecutor v Hadžihasanović and Kubura*, IT-47-A (16 July 2003) paras. 312–318.

group the perpetrator belonged and prove that the accused exercised effective control over that group.[12] The Trial Chamber in *Orić* went one step further; it held that a superior may be held liable for crimes committed by 'anonymous persons'. For the first time, it was held that the direct perpetrator does not have to be a subordinate of the superior. Orić was held responsible for his subordinates' failure to prevent murder and cruel treatment perpetrated by 'opportunistic visitors' who intruded into the detention facilities and maltreated detainees. This is a significant ruling that may be seen to expand the scope of superior responsibility beyond the chain of command.

The *Blagojević* Appeals Chamber, albeit implicitly, endorsed the *Orić* Trial Chamber judgment by holding that liability under Article 7(3) of the ICTY Statute may also attach to the superior whose subordinates have *participated* in a crime through 'committing' under Article 7(1) of the ICTY Statute, for instance by aiding and abetting the commission of crimes. By holding that 'committing' throughout the ICTY Statute is used '[i]n a broad sense, encompassing all modes of responsibility covered by Article 7(1)'[13] and by adopting a purposive reading of Article 86 of AP I[14] the Appeals Chamber affirmed the Trial Chamber's findings in the *Orić* case.

On 3 July 2008, the Appeals Chamber reversed the *Orić* Trial Chamber judgment. It held that since it was not clear on which basis Orić's subordinate Atif Krdžić was culpable for the crimes committed by 'outsiders', the decision that Orić was responsible for those crimes on the basis of superior responsibility could not stand. The judgment does not rule out the possibility that superiors are liable for crimes committed by anonymous perpetrators, nor does it forestall the *Blagojević* appellate ruling that accepts superior responsibility beyond the direct chain of command. As long as the subordinate can be identified and it is clear on which basis the latter is responsible for such crimes, superior responsibility can attach to his superior. The *Orić* appellate ruling emphasizes the superior-subordinate relationship as an element of superior responsibility. As such, the recent *Orić* judgment endorses the *Celebiči* jurisprudence and represents what Bonafè has called a 'rigorous definition' of superior responsibility.[15]

[12] *Prosecutor v Hadžihasanović and Kubura* (n. 11) para. 90.

[13] *Prosecutor v Blagojovic*, IT-02–60, appeal Judgment (9 May 2007) para. 280.

[14] *Prosecutor v Blagojovic* (n. 13) para. 282.

[15] See B. Bonafè, 'Finding a proper role for command responsibility' (2007) 5 JCIJ 602, who argues that superior responsibility is narrowly defined in modern war crimes law and as a result can only be successfully applied in more traditional military-like contexts.

2. System criminality and superior responsibility

The concept of superior responsibility has been developed since the landmark ruling in *Čelebići*. It has expanded in recent ICTY case law by broadening liability beyond the direct superior-subordinate relationship. Yet the Appeals Chamber ruling in *Orić* prevents it from expanding too much. In that sense, the prosecutor's attempt to loosen the link between the superior and the subordinate has been only partially successful. From a prosecutorial point of view, loosening the link between superiors and subordinates serves prosecuting system criminality where those at the highest level, the intellectual perpetrators, are often far removed from those at execution level.

'Delinking' superiors from subordinates further 'fits' the findings of those ICTY Trial Chambers that regard superior responsibility as a separate crime of omission, as a dereliction of duty rather than a 'mode of liability' as the ICTY Prosecutor submitted.[16] However, it is doubtful whether the ICTY Statute and its proceedings warrant such an understanding of superior responsibility. The wording of Article 7(3) of the ICTY Statute suggests that superior responsibility is an extension of 'subordinate responsibility'. Moreover, it does not comply with the practice at the Tribunal to punish a superior for the offence(s) committed by the subordinate(s). The Trial Chamber in *Hadžihasanovićand Kubura* took an unprecedented and innovative step by imposing a sentence distinct from, and much more lenient than, that of the subordinate. By doing this, the Trial Chamber felt it expressed the *sui generis* nature of superior responsibility. This 'new direction' had been endorsed by the Trial Chamber in *Orić*.[17]

This is not to say that the interpretation of superior responsibility as genuine omission liability should not be welcomed. For a long time it was unclear for what the superior was blamed.[18] At least now it has been made clear: superior responsibility is a dereliction of duty. Moreover, one can only agree with the finding in *Hadžihasanovićand Kubura* that superior responsibility as negligence warrants a more lenient sentence. The distinction between intent and negligence where the latter is generally regarded as being lower on the scale of culpability than the former,

[16] See *Prosecutor v Orić*, Prosecution's Appeal Brief, IT-03-68-A (16 October 2006) para. 10.

[17] Since the conviction under 7(3) of the Statute was reversed on appeal, the Appeals Chamber did not express a view on the nature of superior responsibility. See, however, the declaration of Judge Shahahbuddeen to the judgment, paras. 18–26

[18] V. Nehrlich, 'Superior responsibility under Article 28 ICC Statute' (2007) 5 JICJ 655–82.

justifies a lower sentence. On the other hand, when superior responsibility is an intentional omission for instance by 'intentionally permitting the commission of offences',[19] a more lenient sentence would not be appropriate.

Unlike the wording of Article 7(3) ICTY St, superior responsibility at the ICC *is* worded as omission liability. Article 28 ICC St generates criminal responsibility for a superior's 'failure to act'. A superior is punished for his/her own failure, not for the crimes of the subordinate. Superior responsibility in Article 28 is linked to the subordinates' crimes but differently than at the ICTY/ICTR. Crimes committed by subordinates 'trigger' a superior's liability and should be 'a result of' the superior's failure to act (causal link).[20] Instead of a link with a particular *subordinate,* the ICC provision requires a link with a subordinate's *act.* Such a link could, to this author's view, be less specific; anonymous subordinates could trigger a superior's liability under Article 28 of the ICC Statute.

III. Joint criminal enterprise

In 1999, in its sixth annual report, the ICTY informed the UN General Assembly on the application of the 'doctrine of common purpose' in the *Tadić* case.[21] At the time, probably no one realized the impact this doctrine would have on the Tribunal's case law. Common purpose, or joint criminal enterprise (JCE), as it was referred to later, was to shape the way the Tribunal attributes *individual* liability for *collective* wrongdoing.

In *Tadić*, JCE was applied in order to ascribe to Tadić the killing of five men at the village of Jaskici. Tadić had not physically committed these crimes but the Appeals Chamber, applying the concept of common purpose/JCE, ruled that Tadić was responsible for the five deaths,

[19] See e.g. section 9(1)(a) of the Dutch International Crimes Act: 'A superior shall be liable to the penalties prescribed for the offences referred to in § 2 if he: (a) intentionally permits the commission of such an offence by a subordinate.'

[20] Ambos refers to subordinates' crimes as a 'point of reference of the superior's failure of supervision'. K. Ambos, 'Superior responsibility', in A. Cassese *et al.* (eds.), *The Rome Statute of the International Criminal Court: A Commentary* (Oxford University Press, Oxford 2002), p. 851.

[21] Report of the International Tribunal for the Prosecution of Persons Responsible for Serious Violations of International Humanitarian Law Committed in the Territory of the former Yugoslavia since 1991 (25 August 1999) A/54/187 – S/1999/846.

as members of his group committed them and because the deaths were considered 'natural and foreseeable consequences' of the common purpose to 'ethnically cleanse' the Prijidor region to which Tadić had agreed.[22] Since the ICTY Statute does not provide for the concept of JCE, the Appeals Chamber subsumed it under 'committing' in Article 7(1) and justified this by pointing to the object and purpose of the Statute and the inherent characteristics of crimes committed in warlike situations.[23]

According to the Appeals Chamber, relevant case law shows that the notion of common purpose or JCE, encompasses three distinct categories.[24] Tadić was held responsible under the Third Category, also referred to as JCE III or extended JCE. This category concerns cases where 'one of the perpetrators commits an act which, while outside the common design, was nevertheless a natural and foreseeable consequence of the effecting of that common purpose'.[25] The post-Second World War case law, such as the *Essen Lynching* and *Borkum Island* cases that were cited in support of this category as reflecting customary international law, mainly deal with small-scale, mob violence situations.[26]

Since the *Tadić* ruling, the concept of JCE has been applied in many cases, initially only at the ICTY, later at the ICTR as well. From a

[22] *Prosecutor v Tadić*, IT-94-1-A, Appeal Judgment (15 July 1999) paras. 232–3.

[23] See, for the doctrine of common purpose at the ICTY and the principle of legality, M. Boot, *Nullum Crimen Sine Lege and the Subject Matter Jurisdiction of the International Criminal Court. Genocide, Crimes against Humanity, War Crimes* (Intersentia, Antwerp Groningen Oxford 2002), pp. 288–302.

[24] (1) *The first category* relates to cases where all co-defendants possessing the same intent pursue a common criminal design, for instance, the killing of a certain person.
(2) *The second category* concerns the so-called 'concentration camp' cases, where the requisite *actus reus* comprises the active participation in the enforcement of a system of repression, as it could be inferred from the position of authority and the specific functions held by each accused. The *mens rea* element comprised: (i) knowledge of the nature of the system and (ii) the intent to further the common concerted design to ill-treat inmates. Intent may *also* be inferred from the accused's position within the camp.
(3) *The third category* concerns cases where 'one of the perpetrators commits an act which, while outside the common design, was nevertheless a natural and foreseeable consequence of the effecting of that common purpose'. *Tadić Appeal Judgment* (n. 22) para. 204.

[25] *Tadić Appeal Judgment* (n. 22) para. 204.

[26] *Tadić Appeal Judgment* (n. 22) para. 219. Sassòli and Olsen doubt the correctness of this statement as the Italian cases, unlike the *Essen Lynching* and *Borkum Island* cases, represent the application of national rather than international law. See M. Sassòli and L. M. Olsen, 'Prosecutor v. Tadic' (2000) 94 AJIL 751–2.

prosecutorial point of view, JCE has appeal because it captures an array of criminal conduct of those who knowingly participate in the criminal endeavour.[27] Tadić could not have been convicted for the five deaths at Jaskíci on the basis of accomplice liability provided for in Article 7(1) as 'aiding and abetting in a crime'. The prosecution would have had to prove that Tadić had carried out acts specifically directed to assisting, encouraging, or lending moral support to the killings while the support must have had a substantial effect on the underlying crime.[28] JCE thus filled a gap by providing for a group crime concept; a basis for convicting those engaged in the 'mob violence type' of system criminality.

JCE has further been used to prosecute senior political and military figures for crimes committed by others but falling within the object of a certain (criminal) policy formulated by them, for instance the plan to create a 'greater Serbia' and ethnically cleanse certain areas by setting up detention camps.[29] The extended form of JCE can be relied upon to hold leaders responsible for crimes that go *beyond* the plan; detention-related crimes (rape and killing) that can be considered natural and foreseeable consequences of the common criminal policy of which the accused were aware as being the 'possible outcome'.[30]

The difficulty with JCE at leadership level is the link with the physical perpetrator. Political leaders are structurally remote from the battlefield, which makes it difficult to link them to those who actually commit the crimes. The question arises whether proof of an *agreement* between the physical perpetrator and the accused leader is required to sustain a conviction for the latter on the basis of JCE. Such a requirement would appreciate the common plan or agreement as a central element of the JCE doctrine but would render it difficult to prove a JCE liability at leadership level. Another difficult question is whether the physical perpetrator should be a member of the enterprise or can be an 'outsider' who is used as a tool by those within the enterprise. In the *Brđanin* case, both issues were addressed.

[27] See J.S. Martinez and A.M. Danner, 'Guilty associations: joint criminal enterprise, command responsibility, and the development of international criminal law' (2005) 93 *California Law Review* 102–20.

[28] *Tadić Appeal Judgment* (n. 22) para. 192.

[29] For instance, the *Krajisnik, Brđanin, Plavsic* and *Milosevic* cases.

[30] *Prosecutor v Slobodan Milosević*, Second Amended Indictment, IT-02–54-T (28 July 2004) para. 8.

1. *The* Brđanin *case*

Radoslav Brđanin was a fairly high-level political figure within the Serbian Democratic Party (SDS) of Radovan Karadžić. He was vice-president and later president of the crisis staff of the Autonomous Region of Krajina (ARK), an area within the planned Serbian state. He retained this position until the abolition of the ARK on 15 September 1992. Brđanin, together with other military and political Bosnian-Serb leaders, formulated a 'Strategic Plan' to link Serb-populated areas in Bosnia and Herzegovina together, to gain control over these areas and to create a separate Bosnian State from which non-Serbs would be removed. The implementation of the Strategic Plan involved the commission of crimes against humanity and war crimes. Brđanin was arrested by NATO forces on 6 July 1999 and brought before the ICTY on charges of crimes against humanity and war crimes.

a. Trial Chamber judgment

One of the theories of liability alleged by the prosecution was that Brđanin was a member in a JCE that included the membership of the SDS (amongst whom were Karadžić and Plavsić), members of the army of the Repubika Srpška, and members of the paramilitary forces. The alleged purpose of the (first category) JCE was to implement the Strategic Plan. The JCE covered a broad range of crimes, committed over a significant period of time and including a large number of individuals.

In finding Brđanin guilty, the Trial Chamber did not rely on JCE. Instead, the judges convicted Brđanin for instigating, ordering and aiding and abetting war crimes and crimes against humanity. The Trial Chamber held that a conviction on the basis of JCE requires proof of an agreement between the principal perpetrator and the participant(s)[31] and – implicitly – that the physical perpetrator must be a member of the JCE.[32] This agreement must be specified; reference to unidentified individuals, such as 'Bosnian Serb police' was thought to be insufficient. Moreover, the Chamber found that proof of an agreement between senior participants amongst themselves (for instance, the leadership of the SerBiH or the Crisis Staff) did not fulfil the 'agreement requirement' of JCE liability. Furthermore, JCE as a mode of liability does not apply

[31] *Prosecutor v Brđanin*, IT-99–36-T, Judgment (1 September 2004) paras. 344 and 347.

[32] This can be deduced from reading para. 344 together with n. 880 of the Trial Chamber Judgment in *Brđanin*.

to large-scale enterprises such as the Strategic Plan. The Trial Chamber found that:

> Although JCE is applicable in relation to cases involving ethnic cleansing, as the *Tadic* Appeal Judgment recognises, it appears that, in providing for a definition of JCE, the Appeals Chamber had in mind a somewhat smaller enterprise than the one that is invoked in the present case.[33]

The Trial Chamber's ruling made it difficult to rely on the doctrine of JCE in prosecuting those engaged in large-scale enterprises and those occupying senior positions. It was, therefore, hardly surprising that the prosecutor appealed the Trial Chamber judgment on questions of law relating to JCE.

b. Appeals Chamber judgment

In its judgment of 3 April 2007, the ICTY Appeals Chamber rejected the Trial Chamber's findings on JCE. It made three important findings. First, it found that there is support in post-Second World War case law[34] and in Tribunal jurisprudence[35] that the principal perpetrator does not have to be a member of the JCE. Instead, the appellate judges found that '[w]hat matters is … not whether the person who carried out the *actus reus* of a particular crime is a member of the JCE but whether the crime in question forms part of the common purpose'.[36] To hold a member of the JCE responsible for crimes perpetrated by a non-member, it is sufficient to show that at least one member of the JCE can be linked to a non-member. When the latter is used by the former to carry out the common criminal purpose, the other co-perpetrators of the JCE can be held equally liable for the crimes.[37] The Appeals Chamber further held that the extended form of JCE, or Third Category JCE, may also trigger liability when it concerns crimes committed by non-members. As long as it can be shown that the member who uses non-members as tools to carry out the *actus reus* had the requisite intent, i.e. that in the circumstances of the case (1) it was foreseeable that such a crime might be perpetrated by one or more of the principal persons and that (2) he willingly took that risk.[38]

[33] *Prosecutor v Brđanin* (n. 31) para. 355.

[34] *Prosecutor v Brđanin,* IT-99-36-A, Appeal Chamber (3 April 2007) para. 404.

[35] *Brđanin Appeal Judgment* (n. 34) paras. 408–409, referring to the *Prosecuotr v Stakić,* IT-97-24-A, Appeal Judgment (22 March 2006) para. 98 and the *Prosecutor v Krstic,* IT-98-33-A, Appeal Judgment (19 April 2004) paras. 601, 611, 613.

[36] *Brđanin* Appeals Judgment (n. 34) para. 410.

[37] *Brđanin* Appeals Judgment (n. 34) para. 413.

[38] *Brđanin* Appeals Judgment (n. 34) para. 411.

Secondly, the Appeals Chamber found that the jurisprudence of the Tribunal does not support the additional requirement of an agreement between the principal perpetrator and the accused.[39] The judges admit that proving the existence of an agreement may be an appropriate way of establishing that a crime was part of the common criminal purpose but that 'as far as the basis form of JCE is concerned … to impute to any accused member of the JCE liability for a crime committed by another person is that the crime in question *forms part of the common criminal purpose*'.[40] Proof of an agreement is therefore unnecessary and even superfluous when it concerns First Category JCE where proof is required of a shared *mens rea*.

A third and last point relates to the scale of the JCE; the Appeals Chamber held that the Tribunal's jurisprudence does not warrant the conclusion that JCE only applies to small-scale enterprises.[41] Referring to the *Rwamakuba* appeal judgment, where the ICTR Appeals Chamber held that post-Second World War case law supports the contention that '[a]n accused's liability under a "common purpose" mode of commission may be as narrow or as broad as the plan in which he willingly participated',[42] the appellate judges rejected the Trial Chamber's ruling on this point.[43]

2. *System criminality and JCE*

The appellate ruling in the *Brđanin* case can be regarded a break-through in the law on JCE. This judgment enables the prosecutor at the ICTY (and the ICTR) to apply JCE entirely at leadership level, as long as it can be shown that one of the participants is linked to the physical perpetrator who is used as a tool to carry out the crime(s). The *Brđanin* ruling effectively loosens the link between the JCE participants and the principal perpetrator.

[39] *Brđanin* Appeals Judgment (n. 34) paras. 415–419.

[40] *Brđanin* Appeals Judgment (n. 34) para. 418.

[41] *Brđanin* Appeals Judgment (n. 34) paras. 420–425.

[42] *Prosecutor v Rwamakuba*, decision on interlocutory appeal regarding application of JCE to the crime of genocide, ICTR-98–44-AR72.4 (22 October 2004) paras. 24–25; *Brđanin* Appeals Judgment (n. 34) para. 423.

[43] More recently, in the *Karemera* case, the ICTR Appeals Chamber held that it is firmly established in customary international law that in 1994, at the time of the crimes, that JCE liability may apply to a campaign of a vast scale. *Prosecutor v Karemera*, Decision on Jurisdictional Appeals: Joint Criminal Enterprise, ICTR-98–44-AR72.5; ICTR-98–44-AR-AR72.6 (12 April 2006) para. 16.

Such 'delinking' is expressed through the acceptance of non-membership of the actual perpetrator. It is also reflected in the Appeal Chamber finding with regard to *mens rea* of first category JCE.[44] The Appeals Chamber held that determining the link between the JCE member and the non-member does not require proof of a shared agreement. Instead, '[t]his essential requirement may be inferred from various circumstances'. When a JCE member uses a non-member to carry out the crimes and the latter '[k]nows of the existence of the JCE – without it being established that he or she shares the *mens rea* necessary to become a member of the JCE', such knowledge '[m]ay be a factor to be taken into account when determining whether the crime forms part of the common criminal purpose'.[45] In other words, the *mens rea* requirement for participants and non-participants may deviate. First category JCE liability ('sharing the *mens rea*') does not apply to the non-member of a JCE. Thus, the principal perpetrator, when committing crimes within a detention centre set up as part of a policy to ethnically cleanse a certain area, does not necessarily have to share the *mens rea* of the senior leaders who devised and implemented the policy of ethnic cleansing.

The *Brđanin* appellate ruling, rather than endorsing the prosecutor's initial strategy of charging a large-scale JCE with members at leadership level and at 'execution level', all furthering the same common criminal purpose, accepts liability for those participating in *separate* but *linked* JCEs. The leadership JCE and the execution JCE may pursue different criminal objectives but come together in the agreement between representatives of each JCE. While the Appeals Chamber accepts that JCE liability may attach to those participating in large-scale criminal enterprises, the 'interlinked JCE' seems to be the preferred theory in cases such as *Brđanin*, with policy-makers on the one hand and executors or 'foot soldiers' on the other hand.

The concept of JCE, as developed at the ICTY, has evoked strong criticism. It is telling that JCE is referred to as the acronym for 'just convict everyone'.[46] There is a fear amongst those critically following the ICTY and its case law that the doctrine of JCE '[l]ures international law to a point where liability threatens to exceed the scope of moral

[44] See n. 24 for definition of First Category JCE.

[45] *Brđanin* Appeals Judgment (n. 34) para. 410.

[46] For instance, in the title of a commentary on the *Stakić* case: M. E. Badar, '"Just Convict Everyone!" – Joint perpetration from *Tadić* to *Stakić* and back again' (2006) 6 ICLR 293–302.

culpability'.[47] That is why the *Brđanin* Trial Chamber judgment was welcomed; it was seen as an attempt to limit JCE liability and to prevent JCE from straying into a type of collective responsibility.[48] What to think, then, of the *Brđanin* appeals judgment?

A few observations can be made. First, JCE, as applied in *Tadić*, is very different from JCE as developed in the *Brđanin* appeals judgment. In *Tadić* it was applied as a small-scale group crime concept at 'execution level'. As such, the concept had underpinnings in national criminal law, most notably in Anglo-American law, where JCE is a form of complicity to which principles of derivative liability apply.[49] However, JCE has moved away from its Anglo-American roots. In the *Brđanin* appeals judgment, JCE shows traits of *Tatherrschaftlehre* or, as Fletcher translates it: the doctrine of 'hegemony-over-the-act'.[50] This liability theory has been developed by the German scholar Roxin and is premised on the experience of system criminality and state crime in Nazi Germany. It provides for the liability of senior figures (indirect perpetrators) for crimes committed by an anonymous executive machinery (direct perpetrators) who are used as a tool to carry out the crimes planned and instigated by those leaders.[51] From a legality point of view it is problematic that a concept can be 're-conceptualized' over time. The question then is whether the JCE concept of the *Brđanin* appeals judgment is in nature still the same as the 'original'/*Tadić* JCE concept. This is a question that I leave to others to answer but it needs to be answered when scrutinizing recent developments on the concept of JCE at the ICTY.

A second, related observation concerns the customary law status of the interlinked JCE concept. In substantiating the existence of interlinked JCE in post-Second World War, the Appeals Chamber relies on two cases, the *Justice* case and the *RuSHA* case. This, in the author's opinion, is not sufficient. Again, the legality principle seems to argue against such progressive law-making. The judges themselves are aware of the thin legal basis of interlinked JCE when they state that these cases have been

47 M. J. Osiel, 'The banality of good: aligning incentives against mass atrocity' (2005) 105 *Columbia Law Review* 1772. See also Martinez and Danner (n. 27) 137.

48 See H. G. van der Wilt, 'Joint criminal enterprise: possibilities and limitations' (2007) 5 JICJ 91–108; J. Ohlin, 'Three conceptual problems with the doctrine of joint criminal enterprise' (2007) 5 JICJ 69–90; E. van Sliedregt, 'Joint criminal enterprise as a pathway to convicting individuals for genocide' (2007) 5 JICJ 184–207.

49 See van Sliedregt (n. 48) 184–207.

50 G. P. Fletcher, *Rethinking Criminal Law* (Little, Brown & Co, Boston 1978), pp. 655–6.

51 C. Roxin, *Täterschaft und Tatherrschaft* (Walter de Gruyter, Berlin 2000), pp. 242–52, 653–4.

'interpreted as a valid source of the *contours of* joint criminal enterprise liability in customary international law' (emphasis added).[52]

The third observation lies in the loosening of the link between participants in the JCE at leadership level and perpetrators at 'execution level'. This delinking may increase the possibility of guilt by association. In other words, the interlinked JCE concept with principal perpetrators who do not share the common objective of those participating at policy level may increase the risk of violating the principle of *personal* culpability. The Appeals Chamber in *Brđanin* is aware of this risk and emphasizes that 'JCE is not an open-ended concept that permits conviction based on guilt by association'.[53] The appellate judges further point to the elements that require proof before a conviction under the JCE doctrine can be entered (identification of the plurality of persons belonging to the JCE, specification of the common criminal purpose as to scope and content, and that a significant contribution to the JCE is made).[54] The message is clear: JCE liability, also in its interlinked form, stays within limits of criminal law principles. This commentator is hesitant in accepting these reassurances. There are still many questions that remain unanswered. Does interlinked JCE mean that the participants in a JCE can be held liable for crimes for which they had no *mens rea*, not even through the 'natural and foreseeable consequences variant'? In other words, can all the participants in a JCE be held responsible for deaths and killings in a detention camp where guards have been used as a tool by only one of the JCE participants and with whom they – the other JCE participants – do not share the *mens rea*, or whose acts have not been accepted by them as natural and foreseeable consequences of their plan? In other words, can the *mens rea* of the member participant who uses the non-member participant, replace the *mens rea* of all the participants? If so, interlinked JCE would be a form of vicarious liability.

IV. Liability at leadership level

For a long time it appeared that superior responsibility was not the most appropriate route to securing a conviction of senior leaders for crimes committed by others. Superiors at the top end of a hierarchy will not necessarily have knowledge of, and effective control over the crimes committed

[52] *Brđanin Appeals Judgment* (n. 34) para. 415.

[53] *Brđanin Appeals Judgment* (n. 34) para. 428.

[54] *Brđanin Appeals Judgment* (n. 34) para. 430.

by physical perpetrators. More importantly, superior responsibility does not adequately describe the responsibility of those who instigate mass crime rather than fail to prevent it. It is for these reasons that the ICTY prosecutor preferred to rely on JCE rather than superior responsibility when prosecuting those at leadership level. The most conspicuous example of this prosecutorial policy is the case against Slobodan Milosević. In this case, JCE appeared as the primary ground of responsibility on the indictment.[55] Because of the higher evidentiary standards for superior responsibility, which often features as the subsidiary mode of liability on the indictment (also in the *Milosević* case) and which was initially thought to provide the basis for prosecuting senior officials, JCE became the preferred liability theory of prosecutors at the ICTY. The *Blagojevic* appellate ruling, however, accepting superior responsibility beyond direct superior-subordinate relationships may make superior responsibility more 'suitable' for prosecuting those at leadership level. Loosening the link between the perpetrator who commits the crime and the superior who is held responsible may remove some of the restrictions the concept was under in providing a basis for liability at leadership level. Yet, there is a limit to indirect subordination. As the *Orić* appeals judgment insists, the subordinate's relationship to the superior and to the underlying crimes must be specified.

In an essay on the role of superior responsibility in ICTY case law, Bonafè argues that while superior responsibility has a much broader scope than sixty years ago because it can be relied upon to convict civilian and political leaders, its application has been limited to traditional military type contexts. Modern war crimes law, particularly at the ICTY, makes superior responsibility conform more closely to the principle of individual criminal responsibility. Indeed, while the *Blagojević* ruling may be seen to expand the scope of superior responsibility beyond direct superior-subordinate relationships, as a liability theory it is still most likely to be applied to *military* leaders.

A more rigorous development of 'de-linking' may be witnessed with regard to JCE liability. Since the *Brđanin* appeals judgment, it has been possible to convict policy makers for crimes committed by an anonymous

[55] *Prosecutor v Slobodan Milosević* (n. 30) paras. 5–31; *Prosecutor v Slobodan Milosević*, IT-02–54-T, First Amended Indictment, paras. 5–33; *Prosecutor v Slobodan Milosević, Milan Milutinović, Sainović, Dragoljub Ojdanić, Vlajiko Stojiljković*, IT-99–37-PT, Second Amended Indictment (29 October 2001) paras. 16–29.

collective. No longer do principal perpetrators have to be part of the JCE; the JCE can exist entirely at leadership level. The interlinked JCE concept, as accepted in *Brđanin*, is very different from the JCE developed and relied upon in *Tadić*. From a legality point of view, one wonders how far the Tribunal can stretch the limits of the concept to make it fit the facts.

V. Concluding remarks

At the ICTY and the ICTR, the facts dictate the modelling of a criminal liability theory. Unlike the ICC, the *ad hoc* Tribunals cannot rely on a pre-existing conceptual framework laid down in a statute and that can be applied to the facts of an individual case before it. Is that a bad thing? Not necessarily. It is inherent in judicial law-making, which is what the *ad hoc* Tribunals do and *have* to do because of the rudimentary structure of their Statutes. As long as there is intellectual honesty in developing the law and one stays within limits devised earlier, it does not have to be a bad thing. However, it is a risky business when there is no rule of binding precedent or *stare decisis* and at the same time a frequent reliance on fluid rules of customary international law.

The Tribunals have been criticized for adopting a result-oriented approach, for being 'prosecutorial entities'.[56] This was criticism voiced by defence counsel, mainly in the beginning of the Tribunals' existence when there was still a very clear imbalance in means and facilities between the prosecution, on the one hand, and the defence, on the other hand. It is criticism that may be recalled in the closing stage of the Tribunals but from a different perspective. Prosecutors and judges at the Tribunals are under pressure of the so-called 'completion strategy'. By 2010, both Tribunals must have finished their work. Pending cases need to be completed sooner rather than later, 'smaller' cases need to be transferred to national courts and no new prosecutions can be initiated apart from cases against senior defendants still at large (Karadzic and Mladic). The completion strategy carries risks for the Tribunals jurisprudence and legacy. It might engender a result-oriented approach that, at least at the ICTY, causes a reconceptualizing of concepts to make the

[56] H. A. C. Morrison, 'Practice at the ad hoc Tribunals for the Former Yugoslavia and Rwanda', in M. Hallers *et al.* (eds.), *The Position of the Defence at the International Criminal Court and the Role of the Netherlands as the Host State* (Rozenberg Publishers, Amsterdam 2002), p. 43.

law fit the facts. Those who currently stand trial before the ICTY differ fundamentally from the first generation of defendants, like Tadić. Those who have been convicted in recent years have occupied senior positions in military and political circles and have been structurally remote from the battlefield. This is problematic because liability theories like JCE have been modelled on those first generation cases where defendants were often personally implicated in committing crimes and present at – or at least not remote from – the scene of the crimes. The need for reconceptualizing existing liability theories may thus be perfectly justified. However, caution is required, especially since neither Tribunal has at its disposal a clear framework within which a theory of liability is shaped, but where at the same time the legality principle and the culpability principle unequivocally apply.

9

Criminality of organizations under international law

NINA H. B. JØRGENSEN*

I. Introduction

In system criminality the organization itself is central and behind its mask criminal programmes are carried out. In his book, *Shake Hands with the Devil*, General Dallaire describes his meeting with the leaders of the *Interahamwe*. He was expecting 'frothing at the mouth' but his meeting turned out to be with humans.[1] Dallaire's meeting took him behind the mask of the organization known as the *Interahamwe*. One of the individuals he met with is now standing trial before the International Criminal Tribunal for Rwanda (ICTR) on charges of conspiracy to commit genocide.[2]

Justice Jackson referred at Nuremberg to the calculated and decisive part certain organizations played in the ruthless extremes of the Nazi movement: 'They served primarily to exploit mob psychology and to manipulate the mob. Multiplying the number of persons in a common enterprise always tends to diminish the individual's sense of moral responsibility and to increase his sense of security.'[3] Or, as Maurice Punch has noted, the institutional context provides the motive, opportunity and means for 'ordinary' individuals to commit criminal acts.[4]

The frothing at the mouth that Dallaire expected of the individual perpetrators is the image created by the organization, or in other words

* Senior Judicial Coordinator of the Pre-Trial Chamber at the Extraordinary Chambers in the Courts of Cambodia/UN Assistance to the Khmer Rouge Trial.

1 'The three young men Bagosora introduced to me had no particularly distinguishing features. I think I was expecting frothing at the mouth, but the meeting would be with humans.' Lt Gen. R. Dallaire, *Shake Hands with the Devil. The Failure of Humanity in Rwanda* (Knopf, Canada 2003), p. 347.

2 *Prosecutor v Theoneste Bagosora*, ICTR-96-7-I, Indictment (12 August 1999).

3 Nuremberg Trial Proceedings, vol. 8 (28 February 1946) 353, www.yale.edu/lawweb/avalon/imt/proc/02-28-46.htm, accessed 23 June 2008.

4 M. Punch, 'Why organizations kill – and get away with it: the failure of law to cope with crimes in organizations', this volume, Chapter 3, pp. 43, 56

the mask. Masks may be more than a simple disguise. The individual beneath the mask ceases to exist and instead the character of the mask comes to life. In the same way, a criminal organization takes on its own identity. The question to be addressed, therefore, is what role can international law play in confronting the identity of the mask?

The institutional framework for certain criminal acts may take the form of a corporation, a criminal organization or indeed a state. The focus of this chapter is the Nuremberg-style criminal organization and its place in international law when compared with related concepts such as conspiracy, joint criminal enterprise, terrorist organizations, transnational organized crime and hate crime. The chapter first summarizes the essence of the concept of criminal organizations developed at Nuremberg before distinguishing it from the core elements of related concepts. The second part is concerned with the continued relevance of the concept of criminal organizations, the pros and cons of allowing it any future function in international law and what this function might be.

This chapter does not address the domestic law debate on corporate crime[5] or the issue of the criminal responsibility of states,[6] both of which topics have an independent relevance to the discussion on system criminality. The aim here is to explore the mechanisms for ensuring accountability as a reaction to systems put in place for the very purpose of committing crimes. The focus of accountability in this context is on the personal, individual responsibility of the members of an organization judged to be criminal as such. States and corporations may order, encourage, permit or fail to punish international crimes but are distinguishable from groups formed expressly to achieve criminal aims. Moreover, the removal of the criminal element from a criminal organization generally means, or follows from, the disbanding of the organization. Therefore, once the mask is lifted, nothing remains.

II. The concept of criminal organizations[7]

The notion of criminal organizations in international law immediately brings to mind the concept developed at Nuremberg. In a sense the story

[5] See e.g. V. S. Khanna, 'Corporate criminal liability: what purpose does it serve?'(1996) 109 *Harvard Law Review* 1477.

[6] See e.g. D. D. Caron, 'State crimes in the ILC Draft Articles on State Responsibility: insights from municipal experience with corporate crimes' (1998) 92 *American Society of International Law Proceedings* 307; notably, the author uses the phrase 'organizational crimes' to refer to corporate and state crimes collectively.

[7] See generally N. H. B. Jørgensen, *The Responsibility of States for International Crimes* (Oxford University Press, Oxford 2000); E. van Sliedregt, *The Criminal Responsibility*

begins and ends in Nuremberg as the Nuremberg trials and subsequent proceedings provide the only example of organizations being judged and declared criminal by a court applying international law with the result that the individual responsibility of the members of those organizations could be established on the basis of their membership in a criminal organization. The concept was developed because the crimes committed by the Nazis during the Second World War were seen as systematic and highly organized. At the same time they were 'massive' both in terms of the number of victims and the number of perpetrators.

The role of organizations such as the SS and the Gestapo in the commission of crimes, and the best way to deal with their many members after the war was debated extensively both on a political level and by the United Nations War Crimes Commission prior to the London Conference of June 1945. As a result of these debates, the Nuremberg Charter[8] contained three provisions, Articles 9 to 11, on criminal organizations.

Article 9

At the trial of any individual member of any group or organization the Tribunal may declare (in connection with any act of which the individual may be convicted) that the group or organization of which the individual was a member was a criminal organization.

Article 10

In cases where a group or organization is declared criminal by the Tribunal, the competent national authority of any Signatory shall have the right to bring individuals to trial for membership therein before national, military or occupation courts. In any such case the criminal nature of the group or organization is considered proved and shall not be questioned.

Article 11

Any person convicted by the Tribunal may be charged before a national, military or occupation court, referred to in Article 10 of this Charter, with a crime other than of membership in a criminal group or organization and such court may, after convicting him, impose upon him punishment independent of and additional to the punishment imposed

of Individuals for Violations of International Humanitarian Law (TMC Asser Press, The Hague 2003) ch. 1; S. Pomorski, 'Conspiracy and criminal organization', in G. Ginsburgs and V.N. Kudriavtsev (eds.), *The Nuremberg Trial and International Law* (Martinus Nijhoff, Leiden 1990), p. 213.

[8] Agreement for the Prosecution and Punishment of the Major War Criminals of the European Axis, and Charter of the International Military Tribunal (London 8 August 1945), available at www.icrc.org/ihl.nsf/FULL/350?OpenDocument, accessed 23 June 2008.

> by the Tribunal for participation in the criminal activities of such group or organization.

In essence, the theory was that the Nuremberg Tribunal could declare an indicted group or organization to be criminal, which meant that in subsequent proceedings the criminal nature of the group or organization could not be challenged. The Tribunal could not impose a sentence on the group or organization as such and a judgment as to the criminality of an organization was to be declaratory only.

The judges found that there was indeed a crime of 'membership' in an organization declared to be criminal but emphasized that this was a 'far-reaching and novel procedure. Its application, unless properly safeguarded, may produce great injustice.'[9] It was stressed that 'criminal guilt is individual and that mass punishment should be avoided' and that any declaration of criminality would as far as possible be made in a manner to ensure that innocent persons would not be punished.[10] The Tribunal advanced a definition of a criminal group or organization:

> There must be a group bound together and organised for a common purpose. The group must be formed or used in connection with the commission of crimes denounced by the Charter. Since the declaration with respect to the organisations and groups will, as has been pointed out, fix the criminality of its members, that definition should exclude persons who had no knowledge of the criminal purposes or acts of the organisation and those who were drafted by the State for membership, unless they were personally implicated in the commission of acts declared criminal by Article 6 of the Charter as members of the organisation. Membership alone is not enough to come within the scope of these declarations.[11]

The essential requirements were those of knowledge of the criminal purposes of the organization and voluntarily remaining a member. The Tribunal recommended that in no case should any punishment under Control Council Law No. 10, which governed the subsequent proceedings, imposed upon any members of an organization or group declared by the Tribunal to be criminal, exceed the punishment fixed by the De-Nazification Law of 5 March 1946. Further, no person should be punished under both laws.[12] Of the six indicted organizations, three were

[9] Judgment of the International Military Tribunal ('IMT Judgment') (30 September and 1 October 1946) 'The Accused Organizations', www.yale.edu/lawweb/avalon/imt/proc/judorg.htm, accessed 23 June 2008.

[10] IMT Judgment (n. 9). [11] IMT Judgment (n. 9). [12] IMT Judgment (n. 9).

held to be criminal (the Leadership Corps of the Nazi Party, the Gestapo and SD, and the SS).[13]

The prosecution had vigorously argued the fairness of the concept of criminal organizations and made it clear that the only defence denied by the Charter was that of re-litigating the question in a subsequent trial whether the organization itself was a criminal one. An accused would not be precluded from denying that his participation was voluntary, proving that he acted under duress or that he was deceived or tricked into membership, or showing that he had withdrawn or that his name on the rolls was a case of mistaken identity. Conscription was also highlighted as a possible defence.[14] The defence on the other hand pointed to the novelty of the idea and the risk that its broad reach would invariably impact upon the innocent. The defence distinguished the law of conspiracy, under which the conspiracy itself is not judged, but rather the individual participants.[15]

[13] The SA was held not to be a criminal organization on the basis that the group consisted: 'in large part of ruffians and bullies who participated in the Nazi outrages of that period. It has not been shown, however, that these atrocities were part of a specific plan to wage aggressive war, and the Tribunal therefore cannot hold that these activities were criminal under the Charter. After the purge, the SA was reduced to the status of a group of unimportant Nazi hangers-on. Although in specific instances some units of the SA were used for the commission of war crimes and crimes against humanity, it cannot be said that its members generally participated in or even knew of the criminal acts.' With respect to the Reich Cabinet, the Tribunal was of the opinion that a declaration of criminality was not appropriate: '(1) because it is not shown that after 1931 it ever really acted as a group or organization, (2) because the group of persons here charged is so small that members could be conveniently tried in proper cases without resort to a declaration that the Cabinet of which they were members was criminal.' The General Staff and High Command of the German Armed Forces was found not to be a criminal organization on the basis that it did not fall within the definition of a group: 'For this alleged criminal organization has one characteristic, a controlling one, which sharply distinguishes it from the other five indicted. When an individual became a member of the SS for instance, he did so, voluntarily or otherwise, but certainly with the knowledge that he was joining something. In the case of the General Staff and High Command, however, he could not know he was joining a group or organization, for such organisation did not exist except in the charge of the Indictment. He knew only that he had achieved a certain high rank in one of the three services, and could not be conscious of the fact that he was becoming a member of anything so tangible as a "group", as that word is commonly used.' Specific exclusions were made with respect to the Leadership Corps of the Nazi Party (staff officers and party organizations attached to the Leadership Corps other than the Amtsleiters who were heads of offices on the staffs of the Reichsleitung, Gauleitung and Kreisleitung), Gestapo and SD (Border and Customs Protection, Secret Field Police, and persons employed by the Gestapo for purely clerical, stenographic, janitorial or similar unofficial routine tasks), SS (so-called SS riding units); IMT Judgment (n. 9).

[14] Nuremberg Trial Proceedings (n. 3) 359.

[15] Nuremberg Trial Proceedings, vol. 8, 1 March 1946, 415.

It was, as foreseen by the prosecution, the national courts that had to resolve the problems of individual responsibility.[16] In the Subsequent Proceedings, under Article II(1)(d) of Control Council Law No. 10, membership in categories of a criminal group or organization declared criminal by the Nuremberg Tribunal was recognized as a crime. This resulted in convictions,[17] although not on the scale envisaged or feared.

III. How is the concept of criminal organizations legally distinct from related concepts?

1. *Conspiracy*

The Nuremberg Tribunal considered the concept of criminal organizations to be analogous to the concept of conspiracy in Article 6 of the Charter, 'in that the essence of both is cooperation for criminal purposes'.[18] Conspiracy, no less controversial than the criminal organizations theory, was described by the prosecution as being 'the great dragnet of the law and rightly watched by courts lest it be abused'.[19]

Article 6 of the Nuremberg Charter criminalized participation in a common plan or conspiracy to commit crimes against peace, as well as providing that participating in the formulation or execution of a common plan or conspiracy to commit any of the crimes listed in the Charter resulted in responsibility for all acts performed by any persons in execution of such a plan. The Charter intertwined conspiracy as a substantive crime with conspiracy as a mode of participation. Conspiracy to commit crimes against peace was a crime in its own right, while each accused could be convicted of any act committed by others in the execution of the conspiracy. The Nuremberg judgment applied a restrictive notion of conspiracy, and only eight of those forming part of Hitler's senior

[16] Nuremberg Trial Proceedings, vol. 8, 2 March 1946, 468.

[17] See e.g. case of K. Brandt and others: 'The defendants Karl Brandt, Genzken, Gebhardt, Rudolf Brandt, Mrugowsky, Poppendick, Sievers, Brack, Hoven, and Fischer are guilty of membership in an organization declared to be criminal by the International Military Tribunal in Case No. 1, in that each of the said defendants was a member of the SCHUTZSTAFFELN DER NATIONALSOZIALISTISCHEN DEUTSCHEN ARBEITERPARTEI (commonly known as the "SS") after 1 September 1939. Such membership is in violation of paragraph I (d), Article II of Control Council Law No 10.'

[18] IMT Judgment (n. 9).

[19] Nuremberg Trial Proceedings (n. 3) 360. See also R. P. Barrett and L. E. Little, 'Lessons of Yugoslav Rape Trials: A Role for Conspiracy Law in International Tribunals' (2003) 88 *Minnesota Law Review* 30.

leadership who actively participated in the planning of aggressive war were convicted on this basis.

In the Statutes of the International Criminal Tribunal for the Former Yugoslavia (ICTY) and ICTR, conspiracy is only mentioned in relation to the crime of genocide, the definition of which is taken from the 1948 Genocide Convention.[20] In the *Musema* case, conspiracy to commit genocide was defined quite simply as an agreement between two or more persons to commit the crime of genocide.[21] Conspiracy was identified as being an inchoate offence.[22] In the *Nahimana* case, the Trial Chamber stated that '[i]nstitutional coordination can form the basis of a conspiracy among those individuals who control the institutions that are engaged in coordinated action',[23] which seems to link 'institutional conspiracies' with the notion of criminal organizations. However, the key distinctions between the two notions are: first, while both recognize a form of collective responsibility for acts of accomplices, an indictment is not directed against a conspiracy as such, but rather against the individual conspirators, and second, conspiracy is an inchoate crime (although in some instances it may also function as a mode of participation) while the theory of criminal organizations requires the commission of crimes by members of the organization.

2. *Joint criminal enterprise*

The roots of joint criminal enterprise liability are immediately evident in the notion of conspiracy but conspiracy did not form the basis of the theory developed in the ICTY case of *Tadic*.[24] This is surprising, considering the similarities in the manner in which conspiracy was charged at Nuremberg and joint criminal enterprise liability is pleaded before the modern International Tribunals. At Nuremberg, count 1 of the indictment alleged:

> All the defendants, with divers other persons, during a period of years preceding 8 May 1945, participated as leaders, organizers, instigators,

[20] Adopted by Resolution 260 (III)A of the United Nations General Assembly on 9 December 1948, entered into force 12 January 1951. Art. 2(3)(b) ICTR Statute and Art. 4(3)(b) ICTY Statute.

[21] *Prosecutor v Alfred Musema*, ICTR-96-13, Judgment, Trial Chamber (27 January 2000) para. 191.

[22] *Prosecutor v Alfred Musema* (n. 21) para. 193.

[23] *Prosecutor v Ferdinand Nahimana, Jean-Bosco Barayagwiza and Hassan Ngeze*, ICTR-99-52-T, Judgment and Sentence, Trial Chamber (3 December 2003).

[24] *Prosecutor v Dusko Tadic*, IT-94-1, Judgment, Appeals Chamber (15 July 1999) paras. 185–229.

> or accomplices in the formulation or execution of a common plan or conspiracy to commit, or which involved the commission of, Crimes against Peace, War Crimes, and Crimes against Humanity, as defined in the Charter of this Tribunal, and, in accordance with the provisions of the Charter, are individually responsible for their own acts and for all acts committed by any persons in the execution of such plan or conspiracy.[25]

Charles Taylor is charged before the Special Court for Sierra Leone as follows:

> The Accused committed the crimes alleged in the Amended Indictment in the sense of being a co-perpetrator of those crimes, in that, while not physically perpetrating the crimes, the Accused shared the intent to commit the crimes and participated in the common plan, design or purpose which amounted to or involved commission of those crimes … The alleged crimes, amounting to or involved within the common plan, design or purpose, were either intended by the Accused, or were a reasonably foreseeable consequence of the common plan, design or purpose.[26]

Joint criminal enterprise, as a means of dealing with what was described in *Tadic* as 'manifestations of collective criminality',[27] seems to be the preferred method for reaching senior military and political leaders. In this way the accused, who is often an accessory to the physical perpetrator, may be described as a co-perpetrator, avoiding the suggestion of a lesser degree of culpability associated with accomplice liability.[28]

Slobodan Milosevic, for example, was accused of participating in three very large joint criminal enterprises. The Trial Chamber found at the conclusion of the prosecution case that a reasonable trier of fact could be satisfied beyond reasonable doubt that Milosevic was a participant in a joint criminal enterprise that included the Bosnian Serb leadership, and that he shared with its participants the aim and intention to destroy a part of the Bosnian Muslims as a group,[29] notably because '[t]he

[25] Nuremberg Trial Proceedings (n. 3), vol. 1, Indictment: Count 1, www.yale.edu/lawweb/avalon/imt/proc/count1.htm, accessed 23 June 2008.

[26] *Prosecutor v Charles Ghankay Taylor*, SCSL-2003–01-I, Amended Indictment (16 March 2006); note that the Second Amended Indictment of 28 May 2007 amends this wording.

[27] *Prosecutor v Dusko Tadic* (n. 24) para. 191.

[28] See *Prosecutor v Momcilo Krajisnik*, IT-00–39-T, Judgment (27 September 2006) para. 886: 'Gradations of fault within the JCE are possible, and may be reflected in the sentences given. However, a person's conduct either meets the conditions of JCE membership … in which case he or she is characterized as a co-perpetrator, or the conduct fails the threshold, in which case there is no JCE responsibility.'

[29] *Prosecutor v Slobodan Milosevic*, IT-02–54-T, Decision on Motion for Judgment of Acquittal, Trial Chamber (16 June 2004) para. 288.

Accused was the dominant political figure in Serbia and he had profound influence over the Bosnian Serb political and military authorities'.[30] In the *Krajisnik* judgment, the ICTY Trial Chamber stated in response to the defence argument that joint criminal enterprise liability was only applicable to enterprises of small size or scope, that 'JCE is well suited to cases ... in which numerous persons are all said to be concerned with the commission of a large number of crimes'.[31] In fact, it was the only mode of liability considered.[32] In the ICTR case of *Rwamakuba*, the Appeals Chamber held, referring to post-Second World War cases, that: 'liability for participation in a criminal plan is as wide as the plan itself, even if the plan amounts to a "nation wide government-organized system of cruelty and injustice".'[33]

The two notions of joint criminal enterprise and criminal organizations have similar underpinnings.[34] Joint criminal enterprise allows members of the senior political leadership to be characterized as the main players – those bearing the greatest responsibility – which alternative theories of liability such as command responsibility or accomplice liability might not capture. Similarly, condemning the principal Nazi structures was regarded as necessary to expose the current of organized criminal activity that was a feature of Nazi Germany.

There are two key distinctions between the concepts. First, the concept of criminal organizations is not a liability theory – membership in a criminal organization is a crime. Second, criminal liability pursuant to a joint criminal enterprise is not liability for voluntary and knowledgeable membership (or in contrast to a conspiracy, mere planning) – it is necessary to show that the accused took action in furtherance of the common plan.

3. *Terrorist organizations*

It was noted by the prosecution at Nuremberg that it would have been competent for the Charter to name certain organizations as criminal rather

[30] *Prosecutor v Slobodan Milosevic* (n. 29) para. 257.

[31] *Prosecutor v Momcilo Krajisnik* (n. 28) para. 876.

[32] *Prosecutor v Momcilo Krajisnik* (n. 28) para. 877.

[33] *Prosecutor v André Rwamakuba*, ICTR-98–44-AR72.4, Decision on Interlocutory Appeal Regarding Application of Joint Criminal Enterprise to the Crime of Genocide, Appeals Chamber (22 October 2004) para. 25.

[34] See generally A. M. Danner and J. S. Martinez, 'Guilty associations: joint criminal enterprise, command responsibility, and the development of international criminal law' (2005) 93 *California Law Review* 75.

than leaving the criminal nature of the organization open to challenge during the proceedings.[35] But the process of allowing the determination as to criminality to be made following adversarial proceedings was felt to accord better with the rights of the accused. In contrast, in action taken to counteract terrorism, the names of organizations alleged to be criminal are kept on lists maintained by governments, and by the UN Security Council, with potentially far-reaching effect.

In 1999, the Security Council adopted Resolution 1267, which imposed obligations on UN member states to freeze assets controlled by the Taliban.[36] This obligation was extended to include individuals and entities associated with Al Qaida in Resolution 1390 of 2002. Under these resolutions, the UN maintains a list of individuals and entities associated with the Taliban and Al Qaida, as agreed upon by the '1267 Committee', which comprises all fifteen members of the Security Council. Resolution 1373, adopted in response to the 11 September 2001 attacks, imposed further obligations for the freezing of funds of persons or entities involved in terrorism. Follow-up resolutions have regularly been adopted, for example Resolution 1735 of 22 December 2006, which reiterates that the measures set out in the previous resolutions are preventive and 'not reliant upon criminal standards set out under national law'. However, freezing orders, for example, may potentially affect innocent third parties. Resolution 1730 of 19 December 2006 adopted a delisting procedure and established within the Security Council Subsidiary Organs Branch of the Secretariat, a focal point to receive delisting requests. Resolution 1822 of 30 June 2008 recalled previous resolutions and noted the need to ensure that 'fair and clear procedures exist for placing individuals, groups, undertakings, and entities' on the lists, as well as for removing them. At the same time, the 'need for robust implementation' of the previous resolutions was spelt out.

[35] 'Unquestionably, it would have been competent for the Charter to have declared flatly that membership in any of these named organizations is criminal and should be punished accordingly. If there had been such an enactment, it would not have been open to an individual, who was being tried for membership, to contend that the organization was not in fact, criminal. But the framers of the Charter, acting last summer at a time before the evidence which has been adduced here was even available to us, did not care to find organizations criminal by fiat. They left that issue to determination after relevant facts were developed by adversary proceedings. Plainly, the individual is better off because of the procedure of the Charter, which leaves that finding of criminality to this body after hearings at which the organization must, and the individual may, be represented. It is at least the best assurance that we could devise, that no mistake would be made in dealing with these organizations.' Nuremberg Trial Proceedings (n. 3) 357.

[36] For Security Council resolutions related to the work of the '1267 Committee', see www.un.org/Docs/sc/committees/1267/1267ResEng.htm, accessed 23 June 2008.

In the United States, the Secretary of State, in consultation with the Secretary of the Treasury and the Attorney-General, is authorized to designate a group as a foreign terrorist organization if the Secretary of State finds that the group is foreign, engages in, or has the capacity or intent to engage in terrorist activity, and threatens the security of United States nationals or the national security of the United States.[37] While membership of a terrorist group is not a crime in the United States, it may be a ground for removal from the country under immigration laws.[38]

In the United Kingdom, the Terrorism Act 2000[39] makes belonging or professing to belong to a proscribed organization an offence. It is a defence for a person charged with such an offence to prove: (a) that the organization was not proscribed on the last (or only) occasion on which he became a member or began to profess to be a member; and (b) that he has not taken part in the activities of the organization at any time while it was proscribed. The maximum punishment for membership is ten years' imprisonment. Terrorist organizations are so designated by the Secretary of State.

Section 20 of the Indian Prevention of Terrorism Act of 26 March 2002 makes it an offence to belong to or to profess to belong to an organization declared as terrorist.[40] Pakistan's terrorism laws are similarly far-reaching and allow the government to restrict the movement of individuals or authorize their detention if they are activists, office-bearers or associates of a proscribed organization or in any way concerned with such an organization.[41]

The international conventions on terrorism do not deal with membership in a terrorist organization as such but rely on common purpose liability. For example, the 1998 International Convention for the Suppression of Terrorist Bombings[42] provides for liability if a person:

> contributes to the commission of one or more offences... by a group of persons acting with a common purpose; such contribution shall be

[37] See US Department of State website: www.state.gov/s/ct/rls/fs/2002/16181.htm, accessed 23 June 2008.

[38] See further International Bar Association, *International Terrorism: Legal Challenges and Responses* (Transnational Publishers, Ardsley Park, NY 2003) 60 fn. 32.

[39] www.opsi.gov.uk/Acts/acts2000/20000011.htm#aofs, accessed 23 June 2008.

[40] See *International Terrorism: Legal Challenges and Responses* (n. 38) fn. 32.

[41] Anti-Terrorism Act 1997, section 11EE, as inserted by the Anti-Terrorism (Amendment) Ordinance 2002, referred to in *International Terrorism: Legal Challenges and Responses* (n. 38) fn. 34.

[42] Art. 2(3)(c) of the International Convention for the Suppression of Terrorist Bombings.

> intentional and either be made with the aim of furthering the general criminal activity or purpose of the group or be made in the knowledge of the intention of the group to commit the offence ... concerned.

Notably, the Statute of the International Criminal Court mirrors this wording in Article 25(3)(d).[43]

The key distinction between the concept of criminal organizations and the manner in which international organizations and states deal with terrorist organizations is that according to the concept of criminal organizations, a declaration of criminality is a judicial determination, while the designation of an organization as a terrorist organization is essentially a political determination which may result in administrative or penal sanctions against the organization and/or its members. This aspect of anti-terrorism legislation has been criticized, especially where the designation of organizations as terrorist is not subject to judicial review.[44] Article 9 of the Nuremberg Charter provided that any member of an organization which the prosecution intended to put forward for a declaration of criminality would be entitled to apply to the Tribunal for leave to be heard upon the question of the criminal character of the organization.[45] Applications to be heard as a consequence of the Tribunal's order numbered over 100,000.[46]

4. *Transnational organized crime*

Terrorism involves a political element that is absent from organized crime. Organized criminal groups are generally motivated by financial gain and their core activities include action such as drug trafficking and trafficking in human beings.[47] Perceived as a global threat, with increasing links to terrorism, and tending to feed like vultures off the fragmented and corrupt remains of societies emerging from civil conflict, organized crime

[43] Statute of the International Criminal Court ('ICC Statute') A/CONF.183/9.

[44] *International Terrorism: Legal Challenges and Responses* (n. 38) fn. 32.

[45] Nuremberg Trial Proceedings, vol. 42, Final Report on the Evidence of Witnesses for the Defense of Organizations Alleged to be Criminal, Heard Before a Commission Appointed by the Tribunal Pursuant to Paragraph 4 of the Order of the 13 March 1946, 'Colonel Neave Report', http://avalon.law.yale.edu/imt/naeve.asp, accessed 23 June 2008.

[46] Note 45.

[47] See generally M. C. Bassiouni and E. Vetere (eds.), *Organized Crime, A Compilation of UN Documents 1975–1988* (Transnational Publishers, Ardsley Park, NY 1998); P. J. Ryan and G. E. Rush, *Understanding Organized Crime in Global Perspective, A Reader* (Sage Publications, Thousand Oaks, CA 1997).

has been the object of a considerable amount of national and international legislation. Definitional inconsistencies remain, however.

The point to note about the response to organized crime is that it brings together common purpose and conspiracy theories and may also target the formation of the criminal group as such by prohibiting criminal associations as is the practice in some national systems.[48] The UN Convention against Transnational Organized Crime[49] defines an organized criminal group as: 'a structured group of three or more persons, existing for a period of time and acting in concert with the aim of committing one or more serious crimes or offences established in accordance with this Convention, in order to obtain, directly or indirectly, a financial or other material benefit.' Article 5 of the Convention requires states to criminalize participation in an organized criminal group by making the following acts criminal offences:

(i) Agreeing with one or more other persons to commit a serious crime for a purpose relating directly or indirectly to the obtaining of a financial or other material benefit and, *where required by domestic law*, involving an act undertaken by one of the participants in furtherance of the agreement or involving an organized criminal group.
(ii) Conduct by a person who, with knowledge of either the aim and general criminal activity of an organized criminal group or its intention to commit the crimes in question, takes an active part in:
   (a) criminal activities of the organized criminal group;
   (b) other activities of the organized criminal group in the knowledge that his or her participation will contribute to the achievement of the above-described criminal aim.

The Convention does not provide for a declaration of criminality against the group and mere membership of an organized criminal group is insufficient for liability to be incurred. At the European Union level, on the other hand, the concept of criminal and civil liability of legal persons has been introduced in parallel with that of natural persons, for example in Articles 4 and 5 of the Council Framework Decision on Combating Traffic in Human Beings.[50] Legal persons may be held liable for offences committed for their benefit by any person acting either individually or as

[48] A. D. Tripp, 'Margins of the mob: a comparison of *Reeves v Ernst & Young* with criminal association laws in Italy and France' (1996) 20 *Fordham International Law Journal* 263.

[49] UN Convention against Transnational Organized Crime, A/RES/55/25.

[50] Council Framework Decision 2002/629/JHA, 19 July 2002, Official Journal L 203 of 1 August 2002.

part of the organ of the legal person, or who exercises decision-making power. Penalties may include criminal or non-criminal fines and specific sanctions such as a temporary or definitive ban on commercial activities or dissolution. The need for a common approach to participation in the activities of criminal organizations was recognized in the Joint Action of 21 December 1998 on making it a criminal offence to participate in a criminal organization in the member states of the European Union.[51] According to Article 2(1) of the Joint Action, states undertake to make punishable:

(a) Conduct by any person who, with intent and with knowledge of either the aim and general criminal activity of the organization or the intention of the organization to commit the offences in question, actively takes part in:
  - the organization's criminal activities falling within Article 1, even where that person does not take part in the actual execution of the offences concerned and, subject to the general principles of the criminal law of the member state concerned, even where the offences concerned are not actually committed;
  - the organization's other activities in the further knowledge that his participation will contribute to the achievement of the organisation's criminal activities falling within Article 1.

(b) conduct by any person consisting in an agreement with one or more persons that an activity should be pursued which, if carried out, would amount to the commission of offences falling within Article 1, even if that person does not take part in the actual execution of the activity.

Article 3 requires states to ensure that legal persons may be held criminally or otherwise liable for offences committed by the legal person, without prejudice to the criminal liability of the natural persons who were the perpetrators of the offences or their accomplices.

5. *Hate crime*

The 1965 International Convention on the Elimination of All Forms of Racial Discrimination (ICERD) provides in Article 4 that states parties shall declare illegal and prohibit organizations which promote and incite

[51] 98/733/JHA: Joint action of 21 December 1998, Official Journal L 351 (29 December 1998) 1–3.

racial discrimination and shall recognize participation in such organizations or activities as an offence punishable by law. While conceptually similar in approach to organized crime, it is broader, in that it requires states to legislate to prohibit the formation of racist organizations and provides that participation in a prohibited organization may be a punishable offence.

The provision has not been widely implemented. The Bulgarian criminal code, for example, provides that a person who is a member of an organization which has the objective of committing crimes against national and racial equality shall be punished.[52] In Cyprus it is a criminal offence to establish or participate in an organization which promotes organized propaganda or activities of any form aiming at racial discrimination.[53] Article 282 of the Criminal Code of the Russian Federation (2002 Federal Law on Counteracting Extremist Activities) covers the planning and establishment of an extremist community and planning an extremist organization's activities. The establishment of an extremist community means the establishment of an organized group of persons for the preparation for or commission, because of ideological, political, racial, national or religious hatred or hostility, of crimes of an extremist nature.[54]

Article 4 of ICERD is not without its difficulties, as it may be seen to give the green light for draconian laws aimed at combating extremism which impact upon the right to freedom of association and tend to be focused on groups that potentially pose a threat to the state rather than at groups that threaten other groups or individuals, in particular minorities.

IV. Is there a need to engage with the Nuremberg concept of criminal organizations in the context of 'system criminality'?

The above outline of related concepts dealing in various ways with the phenomenon of crimes committed through or by an organization raises the question of the relevance of the Nuremberg concept of criminal

[52] Chapter 3, Section 1, §162(4), see OSCE, Office for Democratic Institutions and Human Rights, *Combating Hate Crimes in the OSCE Region: An Overview of Statistics, Legislation and National Initiatives*, 2005, www.osce.org/odihr/item_11_16251.html, accessed 23 June 2008.

[53] Amending Laws 11/92, 6(III)/95, and 28(III)/99, amending the law ratifying the ICERD, see *Combating Hate Crimes* (n. 52).

[54] See further, European Commission against Racism and Intolerance, Third Report on the Russian Federation, adopted on 16 December 2005, made public on 16 May 2006, www.coe.int/t/e/human_rights/ecri/1-ecri/2-country-by country_approach/russian_federation/russian_federation_cbc_3.asp#P123_14132, accessed 23 June 2008.

organizations in a modern setting. Reasons to abandon the concept, or, rather, to let sleeping dogs lie, might include the following: First, the doctrines of superior responsibility and joint criminal enterprise, plus general principles of accomplice liability, are sufficient tools in terms of ensuring that all perpetrators are punished. Second, the element of a 'system' emerges through joint trials of perpetrators belonging to different military, political, media, administrative, religious or other groups charged with participation in a common plan, without the need to criminalize the group or enterprise as such. Third, the responsibility of organizations can be explored in truth commissions. Fourth, the rights of the accused prohibit a finding of guilt by association, the idea of 'collective guilt' being one of the main objections to the concept of criminal organizations.

The International Tribunals have repeatedly stressed that the joint criminal enterprise doctrine does not present a danger of guilt by association. For example, the ICTY Trial Chamber in the *Stakic* case emphasized that: 'joint criminal enterprise can not be viewed as membership in an organisation because this would constitute a new crime not foreseen under the Statute and therefore amount to a flagrant infringement of the principle *nullum crimen sine lege*.'[55] The accused Stakic argued on appeal that he was being found guilty by association in that he was being considered together with the police, military and other leaders, especially with regard to his role in the Omarska camp. The Appeals Chamber found that his role in relation to the detention facilities of Omarska revealed more than guilt by association, and that the Trial Chamber had found that the Crisis Staff, presided over by Stakic, had a management and oversight function in relation to the camps.[56]

Fifth, groups and organizations are difficult to define. Compare, for example, the SS with the Prijedor Crisis Staff that was the feature of the *Stakic* case or the Revolutionary United Front (RUF) that operated during the conflict in Sierra Leone. In relation to the RUF, the Report of the Sierra Leone Truth and Reconciliation Commission[57] states that 'there was no inspirational or ideological thread that welded the leadership and

[55] *Prosecutor v Milomir Stakic*, IT-97–24-T, Judgment, Trial Chamber (31 July 2003) para. 433.

[56] *Prosecutor v Milomir Stakic*, IT-97–24-A, Judgment, Appeals Chamber (22 March 2006) para. 386.

[57] *Final Report of the Truth and Reconciliation Commission of Sierra Leone*, www.trcsierraleone.org/drwebsite/publish/index.shtml, accessed 23 June 2008.

membership of the movement'[58] and 'it is difficult to talk of a common cause among the members of the movement'.[59] Further, '[p]eople were recruited as long as they could carry a gun ... it did not matter whether they believed in the cause or not. What mattered was numbers. All kinds of tools, including deception and forced recruitment would be deployed on a large scale by the RUF to get people into the movement.'[60] After recruitment, a culture of dependency prevailed with the threat of death for disobedience. All of these factors, particularly that of forced recruitment and the phenomenon of victim turned perpetrator, would make it difficult both to define and prove the criminality of the organization. Interestingly, however, the RUF is on the US State Department's Terrorist Exclusion List, which designates terrorist organizations for immigration purposes.[61]

It is well known that one of the reasons for the development of the concept of criminal organizations was the reality that no system of jurisprudence had yet evolved a satisfactory technique for handling a great number of common charges against a multitude of accused persons. The focus of modern international trials is less on the 'multitude of accused persons' and more on the degree of responsibility of key perpetrators, leaving national trials or truth commissions to address the problem of the guilty multitude. Increasingly, superior responsibility and joint criminal enterprise liability are seen as adequate tools.

However, joint criminal enterprise, in particular, has the potential to lapse into guilt by association if it is not carefully defined, especially where the alleged enterprise spans the membership of, for example, a particular political party, a military group or the crisis staff of a region. The result may be a subtle shifting of the burden of proof in the sense that the accused may feel compelled to establish that despite belonging to such a group or associating with members of that group, he did not intend or take action to further the criminal outcome of the group's policies. This is true both from the perspective of the individuals on trial and the named and unnamed participants who make guest appearances in international indictments.

[58] *Final Report of the Truth and Reconciliation Commission of Sierra Leone* (n. 57) vol. 3a, ch. 4, Nature of the Conflict, para. 233.

[59] *Final Report of the Truth and Reconciliation Commission of Sierra Leone* (n. 57) vol. 3a, ch. 4, para. 234.

[60] *Final Report of the Truth and Reconciliation Commission of Sierra Leone* (n. 57) vol. 3a, ch. 4, para. 235.

[61] Terrorist Exclusion List (29 December 2004), www.state.gov/s/ct/rls/fs/2004/32678.htm, accessed 23 June 2008.

This raises the issue of all those alleged participants who are never in fact put on trial. It may be questioned whether international trials of a handful of key perpetrators are sufficient from the perspective of victims and in terms of revealing the truth behind the mask of the organization. The application of the concept of criminal organizations does not translate into collective punishment so the difficulty really is one of a stigma being attached to members of a particular group. The same stigma may result from joint criminal enterprise liability or indeed the findings of truth commissions.

Action against the threat of terrorism and developments in the field of organized crime provide further reasons to engage with the concept of criminal organizations, if only to guard against the risk of abuse. The manner in which entities or individuals are added to the terrorist list maintained by the UN Security Council and the absence of review or appeal for those listed raise serious human rights concerns. It has been proposed that the Al Qaida and Taliban Sanctions Committee should institute a process for reviewing the cases of individuals and institutions claiming to have been wrongly placed or retained on its watch lists[62] and Resolution 1375 at least addresses the question of de-listing.[63] A declaration of criminality against a terrorist organization by a court applying international human rights standards with evidence against the organization being fully tested might be an attractive alternative to unchecked 'preventive' measures.

V. Conclusion: the concept of criminal organizations in a modern setting

This author has previously advocated a role for the concept of criminal organizations in the context of large-scale international crimes where

[62] See Report of the High Level Panel on Threats, Challenges and Change, 'A more secure world: our shared responsibility', A/59/565 (2 December 2004) para. 152, www.un.org/secureworld/report.pdf, accessed 23 June 2008.

[63] '[T]he Committee, in determining whether to remove names from the Consolidated List, may consider, among other things, (i) whether the individual or entity was placed on the Consolidated List due to a mistake of identity, or (ii) whether the individual or entity no longer meets the criteria set out in relevant resolutions, in particular resolution 1617 (2005); in making the evaluation in (ii) above, the Committee may consider, among other things, whether the individual is deceased, or whether it has been affirmatively shown that the individual or entity has severed all association, as defined in resolution 1617 (2005), with Al-Qaida, Usama bin Laden, the Taliban, and their supporters, including all individuals and entities on the Consolidated List.'

the burden on domestic courts is immense, as for example in Rwanda, where there have been a number of domestic initiatives aimed at bringing the alleged perpetrators of genocide to justice and relieving the burden on the prison system without resorting to an amnesty.[64] The concept of criminal organizations could have provided the ICTR (and therefore the international community) with a means of assisting Rwanda in its efforts to ensure accountability while still maintaining international fair trial standards. Certain groups, such as the *Interahamwe* and the newspaper *Kangura* would have been potential candidates for a declaration of criminality. As the ICTR found in the *Nahimana* case: 'Through fear-mongering and hate propaganda, *Kangura* paved the way for genocide in Rwanda, whipping the Hutu population into a killing frenzy.'[65]

The ICTR Statute might have included an article similar to Article 9 of the Nuremberg Charter providing that the ICTR could, at the trial of any individual member of any group, declare that the group was a criminal organization. An article analogous to Article 10 of the Nuremberg Charter could have stated that the competent courts in Rwanda would have the right to bring individuals to trial for membership in a criminal organization and in any such case the criminal nature of the organization would be considered proven. The ICTR Statute and Rules of Procedure would have been advancements on the Nuremberg concept in: providing a definition of a criminal organization; clearly stating that the prosecution bears the burden of proving an accused was a knowledgeable and voluntary member; specifying the maximum penalty for membership (to remain relatively low if no act beyond mere membership was proven, thereby excluding the death penalty); specifying time periods for the operation of the organization; disallowing any further declarations of criminality of organizations by domestic courts; excluding certain sub-groups (e.g. children recruited as soldiers); and, possibly, providing that a person may only be convicted of membership if he also committed a crime in furtherance of the criminal goal of the group. This last restriction would weaken the effectiveness of the procedure in that the goal of trying large numbers of perpetrators in a short time frame might not be met. However, it would allow for a declaration of criminality against the organization as

[64] N. H. B. Jørgensen, 'A reappraisal of the abandoned Nuremberg concept of criminal organisations in the context of justice in Rwanda' (2001) 12 *Criminal Law Forum* 371–406.

[65] *Prosecutor v Ferdinand Nahimana, Jean-Bosco Barayagwiza and Hassan Ngeze*, ICTR-99-52-T, Judgment and Sentence, Trial Chamber (3 December 2003) para. 950.

such while at the same time ensuring individual accountability along the lines of a more familiar common purpose doctrine.

Some of the difficulties with such a proposal are the absence of documentation in many modern conflicts, the problem of identifying members of the group, the question whether an organization like the *Interahamwe* was a very loose organization which individuals were coerced into joining, and the issue of effectiveness being dependent on cooperation between the international tribunal and the government concerned. These difficulties become clear if the concept is considered in the context of the Special Court for Sierra Leone and domestic Sierra Leonean courts. Some of the key differences in the Sierra Leone context are the amnesty that is applicable before domestic courts[66] and the functioning of a Truth and Reconciliation Commission, for a period simultaneously with the Special Court. It is an interesting, though academic, question whether the concept of criminal organizations could have provided the Special Court with a means of forcing domestic prosecutions of members of organizations such as the RUF in spite of the amnesty, while at the same time preventing the use of the death penalty. As it is, in addition to the former Liberian President Charles Taylor, the Special Court has tried members of each of the three warring factions in three joint trials and the prosecution alleged very broad joint criminal enterprises, for example that the AFRC and RUF acted pursuant to a common plan to take any action necessary to gain control over Sierra Leone.[67] Groups such as the RUF or a smaller entity such as the Kamajors, which fought on behalf of the elected government, do not fall easily into the Nuremberg concept of criminal organizations.

However, it is still possible to envisage a potential role for the concept in the event of future trials at the international level for terrorism as well as

[66] Peace Agreement between the Government of Sierra Leone and the Revolutionary United Front of Sierra Leone, Lomé, 3 June 1999, www.sierra-leone.org/lomeaccord.html, accessed 23 June 2008.

[67] *Prosecutor v Issa Sesay, Morris Kallon, Augustine Gbao*, SCSL-04-15-PT, Corrected Amended Consolidated Indictment (2 August 2006) para. 36. In its judgment in the case of *Prosecutor v Alex Tamba Brima, Brima Bazzy Kamara and Santigie Borbor Kanu*, SCSL-04-16-T (20 June 2007) the Trial Chamber refused to accept the manner in which the joint criminal enterprise had been pleaded. The prosecution was found to have failed to plead an inherently criminal enterprise envisaging a crime under the statute. However, the Appeals Chamber, in its judgment of 22 February 2008, para. 84, found that the common purpose of the joint criminal enterprise was not defectively pleaded: 'Although the objective of gaining and exercising political power and control over the territory of Sierra Leone may not be a crime under the Statute, the actions contemplated as a means to achieve that objective are crimes within the Statute.'

at the domestic level in cases involving organized crime. The safeguards and restraints of the criminal law may indeed make such an alternative preferable to less restrained or unrestrained forms of coercion such as wars, extra-judicial killings, torture and detention without review. The real danger is to dismiss the concept outright as bearing no relationship to more favoured concepts of common purpose liability, thereby portraying those concepts as the benchmarks of fairness when closer scrutiny is warranted. There is a common thread that runs through the doctrines outlined in this chapter. It is only by comparing and contrasting, and examining them under the spotlight of fairness and effectiveness, that the most appropriate way of removing the organizational mask when confronting 'system criminality' in these forms may be revealed.

10

Criminality of organizations: lessons from domestic law – a comparative perspective

ALBIN ESER*

IN COOPERATION WITH

FELIX RETTENMAIER**

I. Introduction

As very simply and decisively stated by Lord Holt in an anonymous case of 1701, over many centuries it was common belief that 'a corporation is not indictable, but the particular members of it are'.[1]

Nowadays, when dealing with the criminal responsibility of organizations, that statement cannot be upheld any more.[2] In fact, as already called for at to outset of the last century by one of the then leading German-Austrian criminal law professors, Franz von Liszt,[3] criminal responsibility for legal and collective entities has been widely achieved, though only to varying degrees and in different forms.

In most European countries the national legislatures have created possibilities to hold legal and collective entities criminally responsible. In so far, one can witness an approximation to the Anglo-American

* Professor Dr. Dr. h. c. mult., M. C. J., Director Emeritus of the Max-Planck-Institute for Foreign and International Criminal Law, Freiburg, Germany, Former Judge at the International Criminal Tribunal for the Former Yugoslavia in The Hague.

** Lawyer with Knierim & Kollegen Rechtsanwälte, Mainz, Germany, Former Research Fellow at the Max-Planck-Institute for Foreign and International Criminal Law, Freiburg, Germany.

1 Cited by J. C. Coffee Jr, 'Corporate criminal liability: an introduction and comparative survey', in A. Eser, G. Heine and B. Huber (eds.), *Criminal Responsibility of Legal and Collective Entities* (edition iuscrim, Freiburg 1999), p. 13.

2 G. Britz, 'Rechtsfolgen gegen das Unternehmen', in K. Volk (ed.), *Verteidigung in Wirtschafts- und Steuerstrafsachen* (Verlag C. H. Beck, Munich 2006), p. 152 with reference to G. Eidam, 'Die Verbandsgeldbuße des § 30 Abs 4 OWiG – eine Bestandsaufnahme' (2003) wistra 448.

3 Cf. R. Scholz, 'Strafbarkeit juristischer Personen?' (2000) ZRP 435, with reference to F. von Liszt, *Lehrbuch des Deutschen Strafrechts* (18th edn., Guttentag, Berlin 1911), p. 128.

jurisdictions, which have known a form of 'corporate criminal liability' since the beginning of the last century.[4]

With introducing criminal responsibility of legal and collective entities, many legislatures of the large industrial nations paid tribute to the ever increasing economic development followed by an increase of 'corporate crimes'.[5] At present, hardly a day passes without media reports of criminal offences committed by enterprises and their executive personnel.

There is no doubt that many legislatures are both aware of this criminal conduct and determined to fight this by new legal measures and sanctions. It is, however, equally true that the legal and procedural problems involved are still far from having been solved in a satisfying and uniform manner. Instead of offering an all-encompassing solution, which would not be possible here anyhow, we will reflect on some comparative lessons that can be drawn from the various legislative efforts undertaken in the past.

We will proceed in four steps. First, by offering an empirical typology, we will illustrate and organize different ways and degrees of organisational formats in which crimes can be committed (section II). Second, we will provide an overview of the main approaches and types of legislation in this field (section III). Third, as there remain countries sceptical of direct punishment of juristic persons, we will present some of the principal arguments pro and contra. For this purpose, we will focus on the German perspective, since the legal issues have been most intensely debated in Germany (section IV). Finally, we will propose a new approach to collective criminal liability (section V).

II. Empirical typology of criminal responsibility – normative classifications and transgressions

When speaking of 'criminality of organizations', everybody supposedly knows what is meant by this terminology. At a closer look, however, it is much less clear which type of crimes committed by or within an organizational structure and of what form and degree shall be covered. Should any cooperation of a certain number of individuals suffice? Should some sort of organizational network be required? Or should only immediate corporate criminality in terms of illegal acts of legal persons or similar collective entities be comprised? Since one can never be sure, when looking at the relevant literature, what people have in mind when they

[4] Scholz (n. 3) 435.

[5] Cf. E. von Bubnoff, 'Ein eigenständiges Verbandssanktionsrecht' (2004) ZEuS 449, speaking of complex and wide-ranging phenomena of criminal activity.

speak of organized crime, of criminality of organizations or of collective responsibility, it seems helpful to identify certain steps within the continuum in which crimes can be committed by a multiplicity of persons. This continuum may begin with parallel action taken independantly beside each other, run through various forms of participation and organization and end in collective action. Different normative-legal formulas apply to each of these stages.

At least three stages can be distinguished in this continuum, as follows.

1. *Various individuals in parallel, but independent commission of a crime (group 1)*

Various individuals may commit a crime in parallel, but independently of one another. This is the case when, for instance, a bank account is electronically invaded and plundered by different hackers at the same time who may or may not know of each other but who, at any rate, do not cooperate in any form of 'participation' in legal terms.

This would be a clear case of individual responsibility: although the crime is committed in parallel time and way and by more than one person, each individual will be dealt with by the 'classical' norms of single perpetratorship.

2. *Cooperative criminality (group 2)*

Acts of cooperative criminality fall into a second group. Although this type of criminality has some sort of cooperation between various individuals in common, this connection may appear – and correspondingly be legally dealt with – in at least three different forms:

(a) The most intensive mode of cooperation exists in 'co-perpetration'. This is, for instance, the case where two individuals jointly rob a bank (group 2a).

(b) Less closely connected, but still in some sort of cooperation that, yet, does not amount to 'co-perpetratorship', criminal cooperation may exist in terms of 'participation'. This is the case where an individual is involved into the crime of another individual (the main perpetrator) as instigator or aider and abettor, as, for instance, when the participant is watching the scene while the main perpetrator is robbing the bank (group 2b).

(c) Finally, more or less tightly knit, cooperative criminality may occur in the form of some organizational network. An example would be the cooperation among drug producers, traffickers and dealers with a bank employee for money laundering (group 2c).

With regard to these different modes of cooperative criminality, the legal treatment in the various jurisdictions is much less homogeneous than in the case of parallel individual responsibility (group 1). In fact, not even the classical distinction of co-perpetration (group 2a) and participation (group 2b) is universally recognized. In international criminal justice, the new figure of 'joint criminal enterprise' complicates matters even further.[6]

Not surprisingly, national divergences go even further when it comes to organized crime in form of criminal networks (group 2c): whereas most countries still rely on the traditional rules of perpetration and participation, other countries, such as Germany, explicitly incriminate the 'formation of a criminal organization' and the 'formation of a terrorist organization' with special provisions.[7] This last form of organized cooperative criminality, however, still needs to be distinguished from an even higher level of supra-individual criminality.

3. *'Collective criminality' of organizations in terms of legal entities (group 3)*

At this third stage, it is not, or at least not only, the responsibility of the natural persons involved in a crime that is at stake, but rather the own direct liability of the collective entity on whose behalf or for whose benefit the crime is committed. Again, the criminal involvement of the legal entity may result from different purposes or causes. Just to mention two varieties:

(a) in the less serious mode, the legal entity may, as a rule, act in accordance with the law and is merely occasionally abused by agents or employees for the commission of crimes (group 3a); or
(b) in the more serious version, the legal entity has been established for the very purpose of committing crimes (group 3b).[8]

[6] See H. van der Wilt, 'Joint criminal enterprise and functional perpetration', this volume, Chapter 7 and E. van Sliedregt, 'System criminality at the ICTY', this volume, Chapter 8.

[7] Section 129 and section 129a German Penal Code.

[8] Cf. A. Eser, 'Comparative observations' in Eser, Heine and Huber (n. 1) 364–5.

4. *Criminality of organizations as distinct from the other forms of crimes committed by a multiplicity of individuals*

Although a multiplicity of persons is involved in all of the modes of criminality mentioned above, differences arise with regard to certain legally relevant features.

First, whereas the parallel commission of a crime by several persons (group 1) can be handled with the same criteria of criminal responsibility that apply to any normal case of 'sole' perpetratorship, cooperative commission of a crime (group 2) may require additional rules for attributing the acts of one co-perpetrator or participant to the others.

Second, while in these cases of classical cooperative perpetration (group 2a) and participation (group 2b) the core of wrongdoing still lies in the finally procured crime (as, for instance, a joint tax fraud by a couple), in the case of the 'formation of a criminal organization'(group 2c) the focus of wrongdoing shifts from the eventually committed crime to the formation of or participation in the illegal organization: as, for instance, in the case that a network of several intermediaries is set up for money laundering of illegal profits gained by drug dealing. Even if in such a setting it never comes to a successful money laundering and, thus, the intended main crime fails, the formation of the criminal organization as such and, thus, the 'front ground' of the true crime is already considered dangerous enough to be penalized as a wrongdoing of its own.

Third, whereas the 'criminal organization' the formation of which is prohibited (group 2c) does not have to be a legal entity but can be any organizational conjunction of a number of at least three persons following a common purpose intended for a certain duration,[9] a new dimension is reached when the particular organization is formed as a legal or equivalent collective entity (group 3). With regard to these – and only these – organizations, the question arises whether they should be held criminally responsible themselves – in addition to or even instead of the individuals acting on their behalf.

5. *The grey zone between 'organized crime' and 'criminality of organizations'*

What does this typology imply for the relationship between 'organized crime' and 'criminality of organizations'?

[9] For more details with regard to section 129 German Penal Code, see T. Lenckner and D. Steinberg-Lieben, in A. Schönke, H. Schröder, T. Lenckner *et al.*, *Strafgesetzbuch* (27th ed., C. H. Beck, Munich 2006) § 129, margin no. 4, 1278.

If we understand 'organized crime', as it was defined by the European Commission, as 'two or more persons' participation in the same criminal scheme for the purpose of obtaining power and profits, for a prolonged or indefinite period of time, each being responsible for specific tasks within the organization',[10] then the natural individuals involved can be held responsible for co-perpetration of, or participation in, the actual crimes committed, or, if the main crime was not completed, for the 'formation of a criminal organization'.[11] On the other hand, the criminal organization as such can be held responsible only if it fulfils certain criteria as, in particular, the requirements of a legal entity.

If this is the case, a further distinction is appropriate: On the one hand, a principally law-abiding corporation (group 3a) on whose behalf merely occasionally some illegal profits have been made, can, if at all, be held responsible only for the accomplished crime (such as, for instance, tax evasion). On the other hand, in case of a corporation purposefully founded for illegal activities (group 3b), criminal responsibility would not only comprise the individual perpetratorship and/or participation of the indivuduals/agents involved and the eventual attribution to the legal entity, but also the fore-field to the 'formation of a criminal organization'. In this situation, 'organized crime' and 'criminality of organization' would overlap. At any rate, this analysis suggests to keep in mind that the scope of 'criminality of organizations' is much more complex and broader than commonly expected.

III. Development of criminal responsibility of legal, corporate or otherwise collective entities in Europe

In this section, we will focus on the own criminal liability of organizations in terms of legal entities, as distinct from the individual responsibility of natural persons who act on behalf or for the benefit of the 'juristic person'.

With regard to terminology, however, we have the problem that different countries use different concepts and terms when declaring certain organizations criminally liable. In order to be as open and neutral as possible, the terms 'juristic person' and 'legal/corporate/collective

[10] Kriterien des K.4-Ausschusses, Beilage C zur Ausarbeitung einer gemeinsamen Ordnung für die Sammlung und systematische Analyse von Meldungen über international organizierte Kriminalität, Brüssel (28 February 1995), cited according to W. Gropp and B. Huber (eds.), *Rechtliche Initiativen gegen organisierte Kriminalität* (edition iuscrim, Freiburg 2001), p. 8.

[11] Provided, of course, that such a prohibition exists in the relevant country.

entities' equally apply to organisms which enjoy a certain independence from their members, organs or other agents and are thus to a certain degree vested with legally acknowledged rights and duties in legal affairs.

Before addressing the various models by which the acts or omissions of individuals may be attributed to a juristic person, it appears appropriate to present a short survey – with particular focus upon Europe – of the various countries which meanwhile have introduced some sort of criminal responsibility of legal entities.[12]

Although the recommendation of the Council of Europe for 'liability of enterprises for offences'[13] can be understood as an impetus for establishing corporate criminal responsibility, so far different ways have been pursued to achieve that end. While some countries locate criminal responsibility of legal entities within 'core' criminal law or other countries prefer quasi-criminal liability in terms of 'regulatory' or 'administrative offences', a growing number of countries is turning to a new model of 'collective liability *sui generis*'.

1. *Regulations in genuine criminal law*

Though notwithstanding certain variations in detail, most European countries have introduced criminal liability of legal entities or corporations in terms of criminal offences. This has been – in chronological sequence – the case with Great Britain (middle of the last century), Ireland (middle of the last century), Netherlands (1951), Norway (1991), Iceland (1993), France (1994), Finland (1995), Denmark (1996), Slovenia (1996), Belgium (1999), Switzerland (2003) and Turkey 2004, limited to safety measures

The same course is taken outside of Europe, in particular, by the USA and Japan. In this connection notice must also be taken of Sweden (1986), Spain (1995) and Romania (2006). In these states, the regulations, however, differ from those of the aforementioned group by providing sanctions

[12] For a comprehensive comparative survey with more details and references than can be given here, and with partly different classifications, cf. the country reports in: Eser, Heine and Huber (n. 1); furthermore, cf. G. Heine, 'Unternehmen, Strafrecht und europäische Entwicklungen', in (2000) 23/24 ÖJZ 871–881; A. Quante, *Sanktionsmöglichkeiten gegen juristische Personen und Personenvereinigungen* (Lang, Bern 2005), p. 175 *et seq.* For a comparative survey on 'organized crimes' as distinct from 'criminality of organizations' in question here (section II. 5) cf. the country reports in W. Gropp and A. Sinn (eds.), *Organisierte Kriminalität und kriminelle Organisationen* (Nomos, Baden-Baden 2006).

[13] See Gropp and Huber (n. 10) 8.

against juristic persons and corporations merely in terms of 'additional consequences' *sui generis*.[14]

2. *Regulatory offences and administrative sanctions*

Countries which, for principal reasons, consider genuine punishment not feasible against non-natural persons, try to proceed on a lower level by treating corporate liability in terms of 'regulatory offences' (*Ordnungswidrigkeitenrecht*), sanctioned with non-punitive fines ('*Geldbuße*'), as in the case of Germany (§ 30 OWiG) and Portugal (1995), or in terms of administrative liability, as in Poland (2003), and in a similar way for the area of economy and competition in Luxemburg (1993) and Greece (2000).

These models, in spite of official terminology, may in substance still be considered 'quasi-criminal'.

3. *Collective liability* sui generis

Different from the traditional approach of merely modifying or expanding ordinary criminal or administrative sanctions to cover offences by or on behalf of collective entities, some countries chose to try out new avenues by criminalizing offences of collective entities by a regulation of its own, both by special provisions for substantive criminal law and for procedure. This is the case with Croatia, Italy (2001) and Austria (2006).[15]

4. *Retainment of traditional individual criminal responsibility*

Since quite a lot of countries which, in one way or the other, have adopted some sort of liability of legal entities have already been mentioned, there seem not many countries left which would restrict punitive sanctions to natural persons. Provided that the sources which have been available at the time being are still valid, the following countries within the European Union have not been reported as having introduced some sort of collective criminal responsibility: Cyprus, Estonia, Hungary, Malta and Slovakia.

[14] See G. Heine, 'Kollektive Verantwortlichkeit als neue Aufgabe im Spiegel der aktuellen europäischen Entwicklung', in D. Dölling (ed.), *Jus humanum. Festschrift für Ernst-Joachim Lampe* (Duncker & Humblot, Berlin 2003), p. 579.

[15] Heine (n. 14) 580.

Whether two other countries which had prepared drafts, namely Czech Republic (1997) and Lithuania (1996), have finalized the legislation, was not possible to ascertain.

IV. Rationales and models of collective criminal liability

Although there are thus rather few countries left still trying to fight corporate crime exclusively with the instruments of individual criminal responsibility, the picture of a vast majority of 'progressive' countries with some sort of collective criminal liability should not make us overlook important differences with regard to the underlying rationale and the respective models of collective liability.

1. Rationales to legitimize criminal liability of 'juristic persons'

(a) 'Representation theories'

Still most common is the proposition that the conduct of organs or other representatives of a juristic person can be attributed to it. In this way, by being represented and acted for by an agent, the legal entity is considered as having acted itself.

This approach which, for example, is prevalent in Belgium, Finland, France, Germany, Iceland, Croatia and – in combination with aspects of 'genuine' liability of the collective entity – in Austria,[16] results in a complete equation of the individual with the collective criminal responsibility. As a consequence of this 'anthropomorphic model',[17] the responsibility of the legal person is doomed to fail when and where responsibility of a natural person cannot be proven.

(b) 'Genuine' recourse to the juristic person

Other jurisdictions, such as Great Britain and Switzerland, try to establish criminal liability of the juristic person by going back to the true 'origin' of the corporate offence (in German termed as *originäres Haftungsmodell*). In so doing, this theory rids itself completely from the requirement of the act of a natural person.

[16] Cf. section 5 to § 3 section 3 n. 1 and 2 *Verbandsverantwortlichkeitsgesetz* (Bundesgesetzblatt für die Republik Österreich, 23 December 2005) 1–10.

[17] As it was termed by Heine (n. 14) 585.

As a consequence, Switzerland does not even allow representatives of an enterprise to function as defendant in the same proceedings.[18] As criminal liability primarily rests with the enterprise itself, it suffices to prove that the legal norm has been violated, that this violation is attributable to the economic activity of the enterprise, and that it results from malfunctioning organization of the enterprise.

(c) Risk-based liability

While the aforementioned foundation of criminal liability still rests on proof of some sort of mismanagement, some states – such as Denmark, Sweden and Poland – have gone a step further by treating the juristic person *per se* as a source of risk. In consequence of this *Veranlassungshaftung* (as it is called in German), the legal entity is held responsible if an offence occurs in the course of establishing or running the organization.[19] As a result, any violation of a criminal provision may trigger liability of the entity.

2. *Basic deficiencies of 'juristic persons'*

Although each of the aforementioned rationales lend some support to collective liability, juristic persons are alleged to suffer from deficiencies which seem to shield them from criminal responsibility. Objections of this sort are raised especially by those countries which are reluctant to impose genuine criminal sanctions on non-natural persons.

As vehemently discussed, particularly in Germany, juristic persons allegedly lack at least two capabilities that are considered fundamental to hold them criminally liable on their own.

The first is the lack of capacity to act. If criminal wrongdoing is based on an act the punishment is supposed to react to, criminal liability requires that an act was committed. As a juristic person has neither hands nor a mouth, it is unable to act by its own. The rights and duties it may be vested with must be exercised by natural persons acting as organs or agents.

The second is the lack of culpability. Even if the lack of a capacity to act may be substituted by natural persons as representatives, a juristic person will hardly meet a second basic requirement of criminal responsibility: the

[18] M. Pieth, 'Strafverfahren gegen das Unternehmen', in J. Arnold *et al.* (eds.), *Menschengerechtes Strafrecht, Festschrift für Albin Eser zum 70. Geburtstag* (C. H. Beck, Munich 2005), p. 609.

[19] For details see Heine (n. 14) 586.

principle of culpability.[20] It requires that the perpetrator can be socially and morally blamed for his wrongdoing as he decided to violate the law in spite of his capability to comply with it.[21] Culpability so construed may rest with the individual actor, but not with the juristic person he or she is acting for.

Consequently, as argued by critics of immediate criminal responsibility of legal entities, since non-natural persons lack the 'capacity of acting differently' – in terms of a choice between law-abiding or norm-deviant conduct – a juristic person cannot be the addressee of criminal norms and commands and, thus, cannot be held criminally responsible on its own.[22]

This insight, however, is not the end of the story. Different efforts have been undertaken to overcome these deficiencies.

3. *Basic models of collective criminal responsibility*

Even if it is generally accepted that juristic persons and similar collective entities are, as such, neither capable of acting in criminal terms nor of doing so in culpable manner, there remain basically three options to sanction collective entities for criminal conduct.

(a) 'Imputation model'

The model that still rather closely keeps in line with traditional propositions of individual criminal responsibility, in particular by way of engaging aspects of the earlier mentioned 'representation theory', would impute the acts of natural persons who are authorized to represent the corporation (as, in particular, members of the board of directors or other leading executives) to the legal entity as such. This way, the natural person acting on behalf of the legal entity also serves as a basis for culpability.[23] The required connection between the natural actor and the juristic person, without which the imputation from one to the other would be hardly

[20] Cf. K. Tiedemann, 'Die "Bebußung" von Unternehmen nach dem 2. Gesetz zur Bekämpfung der Wirtschaftskriminalität' (1988) NJW 1172.

[21] Cf. J. Peglau, 'Unbeantwortete Fragen der Strafbarkeit von Personenverbänden' (2001) ZRP 407.

[22] Cf., in particular, G. Dannecker, 'Kollektive Verantwortlichkeit als neue Aufgabe im Spiegel der aktuellen europäischen Entwicklung' (2001) GA 109.

[23] Cf. J. Peglau, 'Bericht an die Kommission zur Reform des strafrechtlichen Sanktionssystems', in M. Hettinger (ed.), *Reform des Sanktionsrechts* (Berliner Wissenschafts-Verlag, Berlin 2002), p. 20.

justified, may be found in the legal duty addressed to the legal entity and breached by its representatives.

Obviously, if the legal entity is to be sanctioned, the 'classical' criminal penalties need certain modifications and adjustments. For, as rightly noticed by Heine, 'the absence of a human subject to whom individual responsibility can be assigned seems to have reduced the range of options in sanctioning enterprises',[24] or, as drastically phrased by Coffee: 'No soul to damn, no body to kick.'[25] At bottom, these phrases merely acknowledge that legal or collective entities cannot be imprisoned. Nonetheless, corporate entities used to be susceptible to the prospect of severe losses or denial of rights and privileges, be it in form of monetary fines or foreclosure from markets. Thus, an impressive range of sanctions could easily be developed.

(b) 'Evasive model'

Other ways to avoid conflicting with or deviating from the principle of culpability might be sought in inventing a new sanctioning system that would abandon the traditional requirements of culpability in favour of a lesser degree of personal moral reproachability.

This approach could, without requiring a special sanctioning scheme of its own, also be integrated into a general category of quasi-criminal 'regulatory offences' as has been done in Germany. As it would be restricted to 'regulatory offences', however, this scheme could not comprise more serious crimes (as, for instance manslaughter caused by rotten food), which may have been committed on behalf of the cooperation by its agent.

(c) 'System contingent model'

The models considered so far, remain more or less focused on the action of a natural agent. In the alternative, one might also consider a categorically new approach. As a first step, one would have to leave the natural actor behind and to found the liability of a corporation upon the wrongdoing that was caused by, or possibly due to, deficiencies

[24] G. Heine, 'Sanctions in the field of corporate criminal liability', in Eser, Heine and Huber (n. 1) 247.

[25] With reference to the then Lord Chancellor of England, Edward, First Baron Thurlow (1731–1806), see J. C. Coffee Jr '"No soul to damn: no body to kick": an unscandalized inquiry into the problem of corporate punishment' (1981) 79 *Michigan Law Review* 386.

in the corporate system.[26] In this concept, the act of a natural person becomes more or less irrelevant; instead the focus is rather shifted to the legal entity that is held liable for its defective organization or system and blamed for not meeting ordinary social-ethical standards. Thus, the fault of the collective system can be seen in a sort of 'business management culpability' (*Betriebsführungsschuld*). Consequently, the core of the wrongdoing lies in the neglect of the organizational duty of ordinary care in the performance of its affairs and in the prevention of operational risks. This means that, rather than on (proof of) certain individual acts, liability of a legal entity is primarily based on defaults in its organizational system.

In this way, personal governance of individual actors is replaced by functional-systemic governance of the organization.[27]

V. Plea for a complementary collective and individual criminal liability *sui generis*

When comparing and evaluating the various rationales and models of criminal responsibility of legal and similar collective entities, none of them is truly convincing. The following observations may suffice to explain this conclusion.

First, the 'imputation model' and, to the same effect, all 'evasive' models requiring that an act of a natural person be attributed to the legal entity, results in impunity if it cannot be determined what natural person behaved illegally and in which way it did so. In short, imputation of liability to a legal entity is always exposed to failure if a certain individual act may not be provable.

These loopholes in holding legal entities criminally liable are widened if liability of legal entities presupposes proof of an intentional act of a formal representative when, in fact, merely negligence or only misconduct of an employee without any representative powers can be proven.

[26] See, in particular, Dannecker (n. 22) 111.

[27] This proposition is by no means unknown to the German legal system; in particular in the so-called 'Politbüro-proceedings' (*Politbüroprozesse*) the Federal Supreme Court was prepared to accept the principle of 'organizational governance' to be applied in corporate-economic cases; see G. Heine, 'Modelle originär (straf-) rechtlicher Verantwortlichkeit von Unternehmen', in Hettinger (n. 23) Band 3: Verbandsstrafe (2002) 123 with reference to Entscheidungen des Bundesgerichtshofs in Strafsachen, BGHSt 40 [1995] 211ss (236) and 307ss (316), respectively.

Furthermore, if these types of models are to be applied in accordance with the principles of 'classical' criminal law, the juristic person's lack of capacity to act and its lack of culpability appear insurmountable hurdles. Similar problems arise on the sanction side: since 'imprisonment' of the juristic person is out of the question, only monetary penalties seem available.

Second, quite a few of these obstacles could be avoided by applying a 'system contingent model', in which the conduct of natural persons becomes more or less irrelevant while the focus is shifted on organizational deficiencies of the corporate system, resulting in a sort of 'business management culpability'.

The high price which may have to be paid for a complete and one-sided shift of emphasis on systemic faults of the collective entity, however, may be the loss of the ability to give due consideration to the possibly uneven weight of the systemic deficiencies and their causes. So it may, in particular, be difficult to differentiate between intentional or merely negligent conduct of the responsible agents.

Furthermore, it appears questionable whether at all, and if so to what degree, natural persons involved in criminal results of the collective disorder should be relieved from own individual responsibility.[28]

Third, in order to establish immediate liability of the collective entity while maintaining possibly provable individual criminal responsibility of agents, a combination of the 'system contingent model' with the 'imputation model' may appear appropriate. To a certain degree, this option was chosen by the new Austrian 'Law of Responsibility of Collective Entities',[29] which came into force on 1 January 2006.

According to this recent legislation, in principle, an association is criminally liable for any crimes committed in its favour or in violation of its duties.

This apparently 'system contingent' approach, however, is combined with, and thereby curbed by, elements of the 'imputation model'. This results from the law distinguishing between 'decision makers' and other employees: whereas offences committed by a decision-maker render the corporation liable *per se*, with regard to other employees the corporation

[28] See A. Nollkaemper and H. van der Wilt, 'Conclusions and outlook', this volume, Chapter 15, p. 344.

[29] Verbandsverantwortlichkeitsgesetz (VbVG) der Republik Österreich (Bundesgesetzblatt für die Republik Österreich 23 December 2005) 1–10. For details and a critical review, see K. Schmoller, *Strafe ohne Schuld? – Überlegungen zum neuen Österreichischen Verbandsverantwortlichkeitsgesetz,* in G. Dannecker *et al.* (eds.), *Festschrift für Harro Otto* (Carl Heymanns Verlag, Berlin 2007), pp. 453–68.

be held liable only if the employees' misconduct was enabled by a ligent omission of a decision-maker in technical, organizational or personal respects.

Consequently, collective liability in Austria still requires proof of some sort of illegal acts or omissions by natural persons and, thus, as do other 'imputation models', runs the risk of collective impunity.

With regard to the sanction side, by simply transforming imprisonment into fines and, thus, in fact only allowing monetary impositions, the weaponry against legal and collective entities remains rather poor.

Fourth, the general conclusion which has to be drawn from the pros and cons of these models is that it seems impossible to find a satisfactory solution of collective criminal responsibility within the structural corsetry of 'classical' criminal law.

If, on the one hand, the collective entity shall be held criminally liable for systemic deficiencies of the corporate organization without requiring proof of individual responsibility of a certain natural person, and if, on the other hand, the natural representatives of the collective entity shall not be relieved of their own individual criminal responsibility (if sufficiently proven), and if it shall still be possible to differentiate by means of an adequate variety of sanctions with regard to the weight and degree of 'business management culpability' and individual responsibility, then this cannot be achieved but by a regulation of 'collective criminal liability *sui generis*'.

VI. Outlook

If a visionary conclusion is permitted, we will have to take an even more fundamental step further if we want to avoid that the structure of traditional individual criminal responsibility is becoming overstretched and, thereby, perverted.

To illustrate this point of view we should recall that, at least in Europe, the concept of criminal responsibility has been developed from the proposition of a single acting perpetrator; from there the same principles of responsibility were expanded to include the cooperative actions of multiple individual persons, and in a further step to comprise non-natural collective entities.

Now, instead of attempting to handle these completely different situations of a single actor, a variety of co-perpetrators and participants, and finally collective entities from the same set of single-individual responsibility, we should try to develop a tripartite scheme of (1) individual,

(2) participatory and (3) collective responsibility in criminal law: by treating each of them according to special rules of their own – as it was already suggested in the subtitle of a European Colloquium on 'Individual, Participatory and Collective Responsibility' in 1996.[30] This challenge, however, would be no small feat.

[30] A. Eser, 'Eröffnungsansprache', in A. Eser, B. Huber and K. Cornils (eds.), *Einzelverantwortung und Mitverantwortung im Strafrecht: European Colloquium 1996 on Individual, Participatory and Collective Responsibility in Criminal Law* (edition iuscrim, Freiburg 1998), p. 6 and in Diskussionsbericht 360s.

11

The collective accountability of organized armed groups for system crimes

JANN K. KLEFFNER*

I. Introduction

The analytical starting point of the present book is that massive violations of human rights and of the law of armed conflict are committed as part, or with the involvement, of a collective entity, a 'system', which constitutes a central element of the enabling context for their commission.[1] Accordingly, the examination of crimes of genocide, crimes against humanity and war crimes would remain incomplete if one were to lose sight of this systemic environment and were to conceive of these crimes as solely a matter of criminal responsibility, with its focus on individual perpetrators. However, such an examination would run the risk of perpetuating incompleteness, were it to be limited to the *state* as the only conceivable 'system'. The assumption that the collective environment, in which policies of genocide, crimes against humanity and war crimes are implemented or condoned, is a state, may be justifiable in historical terms. In the past, it was, as a rule, states which constituted the collective environment for system crimes. Indeed, when the Nuremberg Tribunal held that system crimes are committed 'by men, not by abstract entities',[2] it was clear at the time that the 'abstract

* Assistant Professor of International Law, University of Amsterdam Law School. I am indebted to Pieter Jan Kuijper and Beth Stephens, who provided invaluable information. Special thanks to Professor Marco Sassoli for his insights and exchanges pertaining to the present subject. The research assistance of Swen Meereboer is gratefully acknowledged. The chapter was prepared as part of the research programme on 'The Role of Law in Armed Conflict and Peace Operations' of the Amsterdam Center for International Law, University of Amsterdam.

[1] This is subject to the possible exception of cases of isolated 'random soldiers on a rampage' and the lone individual who intends to destroy, in whole or in part, a particular group. See further, A. Nollkaemper, 'Introduction', this volume, Chapter 1, p. 3.

[2] Trial of the Major War Criminals before the International Military Tribunal, Nürnberg 14 November 1945–1 October 1946 (Nürnberg, 1947), p. 223.

entity' in question was meant to be a state. It is equally undisputed that the state retains a central role in that respect also today. More recent instances in which system crimes were or continue to be committed – Rwanda, Burma and Zimbabwe to name just a few – bear unequivocal witness to this fact.

However, states are not the *only* systems, which provide the collective context for genocide, crimes against humanity and systematic war crimes. Amidst challenges to the concept of state monopoly of legitimate organised armed violence, *non-state* collective entities have emerged as actors, which initiate, enable, condone, or are otherwise implicated in, these international crimes.[3] Put succinctly, genocide is not necessarily 'democide',[4] nor are crimes against humanity. Even less so are war crimes, especially those committed in non-international armed conflicts, which by definition include one or more non-state actors as parties.

To examine the framework of international legal accountability of non-state systems is the objective of the present contribution. In so doing, I confine myself to a specific sub-species of non-state actors: organized armed groups, i.e. those non-state actors which possess, at the very least, the necessary degree of organization so as to be considered a party to a non-international armed conflict in the sense of Article 3 common to the Geneva Conventions (assuming that such a group partakes in 'protracted armed violence', which reaches the intensity threshold of an armed conflict).[5] This limitation is not meant to suggest that organized armed groups are the only non-state actors, which may constitute 'systems' that are implicated in the commission of system crimes. Indeed, recent efforts to codify or develop international law vis-à-vis transnational corporations

[3] See generally, M. van Creveld, *The Transformation of War* (Free Press, New York 1991); M. Kaldor, *New and Old Wars: Organized Violence in a Global Era* (Polity Press/Stanford University Press, Stanford 2001); H. Münkler, *The New Wars* (Polity, Cambridge 2005); I. Duyvesteyn and J. Angstrom, *Rethinking the Nature of War* (Cass, London 2005); J. Bakonyi, S. Hensell and J. Siegelberg (eds.), *Gewaltordnungen bewaffneter Gruppen – Ökonomie und Herrschaft nichtstaatlicher Akteure in den Kriegen der Gegenwart* (Nomos, Baden-Baden 2006); J. Shultz, H. Richard and A. J. Dew, *Insurgents, Terrorists and Militias: The Warriors of Contemporary Combat* (Columbia University Press, New York, NY 2006).

[4] On the notion of democide as 'the murder of any person or people by a government, including genocide, politicide, and mass murder', see R. J. Rummel, *Death By Government* (Transaction Publishers, Edison, NJ 1994), p. 31.

[5] On these two requirements of organization and intensity, see amongst others, *ICTY Prosecutor v Limaj et al.*, IT-03-66-T, Judgment, Trial Chamber (30 November 2005) para. 84–174; *Prosecutor v Ramush Haradinaj, Idriz Balaj and Lahi Brahimaj*, IT-04-84-T, Judgment (3 April 2008) paras. 37–60.

and other business enterprises and vis-à-vis the responsibility of international organizations indicate that there is an increasing awareness of the possibility that non-state actors violate international legal norms, including those violations which may amount to international crimes.[6] However, in contrast to these other non-state actors, no efforts are currently being undertaken to codify the legal dimensions of accountability of organized armed groups in (quasi-)legal instruments and these dimensions have received considerably less attention in academic literature.[7] Together with the propensity of organized armed groups to commit system crimes, this current relative 'blind spot' justifies the particular focus on organized armed groups in this chapter.

Before proceeding, two caveats are in order. First, the ensuing analysis generically distinguishes between 'accountability' and 'responsibility'. The former is broader than the latter in as much as it encompasses not only formal processes for determining the wrongfulness of a given act and its consequences (e.g. in the form of reparation), but comprises all processes through which the conduct of organized armed groups is being assessed and measured against international legal rules, and the possible consequences imposed on them in case they have violated these rules.[8]

Secondly, I will limit myself to the *collective* accountability of organized armed groups *as such* in the following. Accordingly, I will discard

[6] As far as transnational corporations and other business enterprises are concerned, this is clearly contemplated in the 'Norms on the responsibilities of transnational corporations and other business enterprises with regard to human rights', adopted by the Commission on Human Rights, Sub-Commission on the Promotion and Protection of Human Rights, Fifty-fifth session, UN Doc. E/CN.4/Sub.2/2003/12/Rev.2 (26 August 2003) Section 3 of which provides: 'Transnational corporations and other business enterprises shall not engage in nor benefit from war crimes, crimes against humanity, genocide, torture, forced disappearance, forced or compulsory labour, hostage-taking, extrajudicial, summary or arbitrary executions, other violations of humanitarian law and other international crimes against the human person as defined by international law, in particular human rights and humanitarian law.' As to inter-governmental organizations, see in particular current draft Arts. 44 and 45 adopted by the Drafting Committee on 18, 19, 20 and 25 July 2007, UN Doc. A/CN.4/L.720, which foresees the transposition of aggravated responsibility in cases of 'serious breaches of peremptory norms' under Art. 42 of the Articles on State Responsibility to the responsibility of international organizations.

[7] For exceptions, see L. Zegveld, *Accountability of Armed Opposition Groups in International Law* (Cambridge University Press, Cambridge 2002); M. Sassoli, *Possible Legal Mechanisms to Improve Compliance by Armed Groups with International Humanitarian Law and International Human Rights Law,* Paper submitted at the Armed Groups Conference (Vancouver, 13–15 November 2003) (on file with author).

[8] Cf. D. Curtin and A. Nollkaemper, 'Conceptualizing accountability in international and European law' (2005) 36 NYIL 8; J. Brunnée, 'International legal accountability through the lens of the law of state responsibility' (2005) 36 NYIL 22.

from my analysis aspects of individual (criminal) responsibility of members of such groups.[9] Nor will I address aspects of the criminal responsibility of organizations, since they are being discussed elsewhere in the present volume.[10] What is more, to limit myself to the collective accountability of organized armed groups *as such* entails that the accountability of other collective entities for acts of (members of) organized armed groups are also beyond the purview of the present contribution. Thus, the responsibility of states for acts of (members of) organized armed groups, for example because such a group acts under the control of a state or because a state aids or assists an organized armed group in the commission of system crimes, will not be addressed.

The present chapter is structured as follows: first, I will address why and how organized armed groups can constitute the collective environment for the commission of system crimes (section II). In a subsequent step, I will provide an overview over the responses that have been, and are being, adopted vis-à-vis such organized armed groups, through which states and international organizations have sought to foster accountability (section III). Section IV then examines whether and to what extent international law should, and can, be developed so as to move from these loosely defined modes of accountability to a more coherent legal framework of responsibility of organized armed groups.

II. Organized armed groups and system criminality

Organized armed groups differ widely. On one end of the spectrum are the rare cases in which such groups display many quasi-statal features,

[9] On individual criminal responsibility, see the contributions of K. Ambos, 'Command responsibility and *Organisationsherrschaft*: ways of attributing international crimes to the "most responsible"', this volume, Chapter 6, H. van der Wilt, 'Joint criminal enterprise and functional perpetration', this volume, Chapter 7 and E. van Sliedregt, 'System criminality at the ICTY', this volume, Chapter 8. The rules and principles analyzed in their chapters apply equally to individuals who act as state organs or whose acts can otherwise be attributed to a state, on the one hand, and individual members of organized armed groups, on the other hand. In the main, individuals are criminally responsible for acts of genocide, crimes against humanity and war crimes under the same conditions, irrespective of their status as state organs or other. This is subject to the qualification that some rules, most pertinently international law immunities, pertain exclusively to individuals who assume state functions.

[10] See the contributions of N. Jørgensen, 'Criminality of organizations under international law', this volume Chapter 9 and of A. Eser, 'Criminality of organizations: lessons from domestic law – a comparative perspective', this volume, Chapter 10.

in case of which one might refer to such a group as a quasi-state[11] or a *de facto* régime.[12] Others, while not sharing quite as many of their characteristics with those of states, nevertheless possess highly organized armed forces and have the ability to establish and maintain a relatively stable control over territory and the persons within it. The 1977 Additional Protocol II encapsulates such a high degree of territorial control when referring to organized armed groups which 'exercise such control over a part of [a state party's] territory as to enable them to carry out sustained and concerted military operations'.[13] At the other end of the spectrum are those organized armed groups which are comparatively less organized and lack the ability to control territory. Between these two outer extremes of the continuum is an infinite variance of organized armed groups, which defies to generally treat them as a unitary, coherent category of actors during armed conflicts. Nevertheless, the very context in which *all* organized armed groups operate, i.e. armed conflict, presupposes structures and processes which justify to refer to them as 'systems' in the sense that they can constitute the collective environment for the commission of core international crimes (a). That assertion finds support in normative developments, which have extended the prohibitions of war crimes, crimes against humanity and genocide to (members of) organized armed groups, and in the fact that organized armed groups have in actual fact been implicated in the commission of system crimes (b).

1. *Organized armed groups as 'systems'*

As explained elsewhere in this book, the term 'system' generically refers to 'an organized or connected group of objects', and '[a] group, set, or aggregate of things, natural or artificial, forming a connected or complex whole',[14] which underlines that systems, as understood in the present context 'are more than collections of isolated individuals – key is the connection and the organization'.[15] It is readily apparent that, on a conceptual level, organized armed groups are such collectivities.

[11] On the development of a typology of organized armed groups, in which the quasi-state constitutes the high end of the spectrum, see J. Bakonyi and K. Stuvoy, 'Zwischen Warlordfiguration und Quasi-Staat – Ansätze zu einer Typologie bewaffntere Gruppen', in Bakonyi, Hensell and Siegelberg (n. 3) 38–52.

[12] J. A. Frowein, 'De facto régime' (1992) 1 EPIL 966–8.

[13] Cf. Art. 1(1) 1977 Protocol Additional to the Geneva Conventions of 12 August 1949, and relating to the protection of Victims of Non-International Armed Conflicts.

[14] OED *Online Database*, available at http://dictionary.oed.com/entrance.dtl, accessed 3 July 2008.

[15] See A. Nollkaemper, 'Introduction', this volume, Chapter 1, p. 1.

The law of armed conflict requires a certain degree of organization for a collectivity to be considered a party to an armed conflict. In the words of the ICTR in *Akayesu,* it must 'possess ... an organized military force, an authority responsible for its acts, acting within a determinate territory and having the means of respecting and ensuring the respect for the Convention'.[16] The ICTY also developed indicators for the required degree of organisation in *Ramush Haradinaj et al.*, amongst which are:

> the existence of a command structure and disciplinary rules and mechanisms within the group; ... [the group's] ability to plan, coordinate and carry out military operations, including troop movements and logistics; its ability to define a unified military strategy and use military tactics; and its ability to speak with one voice and negotiate and conclude agreements such as cease-fire or peace accords.[17]

These and other decisions of the international criminal *ad hoc* tribunals indicate that the required degree of organization does not only imply a certain structure, most notably a chain of command, but also other mechanisms through which the behaviour of its members as well as others that support it is being influenced. Indeed, while the complexity and sophistication of these structures and mechanisms differ, it is striking how indispensable they are for the purpose of partaking in armed conflict. No armed force, whether it be that of a state or a 'non-state', will be able to function without orders being followed and without at least a minimum degree of discipline, which enforces obedience, however crude the system for the effectuation of that discipline may be. Perhaps the most obvious way in which the law of armed conflict and international criminal law reflect the existence of such submission to authority and discipline is through the doctrine of command responsibility, which is applicable to all sides also in the context of non-international armed conflicts and, thus, extends to commanders of organized armed groups.[18]

[16] *Prosecutor v Akayesu*, ICTR-96-4-T, Judgment (2 September 1998) para. 619.

[17] *Prosecutor v Ramush Haradinaj, Idriz Balaj and Lahi Brahimaj* (n. 5) para. 60.

[18] Cf. Art. 28 ICC Statute establishing the responsibility of commanders and superiors for 'crimes within the jurisdiction of the Court', which include crimes committed in internal armed conflicts (cf. Art. 8 (2)(c) and (e) ICC Statute) and expressly referring to 'military commander or person effectively acting as a military commander' (Art. 28(a) ICC Statute) and other 'superior and subordinate relationships' (Art. 28(b) ICC Statute). For an overview and analysis of the jurisprudence of the two *ad hoc* tribunals, see E. van Sliedregt, *The Criminal Resonsibility of Individuals for Violations of International Humanitarian Law* (TMC Asser Press, The Hague 2003), pp. 175–9, demonstrating that their jurisprudence is evidence that '[c]onflict classification is not relevant as a jurisdictional prerequisite in triggering the application of superior responsibility'. *Ibid.*, 179.

Beyond the specific question of discipline, organized armed groups and their leadership also influence the behaviour of their members and constituencies on other levels. In the process of 'going to war', as well as during armed conflict, they must be able to project an image of an 'enemy' and find justifications for the suffering of members of the opposing party, which are strong enough so as to mobilize and persuade their constituency to accept the idea that armed conflict is an acceptable, and unavoidable, cause of action.[19] Furthermore, an organized armed group must be able to create and maintain the necessary *esprit de corps* amongst its fighters through means which go well beyond the mere maintenance of discipline. On a deeper, socio-psychological level, armed conflicts imply that an organized armed group and the individual combat unit become the one 'that determines morale, zeal in combat and a large part of the behaviour of a weapons-bearer'.[20] In combat situations, men are motivated to a large extent by group pressure, including regard for their comrades, respect for their leaders, concern to preserve their own reputation and to contribute to the successes of the group. Consequently, individual values are replaced by the group spirit and loyalties which characterize all military organizations.[21] Closely connected to the foregoing is that organized armed groups, much as state armed forces and their governments, must as an existential precondition be in a position to overcome the natural aversion of human beings to kill one another.[22]

Moreover, organized armed groups also possess, and are able to project and implement, policies in the broad sense of the word. Inevitably, organized armed groups pursue a certain objective, which one could loosely refer to as a 'war aim'. These objectives may range from control over territory and access to natural resources, to deposing the incumbent government, to the annihilation of ethnic, religious or other groups perceived to be 'the enemy', to creating and/or maintaining an environment for organized crime. The very existence of such diverse war aims in turn implies that they are formulated by an authoritative body, which devises an overall strategy. An illustrative example in that regard is the Kosovo Liberation Army, which emerged in the 1990s with the aim of liberating Kosovo Albanians from an oppressive Serbian regime by violent means.[23] From an early stage, and certainly long before the situation in Kosovo drew widespread

[19] J.-J. Frésard, *The Roots of Behaviour in War: A Survey of the Literature* (International Committee of the Red Cross, Geneva October 2004), pp. 46–9.

[20] Frésard (n. 19) 50. [21] Frésard (n. 19) 50. [22] Frésard (n. 19) 56–62.

[23] For a concise background to the armed conflict between the KLA and Serbian authorities, see *Prosecutor v Limaj* (n. 5) paras. 36–52.

international attention, the KLA possessed a main governing body in the form of its General Staff. According to the ICTY: '[a]mong other activities, the General Staff issued statements on behalf of the KLA informing the public of its activities, authorised military action, and assigned tasks to individuals in the organisation.'[24] While the KLA may constitute a relatively clear, and well-documented, example of how the war aim and strategy are developed and implemented by organized armed groups, it is by no means exceptional in that respect. Notwithstanding the considerable differences between organized armed groups all of them possess a war aim and an 'authority responsible for its acts' of sorts. This holds not only true for quasi-states but also for groups, which are comparatively less organized and whose aims may be said to be more amorphous, such as the Revolutionary United Front in Sierra Leone,[25] the various clan militias in Somalia[26] or the Bougainville Revolutionary Army in Bougainville.[27]

All of the aforementioned elements inherent in warfare – obedience to authority, mobilization, creation and maintenance of *esprit de corps*, overcoming the aversion of killing, projection and implementation of policies – in turn, are inconceivable without organized armed groups being in a position to create, perpetuate and seek to continuously strengthen these elements. The fact that they dispose of the required structures and processes, which enable them to do so, justifies to liken them in that regard to the 'classic' system of the state.

Besides the innate feature of armed conflict as a situation which is in itself conducive to criminal behaviour,[28] the features which are inherent in warfare and being an organized armed group, which we have addressed in the foregoing, are closely connected to those factors which induce or cause individuals to violate the norms prohibiting international core crimes. Amongst them are the perception by those within an organized armed group that the security of its constituency (an ethnic, racial, religious or other identity-based group, a political movement, or a marginalized section of the society within a state, for example) is under severe threat from either state authorities or other non-state groups, and

[24] *Prosecutor v Limaj* (n. 5) para. 46, footnotes omitted.

[25] For a brief survey over aim and structure of the RUF, see http://en.wikipedia.org/wiki/Revolutionary_United_Front, accessed 12 July 2008.

[26] See e.g. J. Bakonyi, 'Konturen der Gewaltordnung in Somalia' in Bakonyi, Hensell and Siegelberg (n. 3) 98–112.

[27] V. Böge, 'Bougainville – Gewaltordnung jenseits von Markt und Staat', in Bakonyi, Hensell and Siegelberg (n. 3) 312–26.

[28] Frésard (n. 19) 27–8.

the construction and dehumanisation of an 'enemy'; and the functioning of the armed group as an apparatus charged with protecting (or perceived to protect) the security of that constituency.[29]

Furthermore, organized armed groups regularly succeed to create a climate in which crimes are perceived to be in conformity with, rather than a deviation from, standards of behaviour accepted within such a group. The media statements by Taliban commanders and spokesmen, and documents attributed to the Taliban *shura* (council), which indicate that Taliban leaders consider it permissible to attack Afghan government workers and teachers, employees of non-governmental organizations, or anyone who supports the government of President Hamid Karzai exemplify such normative standards. In the case at hand, they are in part even 'codified' in a 'rulebook' issued in December 2006.[30] Another example of how organized armed groups create and reinforce a climate in which crimes are perceived to be in conformity with the group's norms is when Palestinian suicide bombers can expect social respect (expressed through street posters, pamphlets, internet sites, murals, banners, public discourse, and attendance by representatives of organized armed groups at funerals or memorial ceremonies) and are promised the religious reward of ascending to heaven for carrying out their mission with the primary aim to inflict civilian casualties.[31] These examples are illustrative of organized armed groups possessing the powers of authorizing and justifying acts of violence in violation of international legal standards and of routinizing violence by rule governed practice.[32]

Similarly, group coherence, which is an additional factor in explaining how the normative climate is transformed so as to allow for, or even demand, the commission of core crimes, need not be the coherence of a *statal* group. It would seem not to matter much, whether the (military) structure, which replaces individual values with the group spirit and group loyalties, and in turn creates a conducive environment for the commission of core crimes by causing individual autonomy to give way to group coherence,[33] is the structure of a state or a 'non-state'.

[29] On these factors, see H. C. Kelman, 'The policy context of international crimes', this volume, Chapter 2.

[30] Human Rights Watch, *The Human Cost – The Consequences of Insurgent Attacks in Afghanistan* (vol. 19 No. 6 (C) April 2007) 5–6 and 94–7.

[31] Human Rights Watch, *Erased in a Moment – Suicide Bombing Attacks against Israeli Civilians* (New York, NY October 2002), pp. 35–9.

[32] H. C. Kelman, 'The policy context of international crimes', this volume, Chapter 2, p. 27.

[33] Recall above (n. 21) and accompanying text. See also A. Nollkaemper, 'Introduction', this volume, Chapter 1, p. 6.

In sum, it is only a small step from the systemic features of organized armed groups to their translation into the ability of such groups to create a prevailing climate of ordering, encouraging, favouring, permitting or tolerating international core crimes. Indeed, the mechanisms which are at play in inducing or causing individual criminality when the system is a state and when an organized armed group constitutes a system bear a high degree of resemblance. To be clear, it is not submitted here that organized armed groups can generally simply be equated with states. The point is rather that they share some features, which justify referring to them as 'systems' within the meaning of the present book.

2. *Normative and empirical developments*

That organized armed groups can constitute the contextual environment for the commission of system crimes is also borne out by developments in the normative framework governing these crimes. This is most obvious in relation to *war crimes*. Not only has the law of armed conflict been recognised also to bind organized armed groups for a relatively long time (at least since the adoption of Article 3 Common to the Four Geneva Conventions of 1949), but serious violations of that body of law also entail individual criminal responsibility of their members.[34] And besides the examples stemming from the armed conflicts in Rwanda, Serbia and Kosovo, Afghanistan and Israel/the Palestinian Occupied Territories mentioned above, only a random look at recent or ongoing armed conflicts in which organized armed groups are involved also indicates that systematic war crimes are not the exclusive province of states as an empirical matter. This is amply illustrated by the well-documented systematic campaign of deliberately targeting civilians and terrorising the civilian population, collective punishments, rape and other crimes of sexual violence, forced recruitment and use of child soldiers, mutilations, looting and so forth of the Armed Forces Revolutionary Council (AFRC) and Revolutionary United Front (RUF) in Sierra Leone;[35] the widespread

[34] *Prosecutor v Tadic*, Decision on the Defence Motion for Interlocutory Appeal on Jurisdiction, IT-94-1, Appeals Chamber (2 October 1995) 106, 125, 131–2; Art. 4 of the ICTR Statute; Art. 8(2)(c) and (e) of the ICC Statute. For an overview of relevant state practice and case law until 1998, see T. Graditzky, 'Individual criminal responsibility for violations of international humanitarian law committed in non-international armed conflicts' (1998) *International Review of the Red Cross* 29–56.

[35] For some of these crimes and their systematicity, see Special Court for Sierra Leone, *Prosecutor v Alex Tamba Brima, Brima Bazzy Kamara and Santigie Borbor Kanu*,

practice of killing civilians and taking of hostages by the Revolutionary Armed Forces of Colombia – People's Army (FARC) in Colombia;[36] the policy of the Liberation Tigers of Tamil Eelam (LTTE) in Sri Lanka forcefully to recruit and use to take part in hostilities of children, amidst other serious violations of international humanitarian law;[37] hostage-taking, torture and the indiscriminate use of landmines, booby-traps and other explosive devices aimed at causing widespread civilian casualties by Chechen fighters;[38] or summary executions and attacks on civilians, and civilian property by the Ogaden National Liberation Front (ONLF) in Ethiopia.[39]

In addition to systematic war crimes, the prohibition of *crimes against humanity* has also been extended to organized armed groups. While it had been assumed for a long time that these crimes are in the main the manifestation of a criminal *governmental* policy, and still often are today, this confining of the crime to states is no longer a legal requirement, as recognized in relevant international legal instruments such as the Rome Statute,[40] the Statute and case law of the Special Court for Sierra Leone,[41] customary international law and legal doctrine.[42] Crimes against humanity can also be committed by non-state actors. Moreover, in the words of the ICTY Trial Chamber in *Tadic*, the first case that so determined, crimes against humanity can be committed by 'forces

SCSL-04–16-T, Trial Judgment (20 June 2007) and SCSL-2004–16-A, Appeals Judgment (22 February 2008).

[36] See e.g. Inter-American Commission on Human Rights, Report on the demobilization process in Colombia 2004, OEA/Ser.L/V/II.120 Doc. 60 (13 December 2004) paras. 45–52. For statistical information on hostage takings by the FARC between 1996 and 2006, see www.paislibre.org/images/PDF/secuestroestadisticasgenerales%202006%20org.pdf, accessed 12 July 2008.

[37] Report of the Secretary-General on children and armed conflict in Sri Lanka, UN Doc. S/2007/758 (21 December 2007) paras. 7–15. For a summary overview over other violations, see Human Rights Watch, 'Sri Lanka, World Report 2007': http://hrw.org/englishwr2k7/docs/2007/01/11/slanka14837.htm, accessed 12 July 2008.

[38] See e.g. Commission on Human Rights resolution 2001/24, Situation in the Republic of Chechnya of the Russian Federation (20 April 2001) para. 4.

[39] Human Rights Watch, 'Collective Punishment – War Crimes and Crimes against Humanity in the Ogaden area of Ethiopia's Somali Region' (June 2008) 1–56432–322–6, pp. 99–103.

[40] Cf. Art. 7(1) ICC Statute, Elements of Crime, Introduction paras. 2 and 3 ('plan or policy of the State *or organization*'; 'State *or organizational* policy', emphasis added).

[41] Cf. Art. 2 ICC Statute, *Prosecutor v Alex Tamba Brima, Brima Bazzy Kamara and Santigie Borbor Kanu*, Trial and Appeals Judgment (n. 35).

[42] For a summary overview, see G. Werle, *Principles of International Criminal Law* (TMC Asser Press, The Hague 2005), pp. 226–30.

which, although not those of the legitimate government, have *de facto* control over, or are able to move freely within, defined territory'.[43] It has also been suggested that this territorial qualification is not necessary and that crimes against humanity can be committed by any group of people if it has at its disposal the materiel and personnel necessary to enable it to commit a widespread or systematic attack against a civilian population.[44] Be that as it may, the concept of crimes against humanity has evolved so that it is today generally accepted that the system, which provides the enabling context for such crimes, need not be a state but can also be an organized armed group. There is also empirical evidence that organized armed groups commit, condone, or otherwise implicated in, crimes against humanity. The conviction by the Special Court for Sierra Leone of members of the AFRC for crimes against humanity is an example that comes to mind.[45]

Last but not least, nothing in the law governing the crime of *genocide* suggests that this crime can only occur with a state as its enabling, systemic environment. Admittedly, the 1948 Genocide Convention does not speak to the phenomenon and accountability of non-state actors as systems. It is solely concerned with questions of state responsibility and individual criminal responsibility.[46] It is also acknowledged that the two instances, in which genocide had been committed most clearly and visibly in the recent past – the holocaust committed by Nazi Germany and the 1994 Rwandan genocide – concern situations in which the system was a state. However, the findings of the International Court of Justice in its 2007 judgment in the *Case Concerning the Application of the Convention on the Prevention and Punishment of the Crime of Genocide (Bosnia and Herzegovina v Serbia and Montenegro)* quite clearly suggest that acts committed by non-state actors which cannot be attributed to a state in accordance with the rules on attribution as provided for in the law on

[43] *Prosecutor v Tadic*, IT-94–1, Judgment, Trial Chamber (7 May 1997) para. 654. Concurring: *Prosecutor v Kupreskic et al.*, IT-95–16, Judgment, Trial Chamber (14 January 2000) para. 551; *Limaj et al.* (n. 5) para. 213.

[44] Werle (n. 42) 228.

[45] *Prosecutor v Alex Tamba Brima, Brima Bazzy Kamara and Santigie Borbor Kanu*, Trial and Appeals Judgment (n. 35). For the post-AFRC/RUF government period, see in particular (n. 35) Trial Judgment, paras. 233–9.

[46] For discussion of the obligations of states under the Convention and its interface between state and individual criminal responsibility, see *Bosnia and Herzegovina v Serbia and Montenegro* ('Genocide Judgment') ICJ Case Concerning the Application of the Convention on the Prevention and Punishment of the Crime of Genocide, Judgment (26 February 2007) General List No. 91.

state responsibility can nevertheless amount to genocide, provided the definitional prerequisite of Article II of the 1948 Genocide Convention is met.[47] This is strong support for the contention that organized armed groups can commit genocide. Indeed, with contemporary armed conflicts being frequently also fought about identity, it may very well be anticipated that crimes of genocide are increasingly likely to occur within such conflicts and that organized armed groups will be implicated in their commission.

In sum, organized armed groups can and do constitute 'systems' and can commit, and repeatedly have committed, system crimes, be they systematic war crimes, crimes against humanity or genocide.

III. Responses

In light of the foregoing, the question looms large as to how states, international governmental organizations and non-governmental organizations respond to situations in which organized armed groups commit system crimes. In particular, what means and methods do they employ with a view to hold organized armed groups accountable *qua* collective entities, as opposed to approaching the phenomenon via the avenues of state responsibility and individual criminal responsibility of members of organized armed groups?

1. *Monitoring compliance*

Various international actors monitor compliance of organized armed groups with those rules of international law, which relate to system criminality. The available processes for doing so range from relatively formalized ones to those of a predominantly informal nature. They all have in common, however, that they supply processes through which the conduct of organized armed groups is being assessed and measured against international legal rules.

Within the UN system, a prominent set of monitoring mechanisms are available in the context of the human rights machinery, in particular the Special Advisor to the UN Secretary-General on Genocide and

[47] Genocide Judgment (n. 46) paras. 278–97 (concurring with the ICTY that genocide was committed in Srebrenica) and 413–5 (concluding that acts could not be attributed to Serbia and Montenegro).

Mass Atrocities[48] and those operating under the auspices of the Human Rights Council (and formerly the Commission on Human Rights). Various resolutions of the Commission and its successor the Human Rights Council, as well as reports emanating from its Special Procedures (country and thematic) *rapporteurs* indicate the practice of monitoring compliance with human rights and humanitarian law of both state and non-state actors, the latter including organized armed groups.[49] Similarly, regional human rights bodies, amongst which are most prominently the Inter-American Commission on Human Rights, have monitored the compliance of organized armed groups with humanitarian and human rights law.[50] Also, both the UN Security Council and the UN General Assembly have repeatedly denounced serious violations of international humanitarian and human rights law committed by organized armed groups. While such condemnations are regularly not addressed to a specified party to an armed conflict or other identified group, it is clear from the wording of relevant resolutions that their addressees are not only states and their authorities.[51]

48 For the mandate of the Special Advisor, see Annex to the Letter dated 12 July 2004 from the Secretary-General addressed to the President of the Security Council, S/2004/567 (13 July 2004).

49 On the practice and mandate of the Council and Commission as well as the Special Procedures to apply to humanitarian law, see P. Alston and J. Morgan-Foster and W. Abresch, 'The competence of the UN Human Rights Council and its Special Procedures in relation to Armed Conflicts: extrajudicial executions in the "War on Terror"' (2008) 19 EJIL 197–206. See also Commission on Human Rights Resolution 2001/24 (n. 38). For the practice of extending human rights obligations to non-state actors, see e. g. UN Doc. E/CN.4/2005/3 (7 May 2004) CHR, 61st Session, Item 4, Situation of Human Rights in the Darfur Region of the Sudan, where the Human Rights Commission stated that '[t]he rebel forces also appear to violate human rights and humanitarian law'; UN Doc. E/CN.4/2006/53/Add.5 (27 March 2006) 'Report of the Special Rapporteur', Philip Alston, Addendum, 'Mission to Sri Lanka' (28 November to 6 December 2005) especially paras. 24–27 and accompanying footnotes. It should be noted, however, that the practice of applying human rights obligations to organized armed groups is not beyond dispute, also in light of contrary practice of the bodies just referred to: see Zegveld (n. 7) 39–46.

50 See e. g. Inter-American Commission on Human Rights (n. 36); Annual Report of 2007, OEA/Ser.L/V/II.130, Doc. 22, rev. 1 (29 December 2007) Chapter IV (Colombia) paras. 40–83; Inter-American Commission on Human Rights, Annual Report of 1993, OEA/Ser.L/V.85Doc. 9 rev. (11 February 1994) Chapter IV (Peru) at II (1).

51 See amongst the numerous examples for instance SC Res. 1814 (15 May 2008) on the situation in Somalia, para. 16, addressed to 'all parties in Somalia'; SC Res. 1778 (25 September 2007) on the situation in Chad, the Central African Republic and the subregion, Preamble ('activities of armed groups and other attacks in eastern Chad, the north-eastern Central African Republic and western Sudan which threaten the security of the civilian population, the conduct of humanitarian operations in those areas and the stability of those

On the inter-governmental level, compliance of organized armed groups with international law is also monitored by non-governmental organizations. Some NGOs, such as Human Rights Watch or Amnesty International, do so by publicly denouncing system crimes of organized armed groups.[52] The International Committee of the Red Cross, on the other hand, primarily assumes a 'quieter' watchdog function. It monitors compliance with parties to an armed conflict and reacts to breaches of the law of armed conflict by first seeking to establish a dialogue with the parties concerned and only goes public if such attempt proves futile.[53] Another more recent, and intriguing, way of monitoring compliance in the specific context of the ban on anti-personnel mines is the approach adopted by Geneva Call.[54] Geneva Call engages organized armed groups and seeks their committing to such a ban by way of a 'Deed of Commitment for Adherence to a Total Ban on Anti-Personnel Mines and for Cooperation in Mine Action'. These unilateral declarations of organized armed groups include a standard clause on monitoring and verification.[55]

2. *Sanctions*

Besides monitoring compliance, inter-governmental organizations and individual states have imposed sanctions against organized armed

countries, and which result in serious violations of human rights and international humanitarian law'). For further relevant resolutions of the Security Council and the General Assembly pertaining to violations of human rights and humanitarian law committed in the Former Yugoslavia, Afghanistan, The Sudan, Sierra Leone, Ivory Coast, The Congo, Angola, Liberia and Somalia, see C. Tomuschat, 'The applicability of human rights law to insurgent movements', in H. Fischer, U. Froissart, W. Heintschel von Heinegg and C Raap (eds.), *Krisensicherung und Humanitärer Schutz – Crisis Management and Humanitarian Protection, Festschrift für Dieter Fleck* (BWV, Berlin 2004), pp. 577–85. See also P. H. Kooijmans, 'The Security Council and non-state entities as parties to conflicts', in K. Wellens (ed.), *International Law: Theory and Practice: Essays in Honour of Eric Suy* (Martinus Nijhoff, The Hague 1998), pp. 333–46.

52 See, e.g., Amnesty International, 'Afghanistan: all who are not friends, are enemies: Taleban abuses against civilians' AI Index: ASA 11/001/2007 (19 April 2007); Human Rights Watch (n. 30); Human Rights Watch (n. 31); Human Rights Watch (n. 37); Human Rights Watch (n. 39).

53 Cf. Y. Sandoz, 'The International Committee of the Red Cross as guardian of international humanitarian law', originally published in (1996) 43 *Yugoslav Review of International Law* 357–89 (ICRC, Geneva 1998), pp. 28–32.

54 Information available at www.genevacall.org/home.htm, accessed 12 July 2008.

55 Cf. section 3 of the Model Deed, available at www.genevacall.org/resources/testi-reference-materials/testi-deed/gc-04oct01-deed.htm accessed 12 July 2008. At the time of writing, some thirty-five organized armed groups have undertaken such deeds.

groups, which range from the freezing of assets and weapons embargoes, to travel restrictions of members of organized armed groups.

The most prominent organ which has adopted multilateral sanctionist measures is the UN Security Council.[56] In a string of resolutions adopted under Chapter VII, and with increasing frequency since the end of the Cold War, the Council has imposed sanctions on groups as diverse as the Bosnian Serb forces in the former Yugoslavia,[57] UNITA in Angola,[58] the non-state parties to the conflict in Sierra Leone,[59] Al Qaida and the Taleban[60] and foreign and Congolese armed groups and militias operating in the territory of the Democratic Republic of the Congo,[61] to name just some examples. Admittedly, the primary aim of these sanctions, nowadays regularly supervised by Sanctions Committees, is to pursue the objectives set by the Security Council as specified in the relevant resolution(s). It is not, or at least not exclusively, specifically to respond to system crimes, but more broadly to maintain or restore international peace and security.[62] UN Security Council sanctions are therefore regularly responses to a broader set of violations than 'just' system crimes, for example cease-fire violations and breaches of peace agreements, the illicit exploitation of natural resources, and so forth. Only if and when the Security Council agrees that system crimes amount to, or are part

[56] See generally on the role of the Security Council in the context of system crimes, including sanctions, N. White, 'Responses of political organs to crimes by states', this volume, Chapter 14.

[57] Security Council Resolution 942 (1994).

[58] Security Council Resolutions 1127 (1997), 1173 (1998), and 1221 (1999).

[59] Security Council Resolution 1132 (1997). The sanctions regime has been modified by subsequent resolutions, most notably Security Council resolution 1171 (1998).

[60] UN SC Resolution 1267 (1999) of 15 October 1999. The sanctions regime has been modified by subsequent resolutions, including resolutions 1333 (2000), 1390 (2002), 1455 (2003), 1526 (2004), 1617 (2005) and 1735 (2006). The most recent consolidated list of individuals and entities covered by the aforementioned resolutions include groups such as Abu Sayyaf, the Al-Itihaad al-Islamiya, Al Qa'Ida, Ansar Al-Islam, and Al Jamm'ah Al-Islamiah Al-Musallah (GIA), see Consolidated List available at www.un.org/sc/committees/1267/pdf/consolidatedlist.pdf, 54, 57, 58 accessed 12 July 2008.

[61] UN SC Resolution 1493 (2003). The sanctions regime was subsequently modified with the adoption of resolutions 1533 (2004), 1596 (2005), 1649 (2005), 1698 (2006) and 1807 (2008).

[62] But see the 2004 Report of the Secretary-General to the Security Council on the protection of civilians in armed conflict, UN Doc. S/2004/31 (28 May 2004) para. 42, recommending that: '[m]ore serious consideration also needs to be given to the imposition of travel restrictions and targeted sanctions (particularly in respect of small arms and military assistance) against armed groups that blatantly violate international humanitarian law and human rights standards and prevent humanitarian access to populations in need.'

and parcel of, a threat to the peace, breach of the peace, or act of aggression, will those measures under Chapter VII be an available response. Therefore, only some of the relevant Security Council resolutions make express reference to international crimes as (one of the) underlying reason(s) for imposing assets freezes, weapons embargoes, and the like.[63] What nevertheless makes these measures important for our analysis is the fact that the Security Council has operationalised its Chapter VII powers to hold organized armed groups accountable by way of imposing sanctions.

The United Nations is not the only inter-governmental organization which adopts sanctions against organized armed groups. The European Union, for instance, has also done so. Partially as a reaction to sanctions imposed by the Security Council, the EU has adopted a Council Regulation[64] on specific restrictive measures directed against certain persons and entities with a view to combating terrorism. The list designating such persons and entities, in turn, comprises several groups, which are in fact, or were at the relevant time, organized armed groups within the meaning of the present contribution, i.e. parties to an armed conflict.[65] By virtue of the Regulation, all funds, other financial assets and economic resources belonging to, or owned or held by, designated persons, groups or entities are to be frozen.[66] The Regulation also imposes an obligation on EU member states not to make available any funds, other financial assets and economic resources to, or for the benefit of, the designated persons,

[63] Cf. e.g. in relation to Sierra Leone, SC Res. 1171, Preambular para. 3; in relation to the DR Congo, SC Res. 1493, Preambular para. 6 and operative paras. 8 and 13, SC Res. 1807, operative para. 13 in conjunction with operative paras. 9 and 11 (although para. 13 only extends sanctions to individuals (not entities) 'operating in the Democratic Republic of the Congo and committing serious violations of international law involving the targeting of children or women in situations of armed conflict, including killing and maiming, sexual violence, abduction and forced displacement' (cf. operative para. 13(e)); however, by virtue of other provisions, certain sanctions are also imposed on 'entities' (cf. e.g. operative para 13(a)).

[64] Council Regulation No. 2580/2001 of 27 December 2001.

[65] Council Decision 2005/930/EC of 21 December 2005 implementing Art. 2(3) of Regulation (EC) No. 2580/2001 on specific restrictive measures directed against certain persons and entities with a view to combating terrorism and repealing Decision 2005/848/EC. The Decision lists amongst others, the Communist Party of the Philippines, including New Peoples Army (NPA), the Kurdistan Workers' Party (PKK), the Colombian National Liberation Army (Ejército de Liberación Nacional) and Revolutionary Armed Forces of Colombia (FARC), and United Self-Defense Forces/Group of Colombia (AUC).

[66] (n. 64) Art. 2 (1)(a).

groups or entities.[67] Again, as in the case of sanctions imposed by the Security Council, the measures taken by the EU are neither specifically designed nor primarily contemplated as a response to systems crimes, unless one were to qualify the – still undefined – crime of terrorism as a system crime, which is a question beyond the purview of the present contribution. The measures imposed in accordance with the aforementioned Council Regulation nevertheless demonstrates that sanctions constitute one way in which organized armed groups are held accountable.

Individual states have also imposed unilateral sanctions on organized armed groups, independent of those carried out in compliance with their obligations under relevant applicable Security Council Resolutions and, for EU member states, regulations such as the one on specific restrictive measures directed against certain persons and entities with a view to combating terrorism. The United States, for example, designates quite a number of organized armed groups as falling into the reach of Executive Order 13224 on 'Blocking Property and Prohibiting Transactions with Persons who Commit, Threaten to Commit, or Support Terrorism', which was signed by US President Bush on 23 September 2001. The current list extends these measures to groups such as the Colombian FARC, the Sri Lankan LTTE and the Kurdish PKK.[68] Similarly, the United Kingdom has extended unilateral sanctions to organized armed groups, which are subject to neither UN nor EU sanctions, in accordance with its Terrorism Act 2000,[69] for example, and Australia has done so to the PKK under its Security Legislation Amendment (Terrorism) Act 2002.[70]

3. *Reparation*

In contrast to the relatively well-established practice of monitoring the compliance of organized armed groups and imposing sanctions on them, the possibility of claiming reparation for the injury caused by system crimes has thus far remained, in the main, a theoretical one. It is nevertheless worthy of note that some developments suggest an increasing

[67] (n. 64) Art. 2 (1)(b).

[68] List available at www.treasury.gov/offices/enforcement/ofac/programs/terror/terror.pdf, accessed 12 July 2008.

[69] Notably the Baluchistan Liberation Army (BLA), see list at www.homeoffice.gov.uk/security/terrorism-and-the-law/terrorism-act/proscribed-groups, accessed 12 July 2008.

[70] See www.nationalsecurity.gov.au/agd/www/nationalsecurity.nsf/AllDocs/95FB057CA3DECF30CA256FAB001F7FBD?OpenDocument, accessed 12 July 2008.

recognition that organized armed groups can be subjected to claims of reparation.

One such development is the 'Basic Principles and Guidelines on the Right to a Remedy and Reparation for Victims of Violations of International Human Rights and Humanitarian Law',[71] contemplating that '[i]n cases where a person, a legal person, *or other entity* is found liable for reparation to a victim, such party should provide reparation to the victim or compensate the State if the State has already provided reparation to the victim'[72] and that 'States shall, with respect to claims by victims, enforce domestic judgements for reparation against individuals *or entities* liable for the harm suffered and endeavour to enforce valid foreign legal judgments for reparation in accordance with domestic law and international legal obligations'.[73] Another relevant development is the assertion of the International Commission of Inquiry on Darfur in the context of its recommendation to the UN Security Council to establish a compensation commission, that not only states (in the case at hand Sudan) are under an obligation to pay compensation for all the crimes perpetrated by its agents and officials or *de facto* organs, but that a 'similar obligation is incumbent upon rebels for all crimes they may have committed'.[74]

Furthermore, on the domestic level, attempts have been made in the US under the Alien Tort Claims Act (ATCA) and the Torture Victims Protection Act (TVPA) to bring claims against organized armed groups. The case of *Doe v Islamic Salvation Front* (FIS),[75] for instance, involved allegations of war crimes and crimes against humanity, and torture. While that case was ultimately dismissed for reasons unrelated to the question whether groups such as the FIS could in principle be sued under the two aforementioned domestic statutes, it adds further empirical evidence in support of the contention that there are no principled objections to holding organized armed groups through reparations. At the same time, a number of practical problems may prevent such claims of reparations from being successful, for instance in relation to obtaining the personal

[71] Basic Principles and Guidelines on the Right to a Remedy and Reparation for Victims of Violations of International Human Rights and Humanitarian Law, GA Res. A/RES/60/147 (2006).

[72] (n. 71) Basic Principle 15, 3rd sentence, emphasis added.

[73] (n. 71) Basic Principle 17, 1st sentence, emphasis added.

[74] International Commission of Inquiry on Darfur, Report to the Secretary-General (25 January 2005): www.un.org/news/dh/sudan/com_inq_darfur.pdf, para 600, accessed 12 July 2008.

[75] United States District Court, District of Columbia, 993 F.Supp. 3 (D.D.C.1998) (3 February 1998) dismissed (31 March 2003).

jurisdiction over an organized armed group and the actual effectuation of any judgment on damages.

IV. From accountability to responsibility?

While it is clear from the foregoing that organized armed groups can and are being held accountable for system crimes, it is striking that a legal framework of responsibility underlying these accountability mechanisms is at best amorphous, and at worst non-existent. In stark contrast to the areas of state responsibility and responsibility of international organizations, no established rules and principles regulate questions such as the attribution of conduct to an organized armed group, possible circumstances precluding the wrongfulness of breaches of international law, the content of the international responsibility of an organized armed group, and the implementation of that responsibility. While the International Law Commission, in its work on state responsibility, has recognized the possibility that an organized armed group 'may itself be held responsible for its own conduct under international law, for example for a breach of international humanitarian law committed by its forces', it stopped short of exploring the topic further, except for successful insurrectional or other movements,[76] since its mandate was limited to the responsibility of states.[77] Furthermore, the limited practice in this area is insufficient to discern generally applicable legal rules, which might govern the responsibility of organized armed groups.

It is reasonable to assume that the reasons why states have not positioned themselves on the matter of developing a legal framework for the responsibility of organized armed groups, and are likely to remain reluctant to do so, are the same reasons why they have proved to be reluctant to regulate armed conflicts, in which they face these groups: any such regulation is perceived by them to entail the risk of granting legal status and increased authority to such groups, of unduly limiting the freedom of states and of hampering them in taking legitimate measures of repression.[78]

[76] Cf. Art. 10 of the Articles on Responsibility of States for Internationally Wrongful Acts (2001) UNGA Resolution 56/83 of 12 December 2001, and corrected by document A/56/49(Vol. I)/Corr.4.

[77] J. Crawford, *The International Law Commission's Articles on State Responsibility – Introduction, Text and Commentaries* (Cambridge University Press, Cambridge 2002), Commentary to Art. 10, 120, para. 16.

[78] For these concerns raised in the course of the drafting of Common Art. 3, see J. Pictet (ed.), *Commentary to the First Geneva Convention for the Amelioration of the Condition of the Wounded and the Sick in Armed Forces in the Field* (Geneva 1952), p. 44. Such

Normative advances in the primary rules regulating non-international armed conflict and in the rules on individual criminal responsibility applicable in these conflicts suggest that these concerns of states have lessened, although they have certainly not disappeared. However, in contrast to these advances, the development of rules on the collective responsibility of organized armed groups has not followed suit.

It is hard to predict whether it is likely, or even realistic, that this disconnect between the primary norms binding organized armed groups and a body of secondary rules governing their collective responsibility will be overcome through a gradual process of crystallizing practice and codification or, probably even more remotely, through progressive treaty making. A question which, it is submitted, is at least as important, however, is whether the consequences of breaches of international law (and in our case more specifically system crimes) committed by organized armed groups *should* be subjected to international legal regulation. A possible counter-argument would be that the diversity of organized armed groups makes it impossible to develop a framework, which is fitting for all. Yet, such an argument would not seem to be entirely convincing. The fact that inter-governmental organizations differ widely in powers, functions, size and structure has not prevented international efforts to treat them as a uniform category in codifying and developing the legal framework governing their responsibility. The challenge rather seems to be to develop rules, which are *abstract and flexible enough* so as to befit the entire range of organized armed groups.

Another more pragmatic possible objection to the idea of developing a legal framework of responsibility of organized armed groups could be that such an exercise may be counter-productive without the prospect of effectuating it. International law, according to such a view, should only make those promises for which there is a good prospect that it can keep them. Accordingly, a focus on making the more flexible accountability mechanisms more effective might yield more than a forced formalization of rules governing responsibility. However, in my opinion, such a view is equally unconvincing. As in the case of state responsibility or individual criminal responsibility, conceptualising a formal regime for the responsibility of organized armed groups is not the same as effectuating that regime. The challenges to the latter, which emanate from political and

concerns led to the adoption of para. 4 of Common Art. 3, according to which, 'The application of the preceding [paragraphs of Common Art 3] shall not affect the legal status of the Parties to the conflict'. Cf. *ibid.*, 60–61.

other practical constellations, are, and are likely to remain, significant, however sophisticated a formal regime for the responsibility of organized armed groups might be. And yet, rather than suggesting that the project of developing such a regime should be abandoned, these challenges remind us of the modest expectations that one should reasonably have of formalized rules in a decentralized and fragmented system, which remains deeply engrained in power politics. It equally reminds us of the need to understand any such system of responsibility of organized armed groups as being embedded into a broader framework of accountability. In this regard, there is not much difference between the responsibility of organized armed groups and the responsibility of other actors in international law.

While the aforementioned possible arguments against developing a legal framework for the responsibility of organized armed groups are thus refutable, the most fundamental argument in favour of doing so lies elsewhere. States and the United Nations have expressed their support for an international order governed by the rule of law. Such a rule of law, in the words of former Secretary-General Kofi Annan:

> [r]efers to a principle of governance in which all persons, institutions and entities, public and private, including the State itself, are accountable to laws that are publicly promulgated, equally enforced and independently adjudicated, and which are consistent with international human rights norms and standards. It requires, as well, measures to ensure adherence to the principles of supremacy of law, equality before the law, accountability to the law, fairness in the application of the law, separation of powers, participation in decision-making, legal certainty, avoidance of arbitrariness and procedural and legal transparency.[79]

If one takes the rule of law thus understood as the standard against which the responsibility of organized armed groups has to be measured, it is readily apparent that the current situation is wholly unsatisfactory. In the absence of even the first steps towards realizing the rule of law in this area – the development of certain, predictable and stable rules – the realization of all other elements, such as equal enforcement, independent adjudication, and fairness in the application of the law, are impossible. Indeed, the neglect for a legal framework of responsibility of armed groups is particularly startling if one considers the increasing concern of

[79] UN Doc. S/2004/616 (2004) para. 6. See also 'Uniting our Strengths', Report of the Secretary-General, UN Doc. A/61/636-S/2006/980 (2006). See generally on the rule of law on the international level, S. Beaulac, *An Inquiry into the International Rule of Law* (European University Institute Working Paper MWP, No. 2007/14 (2007)).

the United Nations for the rule of law in the light of the recognition by one of its principal organs, the Security Council, of the need for developing further 'measures to promote the responsibility of armed groups and non-State actors' in armed conflict.[80] Coalescing both ambitions would suggest a need to develop a legal framework for the responsibility of organized armed groups.

The foregoing arguments suggest that it is not only desirable but necessary to develop a legal framework for the responsibility of organized armed groups. In pursuing such a project, the question arises whether and to what extent rules and principles can be derived from already existing areas of responsibility of collective entities. In the following, I will examine that question in relation to the most obvious such area: (1) the law of state responsibility; (2) in particular as it relates to questions of attribution; (3) the content and implementation of responsibility; and (4) aggravated responsibility.

1. *State responsibility as a blueprint?*

Organized armed groups resemble states in certain respects. Both are collective entities, able to command, and exercise control over, persons and sometimes (or, in the case of states, always) over territory, project policies, which are formulated by 'an authority', and are in a position to use organized armed violence to a degree of intensity that reaches the threshold of an armed conflict. Indeed, as previously argued, it is because of these shared features that one cannot only qualify states as 'systems', but also organized armed groups. These similarities between states and organized armed groups suggest that the rules on state responsibility may provide a useful starting point for developing a legal framework of the responsibility of organized armed groups.

However, any transposition of these rules to the responsibility of organized armed groups has to be approached with caution for the following reasons. First, the basic assumption underlying the law on state responsibility, much as the entire fabric of international law, is that states have a right to exist, while organized armed groups lack such a right. This pedigree of presumptive legitimacy of states entails that the law of state responsibility stops short of depriving a state of that right as a consequence of an internationally wrongful act. In contrast, the default position

[80] Cf. e.g. the Ten-point platform on the protection of civilians in armed conflict, adopted by the Security Council on 15 December 2003, UN Doc. S/PRST/2003/26, annex at (i).

vis-à-vis organized armed groups is that they are denied a right to exist. That position is certainly taken by the state against whom they are fighting. Third states and the international community may either share that opinion – in particular when organized armed groups commit system crimes – or behave agnostically. Such a situation, in turn, entails that the underlying rationales of a legal responsibility of organized armed groups for system crimes may not only include the termination, prevention of recurrence, prevention in other cases, reconciliation and reparation of such breaches,[81] but also the more far-reaching aim to dismantle organized armed groups.

Secondly, the law on state responsibility is concerned with the responsibility of states for internationally wrongful conduct *as implemented by states.*[82] In contrast to such a relationship between sovereign equals contemplated in the 2001 Articles on Responsibility of States for Internationally Wrongful Acts, the legal relationship under consideration in the present context is not the horizontal one of an organized armed group with another organized armed group. Rather, we are concerned with the identification of generic principles governing the legal responsibility of organized armed groups as such, with one or more states or inter-governmental organizations and possibly individuals implementing and/or invoking that responsibility.

Thirdly, the diversity of organized armed groups defies to simply equate all organized armed groups with states. In considering the question of the transposability of the law on state responsibility to the responsibility of organized armed groups, rules and principles can be utilized when and to the extent that organized armed groups display state-like features, while others will have to be adjusted in order to take account of those features, which are idiosyncratic to organized armed groups.[83] Such an approach would not only require differentiating between those rules and principles of state responsibility which cannot be transposed to organized armed groups *at all* and those, which can as a matter of principle. It would also require to develop rules, which are flexible enough to treat different types of armed groups differently, with 'quasi-states' and *de facto* regimes being treated somewhat more akin to states for purposes of responsibility, than other organized armed groups, for instance relatively loosely organized bands, which lack territorial control.

[81] On these rationales, cf. A. Nollkaemper and H. van den Wilt, 'Conclusions and outlook', this volume, Chapter 15, p. 348.

[82] Cf. Part 3 (Arts. 42–54) of the Articles on Responsibility of States for Internationally Wrongful Acts (2001) (n. 76), Crawford (n. 77) 254–305.

[83] In this vein, see also Zegveld (n. 7) 154; Sassoli (n. 7) 21.

With the preceding considerations in mind, three areas of the law of state responsibility emerge as being of particular pertinence to the development of a legal framework for the responsibility of organized armed groups: the attribution of acts to organized armed groups (section 2), the content and implementation of the international responsibility of an organized armed group (section 3), and the principles governing aggravated responsibility for serious breaches of obligations under *jus cogens* norms (section 4). In the absence of any legal rules and in the light of the very limited practice in these areas, the ensuing considerations will necessarily have to be *de lege ferenda*.

2. *Attribution*

Certain rules on attribution, which have evolved in the context of state responsibility, can be operationalized in the context of attributing conduct to organized armed groups, provided the necessary adjustments are made. To the extent that an individual or group of individuals act as 'organs' of an organized armed group, for instance, there does not seem to be any obvious reason why the principle underlying Article 4 of the Articles on State Responsibility cannot be applied.[84] One fails to see why the acts of members of the armed forces of an organized armed group should be any less attributable to the group as a whole than acts of governmental armed forces are to states by virtue of their being state organs. This is not to suggest that determining the status of (an) indvidual(s) as such an organ will necessarily be an easy task, absent rules of internal organization, which could be equated with 'the law of the state' determining the status of a person as a state organ.[85] However, whether individuals hold a position in the organization of an organized armed group and act on its behalf can, in certain instances, nevertheless be determined. This is even the case with respect to certain 'organs' of organized armed groups other than members of military units. If an organized armed group exercises control over territory in a way which enable it to set up its own quasi-statal institutions, such as a police force, as for instance in the

[84] Zegveld (n. 7). Zegveld refers to practice vis-à-vis the Taliban of the US and of the Special Rapporteur of the UN Commission on Human Rights in Afghanistan in his 1997 report in support of the contention that 'draft Art. 5 on State Responsibility [now Art. 4, JK] may be applied by analogy to armed opposition groups exhibiting state-like features'.

[85] Cf. Art. 4(2). See also Sassoli (n. 7) 21.

case of the LTTE in Sri Lanka,[86] there seems little difficulty in attributing breaches of international law committed by individual members of that police force to the organized armed group.

However, the situations in which Article 4 of the Articles on State Responsibility can be applied by analogy in this way will in all likelihood only be a fraction of instances in which the question of attribution arises. Not many organized armed groups possess the power to exert such stable control over territory so as to replace state institutions and organs with their own. Nor is it always easy to ascertain whether an individual or group of individuals belong to the armed forces of an armed groups and, as such, are 'organs' of that group. In these situations, the question arises whether other rules of attribution found in the law on state responsibility may provide useful complementary parameters.[87] It would seem that the answer is in the affirmative with regard to the principles underlying Articles 5 and 8 of the Articles on State Responsibility.

If individuals or groups of individuals exercise 'elements of the … authority'[88] of an organized armed group, Article 5 of the Articles on State Responsibility could possibly serve as guidance in attributing breaches of international law committed while these individuals are acting in that capacity. An obvious scenario, in which such an analogous application of Article 5 of the Articles on State Responsibility may be warranted, are cases where private military companies exercise elements of the authority of organized armed groups, as has occurred in a number of conflicts.[89]

It is also conceivable that a person or group of persons, while not being an 'organ' of an organized armed group in the sense referred to above, are in fact acting on the instruction of, or under the direction or control of, that organized armed group in carrying out the conduct. This may be the case, for instance, where a commander of an organized armed group exercises *de facto* control over a group of persons within the context of a concrete military operation during which some of these persons commit international crimes, while that group is otherwise operating

[86] Cf. K. Stokke, 'Building the Tamil Eelam State: emerging state institutions and forms of governance in LTTE-controlled areas in Sri Lanka' (2006) 27 *Third World Quarterly* 1021–40.

[87] As argued by Sassoli (n. 7) 21.

[88] Cf. the wording of Art. 5 Articles on State Responsibility.

[89] For examples stemming from Angola and Sierra Leone, see K. A. O'Brien, 'Private military companies and African security 1990–1998', in A.-F. Musah and J. Kayode Fayemi (eds.), *Mercenaries – An African Security Dilemma* (Pluto Press, 2000), pp. 59–60.

independently on its own initiative. Such a scenario was at issue in the case of *Prosecutor v Hadzihasanovic*, where the relationship between the 3rd Corps of the Bosnian Army and the El Mujahedin detachment had to be determined. The ICTY Appeals Chamber ultimately reversed the finding of the Trial Chamber that the accused had effective control over members of the detachment and held that the accused could therefore not bear command responsibility for the violations committed by them.[90] The case nevertheless indicates that situations are conceivable in which persons, who are otherwise acting independently, are receiving and executing orders from the commander of an organized armed group in the context of a specific military operation. Article 8 of the Articles on State Responsibility could be applied by analogy in such a scenario, to the effect that the conduct of such persons should be considered an act of an organized armed group.

3. *Content and implementation of international responsibility*

Turning to the legal consequences of responsibility – referred to in the Articles on State Responsibility as the 'content of responsibility' – the relevant rules of the law on state responsibility can be transposed to organized armed groups without too many difficulties. It would seem to be possible to apply the principle of a continued duty of performing the breached obligation not to commit system crimes,[91] the obligation to cease a continuing system crime and, if circumstances so require, to offer assurances and guarantees of non-repetition[92] also to organized armed groups. The same applies in relation to the obligation to make full reparation for the injury caused by system crimes.[93] Indeed, the transposability of that obligation finds support in the cautious first steps towards recognizing such an obligation of organized armed groups, previously referred to.[94] The various modes of reparation – restitution, compensation and satisfaction[95] – can, in principle, also be applied by analogy.

However, when applying the aforementioned legal consequences of responsibility to organized armed groups, their operationalization is likely to differ in a number of respects. As previously observed, organized

[90] *Prosecutor v Hadzihasanovic*, IT-01–47, Judgment, Appeals Chamber (22 April 2008) paras. 194–232.

[91] Cf. Art. 29 Articles on State Responsibility.

[92] Cf. Art. 30 Articles on State Responsibility.

[93] Cf. Art. 31 Articles on State Responsibility.

[94] Cf. above section III(3).

[95] Cf. Arts. 34–37 Articles on State Responsibility.

armed groups do not have a right to exist under international law and, as a consequence, the objectives pursued by establishing a legal framework governing their legal responsibility may be more far-reaching than those pursued by holding states responsible.[96] This would suggest that a number of limitations on the content of international responsibility of states cannot be transposed to organized armed groups. This would be the case when considering satisfaction as a from of reparation, and, more in particular paragraph 3 of Article 37 of the Articles on State Responsibility, which seeks to protect the 'dignity' of a state by stipulating that '[s]atisfaction shall … not take a form humiliating to the responsible State'. It would seem that such a limitation cannot easily be imported into a legal framework for the responsibility of organized armed groups, unless one were to posit that the law should also concern itself with the protection of the 'dignity' of organized armed groups. What is more, while the law of state responsibility excludes the award of punitive damages,[97] one may very well argue that the legal responsibility of organized armed groups for system crimes should entail such a consequence.

What is more, in contrast to states, which are in principle relatively stable and permanent entities, organized armed groups are not. While there may be some, which exist for a considerable period of time, such as the Colombian FARC, which has fought the Colombian government for more than forty years, the existence of many others is of lesser duration. Many organized armed groups disappear over time, for instance because they are defeated, demobilized or integrated into the armed forces of a state in the course of a peace process. Others may mutate and split up into different rival factions or be absorbed into other organized armed groups. In these situations, it will be problematic, or indeed impossible, to bring claims of reparation against the very group responsible for system crimes. It will therefore be necessary to develop a legal framework of responsibility, which takes due account of the temporary and unstable nature of organized armed groups and provide answers to the question whether and under what conditions the responsibility of organized armed groups shifts to successor organizations, the state or individual members of a defunct organized armed group.

In contrast to the aforementioned rules and principles governing the content of international responsibility, which can be utilized to guide the development of a legal framework of organized armed groups if subjected to the necessary adjustments, it is far more difficult to import

[96] Cf. above section IV(1). [97] Crawford (n. 77) 219.

those governing the *implementation* of responsibility. All the rules on the invocation of the responsibility of a state[98] are so closely tied to the legal relationship between two or more states as sovereign equals, that they cannot be adapted to the legal relationship between one or more states or inter-governmental organizations and possibly individuals, on the one hand, and an organized armed group on the other.

For similar reasons, the general assumptions underlying the Articles on countermeasures[99] are such that most of the relevant provisions cannot easily be used as a blueprint for the responsibility of armed groups. Notwithstanding some resemblance between sanctions referred to previously[100] and countermeasures in the law of state responsibility, the latter are measures 'which would otherwise be contrary to the *international obligations of the injured State vis-à-vis the responsible State*'.[101] It is hard to see what measures, which would be 'otherwise contrary to international legal obligations' vis-à-vis a responsible organized armed group one could think of.[102]

Furthermore, the limited object of countermeasures to only induce a state to comply with its continued duty of performing the obligation breached, to cease such breach and to make full reparation[103] may be too narrow when one considers the object of adverse measures taken against organized armed groups. As already pointed out, nothing would preclude pursuing more far-reaching objectives by such measures, which may go as far as aiming at the dismantling of an organized armed group, which commits system crimes. The fact that organized armed groups do not have a right to exist also is a good ground to approach with caution any possible transposition of the requirement that countermeasures be proportionate to the injury suffered[104] to sanctions imposed on organized armed groups. This is nevertheless not to suggest that some of the other principles, which condition and limit the adoption of countermeasures, could not be utilized in order to develop a legal framework

[98] Cf. Arts. 42–48 Articles on State Responsibility.

[99] Cf. Arts. 49–54 Articles on State Responsibility.

[100] Cf. above section III(2).

[101] Crawford (n. 77) 281 at 1, emphasis added.

[102] That is not to say, however, that measures against an organized armed group may not be 'contrary to international legal obligations' owed to another state. This could be the case, for instance, in which sanctions such as an arms embargo, adopted by state A against a given organized armed group which consists of members and operates from or within the territory of state B, have the (collateral) effect of breaching obligations owed to state B, such as a bilateral treaty on trade in military equipment between the two states.

[103] Cf. Art. 49(1) Articles on State Responsibility.

[104] Cf. Art. 51 Articles on State Responsibility.

for adopting sanctions vis-à-vis organized armed groups. Most pertinently in this context are those obligations, which Article 50(1) of the Articles on State Responsibility identifies as not being affected by countermeasures. Accordingly, in adopting sanctions in response to the commission of system crimes by an organized armed group states and inter-governmental organizations must comply with the obligation to refrain from the threat or use of force as embodied in the UN Charter; obligations for the protection of fundamental human rights; obligations of a humanitarian character prohibiting reprisals; and other obligations under *jus cogens*.

4. *Aggravated responsibility of organized armed groups for system crimes*

When attempting to identify a generic legal framework for the responsibility of organized armed groups by building on the law of state responsibility, a last consideration which is potentially particularly relevant in the context of system crimes committed by organized armed groups relates to the rules governing 'serious breaches of obligations under peremptory norms of general international law'.[105] Most of the system crimes under consideration constitute such serious breaches, if not per definition, then at least whenever they are committed on a gross or systematic scale.[106] The particular consequences attached to the commission of a serious breach by a state should equally apply if an organized armed group commits such crimes.

Thus, states should be considered to be under an affirmative obligation to cooperate to bring such crimes to an end through lawful means,[107] an obligation that is arguably already incumbent on states parties to the Four Geneva Conventions by virtue of its Common Article 1, which stipulates that they undertake to respect and *to ensure* respect for the Conventions (including Common Article 3 applicable to non-international armed conflicts) in all circumstances.[108] Indeed, the

[105] Cf. Arts. 40–41 Articles on State Responsibility.

[106] Cf. the definition of a serious breach in Art. 40(2) Articles on State Responsibility.

[107] Cf. Art. 41(1) Articles on State Responsibility.

[108] Cf. M Sassoli, 'State responsibility for violations of international humanitarian law' (2002) 84 IRRC 401, 421–2, with further references. See also J. M. Henckaerts and L. Doswald-Beck (eds.), *Customary International Humanitarian Law* (vol. I: Rules, Cambridge University Press, Cambridge 2005) Rule 144 obliging states 'to exert their influence, to the degree possible, to stop violations of international humanitarian law'.

practice of imposing collective sanctions on organized armed groups within the context of inter-governmental organizations,[109] could constitute an example of how to comply with both of these obligations, provided such sanctions are adopted as a specific response to system crimes committed by organized armed groups.

States should also be prohibited to recognize as lawful a situation created by system crimes committed by an organized armed group that amount to serious breaches and to render aid or assistance in maintaining that situation.[110] Such an obligation could entail, for example, that states and other relevant actors would be legally barred from entering into treaty or diplomatic or consular relations with an entity created by an organized armed group that has succeeded in establishing itself as the authority over a given territory as a result of the commission of genocide, crimes against humanity or systematic war crimes. Another consequence could be that any claims of rights predicated on system crimes committed by an organized armed group, such as claims of property rights based on the war crime of pillage or of parental rights stemming from the act of genocide of forcibly transferring children of a national, ethnical, racial or religious group to another group, are to be denied any legal effect by other states.[111]

The foregoing suggests that the rules governing serious breaches of obligations under peremptory norms of general international law stemming from the law of state responsibility supply valuable parameters for developing a framework of responsibility of organized armed groups for system crimes.

V. Conclusion

Amidst the various occasions on which organized armed groups have been implicated in the commission of system crimes and a range of responses adopted by states and international organizations, it is submitted that the development of a legal framework of responsibility (and not only looser forms of accountability) is called for. Such a legal framework would create legal certainty about the rights and obligations of states

[109] Above, section III(2). [110] Cf. Art. 41(2) State Responsibility.

[111] Cf., *mutatis mutandis*, S. Talmon 'The duty not to "recognize as lawful" a situation created by the illegal use of force or other serious breaches of a jus cogens obligation: an obligation without real substance?', in C. Tomuschat and J.-M. Thouvenin (eds.) *The Fundamental Rules of the International Legal Order: Jus Cogens and Obligations Erga Omnes* (Martinus Nijhoff, Dordrecht 2005), pp. 99, 117.

and other relevant actors when system crimes are being committed by organized armed groups, as well as about the obligations of these groups. The composite legal rules and principles would have to take account of the distinctive features of organized armed groups and, as such, would eventually have to constitute a framework *sui generis*. The foregoing nevertheless suggests that some rules on state responsibility may provide a useful starting point for developing such a framework. This approach may meet with hesitation from some who perceive the proposition to go too far in treating organized armed groups akin to states. However, the matter is one of taking these groups seriously as violators of international law, rather than as bearers of additional rights. It is also a matter of identifying those rules which, in the absence of any applicable *lex specialis*,[112] govern the behaviour of states and thereby remove their reactions from the nebulous ambit of political responses, which are wholly left to their discretion. To maintain the present situation, in contrast, would perpetuate the current disconnect between primary and secondary rules. Such a disconnect is not only conceptually unsound, but to hold persons or entities – be they states, international organizations or, indeed, organized armed groups – accountable without such accountability to be governed by a legal framework also runs counter to the *leitmotiv* of the rule of law. Without a doubt, it is too optimistic to expect that the situation in which there is some accountability without responsibility will change any time soon. This is not only due to the reluctance of states and a lack of practice, but it equally demonstrates the continuing challenges emanating from the statist assumption underlying international law as a whole. The endeavour to develop a legal framework for the responsibility of organized armed groups can, and should, be seen as part of a larger effort to confront the challenges that non-state actors pose to the fabric of international law.

[112] If one were to succeed in developing a coherent general set of rules of legal responsibility of organized armed groups, its applicability should equally be subject to the caveat that they shall only apply to the extent that no other more specific rules of international law govern the matter, cf. Art. 55 Articles on State Responsibility.

12

Assumptions and presuppositions: state responsibility for system crimes

IAIN SCOBBIE*

This chapter examines state responsibility for system criminality: that is, the remedies available under international law should a state order or encourage, permit or tolerate the widespread or systematic commission of international crimes, even if these are lawful under its domestic law.[1] The analysis here is restricted to acts which threaten core values of international society,[2] such as genocide, torture, and widespread or systematic violations of the law of armed conflict which amount to crimes against humanity. This chapter does not discuss individual criminal responsibility for acts that amount to international crimes,[3] but rather examines the possibilities of engaging the responsibility of the allegedly delinquent state.

As Nollkaemper points out, state responsibility is neither criminal nor civil as we conceive these in domestic legal systems.[4] At its core, a finding of state responsibility simply records that the delinquent state has committed a breach of general international law which binds all states, or of a specific legal obligation which binds two or more states. The aims of

* Sir Joseph Hotung Research Professor in Law, Human Rights and Peace Building in the Middle East, School of Oriental and African Studies, University of London.

[1] Compare the definition of crimes of obedience in H.C. Kelman, 'The policy context of international crimes', this volume, Chapter 2, p. 26, and 'The policy context of torture: a social-psychological analysis' (2005) 857 *International Review of the Red Cross* 125–6.

[2] See *Democratic Republic of the Congo v Rwanda,* Armed activities on the territory of the Congo case (*new application: 2002*) ICJ Rep (2006) separate opinion of Judge *ad hoc* Dugard 89 para. 10 on *ius cogens* norms – 'On the one hand, they affirm the high principles of international law, which recognise the most important rights of the international order … while, on the other hand, they give legal form to the most fundamental policies or goals of the international community'; see also A. Nollkaemper, 'Introduction', this volume, Chapter 1.

[3] A. Nollkaemper, 'Introduction', this volume, Chapter 1, p. 19.

[4] A. Nollkaemper, 'Introduction', this volume, Chapter 1, p. 23.

the ascription of responsibility to a state for system criminality encompass the termination of the unlawful conduct and prevention of its repetition; the vindication and confirmation of fundamental norms of the international legal system; and the reconciliation of the entities and individuals implicated in the delict, whether as perpetrators or injured.[5] Given these objectives, can the law of state responsibility provide an adequate response to acts 'performed in response to orders from authority that [are] considered illegal or immoral by the larger community'?[6]

One aim of the International Law Commission's 2001 Articles on the Responsibility of States for Internationally Wrongful Acts[7] was to move beyond the constraints of the bilateral relationship arising between a state directly injured by another's wrongdoing, where the delinquent state has breached either a peremptory norm or an obligation owed to the international community as a whole. The Articles embodied a conscious attempt to introduce communitarian mechanisms which would also allow a state not directly injured by a breach of these obligations to invoke the responsibility of the delinquent, as all states are thought to have an interest in the observance of peremptory norms and obligations owed to the international community as a whole. The precise nature of what constitutes the invocation of the responsibility of a state is, however, unclear although invocation involves more than a simple condemnation of the breach or a mere protest and apparently requires the presentation of some form of claim against the delinquent. The efficacy of invoking responsibility to obtain a remedy for system crimes is nevertheless prejudiced by the structural dependence of the international legal order on the doctrine of sovereignty.

Sovereignty manifests itself in the principle of consensual jurisdiction to modes of pacific dispute settlement which may frustrate the efforts of both injured and interested states alike to seek and secure satisfaction. Further, any attempt to invoke the responsibility of a delinquent state through the route of diplomatic protection is similarly hampered by its intrinsic state-centric view of international society. The International Law Commission has taken the view that the assertion of diplomatic protection is not an appropriate mechanism for the protection of human

[5] A. Nollkaemper, and H. van der Wilt, 'Conclusions and outlook', this volume, Chapter 15, p. 348.

[6] H. C. Kelman and V. L. Hamilton, *Crimes of Obedience: Toward a Social Psychology of Authority and Responsibility* (Yale University Press, New Haven 1989), p. 46.

[7] See International Law Commission, *Report on the Work of its Fifty-Third Session*, UN Doc.A/56/10 (2001) 26–30.

rights, but generally system crimes are committed by a state against its own nationals.

The assertion of diplomatic protection is, moreover, predicated on the nationality of claims rule, another manifestation of sovereignty, which prevents the presentation of claims on behalf of non-nationals, yet adherence to this rule is, by virtue of the Articles on State Responsibility themselves, a prerequisite for the admissibility of the invocation of responsibility by both injured and interested states. This requirement means that the communitarian aim of the Articles on State Responsibility remain largely unfulfilled: this promise has been stifled by the International Law Commission's formulation of its 2006 Draft Articles on Diplomatic Protection.[8] The only remedies available to interested, as opposed to injured states, appear to be declaratory. Accordingly, the efficacy of state responsibility as a mechanism by which states may respond to system crimes is constrained by the very doctrine which makes these crimes possible in the first place – namely, the centrality of sovereignty in the construction of the international legal order.

I. The nature of state responsibility

The function of the law of state responsibility is principally to provide a reparative response to an internationally wrongful act. It is the mechanism embodied in the international legal order by which states may be called to account for alleged breaches of its substantive rules. The terminology employed by international law to describe this relationship is redolent of that developed by Hart.[9] Substantive norms are primary and require or prohibit certain actions – for instance, Article 1 of the 1948 Convention on the Prevention and Punishment of the Crime of Genocide requires states parties to prevent and punish acts of genocide. In contrast, the law of state responsibility consists of secondary rules which complement primary rules and which may be used to regulate their operation, in particular to determine the existence and consequences of a breach of a primary rule.[10]

[8] See International Law Commission, *Report on the Work of its Fifty-Eighth Session*, UN Doc.A/61/10 (2006), Chapter IV.

[9] See H. L. A. Hart, *The Concept of Law* (Clarendon Press, Oxford 1961). P. A. Bulloch and J. Raz (eds.) (2nd edn, 1994), particularly Ch. 5, 'Law as the union of primary and secondary rules'.

[10] See R. Ago, *Second Report on State Responsibility*, UN Doc.A/CN.4/233 (20 April 1970), reproduced (1970) II YBILC 178 para. 7; 179 para. 11 and 191 para. 41; compare Hart

The basic principles of state responsibility are set out in Articles 1–3 of the International Law Commission's 2001 Articles on the Responsibility of States for Internationally Wrongful Acts. Although these Articles are contained in a 'soft' instrument which does not formally bind states,[11] Articles 1–3 undoubtedly form part of customary international law. More broadly, the United Kingdom has observed that the Articles as a whole 'reflect an authoritative statement of international law and have been referred to by international courts and tribunals, writers and, more recently, domestic courts ... [and] have gained widespread recognition and approval'.[12] Articles 1–3 provide:

1. Every internationally wrongful act of a state entails the responsibility of that state.

(n. 9) 81; for an indication of complexity underneath this apparently simple dichotomy in relation to state responsibility, see S. Rosenne, *Developments in the Law of Treaties 1945–1986* (Cambridge University Press, Cambridge 1989), p. 37.

[11] The General Assembly took note of the 2001 Articles, without vote, in resolution 56/83 (12 December 2001) UN Doc.A/RES/56/83, operative para. 3 of which provided: '*Takes note* of the articles on the responsibility of States for internationally wrongful acts, presented by the International Law Commission, the text of which is annexed to the present resolution, and commends them to the attention of Governments without prejudice to the question of their future adoption or other appropriate action.' This followed the recommendation of the International Law Commission that the General Assembly take note of the Articles and subsequently decide whether to convene a diplomatic conference with a view to conclude a convention on State responsibility – see International Law Commission (n. 7) 24–25 and 25 paras. 61–7 and 72–3; and also J. Crawford, *The International Law Commission's Articles on State Responsibility: Introduction, Text and Commentaries* (Cambridge University Press, Cambridge 2002), pp. 58–60; In 2004, the General Assembly reconsidered this matter, and decided to defer its decision – see J. Crawford and S. Olleson, 'The continuing debate on a UN Convention on State Responsibility' (2005) 54 *International and Comparative Law Quarterly* 959; the General Assembly has since adopted resolution 62/61 (8 January 2008), UN Doc.A/RES/62/61, in which it, once again, commended the Articles to the attention of States 'without prejudice to the question of their future adoption or other appropriate action' (operative para. 1), and included on the provisional agenda of its sixty-fifth session consideration of whether a convention should be adopted, or other appropriate action be taken, on the basis of the Articles (operative para. 4); see also D. Caron, 'The ILC Articles on State responsibility: the paradoxical relationship between form and authority' (2002) 96 AJIL 857.

[12] *Responsibility of States for Internationally Wrongful Acts: Comments and Information Received from Governments*, UN Doc.A/62/63 (9 March 2007), statement of the United Kingdom 6 para. 5: see this document and its addendum, UN Doc.A/62/63/Add.1 (12 June 2007) generally. For a compendium of cases which have employed the 2001 Articles (and earlier draft Articles), see Report of the Secretary-General, *Responsibility of States for Internationally Wrongful Acts: Compilation of Decisions of International Courts, Tribunals and Other Bodies*, UN Doc.A/62/62 (1 February 2007) and its addendum, UN Doc.A/62/62/Add.1 (17 April 2007); I am grateful to Dr Simon Olleson for drawing my attention to these documents.

2. There is an internationally wrongful act of a state when conduct consisting of an action or omission:
   (a) is attributable to the state under international law; and
   (b) constitutes a breach of an international obligation of the state.
3. The characterisation of an act of state as internationally wrongful is governed by international law. Such characterisation is not affected by the characterisation of the same act as lawful by internal law.

This is the basic framework of state responsibility, covering all breaches of general international law and of specific obligations that exist between states.

If a state is responsible for an incident of system criminality, this necessarily entails the breach of a norm of general international law which is unlike the vast majority of international delicts. Included within this category are those obligations whose breach is specifically regulated by Part Two, Chapter III of the International Law Commission's Articles on State Responsibility. The commission of such a delict amounts to 'a serious breach by a State of an obligation arising under a peremptory norm of general international law'. This entails 'a gross or systematic failure by the responsible State to fulfil the obligation'.[13] This approach was substituted for that of 'crimes of state' used in earlier drafts of the Articles as the inclusion of this concept had been opposed by states.[14] Draft Article 19.2 of the 1996 version of the International Law Commission's draft Articles had dealt with 'crimes of State' and had provided:

> An internationally wrongful act which results from the breach by a State of an international obligation so essential for the protection of fundamental interests of the international community that its breach is recognised as a crime by that community as a whole, constitutes an international crime.[15]

Nevertheless, even after this substitution had been made, Japan commented that 'the text … is still haunted by the ghost of "international crime"'.[16]

[13] These definitions are contained in Article 40; for commentary on Chapter Two, Part III, see 'Symposium: assessing the work of the International Law Commission on State responsibility' (2002) 13 EJIL 1053; as A. Nollkaemper, 'Introduction', this volume, Chapter 1, observes, the category of system crimes is wider than breaches of peremptory norms, but the present discussion is restricted to this sub-category.

[14] See Crawford (n. 11) 16–20: the status of the draft Article regulating crimes of state had been placed in abeyance in 1998 by the Commission; Crawford (n. 11) 27.

[15] Reproduced, with commentary www.lcil.cam.ac.uk/Media/ILCSR/Arts.htm#A19, accessed 26 June 2008.

[16] Japan, *State Responsibility: Comments and Observations Received from Governments*, A/CN.4/515 (19 March 2001) 48.

The fact that 'crimes of State' was excised from the International Law Commission's 2001 Articles does not mean that the concept is alien to international law.[17] Indeed, the notion of serious breaches of peremptory norms defined in Article 40 and the discarded notion of state crimes really refer to the same thing. As Zimmerman observes, the distinction between the two is only semantic,[18] and Wyler has termed them 'the twin brothers of horror'.[19] Article 40 provides:

1. This Chapter applies to the international responsibility which is entailed by a serious breach by a State of an obligation arising under a peremptory norm of general international law.
2. A breach of such an obligation is serious if it involves a gross or systematic failure by the responsible State to fulfil the obligation.

The consequences of a serious breach of an obligation arising under a peremptory norm of general international law are set out in Article 41, which provides:

1. States shall cooperate to bring to an end through lawful means any serious breach within the meaning of Article 40.
2. No State shall recognise as lawful a situation created by a serious breach within the meaning of Article 40, nor render aid or assistance in maintaining that situation.

[17] See International Law Commission, *Report on the Work of its Fifty-Second Session*, UN Doc.A/55/10 (2000) 59 paras. 360–2 (also (2002) II(2) YbILC 59 paras. 6–362); there is an extensive literature on crimes of States, see e.g. G. Abi-Saab, 'The uses of Article 19' (1999) 10 EJIL 339; I. Brownlie, *International Law and the Use of Force by States* (Clarendon Press, Oxford 1963), pp 150–66, and *System of the Law of Nations. State Responsibility (Part One)* (Clarendon Press, Oxford 1983), pp. 32–33; G. Gaja, 'Should all references to international crimes disappear from the ILC draft articles on State responsibility?' (1999) 10 EJIL 365; A. de Hoogh, *Obligations Erga Omnes and International Crimes* (Kluwer, The Hague 1996); A. Pellet, 'Can a State commit a crime? Definitely, yes!' (1999) 10 EJIL 425; S. Rosenne, 'State responsibility and international crimes: further reflections on Article 19 of the draft articles on State responsibility' (1997–98) 30 *New York University JILP* 145; C. Tomuschat, 'International crimes by States: an endangered species?', in K. Wellens (ed.), *International Law: Theory and Practice: Essays in Honour of Eric Suy* (Martinus Nijhoff, The Hague 1998), p. 253; and J. Weiler *et al.* (eds.), *International Crimes of State* (de Gruyter, Berlin 1989) part 2.

[18] A. Zimmerman and M. Teichmann, 'State responsibility for international crimes', this volume, Chapter 13; see also E. Wyler, 'From "State crime" to responsibility for "serious breaches of obligations under peremptory norms of general international law"' (2002) 13 EJIL 1147.

[19] Wyler (n. 18) 1159.

3. This Article is without prejudice to the other consequences referred to in this Part and to such further consequences that a breach to which this Chapter applies may entail under international law.

These two Articles exhaust Part Two, Chapter III of the International Law Commission's Articles on State Responsibility. Although, as yet, relatively little judicial attention has been paid to these articles, they have attracted some criticism.[20] In the International Court of Justice's *Legal consequences of the construction of a wall* advisory opinion, Judge Kooijmans was mystified regarding the substantive content of the duty not to recognize an illegal fact placed on states by Article 41,[21] while in the Inter-American Court of Human Rights, Judge Cançado Trindade thought that these Articles were under-developed:

> The relatively succinct treatment of grave violations – and their consequences – of obligations under mandatory norms of general International Law (Articles 40–41) in the ILC's Articles on the Responsibility of the States (2001) reveals the insufficient conceptual development of the matter up to our days, in an international community that is still seeking a greater degree of cohesion and solidarity.[22]

Nevertheless, both articles have been affirmed by domestic supreme courts,[23] and Gattini[24] convincingly argues that Article 41 is declaratory of existing custom.

[20] See also Zimmermann and Teichmann, 'State responsibility for international crimes', this volume, Chapter 13.

[21] *Legal consequences of the construction of a wall in the occupied Palestinian territory* advisory opinion, ICJ Rep (2004) 136, separate opinion of Judge Kooijmans 231–2 paras. 40–45, especially 232 para. 44.

[22] *Myrna Mack Chang v Guatemala*, Inter-American Court of Human Rights (25 November 2003) Ser.C, No.101, [2003] IACHR 4 www.worldlii.org/int/cases/IACHR/2003/4.html#fn1, accessed 26 June 2008, Opinion of Judge Cançado Trindade, para. 8 (note omitted).

[23] Article 40 was affirmed by the German Federal Constitutional Court in case No.2 *B v R* 955/00 (26 October 2004), see *Responsibility of States for Internationally Wrongful Acts: Comments and Information Received from Governments* (n. 12) statement of Germany 15–17 paras. 33–8; it was also affirmed by the United Kingdom House of Lords in *A and others v Secretary of State for the Home Department No 2* [2005] UKHL 71 (8 December 2005), opinion of Lord Bingham of Cornhill, para. 34; further, in *R (on the application of Al Rawi and others) v Secretary of State for Foreign and Commonwealth Affairs and Secretary of State for the Home Department* [2006] EWHC 972 (Admin) (4 May 2006), the English Divisional Court noted and affirmed a ministerial reliance on Articles 40 and 41, see opinion of Lord Justice Latham, paras. 69–70.

[24] A. Gattini, 'A return ticket to "communitarianisme", please' (2002) 13 EJIL 1185–95.

II. 'Injured' and 'interested' states

System crimes, which constitute serious breaches of peremptory norms – such as genocide or torture – will inevitably involve acts which harm individuals. There is, however, no guarantee that civil claims brought by injured individuals before domestic courts against an allegedly delinquent state, whether this is their national or a foreign state, would proceed to judgment: these proceedings could well be blocked by a plea of state immunity.[25] The law of state responsibility functions on the international plane and thus, characteristically, remedies for system crimes will be sought by one or more states against another. In order to assess the adequacy of the response this provides, we must consider which states may avail themselves of remedies within the framework of the law of state responsibility.

The 2001 Articles identify two categories of states which may invoke the responsibility of another. In broad terms, Article 42 provides that a state is entitled as 'an injured state' to invoke the responsibility of another if the obligation breached is owed to the claimant state individually, or to a group of states and the breach of the obligation especially affects the claimant.

This right of this category of states ('injured' states) to challenge the delinquent behaviour of another is clearly established in international law. In contrast, the second category of states ('interested' states) identified in Article 48 of the 2001 Articles was seen by some to involve a degree of innovation. Article 48.1 provides:

> Any State other than an injured State is entitled to invoke the responsibility of another State in accordance with paragraph 2 if:
> (a) the obligation breached is owed to a group of States including that State, and is established for the protection of a collective interest of the group; or
> (b) the obligation breached is owed to the international community as a whole.

Article 48 continues that an interested claimant state may seek the cessation of the delict and guarantees of non-repetition and also reparation in favour of the injured state or the beneficiaries of the obligation breached. In invoking responsibility, however, an interested state must respect the requirements placed on the invocation of responsibility by an

[25] But see, e.g., C. Focarelli, 'Denying foreign state immunity for commission of international crimes: the Ferrini decision' (2005) 54 ICLQ 951; and A. Gattini, 'War crimes and state immunity in the Ferrini decision' (2005) 3 JICJ 224.

injured state. These include the conditions that the injured state has not waived its claim against the delinquent or acquiesced in its waiver, and that the rules regarding the nationality of claims and exhaustion of local remedies are observed.

'Interested' states occupy a conceptually different position from 'injured' states, a matter which has attracted some criticism from states themselves. Some objected to the formulation of the distinction between injured and interested states, and the recognition of the latter category's entitlement to invoke responsibility.[26] In drafting Articles 42 and 48, the International Law Commission elaborated upon the International Court's *dictum* in the *Barcelona Traction* case, which distinguished between obligations whose breach particularly affects one state and those obligations owed to the international community as a whole, in which all states have a legal interest in their protection:

> 33.... an essential distinction should be drawn between the obligations of a State towards the international community as a whole, and those arising vis-à-vis another State in the field of diplomatic protection. By their very nature the former are the concern of all States. In view of the importance of the rights involved, all States can be held to have a legal interest in their protection; they are obligations *erga omnes*.
>
> 34. Such obligations derive, for example, in contemporary international law, from the outlawing of acts of aggression, and of genocide, as also from the principles and rules concerning the basic rights of the human person, including protection from slavery and racial discrimination. Some of the corresponding rights of protection have entered into the body of general international law...; others are conferred by international instruments of a universal or quasi-universal character.
>
> 35. Obligations the performance of which is the subject of diplomatic protection are not of the same category. It cannot be held, when one such obligation in particular is in question, in a specific case, that all States have a legal interest in its observance. In order to bring a claim in respect of the breach of such an obligation, a State must first establish its right to do so...[27]

[26] See, e.g., the comments of France, India and the Nordic States recorded in P. Bodeau, *Comments and Observations by Governments in the 6th Committee, 54th Session – 1999: summary of main points* (1999) 11, www.lcil.cam.ac.uk/projects/state_responsibility_document_collection.php, accessed 26 June 2008; and *State Responsibility: Comments and Observations Received from Governments* (n. 16) the Netherlands (61–2), China (69–70) and Japan (70); by 2001, however, the Nordic States had decided to support the distinction (70).

[27] *Barcelona Traction, Light and Power Co. Ltd case, second phase, final judgment*, ICJ Rep (1970) 32 paras. 33 and 35; compare 47 para. 91; reaffirmed *Legal consequences of the construction of a wall* advisory opinion (n. 21) 199 para. 155; on Article 48 and *Barcelona*

Articles 42 and 48 are not mutually exclusive: a state may be injured within the meaning of Article 42 by another's breach of an obligation owed to the international community as a whole, which thus simultaneously gives rise to the possibility of interested states invoking the delinquent's responsibility under Article 48.[28] While Article 42 expresses an established principle, Article 48 is generally seen as an example of progressive development of the law by the International Law Commission. It attracted a mixed reaction from states[29] and, as yet, has not received judicial scrutiny.[30]

Further, the scope of Article 48 bears a relationship to that of Article 40. Article 48(1)(b) permits states other than the injured state to invoke the responsibility of another where 'the obligation breached is owed to the international community as a whole'. The International Law Commission's view is that peremptory norms and those owed to the international community as a whole are essentially the two sides of the same coin:

> From the Court's reference [in *Barcelona Traction*] to the international community as a whole, and from the character of the examples it gave, one can infer that the core cases of obligations *erga omnes* are those non-derogable obligations of a general character which arise either directly under general international law or under generally accepted multilateral treaties (e.g. in the field of human rights). They are thus virtually coextensive with peremptory obligations (arising under norms of *jus cogens*). For if a particular obligation can be set aside or displaced as between two

Traction, see International Law Commission (n. 7) *Commentary to Article 48*, 126 para. 2 and 127 paras. 8 and 9; Crawford (n. 11) *Commentary to Article 48*, 276–7 para. 2, and 278 paras. 8 and 9; the germ of this development may be traced back to Ago's *Second Report on State Responsibility* (n. 10) 184 para. 23.

28 See International Law Commission (n. 7) *Commentary to Part Three, Chapter I*, 116, para. 3; Crawford (n. 11) *Commentary to Part Three, Chapter I*, 255 para. 3.

29 See *State Responsibility: Comments and Observations Received from Governments* (n. 16) 69–74 (and compare 60–6); and also Bodeau (n. 26) 10–11.

30 In *Democratic Republic of the Congo v Uganda*, Armed activities on the territory of the Congo, ICJ Rep, 2005, 168, separate opinion of Judge Simma 346 para. 32 and 347–8 para. 35; Judge Simma endorsed Art. 48 in his separate opinion, but it is clear that this opinion was expressed on a point which had not been argued by the parties. Elements of an earlier draft Article which do not entirely correspond to Art. 48 in its final form were considered by a 1997 WTO Panel Report in *European Communities – Regime for the Importation, Sale and Distribution of Bananas*, and by the International Tribunal for the Former Yugoslavia Appeals Chamber in the *Blaskic* case (1997): see Report of the Secretary-General, *Responsibility of States for Internationally Wrongful Acts: Compilation of Decisions of International Courts, Tribunals and Other Bodies* (n. 12) 74 and 77–9.

States, it is hard to see how that obligation is owed to the international community as a whole.[31]

Nevertheless, the International Law Commission views peremptory norms and core obligations owed to the international community as having a difference in emphasis. Peremptory norms focus on the scope and priority of the obligations they embody. The focus of obligations owed to the international community is on the interest all states have in compliance through their entitlement to invoke the responsibility of any state in breach.[32] Article 48, however, encompasses a wider class of delicts than Article 40 because it is not restricted to serious breaches of peremptory norms. This is apparent on the face of Article 48: para. 1(a) allows an interested state to invoke the responsibility of another in relation to the breach of an obligation owed to a group of states, in contradistinction to the breach of an obligation owed to the international community as a whole which is addressed in para. 1(b).

III. Calling a delinquent state to account

As Articles 42 and 48 make clear, the implementation of the law of state responsibility requires an injured or interested state to invoke the responsibility of the alleged delinquent state. In contrast, the parameters of invocation are not clear, and this concept is not defined in the 2001 Articles. Some guidance is provided by the International Law Commission's commentary to Article 42, which states:

> invocation should be understood as taking measures of a relatively formal character, for example, the raising or presentation of a claim against another State or the commencement of proceedings before an international court or tribunal. A State does not invoke the responsibility of another State merely because it criticizes that State for a breach and calls for the observance of the obligation, or even reserves its rights or protests. For the purpose of these articles, protest as such is not an invocation of responsibility; it has a variety of forms and purposes and is not limited to cases involving State responsibility. There is in general no requirement that a State which wishes to protest against a breach of international law by another State or remind it of its international

[31] J. Crawford Third Report on State Responsibility, A/CN. 4/507 (10 March 2000), 46–7 para. 106(a); see also International Law Commission (n. 7) 111–12 para. 7; Crawford (n. 11) 244–5 para. 7; and A. J. J. de Hoogh, 'The relationship between jus cogens, obligations erga omnes, and international crimes: peremptory norms in perspective' (1991) 42 *Austrian Journal of Public and International Law* 183.

[32] International Law Commission (n. 7) 111–12 para. 7; Crawford (n. 11) 244–5 para. 7.

> responsibilities in respect of a treaty or other obligation by which they are both bound should establish any specific title or interest to do so. Such informal diplomatic contacts do not amount to the invocation of responsibility unless and until they involve specific claims by the State concerned, such as for compensation for a breach affecting it, or specific action such as the filing of an application before a competent international tribunal, or even the taking of countermeasures. In order to take such steps, ie to invoke responsibility in the sense of the articles, some more specific entitlement is needed.[33]

This definition of invocation entails that a State either 'injured' under the terms of Article 42, or 'interested' within the meaning of Article 48, presents some type of claim or takes measures which go beyond a simple condemnation in relation to the alleged delict. For instance, under Article 54, an interested state may invoke responsibility by taking 'lawful measures' against the alleged delinquent in order 'to ensure cessation of the breach and reparation in the interest of the injured State or of the beneficiaries of the obligation breached'.[34]

Some additional guidance may, however, be drawn from the International Law Commission's Draft Articles on Diplomatic Protection, submitted to the General Assembly in 2006 with the recommendation that they form the basis for the elaboration of a convention.[35] The premise of diplomatic protection is the invocation of the responsibility of an allegedly delinquent State. Draft Article 1 provides:

> For the purposes of the present draft articles, diplomatic protection consists of the invocation by a State, through diplomatic action or other means of peaceful settlement, of the responsibility of another State for an

[33] International Law Commission (n. 7) *Commentary to Article 42*, 117 para. 2 (footnote omitted); Crawford (n. 11) *Commentary to Article 42*, 256 (footnote omitted); and his *Third Report on State Responsibility* (n. 31) para. 105.

[34] See International Law Commission (n. 7) *Commentary to Article 54*, 137–9; and Crawford (n. 11) *Commentary to Article 54*, 302–5; the Commission conceded that countermeasures taken in the general or collective interest by an interested state (or states) to induce a delinquent to comply with its obligations lack a secure legal basis due to a paucity of state practice – see para. 6 of the *Commentary to Article 54* (n. 7) 139 and Crawford (n. 11) 305: compare D. Allard, 'Countermeasures of general interest' (2002) 13 EJIL 1221.

[35] See International Law Commission (n. 8) Chapter IV; the recommendation that a convention be elaborated on the basis of the draft Articles is at p. 15 para. 46, and the draft Articles set out at pp. 16–21; the General Assembly, in Resolution 61/35 (18 December 2006), took note of the draft Articles and invited governments to submit comments on the Commission's recommendation – see UN Doc.A/RES/61/35, operative para 2; states expressed a diversity of views on this – see *Diplomatic Protection: Report of the Secretary-General*, UN Doc.A/62/118 (5 July 2007) and its *Addendum*, UN Doc.A/62/118/Add.1 (2 August 2007).

> injury caused by an internationally wrongful act of that State to a natural or legal person that is a national of the former State with a view to the implementation of such responsibility.

The Draft Articles on Diplomatic Protection thus complement the Articles on State Responsibility[36] and, like them, are secondary rules contained in an instrument which does not formally bind states.[37] The draft Articles regulate one of the principal forms of the invocation, essentially by an injured state, of the responsibility of an allegedly delinquent state 'through diplomatic action or other means of peaceful settlement':

> 'Diplomatic action' covers all the lawful procedures employed by a State to inform another State of its views and concerns, including protest, request for an inquiry or for negotiations aimed at the settlement of disputes. 'Other means of peaceful settlement' embraces all forms of lawful dispute settlement, from negotiation, mediation and conciliation to arbitral and judicial dispute settlement … Diplomatic protection does not include demarches or other diplomatic action that do not involve the invocation of the legal responsibility of another State, such as informal requests for corrective action.[38]

This exegesis of the forms which invocation might take is cast rather widely but, like its counterpart in the state responsibility commentary, it envisions the presentation by the aggrieved state of a specific claim alleging wrongdoing on the part of the delinquent.

Further, although it is clear that mere protest need not necessarily amount to the invocation of responsibility – as protest also, for example, plays an important role in the process of the formation of customary international law – it might be difficult to distinguish protest clearly from invocation where a state is acting under Article 48 in the collective interest. Drawing this distinction could well depend on the circumstances

[36] 'Diplomatic protection [is] not separate from State responsibility; a State acting on behalf of one of its nationals [is] nonetheless invoking State responsibility': International Law Commission (n. 17) 50 para. 286; see also (n. 8) 22 para. 1; this was also emphasized by some states in their comments on the final draft Articles, see *Diplomatic Protection: Report of the Secretary-General*, UN Doc.A/62/118 at 4 (Czech Republic), 6 (Portugal) and 7 (United Kingdom) and its *Addendum*, UN Doc.A/62/118/Add.1 at 2 (France).

[37] On the status of the draft Articles as secondary rules, see International Law Commission (n. 8) *Commentary to Draft Article 1*, 24 para. 2; and J. R. Dugard, *First Report on Diplomatic Protection*, UN Doc.A/CN.4/506 (7 March 2000) 12 para. 35.

[38] International Law Commission (n. 8) *Commentary to Draft Article 1*, 27 para. 8: see also Dugard (n. 37) paras. 41–46, but compare his commentary to his initial, but subsequently discarded, draft Art. 2, 16–22 paras. 47–60, and the summary record of the Commission's discussion in its *Report on the Work of its Fifty-Second Session* (n. 17) 74–6 paras. 430–39.

and terms of the complaint made, but it seems impossible to do so if an interested state requests only cessation and/or non-repetition of the alleged delict as these are inherent in the very notion of protest.

IV. Remedies and responsibility

Calling a state to account for its commission of system crimes aims to terminate and prevent the repetition of the unlawful conduct, confirm the validity of fundamental international norms, and reconcile the actors. Remedies available under the law of state responsibility offer remedies which correspond to some of these aims.

Even where an ordinary delict has been committed, as opposed to a system crime which falls within the ambit of Articles 40 or 48, the delinquent state is under a duty to cease and guarantee non-repetition of the wrongful act, as well as wipe out the consequences of that act by rendering full reparation for the injury caused.[39] Under Article 37, one of the forms that reparation might take is satisfaction where the consequences of the delict cannot be made good by restitution or compensation. This is defined in Article 37(2) as 'an acknowledgement of the breach, an expression of regret, a formal apology or another appropriate modality'. In judicial proceedings, satisfaction may take the form of a declaratory judgment recording the breach. Thus, for instance, in the *Genocide in Bosnia* proceedings, in relation to the injury caused by the respondent's alleged incitement and conspiracy to commit genocide, as well as the consequences of its breach of the obligation to prevent and punish genocide, the applicant (Bosnia) argued that reparation could not lie in an award of monetary compensation:

> Of course, this does not however mean that Serbia and Montenegro is free of any obligation to provide satisfaction to Bosnia and Herzegovina in other forms. Given the judicial context of the present case, the most natural mode of satisfaction, that which springs to mind immediately, also the most common in such circumstances, is obviously a formal declaration by this Court that Serbia and Montenegro has breached its obligations under Articles I to V – inclusive – of the Convention. This is also what Bosnia and Herzegovina asked of you in its Reply and what it continues to request you to decide in this regard.[40]

[39] See Arts. 30 (cessation) and 31 (reparation) of the 2001 Articles: the forms which reparation may take are set out in Arts. 34–7.

[40] *Bosnia and Herzegovina v Serbia and Montenegro,* Application of the Convention on the Prevention and Punishment of the Crime of Genocide, CR 2006/11, oral proceedings

It is possible that a declaratory judgment, or an admission of wrongdoing or apology by the delinquent state, may contribute to the reconciliation of the actors. Further, if a state admits, or an authoritative third party such as a court or commission of enquiry finds, that it is responsible for an internationally unlawful act then the norm in question is vindicated as the required standard of international behaviour.

These remedies are also available in relation to system crimes, whether in relation to a serious breach of a peremptory norm which falls under Article 40, or the breach of an obligation owed to the international community as a whole under Article 48. In addition to the delinquent state's duties of cessation and reparation arising under the general rules of state responsibility, by virtue of Article 41(1), the serious breach of a peremptory norm imposes on all states the duty to cooperate to terminate that breach 'through lawful means'. Under Article 48(2), an interested state which invokes the responsibility of another may call for the cessation and guarantees assuring the non-repetition of the impugned act and also the 'performance of the obligation of reparation … in the interest of the injured State or of the beneficiaries of the obligation breached' and may, by virtue of Article 54, 'take lawful measures against that State' to ensure this outcome. Accordingly, the remedies available under the law of state responsibility appear to match, in principle, the objectives sought in the ascription of responsibility for the commission of a system crime.

V. The replication of assumptions: state sovereignty

Nevertheless, one may question the practical adequacy of the response the law of state responsibility affords to the commission of system crimes by states as the implementation of state responsibility depends on the same assumptions and legal structures that make state criminality possible in the first place.

The key issue is the doctrine of sovereignty. Sovereignty grants a state authority within its territory which is exercised by its government. As Kelman points out, crimes of obedience committed by states rest on the power, or the authority, of the government to control those subject to it, and crimes of obedience are especially likely to occur when

(7 March 2006) argument of Professor Pellet, counsel for Bosnia-Herzegovina, 35–6 paras. 18–20; quotation at 36 para. 20 (notes omitted) (translation by Registry at CR 2006/11 (translation) 26–27).

the legitimacy of the government is challenged.[41] Sovereignty also has an external projection. The classic formulation of the meaning of sovereignty in international law is that of Judge Huber in the *Island of Palmas* case:

> Sovereignty in the relations between States signifies independence. Independence in relation to a portion of the globe is the right to exercise therein, to the exclusion of any other State, the functions of a State.[42]

This gives rise to the legal doctrine of non-intervention in the internal affairs of a state, which has frequently been used as a shield to declare illegitimate external criticisms of a state's human rights record.

More importantly, with regard to the invocation of state responsibility, sovereignty manifests itself in the doctrine of consensual jurisdiction. As the Permanent Court of International Justice ruled in the *Eastern Carelia* advisory opinion: 'no State can, without its consent, be compelled to submit its disputes with other States either to mediation or to arbitration, or to any other kind of pacific settlement.' It observed that this doctrine 'only accepts and applies a principle which is a fundamental principle of international law, namely, the principle of the independence of States'.[43] Accordingly, in attempting to use the law of state responsibility to provide redress in a case of system criminality, consensual jurisdiction presents an immediate potential stumbling block to the presentation of a claim, for instance, before an international tribunal. If the claimant state cannot demonstrate that the respondent state has consented to the tribunal's jurisdiction, then the claim cannot proceed, even if the case concerns serious breaches of peremptory norms or of obligations owed to the international community as a whole.[44] This result is 'resonant of limitations of the international legal system generally, [which] are relics of a past era which need to be revisited',[45] but there are other impediments to the use of state responsibility as an effective remedial response to system criminality.

[41] See, e.g., H.C. Kelman, 'The policy context of international crimes', this volume, Chapter 2, p.32, and Kelman (n. 1) 'The policy context of torture', 128–9.

[42] *Island of Palmas Case* (United States/Netherlands, 1928), 2 Reports of International Arbitral Awards 829, 838; the 'classic' judicial definition of independence is that of Judge Anzilotti in the *Austro-German Customs Union* Advisory Opinion (1931) PCIJ, Ser.A/B, No.41, 57–8.

[43] *Status of Eastern Carelia* Advisory Opinion (1923) PCIJ, Ser.B. No.5, 27.

[44] See *Armed Activities on the Territory of the Congo* (n. 2) 31 para. 64; see also 33 para. 69; 35 para. 78 and 52 para. 125.

[45] *Armed Activities on the Territory of the Congo* (n. 2) declaration of Judge Elaraby 85 para. 10.

One of the aims of the International Law Commission's work on state responsibility was to move its operational framework beyond the strait-jacket of bilateral legal relationships to allow more communitarian responses:

> international law embodies interests which are closely analogous to public law interests in other legal systems. We have not yet succeeded in ridding ourselves of the notion that legal obligation in international law can be analogized to bilateral legal obligations, and their breach to bilateral wrongs. To make progress means creating some (if not too many) additional categories.[46]

The principal mechanism by which this was to be achieved was by recognizing that interested, as opposed to injured, states have the right to invoke the responsibility of another which has committed serious breaches of peremptory norms or of obligations owed to the international community as a whole. The structures embodied in the rules of diplomatic protection, however, again demonstrate the influence of sovereignty by reflecting a state-centric view of international society which impedes the realization of this progressive vision.

The foundation of the rules of diplomatic protection is expressed in the *Mavrommatis* fiction, namely that states have the right to protect nationals who have been injured by internationally wrongful acts committed by another state because:

> By taking up the case of one of its subjects and by resorting to diplomatic action or international judicial proceedings on his behalf, a State is in reality asserting its own rights – its right to ensure, in the person of its subjects, respect for the rules of international law.[47]

Dugard has traced this doctrine to the eighteenth century.[48] He recognizes that it forms the premise of diplomatic protection, but concedes that it is a fiction. Nevertheless, he was 'more concerned with the utility

[46] J. Crawford, *Responsibility to the International Community as a Whole*, Fourth Annual Snyder Lecture (April 2000, Bloomington School of Law, Indiana University) final paragraph: www.lcil.cam.ac.uk/lectures/lecture_papers.php, accessed 26 June 2008; see also his *Third Report on State Responsibility* (n. 31) para. 84.

[47] *Mavrommatis Palestine Concessions Case: Preliminary Objections Judgment* (1924) PCIJ, Ser.A, No.2, 12.

[48] See Dugard (n. 37) 5, paras. 11–13, *Commentary to Draft Article 1*, 12–14 paras. 36–7, and also *Commentary to Draft Article 3*, 22–5 paras. 61–8 (Dugard's initial draft Article 3 was subsequently discarded); and also International Law Commission (n. 8) *Commentary to Draft Article 1*, 25–6 paras. 3–5.

of the traditional view than its soundness in logic'.[49] A consequence of this doctrinal fiction is, however, that a precondition for the exercise of diplomatic protection is the fulfilment of the nationality of claims rule. Further, the Articles on State Responsibility expressly provide that the responsibility of a state may not be invoked, whether by an injured state (Article 44) or an interested state (Article 48(3)), unless the requirements of the nationality of claims rule are fulfilled.

The basic formulation of the nationality of claims rule is expressed in draft Article 3 of the 2006 Draft Articles on Diplomatic Protection. This provides:

1. The State entitled to exercise diplomatic protection is the State of nationality.
2. Notwithstanding paragraph 1, diplomatic protection may be exercised by a State in respect of a person that is not its national in accordance with draft Article 8.

With one exception,[50] the obverse of the nationality of claims rule is that diplomatic protection may not be exercised against a state of which the individual[51] injured by its internationally unlawful act was or is a national. This is expressly stated in draft Article 5(3)[52] and also, more importantly

[49] Dugard (n. 37) *Commentary to Draft Article 3*, 25 para. 68.

[50] The exception, which is supported by international practice and jurisprudence, concerns individuals who have dual or multiple nationality, and is contained in draft Article 7. This provides that a state may not exercise diplomatic protection on behalf of a national against another state whose nationality he also possesses unless the nationality of the claimant state is his predominant nationality, both at the time of the injury and the time of the official presentation of the claim: see International Law Commission (n. 8) *Commentary to Draft Article 7*, 43–7; at p. 47 para. 6, the Commission observes that this draft Article was framed in the negative to emphasize that this situation is exceptional.

[51] Diplomatic protection may be exercised in relation to injury caused to both natural and legal persons, but the link of nationality is, with the exception of draft Article 8 (see below), a prerequisite to the protection of both. The draft Articles contain parallel provisions on the nationality of natural and legal persons. As the types of system criminality under discussion in this paper affect natural persons only – for instance, one cannot commit genocide against a corporation – the focus will be on those provisions which deal with natural persons.

[52] Draft Article 5.3 provides: 'Diplomatic protection shall not be exercised by the present State of nationality in respect of a person against a former State of nationality of that person for an injury caused when that person was a national of the former State of nationality and not of the present State of nationality.'

Draft Article 5 sets out the continuous nationality rule, and provides in para. 1 that a state may only exercise diplomatic protection in respect of an individual who has been its national from the date of injury to the date of the official presentation of the claim – see International Law Commission (n. 8) *Commentary to Draft Article 5*, 35–41; although the

for present purposes, in draft Article 8 which permits a state to exercise diplomatic protection on behalf of stateless persons and refugees who are 'lawfully and habitually resident in that State'. Draft Article 8 was expressly designated as an instance of the progressive development of international law by the International Law Commission: it does not codify custom, and indeed departs from settled jurisprudence.[53] Nevertheless, it was thought justified by the concern that contemporary international law demonstrates for individuals who are stateless or refugees and, despite its innovative character, has broadly been endorsed and supported by states commenting on the draft Articles.[54]

In relation to system criminality, the proposal that states may exercise diplomatic protection with regard to refugees who have fled as a result of atrocities is more pertinent than that concerning stateless individuals. In this connection, draft Article 8 provides:

> 2. A State may exercise diplomatic protection in respect of a person who is recognised as a refugee by that State, in accordance with internationally accepted standards, when that person, at the date of the injury and at the date of the official presentation of the claim, is lawfully and habitually resident in that State.

continuous nationality rule is well established in customary international law, practice and jurisprudence were inconsistent regarding the period during which nationality must be continuous: by stipulating this period, the Commission engaged in the progressive development of international law – see (n. 8) 36 para. 2.

53 International Law Commission (n. 8) *Commentary to Draft Article 8*, 48 paras. 1–2; see also Dugard (n. 37) *Commentary to Draft Article 8*, 57–60 paras. 175–84; and International Law Commission (n. 17) *Commentary to Draft Article 8*, 83–5 paras. 486–94.

54 See *Diplomatic Protection: Comments and Observations Received from Governments*, UN Doc.A/CN.4/561 (27 January 2006) observations of Morocco, the Netherlands, Norway (on behalf of the Nordic countries – Denmark, Finland, Iceland, Norway and Sweden) and Panama (25–6), and the United States (51). In contrast, in this document's *Addendum*, UN Doc.A/CN.4/561/Add.1 (3 April 2006) Belgium took rather a lukewarm view to this proposal, while the United Kingdom thought that this matter did not fall within the scope of diplomatic protection (8). The United Kingdom, in *R (on the application of Al Rawi and others) v Secretary of State for Foreign and Commonwealth Affairs and Secretary of State for the Home Department* [2006] EWHC 972 (Admin) (4 May 2006), maintained before the English Divisional Court that it could not exercise consular or diplomatic protection in relation to non-nationals or refugees (see paras 30, 41, and 47). The court ruled that draft Article 8 was a proposal *de lex ferenda*, thus 'whatever the merits of these proposals may be, they are not yet part of international law' (para. 63, see paras. 62–3). In its comments on the final draft Articles, the United Kingdom reiterated that draft Article 8 amounted to the progressive development of international law, see *Diplomatic Protection: Report of the Secretary-General*, UN Doc.A/62/118 (5 July 2007) at 7; and also 3 (Cuba) and 9 (United States), and its *Addendum*, UN Doc.A/62/118/Add.1 at 3 (France).

3. Paragraph 2 does not apply in respect of an injury caused by an internationally wrongful act of the State of nationality of the refugee.

Although the initial version of draft Article 8[55] did not contain an express exclusion clause equivalent to para. 3, it provided that the right of the state of residence to exercise diplomatic protection only arose 'provided the injury occurred after that person became a legal resident of the claimant State'. The rapporteur commented this was:

> an important qualification to the right to exercise diplomatic protection: in many cases the refugee will have suffered injury at the hands of his State of nationality, from which he has fled to avoid persecution. It would, however, be improper for the State of refuge to exercise diplomatic protection on behalf of the refugee in such circumstances.[56]

This restriction was strengthened in the final version which made the prohibition absolute, as to allow claims against the refugee's national state 'would have contradicted the basic approach of the present draft articles, according to which nationality is the predominant basis for the exercise of diplomatic protection'.[57] Accordingly, the nationality of claims rule hinders the invocation of responsibility by a state which cannot claim to be injured by virtue of an injury caused to its nationals: although a legal fiction, the *Mavrommatis* fiction nonetheless exerts practical results.

Moreover, the evolution of the draft Articles on diplomatic protection demonstrates the influence of the view within the International Law Commission that it is a mechanism unsuited for the general protection of human rights. The initial version of draft Article 4, which was subsequently excised, provided in part:

1. Unless the injured person is able to bring a claim for such injury before a competent international court or tribunal, the State of his/her nationality has a legal duty to exercise diplomatic protection on behalf of the injured person upon request, if the injury results from a grave breach of a *jus cogens* norm attributable to another State.[58]

This draft Article was expressly designated to be an exercise in progressive development, and accordingly was limited to 'particularly

[55] It provided: 'A State may exercise diplomatic protection in respect of an injured person who is stateless and/or a refugee when that person is ordinarily a legal resident of the claimant State [and has an effective link with that State?]; provided the injury occurred after that person became a legal resident of the claimant State' Dugard (n. 37) 57.

[56] Dugard (n. 37) *Commentary to Draft Article 8*, 60 para. 184.

[57] International Law Commission (n. 8) *Commentary to Draft Article 8*, 51 para. 10.

[58] For commentary on this draft Article, see Dugard (n. 37) 27–34.

serious cases'.[59] Moreover, the First Report on Diplomatic Protection envisaged that a subsequent report would include an Article (projected draft Article 10) which would 'deal with the controversial question of whether a State may protect a non-national in the case of the violation of an obligation *erga omnes*'.[60] Presumably, as a result of the Commission's discussion of the First Report, this Article (and the proposed report on the issue[61]) was not produced. The consensus within the Commission was that the subject matter of initial draft Article 4 'was not yet ripe for the attention of the Commission' due to the insufficiency of state practice and *opinio iuris*.[62] Further, some Commission members insisted that a distinction must be maintained between human rights and diplomatic protection and that, 'because of the lack of clear understanding of the meaning and scope of *jus cogens*, the article created great difficulties', whereas others thought that as the rights and interests of the international community as a whole were at stake, and not simply those of nationals, the question did not fall within the ambit of diplomatic protection.[63] If the Commission thought that the implications of an injury caused to a national by a serious breach of a peremptory norm were unclear, then the capacity of a state to assert diplomatic protection in relation to a non-national injured by a violation of an obligation owed to the international community as a whole must have seemed even more opaque. The conclusion can only be that, with the demise of initial draft Article 4, the proposal for the related draft Article 10 evaporated.

VI. System criminality and the nationality of claims

While a state whose nationals have been injured by another's system criminality clearly may assert diplomatic protection to invoke the responsibility of the delinquent state, it is frequently the case – perhaps more often than not – that the sole or primary victims are the latter's nationals. In this situation, state responsibility affords few remedies to the injured as general international law provides no mechanism for individuals to invoke the responsibility of their national state. On the other hand, draft

[59] Dugard (n. 37) *Commentary to Draft Article 4*, 33 para. 88.

[60] Dugard (n. 37) *Commentary to Draft Article 4*, 34 para. 92, note 160.

[61] See Dugard (n. 37) 60 para. 185.

[62] International Law Commission (n. 17) *Commentary to Draft Article 4*, 78 para. 456; see 77–9 paras. 447–56.

[63] International Law Commission (n. 17) *Commentary to Draft Article 8*, 78 paras. 452 and 455.

Article 16 of the 2006 Draft Articles on Diplomatic Protection provides a general saving clause for remedies which may exist under specific regimes, such as human rights conventions:

> The rights of States, natural persons, legal persons or other entities to resort to international law to actions or procedures other than diplomatic protection to secure redress for injury suffered as a result of an internationally wrongful act, are not affected by the present draft articles.

The commentary makes clear that this ensures that remedies available under international law to nationals against their own state are preserved.[64]

Nevertheless, when discussing the subsequently excised initial draft Article 4, some members of the International Law Commission expressed the view that where a state systematically breached an obligation owed to the international community as a whole, 'States not only had the right but also the duty to act', but that this was a matter falling under the 'broader topic of State responsibility' rather than the umbrella of diplomatic protection.[65] Accordingly, the appropriate mechanism to invoke responsibility in order to counter the commission of acts of system criminality by a state against its own nationals lies in Article 48(1)(b). This allows a state, which is not an injured state, to invoke the responsibility of another which has breached an obligation owed to the international community as a whole and demand cessation of the wrongful act as well as assurances of non-repetition. It may also, by virtue of Article 48(2)(b), claim the 'performance of the obligation of reparation ... in the interest of the injured State or of the beneficiaries of the obligation breached'. The International Law Commission conceded that this was an example of progressive development.[66] Reparation in the interest of the injured state need not detain us, given the hypothesis that a state is injuring its own nationals,[67] but

[64] International Law Commission (n. 8) *Commentary to Draft Article 16*, 87–8 para. 3: see 86–9 generally.

[65] International Law Commission (n. 17) *Commentary to Draft Article 4*, 78 para. 455.

[66] International Law Commission (n. 7) *Commentary to Article 48*, 127 para. 12; and also Crawford (n. 11) *Commentary to Article 48*, 279 para. 12.

[67] The capacity of an interested state to invoke the responsibility of another on behalf of an injured state is not without difficulty, see International Law Commission (n. 7) *Commentary to Article 48*, 127, para. 12; Crawford (n. 11) *Commentary to Article 48*, 279 para. 12; and also I. Scobbie, 'The invocation of responsibility for the breach of "obligations under peremptory norms of general international law"' (2002) 13 EJIL 1213–15; the references in that paper to documents held on the Lauterpacht Research Centre website (www.law.cam.ac.uk/rcil) are no longer operative due to a reconfiguration of the

what forms of reparation may an interested state seek for 'the beneficiaries of the obligation breached', namely the injured individuals?

Article 34 of the Articles on State Responsibility provides that 'reparation for the injury caused by the internationally wrongful act shall take the form of restitution, compensation and satisfaction, either singly or in combination'. As the *Genocide in Bosnia* proceedings indicate, where system crimes such as genocide or torture have been committed, restitution is an unlikely remedy: it will generally be impossible to re-establish the situation that existed before the crime was committed. Reparation will therefore be effectuated by the payment of compensation for the injuries caused and/or some form of satisfaction such as an apology or an admission of wrongdoing by the delinquent state. Although the forms of reparation are clear, can these be sought by an interested state on behalf of non-nationals when it invokes the responsibility of another under Article 48?

Article 48.3 expressly makes the invocation of responsibility by an interested state subject to the same requirements as invocation by an injured state, which are contained in Articles 43–5. Article 44(a) provides that a state may not invoke the responsibility of another if 'the claim is not brought in accordance with any applicable rule relating to the nationality of claims', but deferred the definition of this rule to its work on diplomatic protection.[68] It is therefore difficult to comprehend the Commission's claim, made in the commentary to its Draft Articles on Diplomatic Protection, that the invocation of responsibility by an interested state under Article 48(1)(b) is not subject to the conditions set out in Article 44, including the nationality of claims rule.[69] Moreover, the commentary to Article 48 of the Articles on State Responsibility declares:

> a State invoking responsibility under article 48 and claiming anything more than a declaratory remedy and cessation may be called on to establish that it is acting in the interest of the injured party. Where the injured party is a State, its government will be able authoritatively to represent

site: corresponding references in this chapter where the URL starts www.lcil.cam.ac.uk, accessed 9 July 2008, are correct. I am well aware that this is a hostage to fortune.

[68] See International Law Commission (n. 7) *Commentary to Article 44*, 121 para. 2, n. 722; and also Crawford (n. 11) *Commentary to Article 44*, 264 para. 2, n. 722.

[69] International Law Commission (n. 8) *Commentary to Draft Article 16*, 87 para. 2, n. 245; compare E. Milano, 'Diplomatic protection and human rights before the International Court of Justice: re-fashioning tradition?' (2004) 35 NYIL 103–8; and Scobbie (n. 67) 1215–18.

> that interest. Other cases may present greater difficulties, which the present articles cannot solve.[70]

These difficulties were not addressed in the Commission's work on diplomatic protection, and are left untouched by the 2006 Draft Articles. This was guaranteed by its early repudiation of Dugard's initial draft Article 4 on the duty to protect nationals injured by a serious breach of a peremptory norm, and the presumably consequential abandonment of the examination of the protection of non-nationals injured by a violation of an obligation owed to the international community as a whole. The draft Articles on diplomatic protection are predicated on the link of nationality and thus preclude the protection of non-nationals. This ensures that the communitarian promise of Article 48(1)(b) remains largely ineffective. For confirmation, one need only consider draft Article 8 on the protection of refugees. If a state cannot seek remedies for non-nationals established within its territory for injuries caused by their national state, how can it seek the 'performance of the obligation of reparation' for those with whom it lacks all connection? How could it establish that it was acting in their interest?

VII. Interested states acting in their own interest

Nevertheless, an interested state, acting on its own behalf, may invoke another's responsibility for an act of system criminality committed against the latter's own nationals. Rather than seek to obtain reparation for injured non-nationals, an interested state could, for example, seek to obtain a declaratory judgment that the delinquent state is in breach of an obligation owed to the international community as a whole.[71] The *Minority schools* case[72] provides an apposite analogy. Germany alleged that Poland had breached the terms of the 1922 German–Polish Convention regarding Upper Silesia in its treatment of Polish nationals who wished to attend schools established for the ethnic German minority in Polish Upper Silesia. It did not seek reparation in this action, either for itself or for the Polish nationals involved, but rather a declaratory judgment regarding the proper interpretation of the specified provisions

[70] International Law Commission (n. 7) *Commentary to Article 48*, 127–8 para. 12; and also Crawford (n. 11) *Commentary to Article 48*, 279 para. 12.

[71] The availability of this remedy requires that various procedural and jurisdictional conditions are met, see Scobbie (n. 67) 1218–19.

[72] *Rights of Minorities in Upper Silesia (Minority schools)* case (Germany v Poland) (1928) PCIJ, Ser.A, No.15.

of the German–Polish Convention. The compromissory clause of the German–Polish Convention was unusual:

> Article 72, paragraph 3, is the literal reproduction of Article 12 of the Minorities Treaty of June 28th, 1919, and of analogous provisions of other treaties. The jurisdiction conferred by this clause is in every respect very particular in character and goes beyond the province of general international law; for Article 72, paragraph 3, confers on every Power being a Member of the Council [of the League of Nations] … the right of appealing to the Court, and such judicial action is based upon stipulations which relate not to rights of the applicant State or to those of its nationals on whose behalf it might take action, but to the relations between the respondent State and its own nationals.[73]

The legal situation established under Article 72(3) is akin to that envisaged in Article 48(1)(a) of the Articles on State Responsibility, as the German–Polish Convention was concluded to ensure the application of provisions of the Minorities Treaty to the entire area of Upper Silesia. These were 'obligations of international concern … placed under the guarantee of the League of Nations',[74] and thus the matter had a wider significance than the mere breach of a bilateral treaty.

Similarly, a convention-based remedy may be available to an interested state in relation to the commission of a system crime. For instance, Article IX of the Genocide Convention provides:

> Disputes between the Contracting Parties relating to the interpretation, application or fulfilment of the present Convention, including those relating to the responsibility of a State for genocide or for any of the other acts enumerated in Article III, shall be submitted to the International Court of Justice at the request of any of the parties to the dispute.

The significance of Article IX is that it provides a jurisdictional title to an interested state wishing to invoke the responsibility of another under the Genocide Convention. Moreover, in the *Armed activities (Congo v Rwanda)* case, the International Court of Justice affirmed that the prohibition of genocide was a peremptory norm and also that the Convention gave rise to obligations owed to the international community as a whole.[75] It takes no great conceptual leap to posit that a similar remedy must exist in relation

[73] *Minority schools* case (n. 72) dissenting opinion of Judge Huber 50.

[74] *Minority schools* case (n. 72) 9.

[75] *Armed activities on the territory of the Congo* (n. 2) 31–2 para. 64. In this case, Rwanda had excluded Article IX by reservation, and thus the Genocide Convention could not function as a basis of jurisdiction in the case (n. 2) 33 para. 70. This conclusion was strenuously criticized by some judges, see the dissenting opinion of Judge Koroma

to the customary prohibition of genocide, albeit under Article 48(1)(b) rather than 48(1)(a). If an interested state may invoke the responsibility of another and seek a declaratory judgment in relation to the breach of a treaty protecting a collective interest for a limited group of states, and for the breach of a conventional obligation which has peremptory status, surely it may also rely on the doctrine of obligations owed to the international community as a whole in order to enforce a customary peremptory norm?[76]

VIII. Does state responsibility provide an adequate response to system criminality?

The aims of the ascription of responsibility to a state for system criminality encompass the termination of the unlawful conduct and prevention of its repetition; the vindication and confirmation of fundamental norms of the international legal system; and the reconciliation of the parties. When faced with system criminality in the form of genocide, torture, or widespread or systematic breaches of the law of armed conflict which is authorized, condoned, required or encouraged by a state, the remedies available to other states under the law of state responsibility still depend on the nationality of the injured individuals. Despite the development of the doctrines of peremptory norms of international law and obligations owed to the international community as a whole, state responsibility principally remains confined within a bilateral straitjacket and has made little progress towards communitarian responses to serious breaches of international law, including the commission of system criminality. As Judge Trindade observed in the *Myrna Mack Chang* case, we live in 'an international community that is still seeking a greater degree of cohesion and solidarity'.

If a state is, by virtue of the *Mavrommatis* fiction, an injured state because its nationals have been victims, then it may assert diplomatic protection on their behalf and pursue all the forms of reparation available – restitution, compensation and satisfaction – as well as cessation of the delict and guarantees of non-repetition. These remedies, however, are often not coextensive with the injury caused as, typically,

(55), and the joint separate opinion of Judges Higgins, Kooijmans, Elaraby, Owada and Simma (65).

[76] For a much more elaborate argument along these lines, see A. Vermeer-Kunzli, 'A matter of interest: diplomatic protection and State responsibility erga omnes' (2007) 56 ICLQ 553.

a state involved in the commission of system criminality is more intent on harming its own nationals rather than aliens. By virtue of the nationality of claims rule, a state cannot protect the nationals of another and thus cannot obtain reparation on their behalf.

Where the injured individuals are non-nationals, a state wishing to invoke the responsibility of the delinquent is in the position of an interested state, and the remedies available to it are limited. Apart from taking lawful measures under Article 54 of the Articles on State Responsibility, it has the right to seek cessation and guarantees of non-repetition of the impugned conduct and, given the existence of a jurisdictional link, a declaratory judgment recording the unlawful conduct of the delinquent state. There is some authority which indicates that states have a duty to pursue these remedies,[77] but interested states have no right to demand reparation for 'the beneficiaries of the obligation breached'. No doubt this may be sought in diplomatic negotiations, but that is an extra-legal remedy occurring outside the framework of the law of state responsibility.

In the abstract, state responsibility provides the possibility of achieving an adequate response to system criminality on some levels. States may seek to end the wrongdoing and obtain assurances that it will not be repeated. Simply by invoking the responsibility of the delinquent, states reaffirm the validity of the norms breached, which may also be authoritatively confirmed in judicial proceedings brought by an injured or interested state. If the latter occurs, then that may provide 'the most natural mode of satisfaction', namely a determination of wrongdoing, which in turn could contribute to the reconciliation of the parties.

In practice, the law of state responsibility is an unwieldy instrument through which to seek redress. Its implementation cannot rise above the implications of sovereignty, which is the dominant conceptual structure of international law. Because this underlies both the possibility of system criminality committed by a state and the remedial mechanisms provided by state responsibility, although substantive international law might clearly indicate that the delinquent is responsible, it is often – perhaps more often than not – difficult to enforce the law. A state, whether injured or interested, may invoke the responsibility of another to call it to account for its system criminality, but this guarantees neither remedy

[77] See International Law Commission (n. 17) *Commentary to Draft Article 4*, 78 para. 455.

nor resolution. As Kelman has observed, system criminality frequently occurs in time of crisis when a government thinks its legitimacy is being challenged or that the state is under threat.[78] In these circumstances, invoking the responsibility of that state might simply be an exercise in talking to the profoundly deaf.

[78] See, e.g., H. C. Kelman, 'The policy context of international crimes', this volume, Chapter 2, and Kelman (n. 1) 'The policy context of torture' 128–9.

13

State responsibility for international crimes

ANDREAS ZIMMERMANN* AND
MICHAEL TEICHMANN**

I. Introduction

In the ILC Articles on State Responsibility, as they were taken note of by the General Assembly in 2001,[1] the very term of 'crimes' is missing in the overall codification of the law of state responsibility.[2] Even if the term as such has vanished, be it considered a positive or a negative development,[3] it remains to be seen whether instances of 'state criminality' indeed do give rise to specific consequences when it comes down to the law of state responsibility, and if so, what consequences could arise.[4]

Yet there exists, at least *grosso modo,* a significant overlap between the notion of 'system criminality' on the one hand, and that one remaining from the concept of state crimes in the ILC Articles on State

* Prof Dr jur, LLM (Harvard), Director Walther-Schücking-Institute of International Law, University of Kiel.

** Rechtsreferendar, Hanseatisches Oberlandesgericht, Research Assisstant, Helmut-Schmidt-Universität – University of the Federal Armed Forces Hamburg and PhD Student, University of Kiel.

[1] UNGA Res 56/83 (12 December 2001) UN Doc A/RES/56/83.

[2] A. Pellet, 'The new draft Articles of the International Law Commission on the Responsibility of States for Internationally Wrongful Acts: a requiem for states' crime' (2001) 32 NYIL 58.

[3] Pellet (n. 2) 65; see also E. Wyler, 'From "state crime" to responsibility for serious breaches of obligations under peremptory norms of general international law' (2002) 13 EJIL 1159 *et seq.*; for critical remarks against the concept of international crimes see also C. Tomuschat, 'International crimes by states: an endangered species?', in K. Wellens (ed.), *International Law: Theory and Practice – Essays in Honour of Eric Suy* (Martinus Nijhoff, Leiden/Boston 1998), p. 269 and I. Buffard, 'Was wurde aus den internationalen Verbrechen?', in I. Marboe (ed.), *Zwangsarbeiter und Restitution, Streitbeilegungsverfahren im internationalen Wirtschaftsrecht, Dialog der Zivilisationen, Staatenverantwortlichkeit – 26. Österreichischer Völkerrechtstag 14.-16. Juni 2001* (Diplomatische Akademie, Wien 2002), p. 165.

[4] Pellet (n. 2) 67 *et seq.*; see also M. Milanović, 'State responsibility for genocide' (2006) 17 EJIL 559 *et seq.*

Responsibility on the other, namely the concept of serious breaches of peremptory norms of international law,[5] as provided for in Articles 40 and 41 of said articles. Therefore, for the sake of briefness, the term 'state crimes' will henceforth interchangeably be used, although there might exist some specific distinctions between the notion of 'state crimes', 'serious breaches of peremptory norms', and instances of 'state criminality'.[6]

II. The content of the international responsibility of a state in cases of 'international crimes'

There are several different issues arising with regard to the question whether international crimes are specific as to the consequences they entail under the law of state responsibility, namely whether: (1) they are specific in entailing an obligation to guarantee future non-repetition;[7] (2) they also entail an obligation to substantially change the domestic legal and political order that brought about such crimes;[8] (3) they entail an obligation for the responsible state to punish individual offenders as a specific form of satisfaction;[9] (4) such state crimes carry with them the obligation to pay punitive damages;[10] (5) there is an obligation of non-recognition of situations brought about by such international crimes;[11] and, finally, (6) third states may deny state immunity in cases of 'international crimes' as part of a special regime of state responsibility.[12]

In the following, these questions will now be analyzed one by one, starting with the question whether the guarantee of non-repetition is specific to 'international crimes'.

1. *'International crimes' and the guarantee of non-repetition*

In this regard the analysis can be rather brief, since the obligation to offer a guarantee of non-repetition in cases of a violation of any primary rule of international law seems by now to have become generally accepted.[13] In particular, it was the International Court of Justice, which has in several

[5] See W. Czapliński, 'UN Codification of Law of State Responsibility' (2003) 41 AVR 71 *et seq.*

[6] Wyler (n. 3) 1151 *et seq.* [7] See below. [8] See below p. 301.

[9] See below p. 302. [10] See below p. 306. [11] See below p. 307. [12] See below p. 311.

[13] G. Palmisano, 'Les garanties de non-repitition entre codification et réalisation juridictionelle du droit: a propos de l'affaire LaGrand' (2002) 106 RGDIP 781.

cases – starting with the *LaGrand* case,[14] through the *Avena* case[15] up to the case between the *DRC and Uganda*[16] – taken note of the respective request for such a guarantee by the applicant and has acknowledged in each of these cases that the responsible state had, in one way or another, already given such guarantee.

In the *Bosnian Genocide* case, after having rejected Serbia's own responsibility for genocidal acts in Bosnia,[17] the ICJ has not found sufficient grounds for requiring guarantees of non-repetition in regard of Serbia's failure to prevent and to punish genocide and consequently regarded them as being inappropriate for the present case.[18] This was due, however, to the specific circumstances of the case and, probably, not least to the fact that the conflict had ended by 1995, i.e. twelve years before the judgment had been handed down. That judgment should therefore not be taken as an indication that guarantees of non-repetition are generally inappropriate in cases of violations of duties to prevent and to punish international crimes.

Accordingly, there seems to be no doubt that, as of today, and contrary to the arguments brought forward by the United States in the *LaGrand* case,[19] the obligation to offer a guarantee of non-repetition has become part and parcel of customary international law,[20] regardless of the character of the underlying violation of international law.[21] Indeed, both *LaGrand* and *Avena* did deal with 'simple' violations of international law certainly not amounting to 'international crimes'. This *general* application of the obligation to provide a guarantee of non-repetition is also confirmed by the fact that such obligation is contained in Article 30 of the ILC Articles on State Responsibility,[22] i.e. in the general part of

[14] *Germany v United States of America*, LaGrand, Merits [2001] ICJ Rep 513.

[15] *Mexico v United States of America*, Avena and Other Mexican Nationals, Merits [2004] ICJ Rep 69.

[16] *Democratic Republic of the Congo v Uganda*, Armed Activities on the Territory of the Congo, Merits [2005] para. 257.

[17] *Bosnia and Herzegovina v Serbia and Montenegro*, Application of the Convention on the Prevention and Punishment of the Crime of Genocide, Merits [2007] para. 415.

[18] *Bosnia and Herzegovina v Serbia and Montenegro* (n. 17) para. 466.

[19] *Germany v United States of America* (n. 14) 509–10.

[20] Palmisano (n. 13) 781.

[21] See E. Lambert-Abdelgawad, 'La spécifité des reparations pour crimes internationaux', in C. Tomuschat and J.-M. Thouvenin (eds.), *The Fundamental Rules of the International Legal Order* (Martinus Nijhoff, Leiden/Boston 2006), p. 179.

[22] See Commentary on Art. 30 in J. Crawford, *The International Law Commission's Articles on State Responsibility – Introduction, Text and Commentaries* (Cambridge University Press, Cambridge 2003), p. 198.

Part Two and not in Chapter III thereof, dealing with serious breaches of peremptory norms.

It remains to be seen, however, whether the guarantee of non-repetition, as one of the consequences of an internationally wrongful act contemplated in Article 30 of the ILC Articles on State Responsibility, entails specific consequences in instances of international crimes.[23]

2. *State crimes and the possible obligation of the responsible state to alter its domestic political system*

It has indeed been argued that instances of state crimes should lead to an obligation of the responsible state to change its domestic constitutional structure. As A. de Hoogh had put it:

> That State [responsible for international crimes] will further be under an obligation to change its government, to change its constitution to the extent necessary, and to hold free elections so as to prevent the recurrence of criminal acts.[24]

While such ensuing domestic changes are, politically speaking, more than welcome in most, if not all, situations of system criminality, it cannot be argued that they are required under international law as a consequence of previously committed state crimes. Apart from a lack of relevant state practice in that regard as a matter of law, any such proposition is also contradicted by the consideration that even in instances of state-induced widespread violations of basic norms of international law, there is not necessarily a real danger of repetition even without such regime change.

As a matter of fact, such international crimes might have occurred during a war fought in the exercise of the right of self-defence under Article 51 of the Charter, where the military forces of the victim state have committed war crimes on a significant scale, or where they might have used reprisals against protected persons in violation of applicable norms of international humanitarian law. As deplorable as such actions clearly are, such violations of international law must not necessarily lead to a change in the governmental structure of a given state, since, even without such regime change, the danger of repetition might have simply ended

[23] For such a proposition see, *inter alia*, A. de Hoogh, *Obligations Erga Omnes and International Crimes* (Kluwer, The Hague 1996), p. 195: 'scope of guarantees against repetition … ought to be extended in case of international crimes …'

[24] De Hoogh (n. 23) 179.

with the very military conflict or with the exemplary punishment of individual offenders, be it by domestic courts, be it by international criminal tribunals.

Besides, it is worth having a look at the crime of aggression[25] as a further example of a violation of a *jus cogens norm*.[26] It is hard to believe that violations of the prohibition of the use of force, even when committed by democratic states, should lead to a regime change – and if so, to what form of regime change? Furthermore, one also wonders how to reconcile such a proposition of a mandatory regime change forming part of the law of state responsibility with the very idea underlying Article 43 of the Hague Regulation on Land Warfare.[27]

Finally, it was the International Court of Justice which, in all cases, where it had affirmed guarantees of non-repetition as requested by the applicant state, considered it sufficient that the respondent state had either entered into a treaty obligation or had made a binding unilateral statement to that effect – including the case between the *DRC and Uganda*[28] which, *inter alia*, addressed not only violations of the sovereignty and territorial integrity of the victim state, but also serious violations of human rights and international humanitarian law.[29]

3. *State crimes and the obligation to punish individual offenders as a specific form of satisfaction*

Yet another question involves the issue whether serious breaches within the meaning of Article 40 of the ILC Articles on State Responsibility attributable to a given state, i.e. 'international crimes', entail the obligation to punish those individuals who acted on behalf of said state. This is a particularly relevant question in situations where the individuals concerned are *de facto* not subject to the criminal jurisdiction of third states,

[25] The Rome Statute of the International Criminal Court (ICC) by virtue of its Art. 5(1)(d) *de jure* confers jurisdiction over the crime of aggression upon the ICC. However, pending the adoption of a provision in accordance with Arts. 121 and 123, defining the crime and setting out the conditions under which the Court shall act, it may not exercise its jurisdiction with respect to this crime, Art. 5(2), see R. Kherad, 'La question de la définition du crime d'agression dans le Statut de Rome' (2005) 109 RGDIP 331.

[26] On the *jus cogens* nature of the prohibition of aggression see Commentary on Art. 40 in Crawford (n. 22) 246.

[27] See N. Haupais, 'Les obligations de la puissance occupante au regard de la jurisprudence et de la pratique récentes' (2007) 111 RGDIP 125.

[28] *Armed Activities on the Territory of the Congo* (n. 16) para. 257.

[29] *Armed Activities on the Territory of the* Congo (n. 16) paras. 220, 250.

or where, in the alternative, they enjoy immunity with regard to criminal proceedings in such third states.

Arangio-Ruiz in his Seventh Report as Special Rapporteur[30] had still contemplated the obligation of states, which were responsible for international crimes, either to prosecute or to extradite the respective offenders. Yet, the current ILC Articles on State Responsibility have not followed that approach. Instead, Article 37 of the ILC Articles, the scope of application of which, however, extends to all kind of violations of international law and is, therefore, not limited to serious breaches thereof, simply provides that satisfaction, apart from acknowledgment of the breach,[31] an expression of regret[32] or a formal apology,[33] might also include 'other appropriate modalities'. The authoritative commentary of the ILC on Article 37(2)[34] then further provides that such 'other modalities' might include, depending on the circumstances, penal action against the individuals whose conduct caused the internationally wrongful act.

Two questions have to be distinguished in that regard, namely: *first*, whether such an obligation to punish does exist and if so to what extent;[35] and, *second*, where such obligation derives from.[36]

As to the first question, it can be argued that at the current state of international law, there clearly is an obligation to punish individuals who have committed those acts we are currently considering first and foremost, namely acts of genocide, crimes against humanity and war crimes. With regard to genocide, such an obligation is clearly enshrined in Article VI of the Genocide Convention.[37] With regard to war crimes committed in international armed conflicts, such obligation is inherent in the very concept of grave breaches as provided for in the four Geneva Conventions[38] and Additional Protocol I.[39] Yet, even beyond those treaty obligations *stricto sensu*, it can be argued that such obligation does not

[30] A/CN.4/469 [and Corr 1] and Add 1 and 2.

[31] See Commentary on Art. 37 in Crawford (n. 22) 231 *et seq*.

[32] Crawford (n. 31). [33] Crawford (n. 31). [34] Crawford (n. 31).

[35] For a comprehensive analysis on this topic, see C. Tomuschat, 'The duty to prosecute international crimes committed by individuals' in H. J. Cremer, T. Giegerich, D. Richter and A. Zimmermann (eds.), *Tradition und Weltoffenheit des Rechts: Festschrift für Helmut Steinberger* (Springer, Berlin 2002), p. 315.

[36] In favour of such an obligation also as a secondary obligation, de Hoogh (n. 23) 195.

[37] *Bosnia and Herzegovina v Serbia and Montenegro* (n. 17) paras. 439–50; see also M. Milanović (n. 4) 571.

[38] Art. 49 Geneva Convention I; Art. 50 Geneva Convention II; Art. 129 Geneva Convention III; Art. 146 Geneva Convention IV.

[39] Art. 85 Protocol I.

only exist for the respective territorial state, but that its scope, *ratione personae,* extends beyond.[40] Besides, taking into account recent state practice, it seems that such an obligation to punish individual offenders also relates to war crimes committed in non-international armed conflicts, as well as to crimes against humanity, the preamble of the Rome Statute just being one example of a wide-spread *opinio juris* to that effect.[41] Furthermore, human rights monitoring bodies such as, for example, the Inter-American Court on Human Rights, as well as the Human Rights Committee have, and rightfully so, confirmed that states are under a positive obligation to 'prevent, investigate and punish any violation of the rights recognized by the Convention', as stated by the Inter-American Court.[42] Similarly, there is at least a tendency not to recognize as valid amnesties with regard to acts of genocide, crimes against humanity and war crimes,[43] the jurisprudence of the Special Court for Sierra Leone Special being the latest example.[44]

Yet, the question arises whether, conceptually, such a duty to prosecute forms part of a primary obligation, or whether it rather is a secondary obligation forming part of the law of state responsibility. The Genocide Convention and its Article VI might serve as an example in that regard. When reading Article VI of the Genocide Convention, it becomes clear that the obligation to punish acts of genocide indeed forms part of a separate treaty obligation incurred by the contracting parties, any lack of such punishment then giving rise to state responsibility of the unwilling state.[45] Accordingly, the commission of acts of genocide by organs of a

[40] The ICJ has rejected Bosnia and Herzegovina's claim that Serbia and Montenegro had violated Art. VI of the Genocide Convention by not having exercised criminal prosecution of responsible individuals and held that Art. VI obliges only the state on whose territory the genocidal acts have been committed, see *Bosnia and Herzegovina v Serbia and Montenegro* (n. 17) paras 439–42; for a dissenting view, see P. Weckel, 'L'Arrêt sur le génocide: le soufflé de l'avis de 1951 n'a pas transporté la Cour' (2007) 111 RGDIP 328.

[41] In favour of such an obligation regarding war crimes in non-international armed conflicts, Tomuschat (n. 35) 334.

[42] *Velasquez Rodriguez v Honduras* (29 July 1988) IACHR para. 166.

[43] See C. Tomuschat (n. 35) 343 *et seq.*; J. Gavron, 'Amnesties in the light of developments in international law and the establishment of the International Criminal Court' (2002) 51 ICLQ 116.

[44] On 13 March 2004, the Appeals Chamber of the Special Court ruled that the amnesty granted under Article IX of the Lomé Peace Agreement does not bar the prosecution of an accused for international crimes committed before July 1999 before the Special Court, Case No.SCSL-2004–15-PT, Case No.SCSL-2004–16-PT (*Prosecutor v Kallon and Kamara*).

[45] *Bosnia and Herzegovina v Serbia and Montenegro* (n. 17) para. 425.

state, or by individuals whose acts can be attributed to that state, and the non-punishment of such individuals stand side by side as two separate violations of international law. Put differently, it means that the obligation to punish acts of genocide does not simply constitute a consequence of a state organ having previously committed genocide.[46]

This approach was, once again, if there was need, confirmed by the submissions in the Bosnian *Genocide* case. In this case, counsel for Bosnia and Herzegovina rightfully claimed that any *non-prosecution* and *lack of punishment* of acts of genocide would amount to separate violations of the Convention standing side by side with the acts of genocide allegedly committed by the respondent state. Bosnia did not, however, claim that Serbia and Montenegro, and now Serbia, as well as Montenegro, did have an obligation to punish offenders by virtue of being responsible for acts of genocide.[47] The Court in its judgment in turn found that Serbia had not committed genocide, but affirmed, however, that Serbia had violated its obligations under the Convention by having failed fully to cooperate with the International Criminal Tribunal for the former Yugoslavia.[48] Similar considerations would then apply, *mutatis mutandis,* to war crimes and crimes against humanity.

There is, however, at least one more reason why the obligation to punish genocide, crimes against humanity and war crimes and other forms of 'system criminality' is to be considered an autonomous obligation, and therefore does not form part of a specific regime of state responsibility.[49] Under Article 40(2) of the ILC Articles on State Responsibility, violations of a given primary norm only constitute 'serious breaches' provided they involve a gross or systematic failure to fulfil such obligation. Accordingly, and provided one were to consider the duty to punish to constitute a secondary obligation under the law of state responsibility, any such obligation would then only exist once acts of genocide or war crimes had been committed on a wide-scale basis or in a systematic manner.[50] It seems, however, to be beyond doubt that even isolated grave breaches of the Geneva Conventions or single acts of genocide trigger the obligation to punish the respective offender. This is yet another reason, both from a positivistic point of view, but

46 *Bosnia and Herzegovina v Serbia and Montenegro* (n. 17) paras. 439–42.

47 *Bosnia and Herzegovina v Serbia and Montenegro* (n. 17) paras. 64–5.

48 *Bosnia and Herzegovina v Serbia and Montenegro* (n. 17) para. 471.

49 See, in that regard, C. J. Tams, 'Do serious breaches give rise to any specific obligation of the responsible state?' (2002) 13 EJIL 1161, 1178.

50 But see also the viable comments of Wyler (n. 3) 1157 *et seq*.

also policy-wise, why any obligation to punish international crimes should not be considered as constituting a specific feature of the law of state responsibility.

This leads to the next issue, namely the issue of possible punitive damages.

4. *State crimes and the issue of punitive damages*[51]

The very issue of punitive damages evolved significantly during the drafting of the ILC Articles on State Responsibility. The 1996 Draft Articles had still provided in its then Article 45 that in *any* case of 'gross infringement of the rights of the injured State', that state would have been entitled to damages 'reflecting the gravity of the infringement'.[52] It was in 2000 that James Crawford proposed to limit the scope of application of the notion of punitive damages to serious breaches owed to the international community as a whole, and, moreover, tried to avoid the very notion of punitive damages altogether by instead referring to 'damages reflecting the gravity of the breach', while keeping the concept as such alive.[53] It was, however, already the drafting committee of the ILC, and later the ILC overall, which rejected this very idea, which would also have amounted to a clear progressive development and not just a codification of international law[54] and which had also not found much support among states, to say the least.

As a matter of fact, international tribunals have, certain old exceptions notwithstanding, by and large rejected the idea of punitive damages including the Inter-American Court of Human Rights in the *Velasquez-Rodriguez* case, which stated that the idea of awarding damages to deter or to serve as an example 'is not applicable in international law'[55] – a result expressed even more forcefully in one of the concurring opinions in the *Letelier* arbitration.[56]

It is therefore not surprising and in line with the *lex lata* that the claims for compensation in the Bosnian *Genocide* case were limited, apart from material damage, to '*financially assessable damage* which corresponds to damage caused to natural persons … including

[51] See in that regard in particular the extensive studies by N. Jørgenson, 'A reapraisal of punitive damages in international law' (1997) 68 *British Yearbook of International Law* 247 *et seq.*; as well as S. Wittich, 'Awe of the gods and fear of the priests: punitive damages and the law of state responsibility' (1998) 3 ARIEL 101 *et seq.*

[52] YILC (1996) vol. II 63. [53] See Pellet (n. 2) 72. [54] Pellet (n. 2) 72.

[55] Cf. Wittich (n. 51) 138. [56] Wittich (n. 51) 138.

non-material damage suffered by the victims',[57] but did not extent to anything beyond and thus did not include punitive damages despite the fact that, if ever something would be a prototype situation of punitive damages, it certainly would be the acts of genocide allegedly committed by the respondent state in that case.[58]

Accordingly, it seems that, while the concept of punitive or exemplary damages, if implemented, would have constituted the most spectacular development with regard to the law of state responsibility in instances of system criminality,[59] the time simply does not seem ripe yet for international law and its main actors, states, to endorse such concepts, even if certain federal courts in the United States have claimed the contrary to be true.[60]

5. *State crimes and the obligation of non-recognition*

The duty of non-recognition provided for in Article 41(2) of the ILC Articles on State Responsibility with regard to situations created by serious breaches of peremptory norms of international law *incumbent upon third states* is probably one of the most important, if not *the* most important consequence forming part of the special regime of violations of fundamental rules of the international legal order.[61] It demonstrates the international community's legal interest that serious breaches as defined in Article 40 of the ILC Articles on State Responsibility are not committed.

This obligation of non-recognition has, first and foremost, been developed with regard to illegal *de facto* control over territory, the 1971 Namibia Advisory Opinion[62] and the 2004 Wall Advisory Opinion[63] of the ICJ obviously being the most prominent and important steps in that direction. In such a situation, third states are no doubt under an obligation not to recognize as legal the situation prevailing on the ground. It seems

[57] *Bosnia and Herzegovina v Serbia and Montenegro* (n. 17) para. 66 (emphasis added).

[58] It should also be noted that the Court, in its judgment, rejected the Bosnian request for financial compensation altogether: see *Bosnia and Herzegovina v Serbia and Montenegro* (n. 17) para. 462.

[59] Tams (n. 49) 1166.

[60] *Filártiga v Peña-Irala*, 630 F 2d 876 (2d Cir 1980).

[61] Pellet (n. 2) 70 *et seq*.

[62] *Legal Consequences for States of the Continued Presence of South Africa in Namibia (South West Africa) notwithstanding Security Council Resolution 276 (1970)* (Advisory Opinion) [1971] ICJ Rep 16 54 *et seq*.

[63] *Legal Consequences of the Construction of a Wall in the Occupied Palestinian Territory* (Advisory Opinion) [2004] ICJ Rep 136, 200.

to be more difficult to conceptualize, however, the duty of non-recognition in cases of genocide or other forms of violations of fundamental human rights. Stefan Talmon has rightly pointed out[64] that the essential function of non-recognition is to counter an asserted legal status such as statehood, or a title to territory arising from a given factual situation. No such claims to status or title will, however, normally arise in the context of genocide, torture or violations of basic rules of international humanitarian law. This is particularly true where such violations have not given rise to territorial changes, be it because the responsible state was *de facto* militarily unsuccessful in bringing about such changes, be it because the background of such violations was a purely non-international armed conflict.[65]

Nevertheless, even in such situations one might still discern a possible scope of application for an obligation of non-recognition contained in Article 41(2) of the ILC Articles on State Responsibility. The first such example would relate to private property which was *de facto* expropriated by way of acts of genocide or similar crimes, be it that the owners were killed or that they were forced to leave their homes and valuables behind when fleeing, the responsible state attempting to acquire title to such private property. It can be argued that in such a situation third states are, under Article 41(2) of the ILC Articles, when acting as a forum state for private claims, obliged to consider such acts of the responsible state as null and void. Such examples could, for example, relate to looted cultural objects.

Yet another situation might concern a government which has been brought about or been maintained by committing serious breaches as defined in Article 40 of the ILC Articles, such as, for example, the crime of apartheid. If one were to take Article 41(2) of the ILC Articles seriously, third states would be under an obligation neither to enter into dealings with such a government, nor to recognize them as legitimate, the humanitarian exception contemplated in the Namibian advisory opinion[66] notwithstanding. Accordingly, the otherwise doubtful practice of the United Nations with regard to the South African credentials issue[67]

[64] S. Talmon, 'The duty not to recognize as lawful a situation created by the illegal use of force or other serious breaches of a jus cogens obligation: an obligation without real substance?', in C. Tomuschat and J.-M. Thouvenin (eds.), *The Fundamental Rules of the International Legal Order* (Martinus Nijhoff, Leiden/Boston 2006), p. 107.

[65] Talmon (n. 64).

[66] *Legal Consequences for States of the Continued Presence of South Africa in Namibia (South West Africa) notwithstanding Security Council Resolution 276 (1970)* (n. 62) para. 125.

[67] Abbot, Augusti, Brown, Rode, 'The General Assembly, 29th Session: The Decrendialization of South Africa' (1975) 16 *Harvard Journal of International Law* 576; E. Klein, 'Zur

might, all of a sudden, appear in a somewhat different light. State practice in that regard is, however, to say the least, not uniform and, unfortunately, seems to be still willing, certain exceptions notwithstanding, to accept the respective effective government as being the legitimate one regardless of its pedigree.

Furthermore, one might also wonder whether there is no linkage between the notion of serious breaches of international law, Article 41(2) of the ILC Articles on State Responsibility and a possible waiver with regard to the exercise of diplomatic protection.[68] Under international law there is no obligation for states to exercise diplomatic protection. The question accordingly arises what can be drawn from a state's decision not to exercise its right to diplomatic protection. For example one might wonder whether a potential waiver to exercise diplomatic protection on behalf of a group of persons, who have been tortured or subjected to inhuman treatment, could not amount to an implicit recognition of the legality of the underlying serious breach of international law. As a matter of fact, one could indeed argue that the idea underlying Article 41(2) is that the illegal situation, created by a serious breach of international law, should not be petrified, and that instead efforts should be made to reverse such a situation as provided for in Article 41(1) of the ILC Articles on State Responsibility. In contrast to this obligation, the fact that a state effectively waives its right to exercise diplomatic protection in a situation contemplated by Article 40 of the ILC Articles could be perceived as an (implicit) recognition prohibited by Article 41(2). One might, however, distinguish between a waiver of the substantive right, which would appear problematic in light of Article 41(2)[69] on the one hand, and a temporary non-exercise of all or specific forms of diplomatic protection on the other. The latter can certainly not be considered a violation of the duty provided for in Article 41(2) ILC Articles, given that any such purely temporary non-exercise of diplomatic protection in itself demonstrates that the underlying violation of international law has

Beschränkung von Mitgliedsrechten in den Vereinten Nationen' (1975) 23 *Vereinte Nationen* 51.

[68] See, most recently, E. Klein, 'Völkerrechtliche Grenzen des staatlichen Verzichts auf diplomatischen Schutz', in M. Dupuy, B. Fassbender, M. N. Shaw, K.-P. Sommermann (eds.), *Völkerrecht als Weltordnung, Festschrift für Christian Tomuschat* (NP Engel, Kehl 2006), pp. 361, 370 *et seq.*

[69] See, for such a proposition, also B. Graefrath, 'International crimes – a specific regime of international responsibility of States and its legal consequences', in J. Weiler *et al.* (eds.), *International Crimes of States* (de Gruyter, Berlin 1989), p. 165, and also Lambert-Abdelgawad (n. 21) 175.

not been recognized as legal – quite to the contrary.[70] This is even more true so since attempts by John Dugard, as the ILC's special rapporteur on diplomatic protection, to have an individual right of diplomatic protection been included in the ILC Draft Articles on Diplomatic Protection[71] have proved unsuccessful and no longer form part of them,[72] notwithstanding possible regional developments within the European Union, as exemplified by the recent jurisprudence of the European Court of First Instance.[73]

A borderline case would be a situation where the home state, instead of insisting on fulfilling its duty of non-recognition of situations brought about by *jus cogens* violations, enters into negotiations with the responsible state to bring about a situation which might at least improve, be it only partially, the situation of the victims. In that regard, the German Constitutional Court dealing with the consequences of Soviet expropriations in the then Soviet occupation zone of Germany, after quoting Articles 40 and 41 of the ILC Articles on State Responsibility, found in 2004 that such an approach is, even in case of *jus cogens* violations, legally tenable.[74] The court's decision stated that:

> if a factually established situation and differing political interests are involved, the states have merely a duty to cooperate with regard to the consequences [of the violation of a jus *cogens* norm]. Behind this duty of cooperation lies the consideration that it is urgently necessary to create a situation that, while safeguarding the interests on both sides, does actually mitigate the breach of peremptory law as far as possible.[75]

Eventually, one could try to reconcile this approach with Article 41(2) of the ILC Articles by taking into account the Namibia holding of the ICJ, where it stated that any non-recognition of the illegal South-African presence in Namibia should not adversely affect the people concerned.[76]

[70] See Klein (n. 68).

[71] ILC, 'First Report on Diplomatic Protection by the Special Rapporteur, Mr John R. Dugard' 52nd Session (1 May–9 June and 10 July–18 August 2000) 27, UN Doc A/CN.4/506.

[72] See ILC, *Report of the International Law Commission on the Work of its 58th Session* (1 May–9 June and 3 July–11 August 2006), p. 13 *et seq.*, UN Doc A/45/10.

[73] Case T-315/01 *Yassin Abdullah Kadi v Council and Commission* (21 September 2005) CFI para. 276.

[74] BVerfGE 112 1, 36; critical Klein (n. 68) 371.

[75] BVerfGE 112 1, 36 (authors' translation).

[76] *Legal Consequences for States of the Continued Presence of South Africa in Namibia (South West Africa) notwithstanding Security Council Resolution 276 (1970)* (n. 62) para. 125.

6. *State crimes and immunity*

Finally, one last question concerns the issue of state immunity for acts coming within the definition of Article 40 of the ILC Articles on State Responsibility.[77] In the *Ferrini* case, some authors have tried to interpret the attitude of the Italian *Corte de Cassazione* and its denial of immunity as a form of compliance with Article 41 of the ILC Articles on State Responsibility[78] although the court's decision refers to Article 40, but not to Article 41 of the ILC Articles.[79] Any such approach, however, raises significant issues.

First, state practice, including recent domestic decisions such as the British House of Lords decision in *Jones*,[80] is, to say the least, certainly not sufficiently uniform and abundant, and, besides, does neither include the states most concerned, to fulfil the criteria set up by the ICJ in the *North Sea Continental Shelf*[81] case in order for a short period of time to be sufficient to create a new norm of customary international law.

Second, the UN Immunity Convention adopted by the General Assembly in December 2004[82] provides no exception from immunity in cases of *jus cogens* violations.[83] In fact, the respective ILC working

[77] See T. Stein, 'Limits of international law immunities for senior state officials in criminal procedure', in C. Tomuschat and J.-M. Thouvenin (eds.), *The Fundamental Rules of the International Legal Order* (Martinus Nijhoff, Leiden/Boston 2006), p. 249.

[78] Text to be found in (2004) 87 *Rivista di diritto internazionale* 539; see also, for a more detailed analysis of that decision, P. de Sena and F. de Vittor, 'State immunity and human rights: the Italian Supreme Court decision on the Ferrini case' (2005) 16 EJIL 89; A. Bianchi, 'Case-note on *Ferrini v Federal Republic of Germany*' (2005) 99 AJIL 242.

[79] The relevant part of the decision reads in the original as follows:

> Èricorrente l'affermazione che i crimini internazionali «minacciano l'umanità intera e minano le fondamenta stesse della coesistenza internazionale» (così, ad es. Corte costituzionale di Ungheria 13 ottobre 1993, n. 53). Si tratta, infatti, di delitti che si concretano nella violazione, particolarmente grave per intensità o sistematicità (arg. *ex* articolo 40, secondo comma, del Progetto sulla responsabilità internazionale degli Stati, adottato nell'agosto del 2001 dalla Commissione di diritto internazionale dell'ONU), dei diritti fondamentali della persona umana, la cui tutela è affidata a norme inderogabili che si collocano al vertice dell'ordinamento internazionale, prevalendo su ogni altra norma, sia di carattere convenzionale che consuetudinario (Tribunale penale per la *ex* Jugoslavia, 10 dicembre 1998, Furunduzija, 153–155; 14 gennaio 2000, Kupreskic, 520; Corte europea dei diritti dell'uomo, 21 novembre 2001, Al–Adsani c. Regno Unito, 61) e, quindi, anche su quelle in tema di immunità.

[80] *Jones v Ministry of Interior Al-Mamlaka Al-Arabiya AS Saudiya (the Kingdom of Saudi Arabia) and others* [2006] UKHL 26.

[81] *North Sea Continental Shelf Cases* (Merits) [1969] ICJ Reports 4 para. 74.

[82] UNGA Res 59/38 (16 December 2004) UN Doc A/RES/59/38.

[83] E. Denza, 'The 2005 UN Convention on State Immunity in Perspective' (2006) 55 ICLQ 395, 397, 398; H. Fox, 'In defence of state immunity: why the UN Convention on State

group had in 1999, and thus at a time when the ILC Articles on State Responsibility were also still under consideration, made it plain that such an exception had been considered, but that no such exception had been agreed upon. If one were now to interpret Article 41(2) of the ILC Articles on State Responsibility as requiring a denial of state immunity, one would assume that the ILC had, at the very same time, taken two conflicting approaches.

Third, and maybe more important, it has to be stressed once more that state immunity is a procedural rule solely governing the jurisdiction of a national court. Neither does a judgment granting state immunity decide upon issues of substantive law;[84] nor does it recognize alleged serious breaches as legal or lawful, as provided for in Article 41(2) of the ILC Articles. They rather simply divert any dispute to an inter-state method of settlement.[85] Accordingly, denying state immunity is certainly not required by Article 41(2) of the ILC Articles on State Responsibility.

III. Concluding remarks

Regardless of whether one refers to 'international crimes' as 'crimes' or as 'serious breaches of international law' or as instances of 'system criminality', the essential point is that international law provides an arsenal of consequences a responsible state has to take into account when it commits such crimes. Even with this arsenal of weapons international law actually has at its disposal, it is not as comprehensive as some might wish by, for example not providing for punitive damages, or by not providing for the obligation to alter one's domestic legal or constitutional system, yet it still is a quite impressive one. It can be supposed that, instead of further

Immunity is important' (2006) 55 ICLQ 403; R. Gardiner, 'UN Convention on State Immunity: form and function' (2006) 55 ICLQ 409. Other commentators have criticized the Convention, and opposed ratification, precisely because (in the absence of an additional protocol, which they favour) the Convention does not deny state immunity in cases where *jus cogens* norms of international law are said to have been violated outside the forum state: see C. K. Hall, 'UN Convention on State Immunity: the need for a Human Rights Protocol' (2006) 55 ICLQ 411–26; L. McGregor, 'State immunity and jus cogens' (2006) 55 ICLQ 437–45. Note, however, also the Declaration made by Norway upon its accession to said Convention: '... *Finally, Norway understands that the Convention is without prejudice to any future international development in the protection of human rights.*'

84 See, for such a distinction, already A. Zimmermann, 'Sovereign immunity and violations of international jus cogens – some critical remarks' (1995) 16 *Michigan Journal of International Law* 433.

85 H. Fox QC, *The Law of State Immunity* (Oxford University Press, Oxford 2004), p. 525.

extending this set of tools, it is first and foremost necessary that states use them by all appropriate means at their disposal where serious breaches of international law have been or are in the process of being committed. It is therefore more on the *de facto* enforcement and implementation side that the law of state responsibility is weak – but that might, yet again, be another feature the law of state responsibility has in common with international criminal law.

14

Responses of political organs to crimes by states

NIGEL D. WHITE*

I. Introduction

It is worth making it clear at the outset that this chapter is not an essay on whether states can commit crimes under international law or whether, in the words of the International Law Commission's Articles on State Responsibility of 2001, they commit 'serious breaches of obligations under peremptory norms of general international law'.[1] The use of the phrase 'crimes by states' is intended to capture the often integral role of the state in aggression, genocide, crimes against humanity, torture and systematic war crimes.[2] The premise of the essay is that such acts, whether labelled crimes in a technical sense or not, should be confronted and stopped by the rest of the world, what is loosely termed here as the international community. It explores the international community's responses to such crimes beyond those limited avenues laid down by the principles of state responsibility. These have been labelled responses of political organs, to contrast them with the regime of international legal responsibility, though it will be shown that it is not always possible or desirable to keep them apart. It considers the deficiencies of the current political or institutional regime for dealing with crimes by states and explores ways of improving it. It is premised on there being a pressing need to develop a capability to *stop* crimes being committed by states, though responses can also be directed at *preventing* such crimes before they are committed or attempted, or indeed at *punishing* states for having committed them.

* Professor of International Law, University of Sheffield, UK.

1 ILC Articles on Responsibility of States for Internationally Wrongful Acts 2001, Chapter III. For discussion, see J. Crawford, *The International Law Commission's Articles on State Responsibility* (Cambridge University Press, Cambridge 2002), pp. 243–4.

2 For an interesting discussion of modernity and state crimes, see M. Mann, *The Dark Side of Democracy: Explaining Ethnic Cleansing* (Cambridge University Press, Cambridge 2004). See also Z. Baumann, *Modernity and the Holocaust* (Cornell University Press, Ithaca, NY 1989).

II. Background

It is technically correct to state that, following the setting aside of the concept of 'international crimes of states' by the International Law Commission in 1998, the regime of state responsibility is an 'undifferentiated' one, which is based on there being no separation of civil and criminal liability.[3] However, 'this does not prevent international law responding in different ways to different kinds of breaches and to their different impacts on other states, on people and on international order'.[4] Further, this chapter argues that serious breaches by states of peremptory norms of international law necessitate more significant responses both under the rules of state responsibility, and by the political organs of international organizations, though this has not yet developed into a legal duty. Though there is no clearly differentiated responsibility in international law and thus it is not possible to state that there are state crimes in a fully legal sense, it is contended that it is still possible to label the types of breach in question as crimes by states, since they can elicit a different range of responses, and the label is symbolic in identifying acts which are contrary to basic rules and principles of international law, and are acts which are generally heinous, deliberate and devastating.

If a state commits an international crime – for instance aggression or genocide – then the orthodox remedial mechanisms afforded by the international legal system often prove inadequate. The self-help system of the nineteenth century still persists in lawful form today when considering non-forcible measures (countermeasures), and in unlawful form when considering armed reprisals. Such a system will not help the weaker state which is the victim of aggression (unless it has powerful allies willing to help in collective self-defence), nor will it help the victims of genocide or other crimes against humanity (unless they are the nationals of powerful third states), who again will not be able to resist the criminal act. Crimes by states are almost always committed against defenceless victims (states or individuals), and the international legal system of sovereign equals is not really designed to help them.

In the case of aggression, victim states have the right of individual and collective self-defence, but they will only be helped given a confluence of ideological, political, economic and legal factors. For breaches of other peremptory norms, so called 'third states' may decide to take

[3] J. Crawford and S. Ollerson, 'The nature and forms of international responsibility', in M. Evans (ed.), *International Law* (2nd edn, Oxford University Press, Oxford 2006), p. 458.

[4] Crawford and Ollerson (n. 3).

unilateral or multilateral countermeasures against the responsible state, though the International Law Commission was ambiguous on the legality of such measures.[5] Even more controversial is the alleged right of humanitarian intervention by military means in response to genocide and crimes against humanity, which will be invoked in an occasional spectacular military intervention to protect human rights, on the basis of a confluence of similar factors.[6] While NATO acted on behalf of the 'international community' in Kosovo in 1999, there were no saviours for the Tutsis in Rwanda in 1994 or currently for the people of Darfur.

Thus the orthodox system of international law, which is horizontal and consensual in nature, ensures that international crimes by states are generally not confronted nor dealt with in such a way as to bring them to an end. In this situation alternative, more effective, ways of responding to crimes by states are sought, usually through international organizations. Indeed, increasingly they are considered the first port of call when an international crime is being perpetrated by a state. Such violations by their very nature require a collective response. Rather than being seen as alternatives to state responsibility, it has been cogently argued by Vera Gowlland-Debbas that this can be seen as a development of that law by viewing measures taken by the Security Council as being done on behalf of the injured state (perhaps also peoples and groups within states) in matters which affect the interests of the international community as a whole.[7]

Though it may be possible to reconcile responses by political organs to crimes by states with the law of state responsibility, in other words to see

[5] ILC Articles (n. 1) Art. 54 on measures taken by states other than the injured State: 'This Chapter does not prejudice the right of any State, entitled under Art 48, paragraph 1 to invoke the responsibility of another State, to take lawful measures against that State to ensure cessation of the breach and reparation in the interest of the injured State or of the beneficiaries of the obligation breached.' Article 48(1) states in part that: 'any State other than an injured State is entitled to invoke the responsibility of another State … if: … (b) the obligation breached is owed to the international community as a whole.' The commentary to Art. 54 states that 'at present there appears to be no clearly recognised entitlement of States referred to in Art. 48 to take countermeasures in the collective interest', hence Art. 54 'speaks of "lawful measures" rather than "countermeasures"'. See Crawford (n. 1) 305.

[6] For recent discussions, see J. F. Holzgrefe and R. O. Keohane (eds.), *Humanitarian Intervention: Ethical, Legal and Political Dilemmas* (Cambridge University Press, Cambridge 2003).

[7] V. Gowlland-Debbas, 'Security Council Enforcement Action and Issues of State Responsibility' (1994) 43 ICLQ 73.

such instances as part of that legal regime, the reality is that by seeking action by international organizations states are making a choice to deal with such crimes at a political or institutional level. Institutional responses may not be in accordance with the regime of state responsibility, nor does it seem necessary to make them so accord. The term 'political' is used here to denote the dominance of international politics in such organizations. In the Security Council, for instance, the process of dealing with crimes being committed by states is a political one, involving negotiations between member states that *might* produce a political solution. This *may* then be implemented using the legal powers at the Council's disposal.

In general terms the state responsibility doctrine, as well as establishing general principles of state liability, in part institutes a regime of legal responses to wrongful acts, or at least provides the legal foundations upon which institutions such as courts can be built. While legal responses tend to address the issue of responsibility once the crime has been committed, actions authorized by political organs are often directed at stopping crimes from being committed or continued. However, the rules of state responsibility can also be directed at terminating a continuing wrongful act and also depend upon political decisions to invoke them,[8] thus creating an overlap between the legal and political regimes that purport to deal with state crimes.

It has been argued that the Security Council is not a replacement for a court, but is still part of the state responsibility regime as an enforcement body.[9] Certainly, in practice, the Council does not enforce judgments of a court, but this is reflective of the unstructured nature of the law of state responsibility. International actors (states and organizations) can make judgments on whether crimes have been committed by states and take measures, and a court may or may not be called upon to judge on the legality of these measures or whether a criminal act has been committed, and the Council may or may not be employed to enforce those judgments. Further, the lack of structure is shown by the fact that the Council can itself act in a quasi-judicial manner. In the case of Iraq's aggression against Kuwait, the Council not only enforced the norm prohibiting aggression,

[8] ILC Articles (n. 1) Art. 48(2) states that in relation to obligations *erga omnes* 'any state ... may claim from the responsible State: (a) cessation of the internationally wrongful act.'

[9] 'The distinction between the function of the Court and that of the Council in matters of State responsibility is the distinction between *peaceful settlement procedures* and *institutionalised countermeasures*'. Gowlland-Debbas (n. 7) 73.

it also punished Iraq in a resolution that, amongst other things, had procedures within it for legally determining the boundary between Iraq and Kuwait and for compensating the victims of the aggression.[10] None of these measures, or for that matter Iraq's guilt, were ordered or reviewed by any international court. Thus, some of the Security Council's responses have contained within them legal mechanisms such as those mentioned on Iraq in relation to issues of state responsibility, and those on Yugoslavia and Rwanda in relation to individual responsibility in the form of international criminal tribunals.[11]

The result is that there is a regime of state responsibility and a different regime of responses of political organs. These overlap in that the Council may play a role in issues of state responsibility, in punishing responsible states and sometimes in performing a judicial function. However, there is nothing systematic about the Council's role and functions within the state responsibility regime, and further it must be recognized that the Security Council's competence is in matters of peace and security is wider than the aspects state responsibility (for aggression, genocide and crimes against humanity) which come within the Council's remit.

Though they are political arenas most organizations operate within constitutional frameworks that can imbue them with significant powers. Chapter VII of the UN Charter allows the Security Council, as part of its broader competence in matters of peace and security, to deal with international crimes, committed either by states or individuals. Though controversial when considering their extent, the range of express and implied powers – to impose sanctions, take military action, set up international tribunals or compensation commissions, target individuals, or more controversially promulgate international legislation binding on all states – gives the Security Council an impressive array of legal powers. Furthermore, Article 103 ensures the pre-eminence of Council obligations in cases of conflicting treaty provisions,[12] Article 2(7) allows it to circumvent the norm of non-intervention,[13] while a literal reading of Article 1(1) even suggests that principles of justice and international law

[10] SC Res. 687, 3 April 1991.

[11] SC Res. 827, 25 May 1993 (ICTY); SC Res. 955, 8 November 1994 (ICTR).

[12] Article 103 reads: 'In the event of a conflict between the obligations of the Members of the United Nations under the present Charter and their obligations under any other international agreement, their obligations under the present Charter shall prevail.'

[13] Article 2(7) of the UN Charter states that: 'Nothing contained in the present Charter shall authorize the United Nations to intervene in matters which are essentially within the domestic jurisdiction of any State …; but this shall not prejudice the application of enforcement measures under Chapter VII.'

only apply to the peaceful settlement of disputes and therefore by implication not to action under Chapter VII.[14] The attractiveness of the Council thus becomes apparent – it appears to be able to do things about crimes perpetrated by states that perhaps states, and courts, cannot do. Of course, that is only true in a legal sense: militarily, for example, the Council is only able to act when it has resources at its disposal.

However – and here is the weakness – as a reflection of its political character the Security Council's powers, even if constitutional, are discretionary. It is up to the Council to determine whether a threat to the peace, breach of the peace or act of aggression has been committed, and it is up to the Council what 'action' is to be taken, if any, to deal with these situations. It is a mistake to think of the Council as a pure executive organ taking action to combat serious breaches of UN law or international law, its make-up means that there are a number of political barriers to it taking effective action to deal with crimes committed by states or, indeed, other threats to the peace.[15]

Despite this, it is because the Security Council has the competence to take positive action that can be directed at stopping state crimes that it is an attractive mechanism, and one that is likely to be more effective than a pure state responsibility regime. Effective action to combat state crimes has to include military action, over and above consensual peacekeeping. Of course, there are arguments to be had about the role of diplomacy and non-forcible measures in halting or, more realistically, preventing state crimes, but military action is posited here as essential for a credible system to deal with such crimes. All sorts of pressure – political, economic and military – may be brought to bear on the criminal state within the UN and other fora, some of which may result in the halting of the criminal acts, but ultimately if the criminal behaviour continues, then military action must be available. There are suggestions that military intervention will simply make matters worse, that greater human suffering will ensue from such interventions than would have occurred without them, though no realistic alternative courses of action are offered.[16] Of course, military

[14] Article 1(1) states as one of the purposes of the UN: 'To maintain international peace and security, and to that end, to take effective collective measures for the prevention and removal of threats to the peace, and for the suppression of acts of aggression or other breaches of the peace, and to bring about by peaceful means, and in conformity with the principles of justice and international law, adjustment or settlement of international disputes or situations which might lead to a breach of the peace.'

[15] H. Kelsen, *The Law of the United Nations* (Stevens, London 1950), p. 294.

[16] See generally, R. Jackson, *The Global Covenant: Human Conduct in a World of States* (Oxford University Press, Oxford 2000).

intervention should only be resorted to in circumstances of overwhelming humanitarian necessity after agreement within the political organ to take such action, but it is difficult to see how, otherwise, to combat ongoing genocide or other serious crimes against humanity, at least in the short term. The Security Council clearly has this competence under Chapter VII of the UN Charter, while there are considerable doubts about the legality of unilateral humanitarian intervention.[17]

III. Political barriers

While it may be attractive to go to the Security Council in the belief that it has the competence to deal with crimes committed by states, indeed may be the only effective avenue, there are a number of political obstacles that may prevent the Council from taking effective action. It has to be remembered that the presence of these barriers, most of which have been shaped by the constitution or form part of a constitutional development, shows that the Council, in its current form, was not intended to be an 'instrument for action' in any automatic or guaranteed sense.[18] It will, however, be argued that its ability to act should and could be improved in the face of crimes perpetrated by states. Though responses by political bodies may, at first sight, appear more attractive in dealing with crimes committed by states than the regime of state responsibility which seems very restricted, the attraction of the legal powers seemingly at the Security Council's fingertips must be tempered by the presence of political barriers that may well prevent their activation.

The following are the main, often overlapping, political factors which together illustrate the discretionary nature of the Council's competence:

1. The veto.
2. Political will or lack of it.
3. Determination under Article 39.

[17] See N. D. White, 'The legality of bombing in the name of humanity' (2000) *4 Journal of Conflict and Security Law* 27; N. Krisch, 'Unilateral enforcement of the collective will: Kosovo, Iraq and the Security Council' (1999) 3 *Max Planck Yearbook of UN Law* 59. See also the resolution of 133 non-industrialized states (meeting as the G77) condemning humanitarian intervention as illegal under international law – Declaration of the Group of 77, South Summit, Havana, Cuba 10–14 April 2000, cited in M. Byres, 'The shifting foundations of international law: a decade of forceful measures against Iraq' (2002) 13 EJIL 28.

[18] I. Claude, 'The Security Council', in E. Luard (ed.), *The Evolution of International Organizations* (Thames and Hudson, London 1966), p. 83.

4. Choice of type of measure.
5. Willing volunteers in the case of military action.
6. Implementation of the resolution.

1. *The veto*

This is the obvious political barrier to action, an express recognition in the Charter of the role of politics at the heart of the institution. Now more threatened than cast,[19] it still shapes negotiations. Proposals have to avoid the veto to become adopted. While it might occasionally prevent the authorization of inappropriate action,[20] the threat of the veto is not only used for relatively minor political points scoring, but can block an enabling resolution that would otherwise allow action in the face of state crimes. For example, in the Kosovo crisis of 1999, the lack of consensus amongst the P5 meant that the Security Council was unable to authorize a forcible response to the crimes against humanity being committed there.[21]

2. *Political will*

Even if the veto is not being wielded to block authorization, the P5, perhaps also non-permanent members, might not be concerned enough about a relatively self-contained genocide or crime against humanity being committed here, or a minor aggression being committed there. They may have their eyes elsewhere – on the threat from terrorism or weapons of mass destruction for instance. In the case of the invasion of Lebanon by Israel in 2006, the argument that Israel should be allowed some time to deal with Hezbollah prevailed in the Council, and therefore there was not sufficient political will for a number of weeks to try and stop the death and destruction being committed by Israel on Lebanese territory.[22]

[19] But see UN doc. S/2007/14, a draft resolution on Myanmar which was vetoed by Russia and China, S/PV 5619 mtg, 12 January 2007. The draft called upon the government of Myanmar to cease attacks on civilians, and violations of human rights and humanitarian law; to begin without delay a political dialogue leading to democracy (including the release of political prisoners).

[20] As with Iraq in 2003 – see N. D. White, 'The will and authority of the Security Council after Iraq' (2004) 17 *Leiden Journal of International Law* 666–7.

[21] See SC Res. 1199, 23 September 1998; SC Res. 1203, 24 October 1998.

[22] Israel was subject to a Hezbollah attack on 12 July 2006, on 13 July Israel responded by airstrikes and then a ground offensive. The Security Council did not achieve a significant resolution until SC Res. 1701, 11 August 2006 which determined that the situation

3. *Determination under Article 39*

A determination under Article 39, or more significantly a statement that the Council is 'acting under Chapter VII' of the Charter has become harder to achieve as China and Russia have become extremely wary of such determinations or statements given the American and British penchant for enforcing resolutions adopted under Chapter VII even though those resolutions did not expressly provide for enforcement action.[23] This also illustrates the discretionary nature of a determination by the Security Council of a threat to or breach of the peace, or act of aggression under Article 39 of the UN Charter. Even though a crime perpetrated by a state should normally constitute either a threat to the peace (at least in the case of genocide or other crimes against humanity) or an act of aggression in objective terms, there appears to be no legal requirement in current institutional law that the Security Council has to make such a determination – or at least this appears to be the case under the Charter and subsequent practice. Furthermore, if the practice that there has to be a threat to *international* peace is followed,[24] then it could be argued that a self-contained genocide or crime against humanity does not affect regional or international peace and therefore does not come within Chapter VII. In practice though, the Security Council has since the 1990s incorporated

in Lebanon was a threat to international peace; called for the cessation of hostilities; and stated that once a cease-fire had been established there should be a deployment of Lebanese troops and an expanded UNIFIL to southern Lebanon along with an Israeli withdrawal. A cease-fire came into effect on 14 August. SC Res. 1697, 31 July 2006 had expressed concern at the escalation of hostilities in Lebanon and Israel, while calling on the parties to respect the safety of UNIFIL.

[23] For example, SC Res. 688 5 April 1991 (re internal situation in Iraq); SC Res. 1199, 23 September 1998 and SC Res. 1203, 24 October 1998 (re Kosovo). It is noticeable in recent non-proliferation resolutions directed at North Korea and Iran, more care has been taken in agreeing the words perhaps in an attempt to ward-off later arguments that they should be enforced. In the case of North Korea, SC Res. 1695 15 July 2006 made no determination in terms of Art 39 nor a statement that the Council was acting under Chapter VII. A different approach is to be found on the Iranian resolution adopted two weeks later – SC Res. 1696, 31 July 2006 which made it clear that the Council was acting under Art. 40 of Chapter VII 'in order to make mandatory the suspension required by the IAEA'. The resolution continued by making it clear that if Iran did not comply with the Council's demands, *inter alia*, to stop uranium enrichment by 31 August, then it would adopt appropriate measures under Art. 41. By this resolution, the use of specific Chapter VII powers rules out a wider interpretation that the resolution permits enforcement by military means. A similar approach was then taken to North Korea by SC Res. 1718, 14 October 2006, which adopted Art. 41 measures against that state under Chapter VII.

[24] For discussion, see J. Frowein and N. Krisch, 'Article 39' in B. Simma (ed.), *The Charter of the United Nations* (2nd edn, Oxford University Press, Oxford 2004), pp. 720–1.

'grave violations of human rights into the concept' of threat to the peace, as well as increasingly dealt with internal conflicts.[25] Despite these developments, the Council might still choose for political reasons not to intervene in an internal conflict, even one generating massive atrocities, the conflict in Chechnya being an obvious example of this.

4. *The choice of measure*

Even if the Council determines that there has been a threat to the peace, it could just demand that the state stop its crimes (as in the case of Kosovo and the crime against humanity being committed there),[26] or threaten it with non-forcible measures (as initially in the case of Sudan and the crimes against humanity being committed in Darfur),[27] or take such measures (initially in the case of Iraq and its aggression against Kuwait),[28] or it might decide to address the issue of individual criminal responsibility (as in the case of Darfur),[29] when what is really required is military action to stop the international criminal behaviour. Reference to the International Criminal Court is not putting justice first, it is using a mechanism of justice as an excuse for not taking any action that would restore peace but also prevent further crimes being committed. The effective judgment as to what measures to deploy, if any, is left in the hands of the Security Council or groups of states within it, although this might be deplored by other members and actors.

5. *Willing volunteers*

Even if the political barriers to authorizing military action under Article 42 of the UN Charter were to be cleared, under the current system it is still necessary for states to volunteer their armed forces for the task of preventing the continuation of the crime. In reality, military action is only contemplated if there are such volunteers. Indeed, it is normally the volunteers that ask for authority and often draft the enabling resolution. The decentralized nature of the military option is further embedded by the practice that the funding of such operations is in the hands of the contributors even though they have been authorized by the Security Council.

[25] Frowein and Krisch (n. 24).

[26] SC Res. 1199, 23 September 1998; SC Res. 1203, 24 October 1998.

[27] SC Res. 1556, 30 July 2004; SC Res. 1564, 18 September 2004. See later SC Res. 1591, 29 March 2005.

[28] SC Res. 661, 6 August 1991. [29] SC Res. 1593, 31 March 2005.

6. *Implementation*

Finally, though a resolution under Chapter VII may have been agreed, the implementation of it is in the hands of the volunteer state or states. The delegation of authority to member states means that command and control is in the hands of the volunteers not the Security Council, giving wide discretion within the often generous parameters of the enabling resolution. Indeed, as well as deciding what action can be taken under the authority of the resolution, the states acting under it might decide for themselves that the criminal behaviour is over and no longer needs to be dealt with by military means, though it can be strongly argued that any decision to terminate an operation should be made by the Security Council as the authorizing organ.[30] In practice, though, this does not always appear to be a constraint. For example, the decision not to intervene, despite authority to do so, in Zaire in 1996 to deal with a massive refugee crisis was a result of a judgment made by the volunteer governments.[31]

IV. Why responses by political organs?

Politics in the Security Council thus dominates the decision of whether to take effective action to combat crimes perpetrated by states. Why then would the Security Council route be preferred to that of an (enhanced) system of state responsibility? An optimist might declare that the political route can unlock serious power, both legal and practical, contained in Chapter VII of the Charter. The range of responses available to combat state crimes appears so much wider than available under the state responsibility regime, and the impact of them potentially so much deeper. A pessimist might respond by arguing that, in such a political environment, states, especially powerful ones, are in control. Occasionally they may be disgruntled that nothing is being done – for example the United States in relation to Darfur – but in the long term the current system ensures that no action is taken against them or their interests. If military action were really important to a powerful state, then it could dust off the doctrine of humanitarian intervention, or perhaps find a regional body willing to sanction it, knowing that it will be criticized for illegality but, subject to its motives, understood.

[30] See D. Sarooshi, *The United Nations and the Development of Collective Security* (Oxford University Press, Oxford 1999), p. 150.

[31] SC Res. 1080, 15 November 1996.

Even in the case of crimes by states, other states may prefer the shades of grey allowed in political approaches and compromises rather than the black or white solutions preferred in purely legal responses. In the system of individual criminal responsibility established by the Rome Statute in 1998, this reasoning is found in Article 16, which allows the Security Council to defer investigation or prosecution by the International Criminal Court, initially for a year, to enable the Council to deal with the threat to the peace within the political sphere.[32] Such an approach views legal responses simply as one of the tools to be deployed in dealing with threats to the peace, even when they constitute crimes committed by individuals and possibly states.

On a legal level, it could be said that this preference for the political reflects the fact that there is no international criminal justice system for dealing with states.[33] Such a system would require a re-structuring of international relations.[34] While it has been possible to graft on to the current international legal order an international criminal justice element dealing with individual responsibility, this has still caused problems for some of the permanent members especially the United States given the potential for the International Criminal Court to indict US soldiers for war crimes even though the United States has not consented to the treaty.[35] Creating an international criminal justice system based on punishing states when they are responsible for crimes would exacerbate the objections, especially if it included judicial bodies, since it would envisage creating a vertical international legal system. Though it is possible for the International Court of Justice to find that a state has breached international laws prohibiting genocide, or other crimes against humanity, the court is in no real sense a criminal court, nor do the proceedings before it in any way resemble a criminal trial.

This is clearly shown in the recent judgment of the International Court of Justice in the *Case Concerning the Application of the Convention on the*

[32] Article 16 ICC Statute states that: 'No investigation or prosecution may be commenced or proceeded with under this Statute for a period of 12 months after the Security Council, in a resolution adopted under Chapter VII of the Charter of the United Nations, has requested the Court to that effect; the requests may be renewed by the Court under the same conditions.'

[33] For an excellent survey of the problem of incorporating crimes by states under the law of state responsibility, see N. H. B. Jørgensen, *The Responsibility of States for International Crimes* (Oxford University Press, Oxford 2000).

[34] G. Schwarzenberger, 'The Problem of an International Criminal Court' (1950) 3 *Current Legal Problems* 263.

[35] See Art. 12 ICC Statute.

Prevention and Punishment of the Crime of Genocide.[36] The Court found it had jurisdiction in the case solely on the basis of Article IX of the Genocide Convention 1948, which provides that 'disputes' between the contracting parties 'including those relating to the responsibility of a State for genocide', shall be submitted to the Court at the request of any of the parties to the dispute. Though the dispute was about genocide, stated in Article I of the Convention to be a 'crime under international law', the Court was in no way exercising criminal jurisdiction. Rather, the Court treated the case like any other dispute brought before it between two states. Bosnia could only bring the case against Serbia for its actions during the Bosnian war on the basis of the consent of both parties located in Article IX of the Genocide Convention. This meant that the Court could not consider other crimes allegedly committed by Serbia during the conflict, it could only rule on the disputes between the parties covered by the Genocide Convention.[37]

The limitations of the Court as a forum of justice for serious breaches of fundamental rules are made clear when the Court recalled:

> the fundamental distinction between the existence and binding force of obligations arising under international law and the existence of a court of tribunal with jurisdiction to resolve disputes about compliance with those obligations. The fact that there is not such a court or tribunal does not mean that the obligations do not exist.[38]

On the issue of genocide, the Court found that state parties had an obligation not to commit genocide, as well as to prevent its commission by individuals, at one point stating that it would 'not be in keeping with the object and purpose of the [Genocide] Convention to deny that the international responsibility of a State – *even though quite different in nature from criminal responsibility* – can be engaged'.[39] Thus, the Court dealt with the issue of Serbia's liability under the rules on state responsibility

[36] *Bosnia and Herzegovina v Serbia and Montenegro*, Case concerning the Application of the Convention on the Prevention and Punishment of the Crime of Genocide, ('Genocide Judgment') General List No. 91, Judgment, ICJ (26 February 2007).

[37] '[The Court] has no power to rule on alleged breaches of other obligations under international law, not amounting to genocide, particularly those protecting human rights in armed conflict. This is so even if the alleged breaches are of obligations under peremptory norms, or of obligations which protect essential humanitarian values, and which may be owed *erga omnes*.' Genocide Judgment (n. 36) para. 147.

[38] Genocide Judgment (n. 36) para. 148.

[39] Genocide Judgment (n. 36) para. 167 (emphasis added). See also para. 170, where the 'Court observes that the obligation in question in this case, arising from the terms of the Convention, and the responsibilities of States that would arise from breach of such

that do not distinguish between different types of liability. The Court was thus concerned with whether Serbia had breached the 1948 Convention, and it concluded on one of the main causes of the dispute that Serbia was not responsible for the acts of genocide that occurred at Srebrenica in July 1995, since these were neither carried out by organs of the Serbian state, nor by individuals acting 'on the instructions of, or under the direction of' Serbia. On this basis the acts of those who committed genocide at Srebrenica could not be attributed to Serbia under the rules of international law of state responsibility.[40] It did, however, find that though not liable for genocide itself, Serbia was responsible for failing to prevent genocide being committed at Srebrenica since it 'must have been clear that there was a serious risk of genocide' there.[41] The Court further found that Serbia failed to comply with its obligation to punish genocide by having failed to transfer General Mladic, the Bosnian Serb indicted for genocide at the ICTY, and indeed ordered that Serbia should do this in order to fulfil its obligation.[42]

Clearly, the International Court separated in law the issue of individual criminal responsibility to be dealt with by an international penal tribunal such as the ICTY, from the responsibility of states under international law. Though the Court was dealing with the crime of genocide, it was not able to address the criminal responsibility of the state, nor was it asked to do so by the parties.

Despite limitations in the jurisdiction of the International Court of Justice, international law includes fundamental 'rules and principles protecting basic interests of the international community',[43] including those prohibiting genocide and other crimes against humanity, and other *jus cogens*, breach of which gives rise to what Cassese has called 'aggravated responsibility' under international law. Such a 'gross attack on community or "public" values' may lead to collective responses or, if they fail to be adopted, individual third states taking non-forcible countermeasures against the state in breach.[44] Thus, while responses under the law of the state responsibility regime as well as by political organs are permitted (though not yet required), there is no central criminal

obligations, are obligations and responsibilities under international law. They are not of a criminal nature.'

40 Genocide Judgment (n. 36) paras. 395, 413, 415.

41 Genocide Judgment (n. 36) para. 438.

42 Genocide Judgment (n. 36) paras. 449–50.

43 C. Tomuschat, 'International crimes by states: an endangered species?', in K. Wellens (ed.), *International Law: Theory and Practice* (Kluwer, The Hague 1998) 253.

44 A. Cassese, *International Law* (2nd edn, Oxford University Press, Oxford 2005), p. 274.

court, or similar vertical law enforcement mechanism for states as there is for individuals.

It might be argued that the Security Council, characterized by coercive power largely in the hands of the P5, is such a vertical structure, and thus makes up for the deficiencies in the International Court. However, its verticality or the consequences of that are discretionary and above all cannot be directed against the P5 and their allies. Such an organ cannot embody a system of justice for states, certainly not one governed by the rule of law. At times, the Security Council appears to act towards certain states in a judicial manner, determining Libya's guilt for Lockerbie,[45] or Iraq's for its invasion of Kuwait,[46] but these judgments were also accompanied by enforcement action that bound member states. The Security Council thus exercised judicial and executive powers. It also has started to purport to exercise a legislative competence.[47] The Council thus clearly sees itself as having all three powers, but it does not see itself as a court, or a legislature, or purely an executive body, nor does it behave like any of these by, for instance, allowing for greater due process when acting like a court, or consulting widely when acting like a law-maker. It is a political body with an array of significant legal powers, some controversial, others less so.

The preference for politics in responding to state crimes is reflected in the expanding role of the Security Council, which exercises its discretion to deal with certain states that have committed serious breaches of fundamental rules of international law, and in so doing is developing a very broad competence that encompasses a crude judicial function and a supranational legislative as well as executive powers. Powerful states have seized on the potential of the Security Council under Chapter VII as a way of dealing with state crimes creating a widening set of mechanisms that they can control.

As described, the Security Council does not appear as simply a component part of the state responsibility regime. Though it sometimes can perform this role and enforce fundamental rules of international law, it can also play judicial and legislative roles in relation to criminal activity. However, it is true that under the state responsibility regime states normally judge for themselves the wrongfulness of an act and take measures, either bilaterally in the case of most breaches, or perhaps multilaterally in

[45] SC Res. 748, 31 March 1992. [46] SC Res. 687, 3 April 1991.

[47] SC Res. 1373, 28 September 2001. For discussion, see M. Happold, 'Security Council Resolution 1373 and the Constitution of the United Nations' (2003) 16 *Leiden Journal of International Law* 593; S. Talmon, 'The Security Council as world legislature' (2005) 99 AJIL 175.

the case of serious breaches of fundamental rules. The Security Council makes a collective judgment under Article 39, and may take measures to enforce it. In this way the Security Council's ability to act as a judge and executioner is reconcilable with the state responsibility regime, but not its claimed legislative competence.

V. Discretion exercised within the law

It can be argued that the current political system, with its protection of powerful states, and the selective punishment of others such as Iraq, represents the current state of international relations and law, but it is difficult to see this as being a defensible system beyond the justifications of *Realpolitik*. It manifests insufficient concern for the fundamental norms of the international community, and it has failed thus far to provide an effective centralized organ to ensure those norms are respected and enforced.[48] The P5 might prefer it but as a system for dealing with state criminality it has limited effect. One alternative would be to recognize subsidiary responsibility for the General Assembly, or for regional systems – an argument that will be returned to later. Another would be to try and reduce the amount of political discretion allowed within the current system; to move – more realistically nudge – it away from the rule of politics towards the rule of law. Political discretion can, and arguably should, be exercised within the limits set by law.[49]

Returning to the political obstacles in the Security Council, ways can be suggested of regulating that behaviour. Most, if not all, of these proposals are *de lege ferenda*, though if the objective is to stop international crimes from going unpunished then it may be possible to argue that the line between *de lege lata* and *de lege ferenda* is not so strong that it cannot be crossed in the case of clear and serious breaches of fundamental norms.[50]

1. *Limitations upon the veto*

It should be possible to curtail the threat or use of the veto when it is used to try and prevent measures to combat international crimes. Though not dealing with events of the same magnitude, there have been recent

[48] But see Gowlland-Debbas (n. 7) 98. [49] *Admissions* Case, 1948 ICJ Rep. 64.

[50] R. Higgins, *Problems and Process: International Law and How We Use It* (Clarendon, Oxford 1994), p. 10.

criticisms within the Council of spurious vetoes.[51] It could be said that any such prohibition would, like the existing legal limitation on the veto,[52] be honoured more in the breach, or circumvented by technical arguments, but if the overwhelming membership of the UN were to condemn vetoes cast in the face of an imminent catastrophe, then we could have a situation where a Security Council resolution might be accepted as a valid source of authority despite the negative vote of a permanent member, especially if the General Assembly adopted a resolution in support of the vetoed draft.

2. *Duty to act*

It can be argued strongly that as the United Nations has international legal personality, therefore the Security Council, as part of the larger institution, is bound by rules of international law, especially peremptory rules.[53] Thus the Security Council is bound not to commit or assist states in the commission of crimes, but it is harder to argue that it is under a positive duty to combat those crimes. In this regard it is interesting to note that while the International Law Commission's Draft Article on the Responsibility of International Organizations recognises that peremptory rules apply to international organization,[54] early drafts do not either explicitly or implicitly recognize any responsibility for failing to adopt resolutions which would be aimed at preventing the commission of crimes by states.[55]

[51] For example, SC 3730 mtg, 10 January 1997 (re military observers to Guatemala); SC 3982 mtg, 25 February 1999 (re peacekeepers in Macedonia). Both Chinese vetoes were as a result of Guatemalan and Macedonian support for Taiwan.

[52] Article 27(3) – that any member of the Security Council, including a permanent member, should abstain from voting if a party to a dispute being dealt with by the Council. See S. D. Bailey and S. Daws, *The Procedure of the Security Council* (Oxford University Press, Oxford 1998), pp. 250–6.

[53] *Interpretation of the Agreement between WHO and Egypt*, 1980 ICJ Rep. 73 at 89, where the ICJ stated that international organizations 'are bound by obligations incumbent upon them under general rules of international law'.

[54] Draft Art. 23, which is contained in Draft Chapter V (Circumstances Precluding Wrongfulness) states that: 'nothing in this chapter precludes the wrongfulness of any act of an international organization which is not in conformity with an obligation arising under a peremptory norm of international law.' In the commentary, the ILC clearly states that peremptory norms bind international organizations – International Law Commission, Report of the 58th Session (2006), A/61/10, 31.

[55] See Draft Art. 15 in International Law Commission, Report of the 57th Session (2005), A/60/10, 85. Draft Art. 15.1 provides that: 'an international organization incurs international responsibility if it adopts a decision binding a member state or international organization to commit an act that would be internationally wrongful if committed by

Furthermore, Security Council practice does not show any evidence of there being a duty to act to combat state crimes, though it surely severely erodes that organ's legitimacy if it fails to act in the face of genocide, crimes against humanity and aggression. If that legitimacy is eroded to the point of invisibility then other actors, including regional organizations, are going to ignore the Security Council and take measures themselves.

The current discourse concerning an alleged emergence of a 'responsibility to protect' in circumstances of serious violation of fundamental norms in reality shows that, though representing a tentative move towards law, political discretion is still dominant.[56] Although clearly stated in the High Level Panel Report of 2004,[57] the provision in the Final Outcome Document of the World Summit in September 2005 is significant in two respects. First, the 'responsibility to protect' survived all the amendments and deletions, showing a desire of the UN membership to move in that direction, but secondly it became so hedged around in caveats and conditions that it is difficult to see it as a legal duty rather than just as a policy or guideline.

> We are prepared to take collective action, in a timely and decisive manner, through the Security Council, in accordance with the UN Charter, including Chapter VII, on a case by case basis in co-operation with relevant regional organisations as appropriate, should peaceful means be inadequate and national authorities manifestly fail to protect their populations from genocide, war crimes, ethnic cleansing and crimes against humanity.[58]

A legal 'duty to protect' could only be said to arise when the Security Council is bound as a matter of UN or international law to determine that a state crime is a threat to the peace,[59] and to take coercive measures,

the former organization and would circumvent an international obligation of the former organization.'

[56] But see International Commission on Intervention and State Sovereignty, *The Responsibility to Protect* (International Development Research Centre, Ottawa 2001). See further, S. Breau, 'The impact of the responsibility to protect on peacekeeping' (2006) 11 *Journal of Conflict and Security Law* 429.

[57] Report of the High Level Panel on Threats, Challenges and Change (UN, 2004) recommendation 55.

[58] GA Res. 60/1, 24 October 2005, para.139. See also the Report of the Secretary General, 'In Larger Freedom: Towards Security, Development and Freedom for All' (UN, 2005) para 135.

[59] Certainly the Security Council has found that state crimes can constitute threats to international peace and security, evidenced by its creation of the international criminal tribunals, but this does not imply that it has a duty to do so.

either sanctions (when the crime is imminent) or military action (if a serious breach is occurring) under Chapter VII. Ideally, this action would follow an independent judgment by a commission of inquiry that serious violations of fundamental norms were imminent or have occurred. A commission is needed to remove the judgment from the political arena of the Council chamber. It is interesting to see some of this approach taken in relation to Darfur where a commission was established,[60] but the Council has thus far failed to deal with the crimes against humanity being committed in that region of Sudan. It has mandated a large peacekeeping force with Chapter VII elements, including responsibility to protect civilians,[61] but, at the time of writing this has not replaced the weak AU force until the Sudanese government has consented to its presence. Earlier in 2006 the Security Council had stated that peacekeeping and peace-building missions should, where appropriate, have mandates that include the 'protection of civilians, particularly those under imminent threat of physical danger, within their zones of operation' and stated its intention that such 'protections mandates' are implemented.[62] However, though implementation of such mandates by peace operations are difficult, it seems the Darfur situation reveals a more serious problem in the form of a lack of will to ensure that the force is deployed in the first place.

3. *Duty on states as UN members*

The weaknesses of the decentralized military option[63] could be overcome if there were a duty on states to follow Council decisions on international crimes not only under Article 41 regarding sanctions but also under Article 42 regarding military measures. This would be in a sense a revival of provisions already found in the Charter,[64] though it would by-pass the Article that requires prior agreements by states on troop provision.[65]

[60] Report of the International Commission of Inquiry on Violation of International Humanitarian Law and Human Rights Law in Darfur (UN Doc. S/2005/60).

[61] SC Res. 1706, 31 August 2006, paras. 1 and 12.

[62] SC Res. 1674, 28 July 2006.

[63] See further N. D. White and O. Ulgen, 'The Security Council and the decentralized military option: constitutionality and function' (1997) 44 NILR 378.

[64] Article 48 of the UN Charter. But see Bryde and Reinisch, 'Article 48', in Simma (n. 24) 776–7, who state that: 'a duty to place troops at the disposal of the Security Council is subject to agreements under Art 43. This follows from the legislative history ... and from the clear meaning of Art 43 which is to make sure that the Security Council cannot draw on member's military resources without their consent.'

[65] Article 43 of the UN Charter.

Moreover, such a duty may be more palatable to governments since the obligation to take military action would not apply to any threat to the peace only those that constituted serious breaches of international criminal law by states. With any other threats to the peace, the system would still be voluntary. Such an approach might be a way of reconciling the obligation on state parties under Article 1 of the Genocide Convention of 1948 to 'prevent and punish' the crime of genocide with the rules on the use of force. The Security Council could be seen as invoking this obligation when demanding military action to deal with genocide

4. *A role for the General Assembly*

Debates about the role of the General Assembly in response to crimes perpetrated by states have been overshadowed by the controversy surrounding the legality of the Uniting for Peace Resolution of 1950.[66] While not repeating them here, there is arguably a strong role for the Assembly, with its primary competence in humanitarian and human rights matters, in cases of serious human rights abuse that reaches the level of genocide or other crimes against humanity.[67] Though, again, the Assembly is a political arena and thus may choose not to recommend any action, there would not be any great outcry if the vast majority of states in the Assembly purported to authorize a coalition of the willing to prevent genocide or crimes against humanity after a similar proposed resolution had been vetoed in the Security Council. The General Assembly has only been sidelined in the post-Cold War period because of a tacit agreement in the P5 that it should be sidelined. It suddenly did not lose its subsidiary responsibility for peace and security in 1989. The antipathy of the Non Aligned Movement to unilateral humanitarian intervention may evaporate if it were in the hands of the majority in the Assembly.[68]

[66] GA Res. 377, 3 November 1950.

[67] See statement by the International Court of Justice in its advisory opinion on the *Legal Consequences of the Construction of a Wall in the Occupied Palestinian Territory*, 2004 ICJ Rep. para. 27, where the Court accepted the legality of parallel practice by the two organs whereby 'the Security Council has tended to focus on the aspects of such matters related to international peace and security, the General Assembly has taken a broader view, considering also their humanitarian, social and economic aspects'.

[68] See the resolution of 133 non-industrialized states (meeting as the G77) condemning unilateral humanitarian intervention as illegal under international law – Declaration of the Group of 77 South Summit, Havana, Cuba, 10–14 April 2000, cited in Byers (n. 17) .

Furthermore, the Assembly and the Human Rights Council ought to assert their political authority as upholders of international law, just as the Assembly did in relation to the prohibition on the use of force during the Cold War, when it consistently condemned violations of this peremptory norm by states.[69] Such declarations would not only put pressure on recalcitrant states and a reluctant Security Council, but would also provide judgment of a serious breach of a fundamental rule of international law and thus provide justification for states to take measures under the rules of state responsibility.

The simple statement by a political organ that there has been a crime committed by a state overcomes many of the problems associated with the regime of state responsibility where, in practice at least, measures are taken by a third state against a government perceived by that third state to have committed a crime. That judgment may be motivated by other factors. Of course, judgment by a political organ is not free of such motivations, and is not as objective in legal terms as the judgment of a court, but, in the absence of a court having compulsory jurisdiction over states in such matters, the need to achieve a collective view in the General Assembly removes many of the spurious factors that may motivate individual states. Furthermore, the greater impact of consensus resolutions reduces the motivation of the majority of states to utilise the condemnatory power of the Assembly to 'persecute' those in the minority. Past lapses by the General Assembly, for instance in its infamous Zionism resolution of 1975,[70] should not prevent it from becoming the focal point of world opinion.

A General Assembly or Security Council determination of state 'guilt' in the commission of an international crime followed by unilateral or collective countermeasures against the responsible state is a good illustration of how the regimes of political institutions and state responsibility should interact. Of course, the Security Council has the power to impose sanctions, while the Assembly has in its practice recommended sanctions, but often such organs cannot achieve the

[69] See e.g., GA Res. ES-6/2, 14 January 1980 on the Soviet Union's intervention in Afghanistan. There have been a few resolutions on the human rights situation in Sudan, critical of the government, but none directed at condemning and addressing the crimes against humanity occurring in Darfur – see GA Res. 54/182, 17 December 1999; GA Res. 55/116, 12 March 2001; GA Res. 56/175, 19 December 2001; GA Res. 57/230, 27 February 2003. But see Human Rights Council Res. 4/8, 30 March 2007.

[70] GA Res. 3379, 10 November 1975 which determined that 'Zionism is a form of racism and racial discrimination' (adopted by 72 votes to 35 with 32 abstentions). It was repealed in 1991 by 11 to 13 with 25 abstentions – GA Res. 46/86, 16 December 1991.

compromise necessary to utilise these powers, though it may be possible to achieve consensus for a condemnatory resolution. Objections that such political organs are not courts and have not followed axioms of natural justice seem to ignore the realities of international law where the norms are upheld by collective condemnation more than by judgments of a court.[71]

5. *A role for regional organizations*

Regional organizations are pressing for more subsidiary responsibility in the shape of freedom to take action to combat crimes committed by states when the Security Council is deadlocked. Historically, the OAS has taken security measures against member states but not for violation of peremptory rules. In more recent times, ECOWAS and NATO have both taken military action to deal with crimes against humanity, in the latter case against a non-member state, the Federal Republic of Yugoslavia, in relation to Kosovo in 1999. The AU's treaty has provisions under which it can take action, including military measures, to combat international crimes.[72] Despite African protestations that the current security regime is not working for Africa, where the main concern is internal criminal violence rather than external aggression, legally the argument is not easily sustained. Through a combination of Charter provisions,[73] regional organizations when taking military action seem to be under the authority of the Security Council, and if they act without that authority then they

[71] As recognized by the International Court of Justice itself in the *Case Concerning Military and Paramilitary Activities in and Against Nicaragua*, (1986) ICJ Rep.14 at 98. But see E. Lauterpacht, *Aspects of the Administration of International Justice* (Cambridge University Press, Cambridge 1991), p. 42.

[72] Article 4(h) provides for 'the right of the Union to intervene in a Member State pursuant to a decision of the Assembly in respect of grave circumstances, namely: war crimes, genocide and crimes against humanity'. However, it is worth noting that in the 2002 Protocol Relating to the Establishment of the Peace and Security Council of the African Union, there are provisions that show greater deference to the UN Charter rules. Article 17(1) provides that: 'in the fulfilment of its mandate in the promotion and maintenance of peace, security and stability in Africa, the Peace and Security Council shall cooperate closely with the United Nations Security Council, which has primary responsibility for the maintenance of international peace and security …' Article 17(2) further states that: 'where necessary, recourse will be made to the United Nations to provide the necessary financial, logistical and military support for the African Union's activities in the promotion and maintenance of peace, security and stability in Africa, in keeping with the provisions of Chapter VIII of the UN Charter on the role of Regional Organisations in the maintenance of international peace and security.'

[73] Articles 2(4), 53 and 103 of the UN Charter.

will be breaching Article 2(4), recognized itself as *jus cogens*. However, if a regional organization is faced with a genocide which the Security Council is unwilling to tackle then, while the law does not permit the use of force to prevent genocide unless it is sanctioned by the Security Council, it is likely that no measures, even condemnation, will follow genuine humanitarian action. At the moment, the law sees both the use of force and the genocide as breaches of fundamental rules of international law. It could be argued, however, that a use of force committed to prevent genocide cannot be branded an aggression, although it remains a breach of a fundamental rule of international law.[74]

While the emergence of such regional practice does not seem as yet within the bounds of international law, it may have the consequence of forcing the Security Council to act itself or to recognize that the regional organization should act. The Council might recognize the right of the AU and other regional organizations to act in cases of crimes committed by states under strict conditions, but without the need for individual authorizations from the Council. Regional organizations though should not be seen as an alternative *system* for dealing with state crimes, they have defects – often unclear rules, weak forces, lack of resoures and they can be dominated by regional hegemons. They should though be recognized as another imperfect component in an imperfect political regime for dealing with crimes perpetrated by states.

Further, the political institutional system of the UN and other organizations should not be seen as an alternative system to the traditional one of state responsibility. There are some interactions between state responsibility and the political responses outlined above, with the Assembly and Council capable of delivering judgments on criminal behaviour by states, and the Council in particular having the competence to enforce community norms. Rather than alternatives it should be recognized that all of these methods should be deployed to stop such crimes being committed. Of course, it would be more effective if coordination of these different methods were achieved through the United Nations, though that brings us back to the problem of the Security Council. However, as has been stated, if the Security Council is deadlocked, the Assembly may be able to step in and recommend military action and, if not, at least deliver the judgment of the international community upon which states may take lawful measures short of the use of force.

[74] As argued by this author in H. McCoubrey and N. D. White, *International Law and Armed Conflict* (Dartmouth, Aldershot 1992), p. 119.

VI. Conclusion

Given the preference of powerful states for political action it is unlikely that immediate and clear limitations will be placed upon the veto or upon the discretion of the Security Council. However, there may be developments in this direction shown, for instance, by flawed responsibility to protect that emerged in the World Summit. Such developments in reality at the moment do not constitute norms or duties on the Security Council, rather they amount to policies that raise the expectations of the international community that action will be taken. Such expectations might weigh against Security Council inaction in the face of the next Rwanda, Congo or the continuing inadequate response to Darfur. Ultimately, though, if no consistent action is taken by the Security Council in the face of criminal behaviour by states, politics will have prevailed to such an extent that other actors – regional organizations and ultimately states – will make their own political judgments irrespective of the rules of international law on the use of force.

While there is an almost inevitable gap between the state responsibility regime and the actions of the Security Council in enforcing community norms, the Council should be wary of just dismissing this as a consequence of the political environment in which it operates. Its political nature should not blind the Council to the fact that it is central to the international legal order, not only by being part of the regime regulating the use of force in international relations, but by the fact that it has the legal competence to address and tackle other serious breaches of peremptory norms. Further, world opinion expects it to take action. This expectation might not yet find expression in a legal duty imposed on the Council, but a continued failure to meet those expectations will erode its credibility – certainly as a part of the international legal order. In theory, this would still leave the Council's political role untouched, but, with the legal order undervalued and undermined, it may find itself being asked to play a secondary role to other actors, such as NATO, ECOWAS, the AU and the EU, after they have intervened to protect civilians facing state crimes.[75]

[75] See, e.g., SC Res. 1244, 10 June 1999 re Kosovo. See also SC Res. 788, 19 November 1992 on ECOWAS' intervention in Liberia.

15

Conclusions and outlook

ANDRÉ NOLLKAEMPER* AND
HARMEN VAN DER WILT**

The chapters in this book emanated from a shared discomfort amongst contributing authors about a mismatch between the current fashionable focus on individual (criminal) responsibility, exemplified by the mushroom of international criminal tribunals, on the one hand, and the dominant role of larger collective entities in situations of system criminality, on the other. The book has sought to reflect on ways to better address the forms and manifestations of system criminality.

In this final chapter, we will recapitulate the dynamics of system criminality as these have been analysed in this book (section I) and summarize the power and limitations of the various forms of international responsibility in regard to system criminality (section II). We then will reflect on two cross-cutting themes: the relationship between the separate forms of international responsibility (section III) and the objectives that we may realistically ascribe to international responsibility in situations of system criminality (section IV). We conclude with some final observations (section V).

I. The dynamics of system criminality

The search for a more adequate framework of responsibility in regard to situations of system criminality requires an understanding of the dynamics of system criminality. In the first two chapters of this book Kelman and Punch paint a penetrating and disturbing picture of how organizations may breed mass criminality. Whereas Kelman focuses expressly on mass atrocities which are the main topic of this book, Punch

* André Nollkaemper is Professor of Public International Law and Director of the Amsterdam Center for International Law at the University of Amsterdam.

** Harmen van der Wilt is Professor of International Criminal Law at the University of Amsterdam.

widens the scope by showing that the same mechanisms apply for lawful organizations which engage in more colloquial forms of criminality. Starting with the conceptual tools of criminology – methods, means and opportunity – both scholars explain how individuals may get involved in criminal acts through processes of authorization, neutralization, rationalization and dehumanization. They do not suggest that individual culpability is completely irrelevant, but rather point out that holding (only) individuals responsible creates a scattered picture and will never suffice to capture the essence of system criminality. After all, within an organization individuals appear to be capable of committing crimes which they would not even consider when acting alone and they would certainly not be able physically to accomplish on their own.

Would collective responsibility be a better option? Gattini and Simpson describe how the international community has constantly vacillated between collective (in particular state) responsibility and individual responsibility, each feeding on the apparent shortcomings of the other. Simpson even qualifies the quest for accountability for international crimes as a 'perpetual bargain' between the individualist and the collective approach.[1] The initial emphasis on 'blaming the collective' after World War I lost much of its momentum in view of the dismal political consequences and the idea that a whole people should not suffer for the misdeeds of a selected number of criminals. Indeed, the concept of individual responsibility, propagated at Nuremberg, mainly served to cleanse the German people from collective guilt. On the other hand, even at that time this preference for the individualist approach was partially mere appearance. Gattini correctly points out how the Nuremberg Tribunal adhered to the collective dimension by introducing concepts like 'membership of a criminal organization' and 'conspiracy'.[2]

These four chapters then confirm the working hypothesis of this book that the collective dimension of international crimes should not be ignored. The individual cannot be easily severed from the organization or state in whose service he or she commits the crimes. Individual responsibility, which relies, as Simpson argues, 'on the fiction of detachability (between the individual and the state)'[3] does not dovetail with

[1] G. Simpson, 'Men and abstract entities: individual responsibility and collective guilt in international criminal law', this volume, Chapter 4, p. 77.

[2] A. Gattini, 'A historical perspective: from collective to individual responsibility and back', this volume, Chapter 5, p. 111.

[3] G. Simpson, 'Men and abstract entities: individual responsibility and collective guilt in international criminal law', this volume, Chapter 4, p. 83.

mass criminality. Crimes against humanity, genocide and aggression, but to some extent also war crimes and torture, require collective action and the availability of massive resources which can usually only be provided by the state or by other collective entities. This is illustrated by the recognition by the Prosecutor of the ICC that the international crimes in the Darfur conflict were determined by substantial state involvement.[4] Against this backdrop, the resurgent quest for collective forms of responsibility is imperative.

II. Forms of international responsibility

The contributions to this book have examined the strengths and weaknesses of various forms of international responsibility in regard to system criminality. These fall in essentially two categories. While a number of options remain within the realm of individual (criminal) responsibility, but discuss the possibility to give the collective aspect of responsibility more weight and attention, a second category concerns responsibility of a collectivity as such.

Ambos discusses superior responsibility as a possible avenue for dealing with problems of system criminality. Strongly embedded in international humanitarian law, the concept conveys the idea that legal and moral standards in situations of armed conflict will only be observed if soldiers are subject to responsible command. Military commanders can be held accountable if they fail to prevent or repress violations of international humanitarian law by their subordinates. The asset of this legal construction is that it recognizes that military structures and organizations may be conducive to system criminality and that not only those who physically commit the crimes, but also those in the higher echelons who have the power and authority to prevent those crimes should be held responsible. However, the drawback of the concept in relation to system criminality is that it usually fails to identify the intellectual godfathers and architects of mass crimes. Military commanders incur criminal responsibility for negligent behaviour and their fault is considered, especially in recent case law, as a separate crime of omission.

In search of alternative concepts which might more adequately reflect the essential role of the genocidal masterminds, Ambos examines the

[4] Seventh Report of the Office of the Prosecutor of the International Criminal Court to the UN Security Council Pursuant to UNSCR 1593 (2005) para. 98, available at http://www.icc-cpi.int/library/organs/otp/UNSC_2008_En.pdf, accessed 3 July 2008.

German concept of *Organisationsherrschaft*. This concept refers to pivotal politicians or bureaucrats who, by virtue of their control over an organization, employ the organization for the purpose of mass criminality. This concept which is related to 'functional perpetration', as described and analyzed by Van der Wilt, serves useful purposes in depicting the criminal responsibility of the men at the top.

An alternative form of individual responsibility that is pertinent to attempts to deal with situations of system criminality is the joint criminal enterprise doctrine (JCE). This combines elements of time honoured concepts like conspiracy, complicity and participation in a criminal organization. While the concept does reach beyond the level of the individual and can connect to collectivities in which individuals participated, both Van der Wilt and Van Sliedregt express their concern over the rather broad and uncritical application of the doctrine in recent case law of the ICTY. The problem with the doctrine is that it serves as a cloak, covering and uniting participants acting at different organizational levels, without much heed being paid to the actual contributions of those participants and their mutual synergy. In their enthusiastic reception of JCE, prosecutors and courts may easily lose sight of the legal pedigree and predecessors from which the doctrine has emerged.

The quest for appropriate concepts of criminal law which might capture the collective dimension of system criminality remains a difficult one indeed. The choice for a particular concept of collective responsibility seems often to be inspired by political considerations. In a perceptive essay, Mark Osiel argues that the ICTY's preference for JCE might be influenced by the Prosecutor's desire to achieve the conviction of as many suspects as possible, whereas domestic jurisdictions, in their quest for national reconciliation, rather opt for singling out particular culprits on the basis of superior responsibility.[5]

Whereas the previous chapters focus on criminal justice's attempts to widen the scope of punishable participants by calibrating forms of collective responsibility, the contributions of Eser and Jørgensen explore the possibilities of holding the organization as such criminally responsible. Jørgensen recalls the attempts of the Prosecutor in Nuremberg to use the criminality of organizations to widen the net for the prosecution of their individual members. Eser focuses on corporate criminal liability as such. These approaches would arguably better square with observations made

[5] M. Osiel, 'The banality of good: aligning incentives against mass atrocity' (2005) 105 *Columbia Law Review* 1812–21.

in previous chapters that organizations may be crimogenic. Although some legal systems still adhere to the maxim *societas delinquere non potest,* there is a growing inclination to accept corporate responsibility *in criminalibus.* However, this has not been reflected in modern international law. Lack of universal acceptance of corporate criminal responsibility was the prime reason for restricting the International Criminal Court's jurisdiction to natural persons.[6]

After discussing these criminal law responses, the book moved to consider non-criminal forms of collective responsibility. Kleffner discusses the responsibility of non-state actors, in particular organized armed groups. He demonstrates that in this area a significant gap exists in the law of international responsibility. Whereas organized armed groups in many situations may have been factually responsible for international crimes and their role may be described in terms of system criminality, the law of international responsibility is undeveloped. Although in theory elements of the concepts and principles of the law of state responsibility may be applied to responsibility of such groups, and in the area of reparation interesting developments have taken place, generally states seem to have little interest or ambition to develop the law in that direction, relying more on (collective) sanctions and force to redress situations of system criminality. This underscores the diversity of legal responses that are required in response of system criminality, some of which are located squarely in the field of international responsibility, some of which are far removed from that domain, and yet others, as in the case of organized armed groups, have a *sui generis* nature that display some features of an accountability regime, yet in vastly different terms from individual or state responsibility.

The two chapters on state responsibility for system criminality, by Scobbie and Zimmermann/Teichmann, were written against the background of the fact that in positive international law the state as such cannot incur criminal responsibility for mass atrocities. The prospects for changing this situation appear slim. Criminal responsibility of states would require a different institutional organization of the international community with a centralized power. In the absence of this structure, holding states criminally responsible would trespass on the concept of sovereignty and would militate against the idea of inter-state equality.

Starting from the premise that the state's obligation to abstain from system criminality applies *erga omnes*, both chapters examine whether

[6] Compare Art. 25(1) ICC Statute.

the remedies available under the legal regime of state responsibility provide the international community with useful and adequate tools to censure the delinquent state. The conclusions are not very encouraging. Scobbie concludes that state responsibility principally remains confined within a bilateral straitjacket and has made little progress towards communitarian responses to serious breaches of international law, including the commission of system criminality, and that the law of state responsibility: 'is an unwieldy instrument through which to seek redress. Its implementation cannot rise above the implications of sovereignty, which is the dominant conceptual structure of international law.'[7] Zimmermann and Teichmann are somewhat more optimistic and recognize that international law provides an arsenal of consequences a responsible state has to take into account when it commits such crimes. They too, however, conclude that the main problem is lack of enforcement and implementation. The legal consequences of system criminality under the state responsibility regime often have mainly a declaratory and symbolic character. The international community can assess that a state has violated its obligations under international law, it can decide not to recognize the situation which has emerged as a consequence of system criminality and it can insist on obtaining guarantees of non-repetition, but that may not be enough to stop the breach, secure performance of the obligation and secure reparation.

In view of the limited possibilities within the legal framework of responsibility of organized armed groups and state responsibility to remedy or sanction system criminality, in many cases the question will arise whether political organs like the Security Council are properly equipped to deal with mass atrocities and to enforce community norms. White argues that the Security Council, though a political organ operating on the basis of political decisions, acts within the legal context of the Charter which offers ample opportunities to take far reaching and even punitive measures whenever the Council would be satisfied that those measures could contribute to restoration and maintenance of the peace. Major problems remain the discretion of the Council and the veto power. White notes, however, the emergence of practices and policies that may result in some limitations upon the veto or upon the discretion of the Security Council. Short of this, it will be inevitable that regional organizations and also states will take their own action in response to situations of system criminality.

[7] I. Scobbie, 'Assumptions and presuppositions: state responsibility for system crimes', this volume, Chapter 12, p. 269.

III. Relationship between system criminality and individual responsibility

The question that remains to be considered is the mutual relationship between the different responses to system criminality, in particular between forms of individual responsibility on the one hand and collective responsibility on the other.

Criminal lawyers have a natural proclivity to be suspicious of collective guilt. Their conceptual tool box consists of the twin concepts of *actus reus* and *mens rea*, which puts them on the track of inquiring *who* is exactly responsible for *what*. The aspiration to identify the culprits as precisely as possible, and to mete out punishment commensurate to the contribution and the amount of guilt, is one of the most attractive features of criminal law.

On the other hand, it may be said that the very nature of system criminality obliterates the piecemeal approach of criminal law. Criminal law is not capable of capturing the complex mechanisms and relations of organizations which engage in mass crimes. At the end of the day, one is left with a distorted and fragmentized picture of reality which does not comport with historical truth and in which the blame rests on a few individuals who, understandably, resent their being sacrificed as scapegoats. Collective responsibility is an important step towards acknowledgment that responsibility in case of system criminality should focus on higher levels. It epitomizes a more holistic approach which recognizes the responsibility of the wider periphery of bystanders who, though not directly involved, create the breeding ground for mass atrocity.

While the alternatives of individual and collective responsibility may be presented in mutually exclusive terms, and in practice more often than not trade-offs are made, as illustrated by the mass atrocities in Srebrenica when the international community opted for individual over collective responsibility, we believe that they are better conceived as being complementary.[8]

The major challenge is to combine both approaches within an integrated analytical framework in which the disadvantages of one approach are offset by the advantages of the other and vice versa. This requires an analysis and assessment of responsibility at different levels, to which the individual chapters in the book have much contributed.

Starting from the largest forms of systems, the principles of state responsibility provide a useful tool for capturing the collective dimension

[8] See also A. Nollkaemper, 'Introduction', this volume, Chapter 1, p. 20.

of system criminality. The drawback of 'collective guilt' is mitigated by the fact that the current regime focuses on moral condemnation and does not provide for 'punitive damages', and by the fact that collective responsibility is not necessarily distributive, in the sense that the contribution and guilt of the participants to the collective can be easily measured.[9] However, in light of the conclusions of Chapters 12 and 13, much work needs to be done to strengthen the implementation of the law of responsibility in regard to situations of system criminality, in particular of the principles contained in Articles 41 and 54 of the Articles on International Responsibility.

At a lower level, separate organizations which engage in system criminality may incur criminal or civil responsibility. Army battalions, organized armed groups, terrorist groups and even business corporations might qualify for this purpose. For the time being, such corporate solutions can only be tested by domestic jurisdictions, in view of the previously mentioned restriction of the ICC's jurisdiction to natural persons. One of the clearest recommendations which emerges from this study is that this restrictive provision in the Rome Statute requires serious reconsideration, and that the possibilities to seek non-criminal responsibility of such entities, for instance in domestic courts by seeking to drain financial resources, should be encouraged.[10]

Finally, individuals who are, either personally or in cooperation with others, most responsible for mass criminality should face justice in criminal procedures. The available concepts connoting collective responsibility, like superior responsibility, JCE, *Organisationsherrschaft* and functional perpetration should be further developed and refined to this purpose.

Individual and collective responsibilities thus do not exclude each other. On the one hand, for the reasons set out in Chapters 1–3, individual responsibility is unlikely to reach the level of the system, perhaps except in cases where international crimes are committed or induced by a limited number of persons who constitute the leadership of a small group.[11] It is to be recognized, however, that while individual responsibility may not remove the need for legal responses targeted at system level,

[9] Compare on these distinctions: J. Feinberg, 'Collective responsibility', in *Doing and Deserving; Essays in the Theory of Responsibility* (Princeton University Press, Princeton, NJ 1970), pp. 222–51.

[10] In the same vein, Osiel (n. 5) at 1842–8, who recommends the financial drainage of such organizations for being highly effective, while less stigmatizing.

[11] C. Tomuschat, *International Law: Ensuring the Survival of Mankind on the Eve of a New Century* (vol. 281, R de C, 1999), p. 290.

it may have legal and practical consequences at that level, for instance by punishing leaders[12] or by draining resources controlled by individual members of a group.[13]

On the other hand, the emphasis that we have put on the need for collective responsibility by no means removes the legitimate basis for individual responsibility. It is true that the structural dimensions of behaviour, and the related loss of subjective freedom,[14] may cast doubt on the fundamental premise of (international) criminal law: that the individual is 'endowed with free will and the independent capacity to choose his conduct'.[15] The fact that individual crimes are not, as is commonly the case for domestic crimes, contrary to a norm, but rather in conformity with norms that result from collective processes[16] may have profound consequences for our assessment of individual atrocities. Rather than viewing them as necessarily evil, one may also view them as acts that, for the actor, conform to what is right. In the words of Habermas: 'evil is thus the obverse side of the good.'[17] However, there is no ground for excepting legal excuses for individual behaviour, and

[12] P.M. Dupuy, 'International criminal responsibility of the individual and international responsibility of the state', in A. Cassese, P. Gaeta and J.R.W.D. Jones (eds.), *The Rome Statute of the International Criminal Court: A Commentary* (Oxford University Press, Oxford 2002), p. 1085 (noting that 'the promoters of the various international criminal courts undoubtedly intended, by punishing individuals, also to punish the actions of the State to which the acts may be attributed'. Also: A. A. Cancado Trindade, 'Complementarity between state responsibility and individual responsibility for grave violations of human rights: the crime of state revisited', in M. Ragazzi, *International Responsibility Today. Essays in Memory of Oscar Schachter* (Marshall Cavendish, London 2005), p. 265.

[13] Osiel (n. 5) 1842–8.

[14] A.J. Vetlesen, *Evil and Human Agency. Understanding Collective Eveldoing* (Cambridge University Press, Cambridge 2005), p. 84.

[15] A. Cassese, *International Criminal Law* (Oxford University Press, Oxford 2003), p. 137.

[16] I. Tallgren, 'The sense and sensibility of international criminal law' (2002) 13 EJIL 575. Similarly, H.C. Kelman, 'The policy context of international crimes', this volume, Chapter 2. It is to be added, though, with Wells, that this in general will involve a two way process, with acts of criminality not only using a climate for justification, but at the same time contributing to that climate C. Wells, *Corporations and Criminal Responsibility* (Oxford University Press, Oxord 1993), p. 126; this is also implied in G.P. Fletcher, 'The Storrs Lectures: liberals and romantics at war: the problem of collective guilt' (2002) 111 *Yale Law Journal* 1541, referring to the 'climate of moral degeneracy' produced by the 'collective' contribution to the crime.

[17] Cited in Vetlesen (n. 14) 177. Compare M.A. Drumbl, 'Pluralizing international criminal justice' (2005) 103 *Michigan Law Review* 1311 (noting that the violence in Rwanda arose from the conscious implementation of a shared social norm, according to which '[t]he government, and an astounding number of its subjects, imagined that by exterminating the Tutsi people they could make the world a better place.' (citing P. Gourevitch, *We Wish*

individual responsibility, on this basis. It may often be possible to identify degrees of freedom (to resist) that have not been exercised.[18] Indeed, positive law does not accept that systemic causes entirely *preclude* individual responsibility,[19] though it may be reflected in the level of punishment of individuals.[20]

We thus would be inclined to favour a synthesis of both individual and collective responsibility. After all, the regimes of state responsibility and individual (criminal) responsibility are to a large extent each others mirror image and therefore complementary. It stands to reason that these different levels of analysis and decision-making should be integrated by mutual references and benefits in the realm of procedure evidence, legal concepts etc.[21]

In view of the relatively limited contribution that the implementation of the law of international responsibility in itself may make in situations of system criminality, further complementarity should be sought between the law of international responsibility and the potential contribution of responses by the political organs of the United Nations as well as regional organizations. Such responses need not be isolated from the law of international responsibility, but may contribute to its application and enforcement, for instance because of the fact that the General Assembly and Security Council are capable of delivering

to Inform You That Tomorrow We Will Be Killed with Our Families: Stories from Rwanda (Picador, New York 1998).

[18] M. Osiel, *Mass Atrocity, Extraordinary Evil* and H. Arendt, *Criminal Consciousness in Argentina's Dirty War* (Yale University Press, New Haven & London 2005).

[19] See W. Friedmann, *Legal Theory* (Columbia University Press, New York 1967), pp. 65–7; see also Art. 58 of the ILC Articles on State Responsibility. This conclusion appears to be in line with the theory of Hannah Arendt, despite her emphasis on the effect of bureaucracies on human freedom; see analysis in Vetlesen (n. 14) 86.

[20] It may be argued that the relevance for sentencing purposes attached by the ICTY in *Prosecutor v Krstic*, IT-98–33-T, Judgment (August 2, 2001) para. 724, to the role of individuals who hierarchically are higher placed than the author of the act, may be extended to the role of the state for which that author acted. See generally, on the possible influence of collective action on individual sentencing, M. A. Drumbl, 'Collective violence and individual punishment: the criminality of mass atrocity' (2005) 99 *Northwestern University Law Review* 567 *et seq*.

[21] As illustrated by the judgment in *Bosnia and Herzegovina v Serbia and Montenegro*, Application of the Convention on the Prevention and Punishment of the Crime of Genocide ('Genocide Case') General List No 91, ICJ, Judgment (26 February 2007). See, for discussion of some of the connections between individual and state responsibility: A. Cassese, 'On the use of criminal law notions in determining state responsibility for genocide' (2007) 5 JICJ 857–87; A. Nollkaemper, 'Concurrence between individual responsibility and state responsibility' (2003) 52 ICLQ 615–40.

judgments on criminal behaviour by states, followed by individual or collective countermeasures.[22] Though it is common to separate such responses from the law of responsibility, the line between assertions of responsibility and political response in international institutions may be a thin one. Also responses of political organs such as the Security Council may well be premised on alleged breaches of international law.[23] Also in this respect, we suggest that a comprehensive view should be adopted that views the different methods not as alternatives, but as methods that all may have to be deployed to stop such crimes being committed.[24]

IV. Objectives of international responsibility in regard of system criminality

An assessment of the power of the law of international responsibility in respect of system criminality ultimately depends on one's assessment of the aims that may be ascribed to this body of law. Depending, then, on the context and on the interests of the actors involved, the law of international responsibility may serve a variety of purposes.[25]

We need to take into account that we cannot talk in the abstract of objectives and aims of international responsibility in response to system criminality. The question always has to be answered who it is that defines such objectives.[26] Who defines what, for instance, in the case of Darfur should be the aims of international responsibility (for all practical purposes: the responsibility that the ICC seeks to effectuate).

[22] N. White, 'Responses of political organs to crimes by states', this volume, Chapter 14.

[23] See R. Higgins, *Problems and Process, International Law and How We Use It* (Oxford University Press, Oxford 1994), pp. 181–4. A similar broad conception is adopted by O. Triffterer, 'Prosecution of states for crimes of state' (1996) 67 *Revue Internationale de Droit Penal* 343 (referring to the sanctions imposed or authorized by the Security Council as one example of ' "prosecution" of states for crimes of state'). See also M. Herdegen, *Befugnisse des UN-Sicherheitsrates: aufgeklärter Absolutismus im Völkerrecht* (Müller, Heidelberg 1998), p. 20 (stating that 'In der Regel wird eine Friedensbedrohung durch die schwerwiegende Verletzung von Völkerrechtspflichten begründet'); B. Graefrath, 'International crimes – a specific regime of international responsibility of states and its legal consequences', in J. H. H. Weiler, A. Cassese and M. Spinedi (eds.), *International Crimes of States: A Critical Analysis of the ILC's draft Article 19 on State Responsibility* (Walter de Gruyter, Berlin 1988), p. 164.

[24] N. White, 'Responses of political organs to crimes by states', this volume, Chapter 14.

[25] Cf. M. Reisman, 'Legal responses to genocide and other massive violations of human rights' (1996) 59 *Law and Contemporary Problems* 75.

[26] J. Gardner, 'The mark of responsibility' (2003) 23 *Oxford Journal of Legal Studies* 157.

Retribution? Deterrence? Compensation? Incapacitation of the regime? Or all such things? Although the crimes involved in system criminality as defined in this book are crimes in which the international community has an interest,[27] the question is who defines the objectives of the international community. Indeed, in many of the situations in recent years to which the label of system criminality seems proper, particular (groups of) states that, allegedly acting on behalf of the international community, have pursued a political agenda and have set different aims.

For some of these objectives, in situations of system criminality the possible contribution of international responsibility seems marginal at best. This holds in particular for termination. In many cases involving system criminality, international organizations and states seek: 'an immediate response to the breach of public order, terminating the breach and containing the destructive effects of the act.'[28] Although termination is a well-established objective of the law of international responsibility and it seems proper to use this as a benchmark for evaluating the law and its application, the law of international responsibility may not be the first choice on the menu if this is the objective. Alvarez notes that the first lesson of Rwanda is that 'international efforts to prevent the continuation of genocidal acts and other acts of violence must precede attempts at criminal accountability'.[29] Indeed, there seems to be little evidence that in any of the cases involving system criminality in the past decades, international responsibility (whether in the form of individual responsibility, responsibility of states or responsibility of other collective actors) played a significant role in terminating the criminal acts. In respect of this objective, there is little doubt that, apart from unilateral force, responses by the Security Council are potentially the most effective means to combat situations of system criminality.

The deterrent power, in terms of general prevention, of international responsibility in relationship to system criminality seems equally limited. Though it has been said, also in regard to international crimes, that responsibility may have a deterrent effect,[30] the methodological problems are substantial (we may never know exactly how effective and real its preventative effect will be) and the assumptions underlying such

[27] A. Nollkaemper, 'Introduction', this volume, Chapter 1, p. 19. [28] (n. 28).

[29] J. Alvarez, 'Crimes of states/crimes of hate: lessons from Rwanda' (1999) 24 *Yale Journal International Law* 458.

[30] Trindade (n. 12) 266.

deterrence are shaky, both for future individual perpetrators[31] and for collectivities.[32] It seems, for example, doubtful that, say, a determination of state responsibility of Serbia in 1995 would have made a difference for current policies of Sudan in Darfur. While in theory compensation may contribute to prevention, it seems doubtful that compensation by a collectivity (say a state) provides incentives for individual officeholders, as potential wrongdoers.

Both in regard to termination and prevention, it needs to be recognized that while the causal mechanisms identified in the introduction and discussed in detail in Chapters 2 and 3 may and should inform the responses through the law of international responsibility, for a large part they will be immune from the effect of the law of international responsibility.

In respect of other objectives, however, the law of international responsibility may have more relevance in respect of system criminality. This holds in particular for retribution, prevention of recurrence, reconciliation and compensation. The capability of various forms of international responsibility to contribute to these aims in situations of system criminality underscores that individual and collective responsibility are complementary and that each can contribute to different aims.

Perhaps first and foremost, the law of responsibility can be used as a form of retribution. As is well known, retribution in criminal law emanates from the moral imperative that criminal offenders should be punished because they deserve it, irrespective of the question whether punishment serves any other social aim.[33] The Preamble of the Rome Statute, in affirming that the most serious crimes of concern to the international community as a whole must not go unpunished, pledges allegiance to retributive theory. This seems an objective that primarily can be served through the law of individual responsibility. However, the question whether collective accountability (for instance, the responsibility of Serbia as determined by the ICJ in the Genocide Case) could have retributive effects and as such complement individual punishment has been unexplored and would warrant further empirical research.

[31] I. Tallgren (n. 16) 575. See also Drumbl, referring to long-standing criminological research, he notes that the very low chance that offenders ever are accused adversely affects the assumed effectiveness of deterrence theory: M. A. Drumbl, *Atrocity, Punishment and International Law* (Cambridge University Press, Cambridge 2007), pp. 169–70.

[32] Drumbl (n. 20) 589. [33] Drumbl (n. 31) 150.

The law of international responsibility also may be used to prevent the recurrence of the crimes and to stop the actor who engaged in the criminal acts from repeating them. This is a recognized objective of the law of international responsibility.[34] Though prevention of course also is an objective of the law of individual responsibility,[35] the law of collective responsibility may be more powerful. Prosecuting and detaining high-level leaders responsible for system criminality may help to prevent recurrence in situations where the commission of crimes by a state means that a people has fallen prey to a small criminal leadership.[36] But in more complex forms of system criminality that may not be enough. Though state responsibility is not easily used to incapacitate a regime, the law might be relevant here as it provides for the obligation of states not to recognize and to cooperate in order to bring an end to situations that have resulted from system criminality.[37] Beyond this, the options at the disposal of the Security Council may contribute to this aim.[38]

Finally, also in regard to the aim to compensate victims of situations of system criminality individual and collective responsibility have their own role. Compensation, of course, is a recognized objective of the law of state responsibility[39] and now has also found its way into the Statute of the International Criminal Court.[40] However, both forms of international responsibility have quite distinct potential for offering compensation. Compensation as remedy for state responsibility is not compensation of individual person/victims as such, and states may spend their recovery on other purposes. Compensation as part of individual responsibility, though it remains to be developed,[41] will benefit individual victims rather than collective entities. Again, recognizing

[34] See Article 30 of the Articles on State Responsibility.

[35] The preamble of the ICC Statute states that it seeks to 'to contribute to the prevention of such crimes'. The emphasis in international criminal law seems to be on general prevention, although case law of the ICTY incidentally refers to special deterrence as well; compare Judgment of the Appeals Chamber, *Prosecutor v Kordić and Čerkez*, IT-95–14/2-A (17 December 2004) para. 1076: 'both individual (i.e. specific) and general deterrence serve as important goals of sentencing.'

[36] Tomuschat (n. 11) 290.

[37] I. Scobbie, 'Assumptions and presuppositions: state responsibility for system crimes', this volume, Chapter 12 and A. Zimmermann and M. Teichmann, 'State responsibility for international crimes', this volume, Chapter 13.

[38] N. White, 'Responses of political organs to crimes by states', this volume, Chapter 14.

[39] Article 36 of the Articles on State Responsibility.

[40] Article 79 ICC Statute.

[41] Article 75 ICC Statute.

the own distinct role of various forms of responsibility as well as their complementary nature is key.[42]

V. Final remarks

The final conclusions of the book can be briefly summarized.

International responsibility will offer only a relatively modest role to the problems of system criminality. The social processes that facilitate and contribute to system criminality require a combination of political and legal responses, of which international responsibility is only a minor part. The nature, power and interaction between such responses need to be further explored.

The available concepts of individual responsibility connoting collective responsibility, like superior responsibility, JCE, *Organisationsherrschaft* and functional perpetration should be further developed and refined to this purpose, without losing connection with the fundamental principles of individual responsibility.

The restrictive provisions in the Rome Statute on criminal responsibility of organizations requires reconsideration. Moreover, the possibilities to seek non-criminal responsibility of such entities, including organized armed groups, for instance in domestic courts by seeking to drain financial resources, should be explored and the law in this area should be developed.

The implementation of the principle of state responsibility in relation to system criminality needs to be strengthened, in connection with the activities of political organs of international organizations, which thereby could strengthen their role in the enforcement of community values.

Beyond the rethinking of individual modes of responsibility in relation to system criminality, more work needs to be done on the possible and actual interactions between the different forms of responsibility. The questions are in part of an empirical nature. What forms of responsibility have or have not 'worked' in relationship to system criminality (in respect of such aims as termination, prevention, retribution and compensation)? Under what conditions and in what circumstances

[42] T. Franck, 'Individual criminal liability and collective civil responsibility: do they reinforce or contradict one another' (2007) 6 *Washington University Global Studies Law Review* 573 (noting that: 'genocide is a hydra-headed monster. It warrants a multifaceted response. The heralded advent of individual liability should not cloud our understanding of the continued importance of state responsibility'.).

can they supplement each other? Is one form of responsibility able to compensate for the absence of others? There remain also fundamental normative and legal questions unexplored. What are the procedural and normative interactions between various forms of international responsibility? But these interactions cannot properly be understood before the separate forms of international responsibility in relation to system criminality are understood. It is hoped that this book offers a contribution to such understanding.

INDEX